Claire McGettrick is an Irish Research Council postgraduate scholar at University College Dublin, Ireland. She is cofounder of Justice for Magdalenes Research (JFMR) and Adoption Rights Alliance (ARA). She jointly coordinates the multi-award-winning CLANN project with Dr Maeve O'Rourke, as well as the Magdalene Names Project (MNP), which has recorded the details of over 1,900 women who lived and died in Ireland's Magdalen laundries.

Katherine O'Donnell is Associate Professor at University College Dublin, Ireland, and has published widely on the history of sexuality and gender and the intellectual history of eighteenth-century Ireland. She has been principal investigator on a number of funded research projects, including gathering an archival and oral history of the Magdalen institutions funded by the Irish Research Council. As a member of Justice for Magdalenes Research (JFMR), she has shared in activist honours, including the Irish Labour Party's Thirst for Justice Award.

Maeve O'Rourke is Lecturer in human rights law at the Irish Centre for Human Rights, NUI Galway. She is also a barrister (England and Wales) and attorney-at-law (New York). Since 2009 she has provided pro bono legal assistance to Justice for Magdalenes Research (JFMR) and is currently co-director of the CLANN project, an evidence-gathering and advocacy collaboration between JFMR, Adoption Rights Alliance (ARA) and Hogan Lovells International, LLP.

James M. Smith is an associate professor at Boston College, United States. His book Ireland's Magdalen Laundries and the Nation's Architecture of Containment (2007) was awarded the Donald Murphy Prize for Distinguished First Book by the American Conference for Irish Studies. He is a member of the advocacy group Justice for Magdalenes Research (JFMR).

Mari Steed was one of more than 2,000 children exported from Ireland to the United States and was born in the Bessborough Mother and Baby Home in Cork, where she also endured being part of the vaccine trials. Mari's mother spent time in a Magdalen laundry. She serves as US coordinator with the Adoption Rights Alliance (ARA). In 2003 Mari cofounded Justice for Magdalenes Research (JFMR), an advocacy organization that successfully campaigned for a state apology and restorative justice for survivors of Ireland's Magdalen laundries. She currently serves on the group's executive committee.

Ireland and the Magdalene Laundries

A Campaign for Justice

Claire McGettrick, Katherine O'Donnell,
Maeve O'Rourke, James M. Smith
and Mari Steed

I.B.TAURIS
LONDON • NEW YORK • OXFORD • NEW DELHI • SYDNEY

I.B. TAURIS
Bloomsbury Publishing Plc
50 Bedford Square, London, WC1B 3DP, UK
1385 Broadway, New York, NY 10018, USA
29 Earlsfort Terrace, Dublin 2, Ireland

BLOOMSBURY, I.B. TAURIS and the I.B. Tauris logo are trademarks of Bloomsbury Publishing Plc

First published in Great Britain 2021
Reprinted 2021

Cover design by Dani Leigh
Cover image © Evelyn Glynn

A catalogue record for this book is available from the British Library.

A catalog record for this book is available from the Library of Congress.

ISBN: HB: 978-0-7556-1748-7
PB: 978-0-7556-1749-4
ePDF: 978-0-7556-1751-7
eBook: 978-0-7556-1750-0

Typeset by Deanta Global Publishing Services, Chennai, India
Printed and bound in Great Britain

To find out more about our authors and books visit www.bloomsbury.com and sign up for our newsletters.

This publication was grant-aided by the Publications Fund of National University of Ireland Galway / *Rinneadh maoiniú ar an bhfoilseachán seo trí Chiste Foilseachán Ollscoil na hÉireann, Gaillimh*

This book is dedicated to the memory of Josie Bassett, Martina Keogh, Mary Newsome, Kathleen R., Catherine Whelan, and Beth, and to all survivors of Ireland's Magdalene Laundries.

It is also dedicated to all of the women who died while in the laundries and to those still institutionalized after the laundries' closure.

The authors have had the privilege of listening to hundreds of survivors of the Magdalene Laundries and understand that the women wish to ensure that the abuse they experienced never happens again. In the name of all of the girls and women held in Ireland's Magdalene institutions we are donating all authors' royalties to the charity Empowering People in Care (EPIC) to advocate for the rights of children and young adults in the care system and aftercare and enable their voices to influence positive change in their own circumstances and the care system.

Contents

Plates

Acknowledgements

Countless volunteers and allies have given their time, energy and expertise at crucial junctures since the foundation of our organization. Their friendship and support was indispensable to achieving our goals. We hope that the very many people who so generously assisted Justice for Magdalenes will find their names and contributions acknowledged in the pages of this book or in the accompanying archive at www.jfmresearch.com/bookarchive.

The authors would also like to thank our families for their patience and loving support during our extended campaign for measures of justice. Many thanks to A&L Goodbody and Ciarán Ahern for their ongoing assistance with the corporate governance of Justice for Magdalenes Research.

Nuala and Sean Fenton twice provided us with beautiful accommodation for week-long writing retreats, which enabled us to start and continue the writing of this book. Go raibh míle maith agaibh. Special thanks to Dr Colleen Taylor for her invaluable assistance preparing the manuscript for production.

We are pleased to acknowledge the *Feminist Review* trust for an early grant to conduct a pilot study of the Magdalene Oral History Project and the Irish Research Council for further funding which allowed for an invaluable collection of Magdalene survivors' voices to emerge. Likewise, we are grateful to The Ireland Fund of Great Britain and also to Atlantic Philanthropies, for seed funding at the early stages of our work.

Thanks are also due to the Moore Institute at the National University of Ireland Galway for generously supporting this publication through its Grant-in-Aid scheme. The Moore Institute also funded Jim as a visiting scholar in spring 2012, and his research from that time flowed directly into JFM's campaign.

We also thank Boston College's Morrissey College of Arts and Sciences for generously supporting this publication through subvention funding and for its continuing support of our campaign since 2009.

Abbreviations

AG	Attorney General
AII	Amnesty International Ireland
ARA	Adoption Rights Alliance
BCI	Boston College Ireland
CICA	Commission to Inquire into Child Abuse
CICA Act	*Commission to Inquire into Child Abuse Act, 2000*
CICA Final Report	Final Report of the Commission to Inquire into Child Abuse
CORI	Conference of Religious of Ireland
DCC	Dublin City Council
DED	Dáil Éireann Debates
DHM	Dublin Honours Magdalenes
DoEnv	Department of the Environment
DoH	Department of Health
DoJ	Department of Justice
DML	Donnybrook Magdalene Laundry
DPP	Director of Public Prosecutions
ECHR	European Convention on Human Rights
EHO	Environmental Health Officer
FGM	Female Genital Mutilation
FLAC	Free Legal Aid Centres
FOI	Freedom of Information
GDPR	General Data Protection Regulation
GRO	General Register Office
HAA Card	*Health (Amendment) Act, 1996* Card
HSE	Health Service Executive
HIQA	Health Information and Quality Authority
ICCL	Irish Council for Civil Liberties
IDC	Inter-Departmental Committee to establish the facts of State Involvement with the Magdalen Laundries
IDC Report	Report of the Inter-Departmental Committee to establish the facts of State Involvement with the Magdalen Laundries

IHRC	Irish Human Rights Commission
ILO	International Labour Organization
INMH	Irish National Maternity Hospital
IPRT	Irish Penal Reform Trust
IPP	Irish Parliamentary Party
IWSSN	Irish Women Survivors Support Network
JFM	Justice for Magdalenes
JFMR	Justice for Magdalenes Research
LAB	Legal Aid Board
LSS	Department of the Environment's Local Services Section
MBHCOI	Mother and Baby Homes Commission of Investigation
MMC	Magdalene Memorial Committee
MNP	Magdalene Names Project
MOHP	Magdalene Oral History Project
MST	Magdalene Survivors Together
NAI	National Archives of Ireland
NGO	Non-Governmental Organization
NWCI	National Women's Council of Ireland
OLC	Sisters of Our Lady of Charity
Quirke Report	*The Magdalen Commission Report: Report of Mr Justice John Quirke*
PILA	Public Interest Law Alliance
PQ	Parliamentary Question
PR	Press Release
RIRB	Residential Institutions Redress Board
RTÉ	Raidió Teleifís Éireann
RSC	Sisters of Charity
RSM	Sisters of Mercy
RWRCI Act	*Redress for Women Resident in Certain Institutions Act*, 2015
SGS	Sisters of the Good Shepherd
SOCA	Survivors of Child Abuse
TD	Teachta Dála/Member of Parliament
TUSLA	Child and Family Agency
UCD	University College Dublin
UNCAT	United Nations Committee Against Torture
UNUPR	United Nations Universal Periodic Review

Foreword

Mari Steed

I have often said that I represent the nexus of what my friend and colleague Dr Jim Smith calls Ireland's 'architecture of containment'. My family embodies the generational legacies of just about every institution and social-control response that the State enforced upon those who didn't quite meet the 'standards' of morality, purity or whatever was deemed the norm in twentieth-century Ireland.

I was born in 1960 at the Bessboro Mother and Baby Home in Blackrock, Cork, to an unmarried mother, Josephine (or Josie, as she preferred). This home and two others at Sean Ross Abbey, Roscrea, Co. Tipperary and Castlepollard, Co. Westmeath were run by the Sisters of the Sacred Hearts of Jesus and Mary, an English-based religious order that came to Ireland even as the nation was birthing itself into political independence. Bessboro opened in 1922, with a capacity for some 140 women and children. The buildings and grounds of all three homes were once Anglo-Irish manor houses bequeathed to the order. And they were but 3 of more than 100 such homes, institutions, hostels, private nursing homes and individual brokers who orchestrated the placement of children born to unmarried mothers, so-called first offenders.[1] Prior to the passing of Ireland's first adoption legislation in 1952, these placements were considered informal or ad hoc: children were boarded-out, fostered and quasi-adopted. The households who took in these children at the time were sometimes paid a stipend by the local county or city government authority. Some parents convinced themselves that these arrangements constituted formal adoptions and would have the child's name changed by deed poll to their family surname. In other cases, the child was treated as an extra pair of hands on the farm or in the home, and no formal procedures were taken to alter her or his status within the family.

Before the *Adoption Act, 1952*, the Sacred Heart homes were rife with problems. Historical records show that infant and mother mortality rates in these institutional settings were far in excess (three to five times) that of the national average. Death certificates for children, in particular, list many highly preventable or treatable maladies such as marasmus (malnutrition) and other common early infant ailments which, even in pre-1952 Ireland, were survivable given proper care and medical intervention. There were no trained midwives working in these homes, so mothers laboured (and not infrequently died) under horrendous conditions. After Bessboro was briefly shut down in 1944 by Chief Medical Officer James Deeney, the nuns finally hired a qualified midwife by the name of June Goulding. In the late 1990s June wrote a book detailing these conditions and her own experience over the nine months she served the women at Bessboro.[2]

It was also during this period (1940–52) that the Sisters of the Sacred Hearts and other religious orders running these State-licensed institutions discovered that a lucrative market existed abroad, particularly in America, for Irish babies. American servicemen stationed in the UK during and immediately after the Second World War began hearing stories of children available for adoption and began to make inquiries via the Irish embassy in London and via intermediaries within the network of Catholic clergy. Other American families soon followed suit. Absent any formal legislation, the Irish Department of External Affairs was reluctant (and in some memoranda, outright horrified) to facilitate Irish children being sent abroad to completely unvetted homes. But as the demand increased and after the intervention of the all-powerful Catholic archbishop of Dublin John Charles McQuaid, who put in place criteria protecting the religious identity if not quite guaranteeing the health and welfare of the child, the Department was satisfied to look the other way.

My mother, Josie, was born in Co. Wexford in 1933, well over a decade before these children were being banished overseas. She, too, was the child of an unwed mother, Johanna. Although Mother and Baby Homes were operating at the time, Johanna was sent to the Enniscorthy County Home where Josie was born – the youngest of four non-marital children and the only one not raised in Johanna's family. Details of Josie's early life remain obscure, but it appears that she was sent to St Dominic's Industrial School, managed by the Good Shepherd Sisters in Waterford, at an early age. When she turned fourteen, Josie was transferred to a small training centre/sewing room run by the Sisters of Mercy at St Maries of the Isle, Cork, and then transferred on to the Magdalene Laundry sewing room at Sundays Well, Cork. This institution too was run by the Good Shepherd Order, and my mother remained there sewing for ten years, until she was released to the care of the Daughters of Charity to work at Our Lady's Hospital in Crumlin as a ward aide.

My mother, having spent twenty-six years of her life in the care of religious women, no doubt entered society with very little understanding of men or sex. She also lacked the affection of family and friends to nurture her. So, it is hardly surprising that on a rare evening out at a local dance hall, she met my father and became pregnant. Soon thereafter she was sent through another set of revolving institutional doors – first to St Patrick's Home on the Navan Road, Dublin, for a few weeks, then out to a local barrister's family as holiday help, then on to Ard Mhuire at Dunboyne, a Good Shepherd-run Mother and Baby Home, and finally down to Bessboro near the end of her pregnancy. She suffered from toxaemia, and mine was a difficult, fraught caesarean delivery at the nearby St Finbarr's Hospital in Cork. I cannot help but think that had she experienced the same labour just ten years earlier, both she and I would have died.

My mother, with her intimate first-hand experience of the nation's 'architecture of containment', told me many years later that she begged the nuns in Cork to have me adopted by an American family. She knew there were no supports or resources (or societal acceptance) that would allow her to keep me. Likewise, she knew there was a chance I might not find an adoptive home in Ireland and would simply repeat her own institutional history. So off to the United States I went in December 1961, just shy of my second birthday. I was one of the some 2,000-plus Irish babies to take this life-altering journey.

I was raised in a fairly progressive, comfortable home by Irish-American Catholics in Philadelphia. In fairness, I had a good upbringing and was afforded material comforts, education and opportunities I might not otherwise have enjoyed in Ireland, especially considering the status of my birth. But that all changed when I found myself pregnant at seventeen, as a senior preparing to graduate at a Catholic High School. My adoptive mother was not, unfortunately, progressive enough to handle the 'shame' of an out-of-wedlock birth, and despite offers of support from the baby's father, his parents and even some of my own adoptive relatives, my mother insisted I be sent to a Catholic-run home in Philadelphia where I too was forced to give my eldest daughter Kerry up for adoption. As it happened, Philadelphia in 1977 was not all that different from Cork in 1960: there were few supports for young women to make independent choices.

Twenty years later, having raised two more children with my husband, and surviving the abusive horror that was our marriage (ending in a murder–suicide attempt which I survived but my husband did not), I felt sufficiently strong to start on the journey to rediscover simultaneously my own roots and my lost daughter. I found Kerry first in 1997, and we joyously reunited and continue to enjoy a close, wonderful relationship. The journey through Ireland's history and my place therein proved more fraught: obstruction, secrecy and lies greeted me at every turn. I was determined, as I uncovered each new clue, to be open and truthful about what I discovered, which led me to create a website back in 1996, documenting my journey and the history I was attempting to navigate.

One of the first things I learnt was that my mother had been in a Magdalene Laundry for ten years. Back in 1996, I had no idea what these institutions were, despite the fact that Philadelphia hosted one of America's first Magdalene societies, operating from 1800 until 1915. But I was already connected to advocates in Ireland on the adoption side, so they were able to bring me up to speed, help me with contacts within the Good Shepherd Order to learn more of my mother's history (although they offered very little), and otherwise fast-track my education on Ireland's dark history of coercive institutions. I learnt about vaccine trials that had been conducted in many of these homes, including at Bessboro during the eighteen months I had been resident there. Further investigative work and *Freedom of Information Act* data requests led me to discover that I had actually been a trial subject in a 4-in-1 combination vaccine trial conducted by (then) Burroughs Wellcome Foundation (now GlaxoSmithKline PLC).

In the midst of this educational tsunami, I found and reunited with my mother Josie, who had married and was living in Swindon in the UK. She was overjoyed and had been waiting patiently for the day I would find her. I became even more determined to share, with her permission and as much as she would allow, her history. I was determined to understand how religious women who had vowed to serve their God and perform acts of mercy, charity and kindness could have treated women like my mother or babies like myself so cruelly. I found two equally determined comrades in the form of Angela Newsome, who like me had been adopted, and only much later discovered her own mother had spent nearly her entire adult life between the High Park, Drumcondra, and the Donnybrook Magdalene Laundries, and Claire McGettrick, another fellow adopted person with a keen mind and an equally honed sense of justice.

In 2003, just two years after I had first physically reconnected with my mother, Josie, the three of us formed Justice for Magdalenes (JFM). For the better part of five or six years, we toiled together collecting and investigating as much history as we could, helping former Magdalene women and planting the mustard seed that would eventually result in justice. Our work had not gone unnoticed: here in the United States, Boston College professor Jim Smith had endeavoured to research and write about the laundries and, in his research, had stumbled upon my website. Originally approaching the topic from an academic standpoint, Jim quickly became a passionate advocate and valuable contributor to our 'Little NGO That Could'.[3] We were soon joined by other academics, including the formidable Dr Katherine O'Donnell at University College Dublin, and the incredibly gifted Dr Maeve O'Rourke, who is one of the most brilliant legal minds I have ever had the honour to come across.

This little mustard seed soon grew into an incredibly powerful thorn in the Irish government's side in demanding justice for all victims and survivors of the Magdalene Laundries. Throughout the narrative that follows, you will read more about how we walked that road, what we have all learnt from the experience and how it has come to form a meaningful template for real restorative, transitional justice and truth-telling. The illustrious voices captured here grew from that mustard seed as well, because these advocates and activists knew it was important to listen to the voices of the marginalized – to hear our narratives and help us reach a wider platform. To lift us up when we needed it most.

I cannot say enough about my closest colleagues and friends who have walked this path with me. And I am equally grateful to the many other academics, historians, brilliant legal scholars, human rights advocates, allies from the NGO community, and fellow travellers from all walks of marginalized and oppressed life in Ireland. They have all lifted us up and recognized the fact that without truth, without truth-telling, there can be no justice. This is not a story about the 'good holy nuns or priests'; this story is about what survivors and victims endured and continue to endure. And how important it is that our story be affixed to the national narrative. I am proud to know and be associated with all of the individuals who have contributed to this important work.

As a coda to my story, I learnt over the last year from my eldest daughter Kerry that sadly, she, too, had been forced to place a daughter for adoption in 1993, when she was fifteen years old. She was recently found by her daughter, Kerrie (now twenty-seven), and they have spent the last two years getting to know one another and are enjoying a closeness and healing very similar to what Kerry and I enjoyed over the past two decades. It breaks my heart that even though Kerry and I have always been close – and she is so well aware of our family's generational legacy and my insistence on truth-telling – the stigma was still such that she could not bring herself to tell me. I understand that fear and most certainly do not hold her responsible for it or think any less of her for being unable to share it right away. But it is nevertheless amazing that this generational trauma continues unabated. It is my sincere hope that our past work, this book and the marvellous works done by other advocates and organizations will put an end to it finally.

Introduction

Ireland and the Magdalene Laundries: A Campaign for Justice

'I'm still there.'

These words were spoken by a survivor of Ireland's Magdalene Laundries at a Listening Exercise organized by JFMR as part of the DHM event in June 2018.[1] Known to us as 'Charlotte', this woman was living in a nursing home on the grounds of a former Magdalene institution run by the OLC, almost twenty-two years after the last Magdalene laundry ceased operation in 1996. At that time, she had spent a total of forty-one years in the nuns' 'care'. Given the opportunity to speak her truth, Charlotte wanted her voice to be heard, and she was not alone.

Some 146 survivors – from all across Ireland, the United Kingdom, United States and Australia – took part in the Listening Exercise. Sitting at tables of up to eight women, with a facilitator and scribe to record their conversation, they responded to three questions: 'What should we all know about the Magdalene Laundries? What lessons should we learn from what happened in the Magdalene Laundries? How – in what ways – should we remember what happened in the Magdalene Laundries?' In the ensuing conversations, the women spoke to their fellow survivors, shared personal histories and affirmed each other's experience. We begin this book by foregrounding the women's appeal that we 'listen to them' and 'hear what happened to them' so as to ensure it 'never be forgotten'. Woman after woman insisted that the 'truth' be told. They called for a national memorial, a museum and educational initiatives directed at Ireland's younger generations. They insisted that their story of abuse, neglect and exploitation 'be in the history books'. Taking our inspiration from these remarkable and resilient women, *Ireland and the Magdalene Laundries: A Campaign for Justice* responds to the women's requests.[2]

We five members of JFMR understand that our book offers but one account of this history. We do not claim a monopoly in telling the story of either the Magdalene Laundries or the fight for justice. But we believe it is important that survivors and their family members hear directly from us as to how we experienced the campaign that we fought on their behalf. It is now more than ten years since UNCAT recommended that the Irish State conduct a 'prompt, thorough and independent investigation' and ensure that survivors 'obtain redress' for the human rights abuses suffered in Ireland's Magdalene institutions. The one-decade anniversary of the IDC (the so-called McAleese investigation) and its *Report* is fast approaching. Because we continue to lose survivors to the ravages of time, we feel that now is the right moment to share our story.

Publishing JFMR's account of the campaign is consistent with the group's commitment to counter the epistemic injustice that, to date, has defined the Irish State's response to survivors and family members of the women who worked, and in some cases died, in the Magdalene Laundries. By 'epistemic injustice' we mean the State's unfair treatment of these citizens with respect to what counts as knowledge, whose understanding is considered credible and who gets to participate (and who does not get to participate) in establishing facts and deciding what is important to know and what questions need addressing. Legal scholars Máiréad Enright and Sinéad Ring argue compellingly that the Irish State's response to victim–survivors enacts a refusal to listen (testimonial injustice) or to alter the conditions under which victim–survivors can be heard (hermeneutical injustice).[3] This book reveals how the Irish State refused to adopt international human rights best practice in listening to survivors' testimony during the IDC and the ensuing restorative justice processes. The Irish State returned survivors' personal information to the four religious orders and destroyed all copies. The DoJ then placed the IDC's archive of State papers and administrative files in the care of the Taoiseach's Department whereupon officials rendered it inaccessible, stipulating that the archive is not subject to FOI data requests. The Irish State has continued to promote the view that the so-called McAleese Report is an official, fact-based narrative that disproves allegations that human rights violations ever took place in these institutions. The State claims that the Magdalene Laundries were not places of arbitrary detention, servitude or forced labour, or cruel or unusual punishment:

> No factual evidence to support allegations of systemic torture or ill treatment of a criminal nature in these institutions was found. . . . The facts uncovered by the Committee did not support the allegations that women were systematically detained unlawfully in these institutions or kept for long periods against their will.[4]

Ireland and the Magdalene Laundries: A Campaign for Justice disproves these assertions and shows how the State's own McAleese Report in fact reveals much evidence to the contrary. In offering a counter-narrative, we indict the State's treatment of women and girls in the past and in the present. We seek to make new and additional knowledge available so that survivors' experiences can be listened to and understood, and their voices can finally be heard. We hope, therefore, that this book models a way of understanding the treatment meted out to the socially vulnerable in Irish society, one that insists on knowledge production informed by the archive while also privileging survivor testimony as an opposing force.

This book compiles contemporaneous documentation related to the JFM campaign from diverse sources – survivor testimony, historical archives, the Dáil record, legislative and judicial debates, human rights submissions and assessments, FOI requests, investigative journalism, scholarship, creative literature and the arts – to build and share an archive of information and by so doing to fill in the void of silence cultivated by the official State practice outlined above. Our archive puts politicians, senior government officials, Church representatives and others on the record by directly quoting their own words in support of our analysis. In addition, we point readers to the JFMR website – jfmresearch.com – because our goal is to challenge knowledge suppression by making available the source materials cited in this book and a raft of additional materials, including transcripts from the MOHP, detailed analysis of the women's graves from the MNP, full-text access to all of our submissions to the Irish State and United Nations human rights bodies, and reports of our ongoing advocacy for a dedicated National Archive of Institutional, Adoption, and other 'Care'-Related Records at the site of the former Magdalene Laundry on Sean McDermott Street in Dublin.

Lastly, we offer this book as a model of social justice campaigning that merges academia, advocacy and activism. Many such books exist recounting similar campaigns in different national arenas, but *Ireland and the Magdalene Laundries* details a kind of work that was still relatively new in Ireland when our 'political campaign' began in 2009. In pursuing our goals, and in writing this book, we sought to disturb the establishment status quo by uncovering facts about these institutions. Writing in *The Irish Times* in September 1993, in the days following the exhumation of the human remains of former Magdalene women buried on the grounds of the High Park Laundry in Drumcondra, Fintan O'Toole evoked an image of bodies being unearthed, cremated and reburied in an unmarked mass grave at Dublin's Glasnevin Cemetery before concluding that 'It was a haunting image of a history that remains largely unwritten, a history that in being disturbed still has the power to disturb'.[5] As we suggest, Ireland's Magdalene Laundries continue to disturb contemporary society precisely because the hegemonic forces of State and Church again seek to bury this history in the present and thereby render survivors' truth unknown.

Our book begins with a description of how the nineteenth-century rise of the Catholic middle class was interdependent on the spectacular expansion of Catholic religious orders. There is a steady consistency in the rhetoric of Catholic fundraisers throughout the nineteenth century: they deploy emotional appeals to overcome the defeats of the Reformation and British colonization, and they encourage the forging of a proud, national identity of morally upright, economically stable and hence respectable Victorian Irish Catholics. The growing Irish middle class generously funded their Church which also was adept at seizing on funding opportunities available through the British colonial administration. The idealization of women in nineteenth-century Ireland was compatible with British Victorian idealization in general terms, and the Magdalene institutions were understood to be part of the 'rescue' movement so evident throughout the British Empire. By 1922 when twenty-six counties achieved independence and established the Irish Free State, we see that the ten Magdalene institutions, run by four Catholic religious orders, were already in place to perform their part in the purity project of nation-building. Their work was to contain the perilous bodies of those considered to be the most disrespectable: economically vulnerable girls and women. This chapter provides a broad outline of the ways in which the Irish State facilitated and supported the Magdalene institutions, and we hear first-hand testimony from survivors who endured the punitive, carceral regime.

Chapter 2 provides an account of the genesis of the JFM campaign which began as a response to the way in which the remains of former Magdalene women were hastily exhumed and cremated when the nuns at High Park wished to sell the women's gravesite to a property developer. The chapter details the immediate political context of the JFM campaign, focusing on how survivors of institutional abuse began to make their voices heard in the 1990s and on the State's response to that movement in the establishment of the CICA and eventually the RIRB. Survivors of Magdalene institutions were excluded from the RIRB, which was certainly unjust; yet we in JFM could also see how creating the CICA and the RIRB had enabled the Church/State establishment to prevent the legal justice system from addressing horrific crimes against Ireland's most vulnerable populations. We hoped to chart a different route to justice.

Chapters 3 and 4 offer an 'anatomy' of JFM's 'political campaign', which ran from 2009 to 2013. Chapter 3 traces the campaign's origins to survivor Catherine Whelan's initial phone call where she laid the challenge, 'what are we going to do about it'? The chapter describes the strategies adopted as our all-volunteer group set to work. Two core tenets were foundational: 'It's about the women' and 'Do no harm'. Clear objectives developed over time in consultation with survivors and family members, including the need for an apology, redress, and restorative justice measures. In detailing some of the strategies we deployed we hope this chapter will prove instructive to other campaigners for social justice. Ireland's political elite found ways to stymie our best efforts – a response captured best by survivors who understood such tactics as tantamount to an official policy of 'deny 'til they die'. The four religious congregations that operated the Magdalene Laundries ignored our attempts at fostering dialogue.

Chapter 4 outlines JFM's countervailing strategies, as we refused to compromise in the pursuit of justice for a community of women who were increasingly trusting us with their testimony. Many of these women became our friends. Inspired by their resilience, we took their case to the UN and argued for international recognition of their human rights. We contended that the abuse in Ireland's Magdalene Laundries amounted to 'slavery, servitude and enforced labour' and we pointed to the Irish State's obligation to ensure that the women obtain redress. We promoted survivors' testimony and our archival research as indispensable evidence of gross human rights violations. As Chapter 4 reveals, our approach met with success at the IHRC, UNCAT and an array of other national and international human rights bodies, and it contributed in no small part to forcing the Irish government's hand in establishing the IDC. The chapter details JFM's cooperation with the government's stated policy to respond to survivors' calls for justice. In retrospect, the chapter perhaps betrays our naïveté in failing to expose what one commentator characterized as the government's 'cruel, nasty, and cynically evasive' failure to act. Chapter 4 concludes by offering an overview of the massive effort to win the hearts and minds of the Irish public in our attempt to make it politically untenable for the government not to apologize and introduce redress upon publication of the *IDC Report* in early February 2013.

Chapter 5 begins on the morning of 5 February 2013, the day the *IDC Report* was published. The chapter recalls the events surrounding JFM's 'campaign within the campaign' that began immediately after Dr Martin McAleese's briefing to journalists and advocates, during which he alleged that there was no physical abuse in the Magdalene Laundries. The two weeks that followed saw a short, intense campaign necessitating new strategies which would ultimately lead to a State apology to Magdalene survivors. Throughout this campaign we were committed to generating public knowledge in terms of bringing survivors' ongoing trauma to public awareness and further demonstrating for Irish politicians and civil servants – from the State's own archives – how the State had facilitated and interacted with these institutions and in doing so had broken the law. Our research, teaching and activist skills equipped us to take on those tasks. Yet these same skills created a significant blind spot where we assumed that all we had to do was to scrupulously collect the evidence, rigorously construct compelling arguments and disseminate information so that the public might support the apology and restorative redress scheme that we proposed. We did not appreciate that those with power are adept at maintaining their power by a belligerent ignorance.

Chapter 6 analyses the *IDC Report* as a model of the distinct strategies by which the Irish establishment supresses 'unsettling knowledge': in other words, the kind of knowledge that challenges the status quo of those who govern and the bases of respectability and control of knowledge on which they assume and enact their superior power. We were to learn the hard way that even though the vast majority in the Republic might warmly support a call for justice for Magdalene survivors, those charged with the administration of justice regularly felt affronted at the idea of justice for these women. The knowledge produced by their testimony, the knowledge produced by our archival research and the knowledge produced by our legal arguments would all be routinely and systematically 'unknown'. We began to realize that the Church/State, those respectable people in power, would insist on preserving their ignorance and prejudice, which had rendered null and void the rights of the citizens incarcerated in Magdalene institutions and marred their lives. Ireland's establishment would deploy strategies of ignorance to render justice for Magdalene women unimaginable and therefore unattainable.

Chapter 7 recounts through a painstaking revisiting of individual case files, records of our interactions with State bureaucracy and internal departmental notes obtained by Conall Ó Fátharta, how the women were treated once the glare of public attention dissipated. Following Enda Kenny's apology, the government tasked Mr Justice John Quirke with devising an 'ex gratia' scheme, meaning that 'redress' would be offered as a gift rather than as of right. This philosophy, coupled with the decommissioning of survivors' legal rights against the State by forcing them to sign a waiver as a condition of entry to the scheme, led to profound re-abuse that continues to this day – contrary to the promise of Judge Quirke's interactions with more than 300 women which many of them reported to be cathartic. The chapter details how the DoJ refused to treat survivors' testimony as evidence for the purpose of supporting their redress applications; wherever the religious orders' records or assertions contradicted the women, the nuns were believed. The chapter sheds further light on deficient State structures by describing how the DoJ 'deemed' numerous women to lack sufficient capacity to apply to the scheme and then abandoned them as the government failed (and continues to fail) to commence the *Assisted Decision-Making (Capacity) Act 2015*. The extensive health and social care package which formed Judge Quirke's very first recommendation has never been provided by government, despite our best efforts at political advocacy leading to us being roundly defamed under parliamentary privilege. Meanwhile, the Dedicated Unit which Judge Quirke recommended to provide advocacy assistance to the women and a mechanism for them to meet and supervise the State's memorialization activities remains un-implemented.

Chapter 8 comes full circle and returns to the original motivations for the JFM campaign, which began in 2003 on the discovery of anomalies surrounding the exhumation of 155 human remains from the OLC Magdalene Laundry at High Park a decade earlier. Using sources ignored by the IDC, this chapter demonstrates that 110 women could not be identified during the exhumations and that in the vast majority of cases the identities of the exhumed remains did not correspond with the names provided to the DoEnv by OLC. The chapter reveals major failings by the DoEnv, the Gardaí and the IDC, all of whom neglected to adequately investigate the exhumations. We further demonstrate that the land sale and subsequent exhumation and cremation of the women's remains were motivated by OLC's financial concerns. Chapter 8 closes with an analysis of the fundamental flaws in the OLC-commissioned research directed by Dr Jacinta Prunty and disproves the *IDC Report*'s claim that all 155 exhumed women have been accounted for.

Our concluding chapter asks, as the Republic of Ireland enters its second century of independence, 'Who do we want to be?' We contend that the experiences of the former Magdalene women, as we have witnessed them, demonstrate the necessity of truth-telling to redress and of institutional change to honouring the dignity of those who have suffered State/Church abuse. 'Transformative' reparations are a matter of rebalancing power. Justice requires inviting those who are affected to define the harms perpetrated, the ways in which harms persist and the manner in which they might be remedied. This final chapter of our book reflects on the DHM Listening Exercise and Event in summer 2018, which has spurred us and an ever-growing movement onwards in pursuit of the education and testimonial justice which survivors wish to see for the sake of present and future generations. The women and their families who gathered for DHM extended their generosity and friendship, not only to each other but to all of us, as they discussed the truth of what our nation has been and who we could be, should we care to listen to what they know. The challenge that we take on, and that we invite the Irish establishment to accept, is to work to ensure – as the women request – that similar abuses cease and are never allowed to happen again.

1

Ireland's Magdalene Laundries and the lives lived there

The notorious eighteenth-century Penal Laws denied Catholics in Ireland not only religious freedom but also the rights to a formal education and entry into the legal profession and government. Their rights to own and inherit land were also severely curtailed. The result was that the Irish Catholic elite largely became merchants and were educated on the Continent, and an increasingly wealthy Catholic mercantile class became more evident by the end of the eighteenth century. With the outbreak of the French Revolution, a National Seminary was established in Maynooth as Catholicism came to be understood by the British colonial powers as a bulwark against the radical Republicanism that appeared as an imminent and menacing threat. The early decades of the Irish nineteenth century saw a zeal for Catholic emancipation, which became a mass movement led by Daniel O'Connell. The eventual passing of the Emancipation Act of 1829 led to further consolidation of Catholic cultural, social and economic power on the island.[1] Between 1790 and the Famine of 1847 more than 2,000 Catholic Churches were built in Ireland,[2] even as the vast majority of the country's Catholic population suffered from exploitation by landlords, starvation due to unequal access to land-holding or coerced emigration. The Catholic Repeal and Revival movements were experienced by Catholics of all classes, wealthy and poor alike, as a resistance to the inequities of colonization. The obligation on all to pay significant taxes to the Protestant Church of Ireland was keenly felt as an injustice by Irish Catholics – all the more so because the foundations of many of the Anglican churches were formerly Roman Catholic in the pre-Reformation era, before the brutal subjugation of the country by Cromwell's army in the 1640s. As the bishop of Kildare and Leighlin expressed it in the 1820s, 'They [Catholics] still are bound to rebuild and ornament their own former parish church and spire, that they may stand in the midst of them as records of the right of conquest, or the triumph of law over equity and the public good.'[3] Another contemporary Catholic commentator concurred: 'It is not right that those who live upon potatoes and sour milk, should be called on to build elegant churches for those who fare sumptuously and drink wine every day.'[4] (The irony appears to be lost on the commentator that the Irish poor were also called upon and indeed responded to the consistent fundraising efforts led by the Catholic hierarchy and clergy.) There is a remarkable consistency in the rhetoric of Catholic fundraisers throughout the nineteenth century: they deployed emotional appeals to overcoming the defeats of the Reformation and colonization and forging a proud national identity of morally upright, economically stable and hence respectable Victorian Irish Catholics.[5]

The Great Famine of 1845–53 resulted in a near annihilation of the cottier class who lived in the worst housing: in the fourth-class cabins with an acre attached to grow their food (potatoes being the favoured crop). Yet in this post-Famine era we see what historians describe as an upward Catholic socio-economic transition – a 'Catholic embourgeoisement' – that is a distinct 'upward' social mobility, where an increasing number of Catholics entered the respectable and economically secure ranks of the middle class.[6] The rise of the Catholic middle classes was most evident from the 1860s and is indivisible from the expansion of Catholic religious orders, which offered the Catholic middle class an education and an affirmation of respectability. The growing Irish middle class generously funded their Church which also was adept at seizing on opportunities available through State funding. As James M. Smith describes it,

> The governing burden of the British colonial administration was lightened as it increasingly ceded responsibility to the Catholic Church for areas of social welfare including education, health care, and institutional provision. Irish society in general, especially the emerging Catholic middle class, strengthened its identity as a nation; its sense of modernization and progress was increasingly vested in notions of social and moral respectability.[7]

As modern democratic and nationalist states came to be established throughout Europe in the nineteenth century and as European imperialism expanded globally, the Catholic Church hierarchy operated a policy of setting up 'voluntary' organizations run by religious orders or laypeople with express allegiance to the institution, in order to assert its power and maintain its relevance within the dominant political structures. The increasing number of Victorian Catholic enterprises across the island of Ireland made manifest the new social, cultural, political and economic successes of Catholics more generally. Irish middle-class women became nuns in significant numbers; at the very beginning of the nineteenth century there were 120 nuns in Ireland and by 1901 there were 35 religious orders of about 8,000 nuns living in 368 convents. This increase occurred at a time when the Irish population went from 6.5 million recorded in the 1841 census to 3.3 million in 1901. In 1800 nuns made up approximately 6 per cent of the Catholic Church's ordained workforce; by 1851 they comprised about 38 per cent and they were 64 per cent of the Catholic ordinations by the end of the nineteenth century.[8] The idealization of women in nineteenth-century Ireland was compatible with British Victorian idealization in general terms, and the Magdalene institutions were understood to be part of the 'rescue' movement so evident throughout the nineteenth-century British Empire.[9] The object of 'rescue' was the prostitute or 'wayward' female who was regarded as 'fallen' even from the status of 'woman', that idealized paragon who was without sexual drive or sexual experience apart from a dutiful response to facilitating her husband's desire. The religious sisters were universally admired for embodying sexual chastity, a 'purity' essential to idealized womanhood, and the religious sisters of the Magdalene institutions were further admired for sacrificing their pure lives to the rescue of the 'impure' and trying to elevate the 'fallen woman' to a respectable standard of womanhood. As the nineteenth century turned into the twentieth, an overwhelming majority of the Catholic middle classes supported the IPP who argued that they were capable of Irish nationalist self-governance or 'Home Rule' within the British Empire. The Sisters in Ireland's Magdalenes played their part in confining the disreputable women or the daughters of disreputable women and putting them to penitential hard labour where they could atone for their sins.

From 1895 the IPP lobbied assiduously to ensure that businesses run by religious sisters such as laundries and needlework enterprises would not be subject to legislative oversight. British House of Commons' debates in 1901 and 1907 reveal how the IPP fought for exemptions from health and safety regulation on behalf of the nuns. The leader of the party, John Redmond, sought to exclude Magdalene Laundries from the *Factory and Workshop Act 1901*, explaining that these institutions' mission was to prevent 'fallen women . . . from continuing with their evil courses' and that 'the great object [of the religious orders] was to keep these girls in those institutions'. The Good Shepherd Sisters were 'unanimously of the opinion that the introduction into their institutions of an outside authority in the shape of Government inspectors would completely destroy the discipline of their institutions', Redmond maintained.[10] Irish MPs remained steadfast even when English MPs presented evidence of serious abuses involving forced labour in laundries run by the Good Shepherd Order in France. The IPP's position, so tenaciously defended in Westminster, was to become official Irish Free State policy.

Ireland's War of Independence, which concluded in 1921, led to the end of British rule in twenty-six of the island's thirty-two counties and established the Irish Free State / *Saorstát Éireann*. In the newly independent Ireland, the ten remaining Magdalene institutions, all Catholic in ethos and operated by four congregations of nuns, were about to receive a renewed lease of life.[11] As Maria Luddy notes, in Ireland's revolutionary period and in the early years of independence, the Magdalene institutions became carceral institutions rather than temporary refuges.[12] Irish patriots, with the support of the newly empowered Catholic hierarchy, were eager to establish control in symbolic and material terms. Maternity and social reproduction became significant territory on which to assert a national patriarchal discourse of moral probity and purity, particularly when opposed to the former colonizer. The British Empire might possess vast wealth and political power, but the fledging Free State would cultivate supremacy on the high moral ground – or so the argument ran. Ireland would be triumphantly Catholic above all else.

Political discourse in support of this aspiration was distinctly gendered in the Free State: men immediately began to establish their new-found powers of self-governance by demonstrating control over the firepower of militarized men and the sexuality and reproductive powers of women, in particular the bodies of impoverished women and their children. The Irish establishment was keen both to demonstrate to their former British overlords that they could maintain law and order and to gain international recognition for the high moral order of the country. This morality became most evident in the State-sanctioned Catholic religiosity of the nation. Irish society's ubiquitous religious expression was not something imposed on the everyday culture of the people by dominant powers; rather, it was understood by the vast majority of the people to be intrinsic to the freedom won from colonial oppression. The allegiance of the overwhelming majority of Free State (and later Irish Republic) citizens to the Catholic Church was deep; the people had a profound and intimate attachment to the moral teachings, metaphysical view, folk and canonical rituals, and consolation provided by a much-loved Church.[13]

The Irish establishment, meanwhile, emerged from the symbiotic dyad of Catholic Church and State bodies that combined to copper-fasten a monopoly on power in the new country. In 1931 the publication of a Papal encyclical by Pope Pius XI entitled *Quadragesimo Anno* provided a clear manifesto and rationale for the Catholic Church's practice of establishing voluntary bodies to run educational, health, social welfare and carceral institutions. The encyclical called for harmony between the social classes in order to defeat the spread of socialism. It argued against a strong State and big government in favour of the principle of 'subsidiarity', claiming that it was a disturbance of the Natural Law to assign to a higher association (government) what lesser and subordinate organizations could do. The Pope recommended that the State should merely regulate subsidiary organizations' provision of social services. The Catholic Church hierarchy applied this policy in earnest and were masterful at harnessing State resources to social and educational initiatives which were managed by clergy, Catholic religious orders and lay Catholic organizations.[14] John Charles McQuaid, who served as archbishop of Dublin from 1940 to 1972, was particularly adept at persuading successive Irish governments to finance Church involvement in what is still a large 'voluntary sector' while retaining ecclesiastical control of these projects.[15] The Catholic Church's pre-eminent political and cultural position in mid-twentieth-century Ireland can be seen most clearly in its resounding defeat of Dr Noël Browne's 'Mother and Child Scheme' which was rejected because it was a plan for socialized medicine.[16]

Concern for the plight of the girls and women confined in Magdalene Laundries continued to be voiced throughout the twentieth century, yet time and again the governing elite ignored all complaints. Early on, the Irish State strengthened the religious orders' hand by deliberately excluding their commercial operations from the Census of Production after the 1926 Preliminary Report on Laundry, Dyeing and Cleaning Trades revealed that nearly half (thirty-seven) of the eighty returns for commercial laundry work came from religious institutions ('Convents, Penitentiaries, Female Industrial Schools, etc.'). The report states that 'The amounts charged to customers in 1926 for laundry work done by such institutions amounted to £97,325'. It further acknowledges that the workers (referred to as 'inmates') engaged in this commercial laundry work were not paid for their labour.[17]

In 1936, the *Conditions of Employment Act* exempted all institutions 'carried on for charitable or reformatory purposes' from the requirement to pay wages to their industrial workers.[18] While this legislation otherwise applied to the Magdalene Laundries, as did the *Factories Act 1955* and subsequent regulations, State records show that only piecemeal inspections of Magdalene Laundries took place from 1957 onwards. The records also show that the factory inspectors merely ensured that the machines and processes of production met health and safety regulations, and none spoke to the incarcerated workforce or inquired into their living conditions, or lack of wages and social security payments.[19] The archives show that State officials were involved in directing and escorting girls and women to the convents, in particular Court Probation Officers, but there is not one instance recorded of State officials ensuring their release at the end of the appointed sentences.[20]

It was not until 1970 and the publication of *The Reformatory and Industrial Schools Systems Report* (known as the *Kennedy Report*) that we see a published official objection to the use of Magdalene Laundries as places of arbitrary detention. The *Report* stated that 'at least 70 girls between the ages of 13 and 19 years' were confined in the laundries when they 'should properly be dealt with under the Reformatory Schools system'; the *Report* concluded:

> This method of voluntary arrangement for placement can be criticised on a number of grounds. It is a haphazard system, its legal validity is doubtful and the girls admitted in this irregular way and not being aware of their rights, may remain for long periods and become, in the process, unfit for re-emergence into society. In the past, many girls have been taken into these convents and remained there all their lives.[21]

The *Kennedy Report* did not result in any official remedial action.

The governing establishment that came to power in the 1920s still holds significant sway in twenty-first-century Ireland, as demonstrated by the fact that much of the Irish national education and health services continue to be State-funded and Church-run. The vast majority (over 90 per cent) of primary schools in Ireland are owned and managed under the patronage of the Catholic Church.[22] The sole shareholders of the two main teaching hospitals of UCD (the Mater and St Vincent's public hospitals) are the RSM and the RSC, respectively. These congregations each operated two Magdalene institutions for much of the twentieth century. They also managed other residential institutions for children, which received damning assessments in the *CICA Final Report* (widely known as *The Ryan Report*). In 2017 the RSC was handed sole ownership of the proposed development of a new INMH, to be built at the cost of €300 million and funded solely by the Irish Exchequer in spite of stated concerns by the Institute of Obstetricians in Ireland.[23] Significant protest against public funding ensued in part because Catholic religious teaching forbids services routinely carried out by medical staff in maternity hospitals in other countries (such as elective sterilization, IVF and terminations of pregnancies). The public scrutiny forced the government to acknowledge critical flaws in the development deal, and the minister for health began exploring public ownership, long-term lease and compulsory purchase options. However, it still remains unclear to what extent the RSC will exert influence and control over the proposed INMH.[24]

Reproductive injustice

The governing class throughout twentieth-century Ireland consistently denied women reproductive justice. Reflecting human rights values, the concept of reproductive justice declares that those who can get pregnant alone ought to decide if and when they will have a baby and the conditions under which they will give birth.[25] Likewise, it maintains that those who are pregnant should be enabled to decide if they will not have a baby and exercise their options for preventing or ending a pregnancy. Finally, it holds that those who give birth should be allowed to parent the child with the necessary social supports in safe environments and healthy communities, and without fear of violence from individuals or the government. For most of the past hundred years, the Irish government denied access to contraception. While Irish marriage rates were the lowest in twentieth-century Europe, family sizes were by far the biggest, with poorer women having less access to information and support on how to limit family sizes.[26] Abortion was legally prohibited until 2018, forcing Irish girls and women to go abroad in secrecy and at great expense and personal anguish to seek terminations; limitations in the current law still force some to do so. There were a number of high-profile cases where the constitutional ban on abortion, introduced by referendum in 1983, was shown to cause extreme suffering and even death.[27] Some Irish hospitals until the 1980s also inflicted symphysiotomies on women giving birth rather than provide caesarean sections.[28] The same establishment – through the judiciary, legal and medical professions, and religious and lay social workers – was busy taking away the children of poor women and working-class widowers, and putting those children into Church-run/State-funded industrial and reformatory schools where abuse was endemic. It also declared unmarried mothers 'a problem'; it set up county homes and funded Mother and Baby Homes for the confinement (and to a large extent incarceration) of these women, who routinely found themselves giving birth without pain relief and then separated from their baby without consent.[29] As Maria Luddy explains:

> Representing possible immorality, a drain on public finances and someone in need not only of rescue, but also of institutionalisation, the unmarried mother had become, by the foundation of the Irish Free State in 1922, a symbol of unacceptable sexual activity and a problem that had the potential to blight the reputation not only of the family but of the nation.[30]

The so-called 'illegitimate' children born in these maternity homes died in disproportionately large numbers; infant mortality rates in institutional settings suggest an egregious lack of care for the nation's most vulnerable citizens.[31] Those infants who survived were separated from their mothers and 'boarded out', placed in an industrial school, or, after the commencement of adoption legislation in January 1953, formally adopted under a closed, secret and scarcely monitored system. Others were banished without legislative authorization (but with the participation of the Department of Foreign Affairs) to adoptions abroad, with little or no oversight to ensure their safety.[32] Access to sterilization was forbidden and fertility treatment was and still is curtailed. It was not until 1973 that the government introduced a social welfare allowance for single mothers. The powerlessness of unmarried girls and women to maintain custody of their child is illustrated by the fact that, in 1967, a full 97 per cent of children born outside of marriage were adopted.[33] When we consider these factors, together with others (e.g. divorce was not introduced until 1995; services to address domestic and sexual abuse are minimal; and sex education is still not taught in a systematic way in schools), then we begin to apprehend the contours of reproductive oppression in post-independence Ireland up to the present day.[34] Its effects are manifest in the individuals directly impacted, in their families, and in multi-generational reverberations of trauma and loss. The remnants are visible even today in the Irish Constitution of 1937, such as in Article 41.1 which declares that the family (historically interpreted as the heteronormative family based in marriage) is the 'natural primary and fundamental unit group of society'. Article 41.2 proceeds to define the circumscribed position of the woman/mother within this moral institution, as follows:

1 In particular, the State recognises that by her life within the home, woman gives to the State a support without which the common good cannot be achieved.
2 The State shall, therefore, endeavour to ensure that mothers shall not be obliged by economic necessity to engage in labour to the neglect of their duties in the home.[35]

In this context, Ireland's Magdalene institutions are best understood not as an aberration but as a logical function within the ideology of the Irish establishment whereby law and policy have purposefully and systematically controlled and exploited women's sexuality, labour and bodies. Ultimately, their function impacted poor and vulnerable women disproportionately, the population deemed most threatening to establishment sensibilities.

This ideology and practice began to form even in the midst of the Civil War of 1922 when W. T. Cosgrave, first president of the Executive Council, found money and large premises to give to Frank Duff (1889–1980), who established the Legion of Mary in 1921 and made the eradication of prostitution in Dublin a particular focus of his mission. Duff was a prominent civil servant who, like most of his peers, was initially trained in the British colonial administration in Dublin. Prior to Irish independence all Irish cities and most large towns included a visible population of garrisoned British soldiers, and these urban districts witnessed an active trade in prostitution that serviced the military.[36] Irish nationalist discourse depicted the British military as carriers of syphilis. Joyce's *Ulysses* illustrates this hackneyed denunciation when the fulminating Irish nationalist 'Citizen' in the Cyclops chapter denounces British colonial rule and civilization as nothing more than a 'syphilization'.[37] Irish feminists specifically sought to counter the misery that venereal infection caused to women and their children.[38] Irish Citizen Army medical officer Dr Kathleen Lynn and her feminist colleagues founded St Ultan's Hospital in 1919 in an effort to combat the suffering of poor children, many of whom were suffering from congenital syphilis. Dublin's child mortality rates were the worst in Europe (and the city had the worst housing in the UK).[39] However, Lynn's enlightened approach was swiftly sidelined with the establishment of the Irish Free State.[40] In the decades following independence, the prostitute was a reminder to the new Ireland of the evils popularly associated with British military rule. Dublin's prostitutes could be seen visibly operating in areas of the city such as the Phoenix Park, the docks, around St Stephen's Green and most famously in the Monto district, Europe's largest 'red light' district (an area of less than 1 square mile just to the east of the city's main thoroughfare of Sackville Street, now known as O'Connell Street).[41] Within weeks of the

Free State's establishment, the women who sold sex in this area fell under the attention of Duff's Legion of Mary, one of the earliest State-funded/Catholic-run organizations in twentieth-century Ireland. Duff recruited powerful supporters for his social purity campaign, most notably the outspoken Jesuit Fr R. S. Devane and Major General W. R. E. Murphy (Liam Ó Murchadha), deputy commissioner of An Garda Síochána.[42] On the night of 12 March 1925, the social purity crusade made an organized assault on the brothels of the Monto. The police made over 120 arrests; a priest blessed every house and the area ceased to be a red-light district. The most prominent site in the area remained the Magdalene Laundry on Gloucester Street (later renamed Sean McDermott Street) whose presence marked the northern boundary of the old Monto district.

The new Free State, with its emphasis on ensuring social purity and sexual respectability, maintained a system of incarcerating vulnerable women and children. It did so by utilizing the largely inherited British colonial system of massive Victorian institutions funded by the State and managed by Catholic religious orders, which had provided basic levels of relief to the Irish poor. The mass institutionalization of the socially and economically vulnerable (particularly women and children) continued post-independence and was maintained by a system of capitation payments to the religious orders from the Irish State exchequer for most of the twentieth century.[43] Ireland's prison population was a relatively negligible percentage of the population by mid-century (there was an average of just fifty women annually held in Irish prisons), yet by 1951, about 1 in every 100 Irish citizens was coercively confined in an institution operated collaboratively by the Church/State establishment, including psychiatric hospitals, industrial and reformatory schools, residential schools for disabled children, Mother and Baby Homes, county homes and Magdalene institutions.[44] Scholars refer to this coercive confinement as Ireland's 'architecture of containment', and we can see that its policing had a gender, class, ethnic and disability focus that upheld patriarchal, married, middle-class, white, settled and able-bodied norms.[45] The architecture of containment concentrated on the surveillance and monitoring of all girls an women and, where considered necessary, the incarceration of poorer women and their children; but, it also contained Travellers, so-called 'illegitimate' children, children designated as 'mixed race', and children and adults with disabilities. Legacy issues stemming from this system of surveillance, punishment and incarceration are still manifest in twenty-first century Ireland: one prime example being that adopted people are denied their rights to their birth certificates and other personal data from their adoption files, and other examples being the continuing institutionalization (with capitation payments from the State to private commercial enterprises providing institutional care) of older people, people with disabilities, homeless families and people seeking asylum.

Class and the exodus of Irish women and Irish nuns in the twentieth century

About one in every two people born in nineteenth-century Ireland left: by 1900 nearly as many people born in Ireland lived outside the country as in it.[46] After 1922 mass emigration continued, albeit not at the same alarming rate. Yet women left in even greater numbers than men, and Ireland had by far the highest rate of female emigration of any European country between 1945 and 1960.[47] The Irish patriarchal establishment worried about the exodus of young Irish women (two-thirds were aged between fifteen and twenty-four), particularly the 'servant class' when there were so many vacant positions for domestics among the Irish middle class. Throughout the 1930s, 1940s and 1950s, government officials were also concerned about the moral downfall of young Irish women emigrating to the UK. The popular Catholic press referred to this exodus as 'unnatural' and 'evil'.[48] A memo from the Department of External Affairs in 1947 euphemistically mused that 'the abnormal emigration of young girls' must lie in their sexual drive: 'those obscure, traditional, psychological factors in which it has its principal roots'.[49] The newly independent nation had become an increasingly stultifying and hostile place for women and many left when they could.[50]

Irish women religious also left in significant numbers throughout the nineteenth and twentieth centuries and were instrumental in the establishment of welfare and educational systems in American cities as well as the provision of education, healthcare and social welfare in the UK. Studies show that the religious congregations made prudent use of the dowries that women joining the orders were generally expected to bring (commensurate with the money that a middle-class woman would bring with her into a marriage).[51] The dowries allowed the nuns the financial wherewithal to establish their institutions and to maintain forms of independence from bishops who sought to exert their dominance over the Sisters.[52] The dowry system lasted largely until the late 1960s, thereby ensuring that Irish women religious commanded respect on class grounds as well as on the grounds of reverence for their spiritual vocations, called by God to live a holy life, as brides of Christ.[53] Irish women joined Catholic religious communities in England in large numbers, accounting for 75 per cent of membership in some orders, proliferating mostly in the prosperous south east, especially London. While the influence of Irish nuns has been well documented in histories of education, healthcare and social welfare outside Ireland, there remains a curious dearth of scholarship focused on the impact of female religious in Ireland.[54] Barbara Walsh's work on Irish women religious in twentieth-century England might give us the closest picture of how congregations of Irish sisters operated in the Free State and Republic. The Sisters predominantly came from the middle class of strong farmers, cattle dealers and small-town merchants and from the best farming land in Ireland, that is, Munster and South Leinster.[55] Walsh charts the financial strategies that allowed for the development of these religious communities from small and impoverished beginnings to their becoming 'custodians and administrators of vast wealthy and efficient corporate institutions' by the outbreak of the Second World War.[56] She notes that religious sisters' wages as teachers, nurses, medics and the payment to congregations by local and national government for the health, education and social services they ran, as well as dowries of choir sisters, were all subject to investment policies in property, shares and expansion of services and revenue-generating income streams which were 'enviably successful'.[57] Walsh asks:

> Why were these daughters of the strong farmers and middle-class merchants so successful in their chosen careers? Perhaps they brought to convent life an

> overlooked bonus in that their family backgrounds had fostered in them an inherent business acumen and authority. It was knowledge gathered in the most traditional and basic way since childhood by listening to the talk round the table. These girls had grown up understanding the negotiating skills required by self-employed farmers for striking deals, for haggling and manoeuvring over a price. If not exactly 'street-wise' in the urban sense, it might be said that they were most certainly 'market-place aware' when it came to financial matters. They were accustomed to the supervision of farm servants and other staff and they were familiar with animal husbandry – which was useful if a convent ran a small farm, as many did. As 'daughters of the house', young Irishwomen knew how to run a middle-class household. Convent households were, in essence, exactly this and they had to conduct their affairs in a business-like manner to survive.[58]

Those nuns who remained in Ireland played an even greater role in shaping the nation's economic life and society than their sisters abroad. Margaret MacCurtain O. P., a pioneer of Irish women's history and a Dominican Sister, describes how 'the involvement of female religious orders with state projects, education, hospitals, and social welfare organizations has been of staggering proportions. . . . Elites and power players have not been examined to any great extent in twentieth- century Ireland. Leaders of women's religious orders were both.'[59] At the beginning of the twentieth century there were just over 8,000 nuns in 35 orders living in 368 convents on the island of Ireland. Admissions to novitiates climbed steadily, peaked around 1960, remained stable until 1972 and then declined decisively. In the last decade of the twentieth century, there were 128 religious congregations of women and 24 monasteries of women contemplatives in the Republic of Ireland. Historian Diarmaid Ferriter has noted that MacCurtain provides us with some understanding of how nuns were often situated in an invidious position: culturally very powerful in the wider society, yet with very little political power within the patriarchal hierarchy of the Church.[60] MacCurtain suggests that it was difficult even for powerful indigenous Irish orders, such as the RSM, to resist the hierarchy when they wished to appropriate the nuns' successful enterprises.[61]

The Catholic Church's Second Ecumenical Council of the Vatican (commonly known as Vatican II) occurred from 1962 to 1965 and addressed relations between the Church and the modern world. It might be argued that the position of nuns post-Vatican II was rendered largely untenable or certainly greatly challenged by the dicta of the Church hierarchy. The message as relayed from the Vatican by cardinals, archbishops and bishops was that nuns had to 'modernise'; their habitual dress, their monastic enclosure, the precepts and disciplinary procedures of their religious formation, the class system of dowry and lay sisters, and even their religious names were to be eschewed. Every aspect of a nun's life and community was overhauled without any clear guidance on how they were expected to constitute and conduct themselves. The centuries-old traditions to which they had dedicated their lives were, within a brief number of years, rendered old-fashioned, austere and regimented. The obsolescence of convent life seemed mandated, and yet reformation stopped short of allowing for the ordination of women as priests. Indeed, as MacCurtain rather wryly notes, 'In the same decade [immediately post Vatican II] apostolic religious orders of women, what used to be known as the active orders discovered that they were members of the laity.'[62] In other words, the Church hierarchy decreed that nuns who were not part of a contemplative order held the same rank and status as non-ordained lay people.

Magdalene lives in the Irish Free State and Republic

Ireland's Magdalene institutions remained in existence for most of the twentieth century; the last one, on Sean McDermott Street in Dublin, abutting the old Monto district, closed in 1996.[63] They were operated by four religious congregations – the OLC ran Laundries at High Park, Drumcondra, and Sean McDermott Street in Dublin; while the SGS ran Magdalenes in Cork city (Sundays Well), Waterford, Limerick, and New Ross, Co. Wexford.[64] The RSM ran laundries in Galway and Dún Laoghaire, and the RSC operated Magdalenes in Cork (Peacock Lane) and Dublin (Donnybrook). All four orders also owned and managed residential industrial schools where poor children considered 'wayward' or 'neglected' were held. The OLC ran a reformatory school for girls at Kilmacud, Stillorgan, while the Good Shepherds ran a reformatory school in Limerick and later a Mother and Baby Home at Dunboyne, Co. Meath.

After 1922, the ten Magdalene institutions cannot be understood as rehabilitative: they were not residences that were primarily offering temporary asylum and opportunities for women to train for a career in service. They were operated less by a rationale of benign penance and were deliberately punitive, and as the century progressed, they became increasingly carceral. There was a general assumption in Irish culture that the girls and women confined in these institutions had to atone for sins (generally 'sins of the flesh') that they were adjudged to have committed or be at risk of committing. Survivors who gave their testimony to JFM and who participated in the MOHP say the girls and women incarcerated in the laundries were generally young and motherless, and in a relatively small number of cases, they may have given birth outside wedlock.[65] Other women were intellectually disabled; some had committed minor crimes. Many were raised as children in industrial schools and transferred 'on licence' to the laundries, typically upon reaching their sixteenth birthday when the State capitation grant payments ended (and sometimes at a younger age as punishment). Most strikingly, girls who were committed to Magdalene institutions were regularly victims of incest, sexual assault and rape.[66] In the words of one survivor who found herself incarcerated in a Magdalene after she complained to the Gardaí that her father was sexually assaulting her, she was told by the nuns:

> It was my fault I was in there because I made 'behavioural suggestions' . . . towards my father. . . . I don't know how many times I went up to the police after Mum died. And told them what was going on, and they still ignored it. And he got away with it. Yet I'm the one who's punished for telling the truth. And yet nobody heard me, nobody listened. I was just a child . . . why weren't we heard . . . why weren't the

men questioned? Why was it always the woman's fault? You know, why was I the only one punished? Why wasn't my father punished?[67]

Survivors of Ireland's Magdalene institutions are making their testimonies available in an increasing number of publicly available documents and databases, and many and diverse voices uniformly attest to a brutal regime.[68] These testimonies, which are further corroborated by other witnesses, compensate for the fact that the religious orders will not release Magdalene records for the twentieth century, even in redacted form.[69]

The nuns held the Magdalene girls and women under lock and key.[70] Once inside the convents, girls and women were imprisoned behind locked doors, barred or unreachable windows and high walls (oftentimes with barbed wire, spikes or broken glass cemented at the apex).[71] The gates to the street were locked. Internal doors were also locked, including the doors to the dormitories at night-time.[72] As one survivor, 'Maisie K.' describes it:

> You couldn't look out a window. They were high but the windows where I was in the room with the calendar and the ironing room there was six inch thick glass . . . you could see shadows but you couldn't see out. You didn't know anything about what went on outside. You weren't even allowed to stand and look out. If you'd seen a gate open or a door it would be immediately closed. It was like you know you were wiped out of that area of the world. You couldn't see out the windows and in the dormitories they were too high up to look outside as well.[73]

The women were given little information as to when or even whether they would be released: they experienced the institutions as prisons. The Sisters cut the hair short of girls and women brought into their institutions. As one survivor remembers,

> I saw the scissors in her hand. . . . They forced me on my knees and she cut my hair . . . she left me with nothing only bits sticking out here and there in my head and it was then I think that my whole attitude towards nuns . . . changed – changed completely. . . . It was the first time in my life that I learned to hate somebody.[74]

Upon entry, the girls and women had to strip, and their clothes were taken away and replaced with drab work uniforms. The Sisters gave them a religious name and sometimes also a number. This was the name and number by which they were identified inside the institution, as the nuns sought to erase their former identity and insist on treating the Magdalenes as 'penitents', regardless of the reasons they found themselves in the institution. Survivor 'Kate O'Sullivan' says of her experience at Sundays Well: 'if they opened the window it wouldn't be too bad, they wouldn't open the window, no, "you're here for your sins", that's what we were told.'[75] A survivor who was incarcerated in High Park describes it thus:

> You weren't in there for sympathy, you were in there to be punished. And that's basically what it was all about. You did wrong and you've heard of people saying,

> 'I'll make your life hell.' Our lives were made hell, literally made hell. And because you did wrong. And it wasn't just a sort of 5-minute punishment. You were being punished. And you were reminded of why you were in there. You know? . . . And as far as they were concerned you did wrong. And the person who actually did wrong got away with it. So you were being punished for nothing.[76]

Many women recall being instructed not to speak about their home-place or family. Visits by friends or relatives were not encouraged and were often monitored when they did occur. Letters were censored or undelivered. Figures relating to the three Dublin Magdalene convents at the end of 1983 reveal that nearly a quarter of the women confined had not seen their siblings since entering the institution; most had not seen other relatives or friends, and while just over half of the women had children, approximately 6 per cent of those Magdalene women who were mothers saw their children after incarceration.[77] Survivors repeatedly recall being told: 'Nobody wants you, that's why you're here.'[78] As one survivor describes it,

> The older I get I find these years haunt me, I will carry it to the grave with me. . . . The nuns made you feel as if you're a nobody and you never have any roots. . . . As the years go by you try not to be spiteful, I try not to be bitter. . . . I have bad days and then I have good days.[79]

The girls and women rose very early in the morning and went to Mass and then worked without pay, usually six full days a week at laundry or needlework. They also had general chores relating to the running of the institution. All the survivors describe how the work was endless, repetitive, compulsory, forced and unpaid. Kate O'Sullivan says of Sundays Well, 'you were told to be up at seven . . . start work at seven.. . . Work all day . . . in the heat.' She says the women had to work six days a week with no breaks, 'No . . . your recreation was on a Sunday, to sit down and sew scapulars, that's no lie. . . . And anyone then that was able to sew, had to make dresses and they never seen money for them either. No, no, no there was no outings, no nothing. Nothing. No. No.'[80]

The women slept in dormitories or individual cells and they were often cold. The food was meagre and poor; sanitary and hygiene facilities were degrading. Survivor Catherine Whelan says of her time at New Ross, 'I did not receive the basic components of a balanced diet for four years. Our diet did not contain fruit or vegetables and very little protein. . . . I was extremely thin and sickly for my first year. I never began my menstrual cycles until the age of 19.'[81] Sara W. says, 'We got one egg a year' on Easter Sunday morning. Other than that, 'you might get a bit of cabbage, you might get a potato and a bit of meat you know, about that size [about 3 cms] and then you'd get porridge in the evening time, that was your supper, porridge . . . you'd get porridge again for your breakfast, a cup of tea and a slice of bread.'[82]

Close relationships between the women (designated 'particular friendships') could result in a transfer to a different institution. The rule of silence and prayer between the inmates was strictly applied, enforced through an internal system of intimidation and physical punishment that sometimes involved older, institutionalized women coercing more recent arrivals to conform. Survivor Rita M. says, 'It didn't matter how ill you were, you still had to work that day.' Rita was put to work at High Park, 'I knew I had no choice, I had to do it . . . or else I would get a good slapping and I didn't want a slapping. So I had to persevere and just get on with the work.'[83] Sara W. says that if you did not want to or could not work, 'You'd be beaten down the stairs, you'd be beaten up and brought down and made [to] work.'[84]

The frightening disappearance of co-inmates without notice or explanation recurs as a trope across women's testimony: perhaps the nuns transferred them to a different laundry, committed them to a mental hospital or placed them in another menial working situation at a different Catholic religious institution, perhaps they escaped, or perhaps they died. The girls and women left behind in the Magdalene were rarely told what happened to their fellow inmates. Mary, who was in the Good Shepherd in Limerick, says, 'the women just . . . never saw a funeral . . . but I know lots of people would have died and . . . they wouldn't say too much to you so's you didn't ask many questions.'[85] Pippa Flanagan was also in Limerick: 'you'd wonder where that person went to, you'd be looking and you'd be wondering, and you can't ask what happened. They would just tell you that . . . their relations came for them, but they didn't.'[86]

Girls as young as nine were committed to Magdalene institutions and never received an education.[87] Survivors dwell on this fact as determining their loss of opportunity in later life. One survivor describes that when her foster mother died, she was fourteen and enjoying secondary school. One day, while at school, she was told that there was a job for her in Galway and 'in my innocence . . . I was delighted. I thought . . . I'll get a job now. I will be able to learn and I will have some money for myself.'[88] When she arrived at the laundry, her schoolbag was taken away from her. As she describes it, 'One of the women already there, said to the nuns, "Ye ought to be ashamed of yer selves taking children out of school in here. What is wrong with ye? Have ye any shame?" And the nuns didn't answer her. And that was my entrance into the Magdalene laundry with my school bag on my back.' She was put to work straight away on a roller machine. About a week later, she asked one of the nuns, 'why wasn't I going to school? . . . and she said with a sneer and a laugh at me: "You're in the finishing college now".' This survivor, who eventually managed to escape from the Galway Magdalene, would have loved to have trained to be a nurse: 'But I couldn't train because nobody would take anybody on with a record like that. . . . the fact that the Magdalene came out, that was taboo entirely.'[89] Regardless of how they entered the Magdalene, all survivors endured the stigma attached to these institutions, but the loss of an education at a young age made it all the more difficult to overcome this deficit in later life.

Many Magdalene institutions operated a rewards system for good behaviour, that is, for being compliant, a docile worker, not resisting the rules. This system differed depending on the religious congregation, but features include encouraging inmates (referred to as 'children') to graduate between various 'classes' and rewarding them through quasi-religious rituals. After periods of probation, women, for example, could become 'a child of Mary', and if willing to accept life-long incarceration as a 'vocation', graduate yet again and become an 'auxiliary' or 'consecrated Magdalene'. 'Auxiliaries' regularly reported to the nuns upon witnessing infractions of the rules by their fellow inmates; they were allowed to give certain orders to the other women and sometimes participated in enforcing punishments.[90] These auxiliaries were rewarded with the promise of a distinguished burial on the convent grounds as distinct from the 'ordinary penitent' who was buried in the local cemetery, typically in an unmarked grave.[91] Kathleen R, who was in Sundays Well in Cork, says that the Magdalene girls and women were allowed to attend the funerals of 'auxiliaries' buried on the grounds of the convent, but were not permitted to attend the burial of 'non-auxiliary' women, who were buried in St Joseph's Cemetery in Cork city.[92] When asked if proper funerals took place for women at Galway's Magdalene Laundry, Mary C., who was a hired worker, says that only two or three people would attend, herself and '[a]nother paid hand. And whoever was driving the hearse and another fellow then to throw it into the coffin and that was it. I can't remember a priest being there either.'[93] Asked if the nuns would attend, Mary C. says, 'Not at all, why would they?', before adding, 'The nuns would be waked, but not the poor creatures that made the money for them.'[94] The girls and women feared that they would die inside the Magdalene institution. Moreover, the identities and graves of many women who died in Magdalene Laundries remain unknown.[95]

Some women attempted to escape although it was difficult given that they were held under lock and key and behind high walls.[96] If successful – perhaps in the back of a laundry van, out an open door at delivery or collection time, or by scaling the high walls – these women were hunted, and often captured and returned by the police (known in Ireland as the Gardaí).[97] Upon return, they suffered punishments – including hair-cutting, solitary confinement or forced humiliation before their peers – and in many cases were transferred without warning to a different Magdalene Laundry, which had the effect of deterring further attempts by them or others. Girls and women did on occasion leave these institutions, taken out by very determined family members.[98] Some were placed in employment 'situations', typically menial service positions in hospitals, schools or other religious-run institutions. It would appear that many so-called preventative cases, that is girls transferred from industrial schools (to prevent them from 'falling into sin'), were released in their early or mid-twenties, but their release was neither assured nor systematically applied. Invariably, these girls were not informed that they were being placed 'on licence' and transferred to a Magdalene institution for their own 'protection'; nor were they informed how long they were to remain there.[99] Survivors were ignorant of the policy underpinning such arrangements, which also stipulated their release on or before their twenty-first birthday.[100] Testimony indicates that from the 1960s onwards some women managed to leave the Magdalene institutions after consistently agitating for release. Their exits invariably happened without advance notice. There was no opportunity to say goodbye to other inmates. Rather, they were told to get out of their uniform and into an outfit of clothes provided by the nuns, and they found themselves placed on the street or in menial, low-paid or even unpaid jobs in other religious-run institutions or with families who had close connections to the religious sisters.[101] The women typically did not have a suitable wardrobe (such as a change of clothes) nor, more importantly, any funds to enable them to transition into society.

A number of oral histories reveal that there were underground support groups organized to help girls and women to escape from the Galway Magdalene Laundry, demonstrating a public willingness to support those who sought to flee. It might be argued that the Galway institution, and its treatment of the girls and women, was public in ways that the other Magdalene Laundries were not.[102] The building was unique in having 'Magdalen Home Laundry' painted in gothic gold script under the apex of the roof, prominently displayed and visible from the public thoroughfare. Galway was notable, too, in that it was a stand-alone institution with just a small convent attached and was located in the heart of the city centre. Furthermore, the laundry's commercial profile was evident across Connaught, the Western Province of Ireland, through the fleet of delivery vans operated by hired hands.

Veiling the past

One of the striking aspects of researching Ireland's Magdalene Laundries is how often religious orders, civil servants and politicians insist that the era in which they operated relates to the mores of previous generations: the laundries they tell us are decidedly 'tales of other times'. The words of a Mercy nun, Sr Meta Reid, provide an apt summary of this argument. Speaking to *Sunday Tribune* journalist Susan McKay in 1993, Sr Reid claimed: 'Society didn't want these women, and their families didn't want them. There was no place else for them to go. Yes, we were unjust, but we were unwittingly facilitating a system that was unjust.' Notably, this was the very same year of the secretive exhumation, purportedly of 155 human remains, at High Park Magdalene in Drumcondra and 3 years before the last Magdalene Laundry ceased its commercial operations in October 1996. Sr Reid, it should be noted, was one of the few religious sisters who spoke to the media (it is stressed that she spoke 'in a personal capacity'). Other religious sisters refused to answer McKay's questions. Sr Reid added an interesting caveat to her admission of culpability: 'However, if church congregations are now to be seen as credible voices for justice, we need to consider acknowledging our participation in injustice and apologising for it.'[103] Yet the religious sisters consistently refuse to publicly engage in discussion about the Magdalene Laundries. On the rare occasion the congregations comment at all, they invariably dismiss the institutions as ancient history from unenlightened times where nuns were merely put in the invidious position of operationalizing other people's prejudice. (In fact, most Magdalene institutions continued to be run as commercial entities into the 1980s, with three operating into the 1990s.)[104] This response fails to account for the fact that the religious sisters were a pre-eminent cultural and material force in the spheres of Irish education, health and social welfare and in the shaping of public mores. Sr Lucy Bruton, the Reverend Mother of the Sean McDermott Street Magdalene, speaking to *The Irish Times* in the final weeks of its commercial operation as a laundry in 1996, is illuminating this respect:

> What we tried to do, in some cases successfully, was to provide money and protection for women in need. Of course we failed, we made mistakes. One of my greatest regrets is that we continued with the status quo rather than pioneering change. If a woman came in today with her daughter I'd tell her to get lost. I'm not

> saying I'd refuse to take the girl but I'd indicate to the mother that you don't hide people away.[105]

Contrary to Sr Bruton's suggestion, the State's inquiry into its involvement in the Magdalene institutions revealed that it was not common for a family member to place a girl in these institutions.[106] Moreover, survivors unanimously refute suggestions that they were provided with payment other than so-called pocket money to purchase hygiene products and, perhaps, sweets. More disturbing, however, is the fact that *The Irish Times* article reveals how the Sean McDermott Street Laundry still relies on the women's unpaid labour:

> First impressions of the laundry building are of austerity, of a large, grim interior with high ceilings. The pounding, steam driven machinery adds to the Victorian atmosphere. These days many of the women there are old and frail, their duties now described as occupational therapy. The laundry does the washing for nearby Mountjoy Prison and the prisoner clothing is collected once a day.

The extraordinary magical temporal thinking used by the religious orders (what is happening currently has actually ceased to happen decades ago) can be seen in the journalist's declaration that 'From the early 19th century until the middle of this century, thousands of Irish women were condemned to a life of servitude and confinement, with the knowledge, coercion and approval of family, Catholic church and State'. Yet the question of how these lives of servitude and confinement might be ameliorated remains unasked, even as the journalist witnesses elderly and frail women continue with laundry duties of 'occupational therapy'. We are told that

> Seven men work in the laundry now and do the hard washing part of the work. The women mostly do 'cylinder work' pressing sheets, pillowcases and towels. Attempts are being made to find other types of 'industrial therapy' work for them when the laundry closes.
>
> 'I'm not saying we run a paradise here,' Sister Lucy says. 'If you had a group living in the Blackrock Clinic you would still find someone who was disaffected.'

The religious sisters have, to the present day, evaded scrutiny not only because they cultivated alliances with Ireland's political establishment but also because of their traditional silence coupled with occasional bouts of assertive obfuscation – on the one hand indicating the Magdalene regime was a thing of the past and the wider society was to blame, while on the other hand planning for 'other types of "industrial therapy"' in the future. They evade the issue of how they might improve the lives of Magdalene women still in their care and thereby avoid any public assessment of their role in this abusive system. There is no evidence that they have reflected on the lessons which they might take from their work in Ireland and apply in other countries where they are currently expanding their enterprises.[107]

2

Survivors begin to be heard

Given that the religious orders refuse researchers access to Magdalene records and in recent decades refuse to speak publicly on the issue, it is fortunate that Sr Stanislaus Kennedy, a RSC, provides a study of life in Irish Magdalene institutions at the end of the twentieth century.[1] Sr Stanislaus is a household name in Ireland, best known as 'Sr Stan' or simply 'Stan'. She has been the recipient of four honorary doctorates among a host of other awards such as being voted Ireland's Greatest Woman in 2014 by readers of the *Irish Independent*.[2] Sr Stan's book, published in 1985 and entitled *But Where Can I Go?: Homeless Women in Dublin*, provides us with a snapshot of life in three Dublin Magdalene institutions in 1983–4. The RSC operated Magdalene Laundries in Donnybrook, Dublin, and Peacock Lane, Cork, as well as a number of industrial schools. Early in her career Sr Stan ran the first ever childcare course in Ireland, lending particular import to her analysis. Her research findings are all the more noteworthy for being both qualitative and quantitative.[3]

But Where Can I Go? runs to 218 pages, and yet the term 'Magdalene' does not appear, not even in a chapter entitled 'Historical Perspective', which recounts that[4]

> During and after the Famine many other voluntary and religious bodies emerged to respond to the needs of the homeless. For example, in the nineteenth century two hostels were opened by the Sisters of Our Lady of Charity for homeless women – one in High Park and the other in Sean McDermott Street; . . . the Irish Sisters of Charity established a home in Donnybrook in 1837 to provide care and protection for homeless women and girls.[5]

In reality, the 'two hostels' and the 'home' were Magdalene institutions which operated laundries into the closing years of the twentieth century. Sr Stan refers to these institutions as 'three large nineteenth century long term hostels'.[6] More remarkable still, she contends that they 'provide employment and occupational therapy' and uses this shorthand reference – 'providing employment and occupational therapy' – throughout her book to distinguish the three Magdalene institutions from the other 'hostels' in her study.[7] Sr Stan alludes to their actual identity twice: once when she acknowledges that 'The three older hostels were originally places of penitence, especially for unmarried mothers, a concept which is now outdated' and again when she states, 'In the old days, these were houses of penance, and the residents were generally referred to as penitents. . . . The three hostels have since their foundation provided work as an occupation or therapeutic rehabilitation.'[8]

Sr Stan's book includes a forty-six-page chapter entitled 'The Women's Stories', but none of the testimony comes from women in the three Magdalene institutions.[9] Later, in Chapter Nine focused on the long-term hostels, she explains that '[a]fter participant observation and on the advice of staff . . . we decided not to interview the women. Instead, we held group discussions with those who wished to talk.'[10] Moreover, she cautions that '[t]he information on women in long-term hostels [*sic*] must be treated with some reserve, as none of it is based on personal interviews with the women themselves.'[11] Yet Chapter 9 includes three pages of comments from Magdalene women which provide ample testimony as to the punitive regime they experienced. The first witness, aged sixty-six and institutionalized since she was sixteen years old, describes her first Magdalene uniform: 'uniforms down to your ankles and a starched white cap'. Her friend 'B', who has lived in the institution even longer, speaks of her hatred of the open dormitories and the lack of any private space, 'it was awful, I hated it'.[12] These two women are the only two informants given any kind of personal descriptors. The two pages that follow offer a collection of block quotes that are not attributed to any particular speaker and are introduced as follows by Sr Stan: 'Overall the picture of the past described by different women was one of hard work, isolation from the outside world, long hours, strictness mingled with humour.'[13] The quotes selected reveal little 'humour' and instead depict a regime fuelled by fear and punishment. For example:

> We used to get up for Mass at half-past six and we worked in the laundry all day. I loved ironing – they had glad irons and gas irons, but it's all new machinery now. I like a hand iron. First of all, you'd be put on pillow slips, to learn. The nun would examine it and, if there was a wrinkle, back it went!
>
> You never got out and there were holy readings at all the meals – breakfast, dinner and tea. You had to sit in silence and ask permission to leave. And if you did anything wrong or out of the way and were getting corrected, you were brought up to the Oratory, it was called, and you'd have to apologise and kiss the floor. It was the same getting the Children of Mary medal. I went in and kissed the floor and she said: 'Do you think you're worthy?' Well, I didn't know what to say, so I just said: 'Oh yes, Mother.'
>
> It was strict all right. Sometimes you'd get locked up. One day, I was locked up in the bathroom. I was just starving. . . . Then Sister — came in. She said: 'If I make you a nice cup of tea and bread and jam, will you be a good girl and go back to work?' All I could think of was the bread and jam, so I said, 'Oh yes!' But when I got it, I wouldn't go. Well I got a good malevoguing for that. They bet sense into me. They thought it was for my own good, but I didn't like the beating.[14]

The editorial emphasis serves to suggest that the Magdalene Laundries era is in the past, even as the women are still working for no pay in the institutions. Further unattributed quotes from the Magdalene participants reveal the present-day conditions:

> All we do is work in the laundry – all the rest is arranged by Sister. But we wouldn't mind if we were more involved, but what's best here is the peace and quiet and no worry . . .

> We don't go out in the evenings in the winter. We go in the summer and you can go up to the shops near here – but in winter it's too dark . . .
>
> We do our own little jobs and keep our own apartment clean and tidy . . . it fills in the time. Sunday can be very long and boring . . .
>
> We go out to town every week on a Saturday; we have pocket-money for small items. Sister caters for the rest. Sometimes, we have a party . . .
>
> It's better to be in a big place like this, than in a house; where there's someone in authority and where there's some security.[15]

The experiences of a different cohort of women studied by Sr Stan ('Group 2'), who live in an unnamed hostel, are illuminating because of the contrast between their treatment and that of women institutionalized in the three Magdalene Laundries at the same time. Sr Stanislaus explains that the women in 'Group 2' reside in a hostel which, 'unlike the larger institutions, do[es] not provide work or therapeutic care [*sic*] for the women. The residents are less protected, have more freedom and are more mobile.'[16] The women in 'Group 2' speak for themselves in answering Sr Stanislaus's questionnaire. Notably, the women in 'Group 2' are significantly younger; their duration of stay in the hostel is significantly shorter; a number of these women come and go from the home; some of them had been rough sleepers or availed of night shelters (this is not the case for the so-called 'homeless' women of the Magdalenes); a significant number (19 per cent) had come to the institution directly from a psychiatric hospital; and many of them were suffering from mental illness, 'mental handicap', drug addiction or alcoholism.[17] These factors point to an anomaly in the logic of the religious orders operating Magdalene Laundries, who repeatedly insist that their institutions should be judged in the context of the times in which they operated. As evidenced in the profiles of the 'Group 2' women, and despite the fact they these women too experienced suffering and deprivation, the 'short-term hostel' supported their specific needs without demanding unpaid labour, and it supported their agency and autonomy as individuals with rights. The Magdalene institutional regime was doing the opposite at precisely the same moment in time.

Many Magdalene survivors have spoken to JFM(R) about how the older women in the laundries became 'institutionalised' – that is, utterly lacking in expression of agency and will. They are described as 'zombies' by survivors who were incarcerated as children, who report how frightening these women seemed. As one survivor describes working in the Sundays Well laundry,

> And the sheets coming off and it boiling hot and oh terrible, prospect [Perspex] glass over you and sweat pouring off you. I drank me sweat Claire, drank my sweat, girl I did there. Then I was kind of afraid I thought . . . and I was looking around at all the old women, you know, I was saying, 'God I'm never going to be here all my life am I?'[18]

Sr Stan provides us with stark insights into the effects of institutionalization through her discussion of a census she undertook on 1 December 1983; she found that there were 241 women in the 3 Dublin Magdalene institutions.[19] She provides alarmingly high figures for mental and physical illness and 'handicap' among the women in the three Magdalene institutions: only 5 per cent of the observed population do not have any.[20] The study reveals that 17 per cent of these women had a mental illness yet only 1 per cent were recorded with a mental illness upon entry. An astonishing 80 per cent of the women are 'deemed mentally handicapped', yet only 4 per cent were considered 'mentally handicapped' on entry.[21] Sr Stan acknowledges that the 'very large discrepancy' between the mental health of the women on entry and their current state might 'be explained by the fact that the staff in these hostels [*sic*] may have defined mental handicap in a much broader sense than is normally the case. They may use the term "mental handicap" to describe symptoms of severe institutionalisation.'[22]

There is additional evidence from other religious sisters that a life spent as a Magdalene often resulted in disabling mental illness as well as an obliteration of agency so severe that those locked into a relentlessly punitive system were over time rendered incapable of living independent lives outside that system. Patricia Burke Brogan, a former novice nun in the Mercy Order who left after her brief experience providing summer relief at the Galway Magdalene, said: 'It was shocking, like going underground. It was dark, and doors were closed and locked behind me. There was the noise of the engines, steam everywhere. . . . Some of the women had become like machines themselves.'[23]

Sr Stan claims that by the mid-1980s changes had been introduced to the 'old institutional way of life, with old open dormitories, bare walls, large and impersonal dining and siting rooms'. In one of the three long-term institutions, 'some women have their own bedrooms and a few have their own televisions. In the other two large hostels [*sic*] the dormitories have been divided into small curtained cubicles.'[24] The women's testimony credits the Second Vatican Council for these positive changes in the regime:

> The idea of leaders started over ten years ago; part of the changes in Rome with the Vatican. We had a mistress, a nun, she was gallant and she selected the people. Twelve, I think there were. There's three of the first ones still here. I suppose you could say the Holy Ghost came down and picked us! We have special responsibilities – bringing girls into town, minding them, helping them with their shopping. And we serve in the dining room one day a week, ringing the bell to get the girls in. There are no special groups. Everyone is very reasonable.
>
> . . .
>
> By now we all have our own place. Every girl has her own room, a cubicle, and you can have your things, ornaments and that, and some of the girls have radios, and your own bedspread. We're in groups now and every group has their own sitting room with television and a kitchen where we can make tea for ourselves. We're delighted with the changes. God bless that little Pope that started it all – John XXIII. But the best part of all was getting out.
>
> I was up in the Sacristy one Sunday and Mother — came in and said to me, 'I want you to go over to — Street.' I said, 'I'm not going over to — Street.' I didn't know what was going on. Then Mother —, another nun, came in and she said, 'Why are you not going? If you don't go, you'll be overlooked.' So that must have been the start of it. I went over the next day. Sister — brought me. And I only

> resigned there last year. I just loved it, for you mixed with people you know, a lot of people, all sorts. And you were off at the weekend and you could go into town and see the changes, or get home. Some of the girls go out and do weekend work. And we can go off on our holidays – we have a house we can go to, in —. First it was for a week; now we go for a fortnight. Father — got it for us.[25]

It is consoling to note the relaxation in the punitive regime in the early to mid 1970s for some of the women held long-term. That said, oral testimony from younger women sent into these same institutions in the 1970s and 1980s reveals that they were still kept under lock and key and forced to work long hours for no pay. Furthermore, it is depressing to observe that even as late as 1983 when Sr Stan conducted her study, the women are still working for the nuns, their old-age pensions are being taken from them (some of it allotted back as pocket money), and little is being done to enable them to live more independent and self-directed lives.

Turning to the operational and financial aspects of the Magdalene Laundries, Sr Stan states that 'These hostels have a life-long commitment to their residents and have modernised to meet their needs. However, this has left them in a position where they have practically no space to admit new residents and only a few women have been received into them in recent years.'[26] Sr Stan concludes that there are 'gross inequalities in the statutory payments to homeless women and to the hostels that cater for them'.[27] In describing the Magdalenes as 'hostels for homeless women' and showing elsewhere in her book the acute need for services for homeless women, particularly those escaping from domestic violence, Sr Stan argues that these three institutions deserve more direct State financial subvention than they receive. Moreover, she continues: 'Despite the differences between the hostels, the variation in the access they have to statutory funding is inexplicable, and it seems that hostels run by religious orders fare worse than any of the hostels run by other voluntary organisations.'[28] While acknowledging that the 'three large nineteenth-century long-term hostels . . . continue to provide work', she ignores the income generated by their inmates' unpaid labour. Instead, she lobbies for additional State financial support:

> In the remaining three long-term hostels, which are run by religious orders, none of the women receives statutory benefit or assistance, apart from the old-age pensioners. Residents pay most of their pension towards their keep in the hostels. The state gives no statutory benefit or assistance to women under sixty-six years of age admitted to these hostels. Instead, it pays a grant of between £11 and £13.50 per woman per week to the hostel. If the women were not in these hostels, they would receive at least three times as much in statutory entitlement. At the moment, residents in these three hostels receive pocket money in the region of £5 a week from the hostel administration.
>
> One of the hostels catering for young women is paid almost seven times the amount per resident per week that is received by these three long-term hostels.[29]

The publication of Sr Stan's book had the desired effect in that she received State funding to establish an organization that is now one of the largest and most respected housing organizations in the country: 'Focus Ireland was founded by Sr Stanislaus Kennedy as a result of the finding of research into the needs of homeless women in Dublin.'[30] As explained on its website, 'In 1985, two years after the initial research Focus Point (now Focus Ireland) opened its doors in Eustace Street, Dublin'. Sr Stanislaus is 'Founder and Life President' of Focus Ireland, which receives approximately 50 per cent of its funding from the Irish Exchequer and the rest from charitable donations. In 2018 Focus Ireland had funds in excess of €25 million to spend on its activities and properties estimated to be worth over €102 million.[31]

State subvention

The Irish government used Magdalene Laundries as alternatives to prison, paying for the detention of girls and women following conviction and on probation and remand.[32] Following representations made by the archbishop of Dublin to the then Taoiseach, Éamon de Valera, the Sean McDermott Street Magdalene was used to hold young women in pretrial detention 'on remand' in spite of some opposition from senators. In a debate on the 1960 Criminal Justice Bill, Senator Nora Connolly O'Brien pointed out that a girl who had been sent to the laundries would suffer a life-long stigma. She declared that

> If I were asked to advise girl delinquents, no matter what offences they were charged with, whether to go to prison on remand, or to go to St Mary Magdalen's Asylum on remand, I would advise them wholeheartedly to choose prison, because I think having a record of being in prison as a juvenile delinquent would not be so detrimental to the after life of the girl as to have it legally recorded that she was an inmate of St Mary Magdalen's Asylum.[33]

Correspondence between the religious orders and the courts reveals that the nuns actively sought committals and that they intended to do their utmost to keep the women at the Magdalene Laundries even after their sentences had elapsed.[34] For example, a letter to the court from the Superioress of the RSC's Cork Magdalene dated 2 December 1934 stated that the Magdalene Laundry was prepared to take a woman convicted of the manslaughter of her newly born child. The woman had been sentenced to a year's detention, yet the nun wrote: 'we will do our best to keep her in safety even after her time has expired.'[35]

The State paid members of lay organizations (e.g. the Legion of Mary, acting as Voluntary Probation Officers, and the National Society for the Prevention of Cruelty to Children, acting as social workers) to place girls and women in Magdalene Laundries.[36] The State also paid the Magdalene Laundries pursuant to the *Health Acts*, for the care and custody of women 'where public authorities would otherwise have had to make alternative arrangements for the maintenance of those persons' – that is, because it was cheaper for the State to outsource its social care responsibility.[37] Making sure to get the most competitive rates,[38] the State awarded countless laundry contracts to the religious sisters – in the full knowledge that the women and girls received no wages for their work.[39] The laundry the women and girls washed therefore came not only from the public, local businesses and religious institutions but also from numerous government departments, including the Defence Forces, public hospitals, public schools, prisons and other State entities such as Leinster House, the Chief State Solicitor's Office, the Office of Public Works, the Land Commission, CIE (the national transport company) and the president of Ireland's residence, Áras an Úachtaráin.

Not only did the nuns pay no wages to the girls and women working in Magdalene Laundries and their fine needlework factories, but they paid no contributions ('stamps') on the women's behalf either, even to mandatory statutory pension schemes.[40] What is more, the Revenue Commissioners gave the religious orders charitable tax exemptions on the legal ground that the incarcerated girls and women were the 'beneficiaries' of the industrial work that they were doing.[41]

Survivors' voices gain attention

In 1990, the feminist legal (and campaigning) scholar, Mary Robinson, was elected president of Ireland. Robinson, a constitutional lawyer by training, found ways to revise and vitalize the largely symbolic and hitherto low-key office of the presidency. She brought a dynamic energy of inclusion and thirst for social justice to the role. Travellers, feminists, community activists, leaders of the Irish Diaspora and LGB people (even before the decriminalization of gay men in 1993) were all early guests to official receptions in the Áras. Robinson's presidency was crucial in creating a political ecosystem that allowed for the emergence of marginalized voices within public discourse. Yet, at precisely the same time, Patricia Burke Brogan, a former Sister of Mercy (RSM) novice, could not find an established Irish theatre company to stage her play *Eclipsed*, based on her experience at the Galway Magdalene Laundry. *Eclipsed* was taken to the Edinburgh Theatre Fringe Festival in 1992 by a small company called Punchbag where it was awarded a Fringe First prize.[42] Four years later, Christine Buckley was the focus of an Irish television documentary *Dear Daughter*, which narrated the relationship with her father, a Nigerian doctor, and the horrors she endured in the RSM Goldenbridge Industrial School. This documentary galvanized many other institutional abuse survivors to come forward and recount how the manifold forms of torture they endured had severely affected their lives. In 1998, on Britain's Channel Four, a documentary entitled *Sex in a Cold Climate* comprised interviews with Irish women who had survived incarceration in Magdalene Laundries. The decade ended with the Irish public being shocked by a three-part television documentary *States of Fear*, independently produced and directed by Mary Raftery and broadcast by RTÉ (the Irish national broadcaster) in April–May 1999.

States of Fear revealed decades of State inertia and Church cover-ups concerning the systematic abuse of poor and disabled children in institutions managed by religious congregations but licenced and generously funded by the government. The 1990s had seen a growing public awareness of how State/Church hegemony in running the country led to corruption in both entities.[43] The revelation in 1992 that Bishop Eamonn Casey had fathered a child shocked the nation, and every year thereafter one clerical sexual abuse scandal followed another.[44] From 1993 there was a continuous stream of stories of physical and sexual assaults on children by priests. The perception that Ireland's AG's office had been negligent in extraditing child rapist, Fr Brendan Smyth, to answer charges in Northern Ireland, led to the downfall of Albert Reynolds's Fianna Fáil/Labour coalition government in 1994. The revelations continued throughout 1995 that populist demagogue, Fr Michael Cleary, had fathered a number of children with his young housekeeper, herself a survivor of Ireland's industrial school system, and that he had coerced at least one adoption of his own children. Just when it seemed the scandal could get no worse, there came the exposure of the horrific rapes perpetrated by Fr Seán Fortune, which in turn led to the establishment of the Ferns Commission of Investigation. Ireland's Catholic clergy, which had long demanded and received not only deference but reverence, was now exposed as having run the gamut from negligent ignorance, through cynical indifference, to sadism. The revelations might have been understood to pertain to the actions of a corrupt few were it not for the evidence of systematic institutional protection by the Catholic hierarchy of child torturers and rapists and the failures of the Garda Síochána (police) to properly investigate reported incidents.[45] The institutional church was exposed as hypocritical in enforcing puritanical sexuality on the public while privately facilitating the sexual abuse of children: in particular, by routinely transferring abusers from parish to parish and maintaining a policy of not reporting crimes to the civic authorities. Further pain was inflicted by the spectacular unwillingness of the Church to apologize in any arena where abuse occurred. The Catholic Church demonstrated a greater fear of litigation and potential financial compensation than pastoral care towards its flock – protecting its financial assets and reputation was everything. In 1990, 85 per cent of Irish adults in the Republic attended weekly Mass; just seven years later this had fallen to 65 per cent.[46]

Raftery's *States of Fear*, which prominently featured the voices of survivors of institutional abuse, energized a new zeitgeist. Her documentary was electrifying in that it conclusively demonstrated systemic abuse, in different kinds of institutions, across different cohorts of survivors, not merely in the past but also in the present. The public anger, following episodes one and two, was responded to with alacrity by the Fianna Fáil Taoiseach, Bertie Ahern, who made an official apology, hours prior to the final episode airing on 11 May 1999:

> On behalf of the State and of all citizens of the State, the Government wishes to make a sincere and long overdue apology to the victims of childhood abuse for our collective failure to intervene, to detect their pain, to come to their rescue.[47]

The apology came against a backdrop of hundreds of court cases alleging physical and sexual abuse against the eighteen religious congregations that managed child residential institutions funded and inspected by the State. On the night of the apology, Mr Ahern announced a series of redress measures, including creating a Commission of Investigation and the establishment of a compensation mechanism for survivors.

The Commission to Inquire into Child Abuse

In the ensuing months of that momentous year, after lengthy Dáil debates, massive street protests and global media attention, the Irish government established the CICA to investigate abuse in State-financed, Church-run residential institutions for children. The CICA would investigate 18 religious orders that ran 215 residential institutions for an estimated 40,000 children since 1922, which formed a key part of the landscape of Ireland's architecture of containment.[48] The Commission was initially chaired by Ms Justice Mary Laffoy.[49] Her 2003 *Interim Report* summarized the testimony of 771 witnesses who at that point had given evidence to the CICA's Confidential Committee. The survivors described 'being beaten on every part of their body: the front and back of hands, wrists, legs, back, buttocks, head, face and feet. Some beatings were administered in public and witnesses reported that they were sometimes made to remove all their clothing for these public beatings.'[50] Among the instruments witnesses described as being used to punish children were: 'canes, sticks, pointers, chair legs, sewing machine treadle belts, leather straps, rulers, scissors, keys, rosary beads, coat-hangers, hand-brushes, hairbrushes, yard-brushes, rungs of chairs, broom handles and tree branches'.[51] The physical violence was routinely accompanied by sexual abuse which 'ranged from inappropriate kissing, fondling, and masturbation of abuser by the child, oral intercourse, use of instruments for vaginal penetration and rape by one or more people'.[52] The CICA also reported that it had heard extensive testimony of severe emotional and psychological abuse. There was pervasive and forced child labour: in farming, cleaning and maintenance, caring for other children and making rosary beads, as well as being hired out for commercial activities. The CICA heard about the persistent and general neglect of hygiene, clothing, accommodation and medical attention needs; lack of food leading to starvation; as well as a lack of play. Many survivors emphasized that the absolute neglect of their education while resident in these institutions was paramount among the abuses they endured. Finally, survivors recalled childhoods spent in environments of fear, which in girls' institutions included the ever-present threat of transfer to a Magdalene Laundry.

The workings of the CICA were not without considerable controversy and legal challenge. This resulted, for example, in the CICA having to abandon its investigation into children in residential settings being used in vaccine trials.[53] The approach of the religious orders was described by the Commission in 2003 as 'adversarial and legalistic', and the CICA was so beset by legal obstacles mounted by the congregations that these threatened to fatally undermine its work. The Department of Education, whose duty it was to inspect and regulate the bulk of the institutions, also refused to cooperate fully with the CICA's requests for archival documents. It also subjected the CICA to a review of its costs and resources. This review was chaired by a barrister called Seán Ryan and delayed the CICA for nine months. On completion, the government promptly announced a second review leading the much-respected Ms Justice Laffoy to resign in protest. She alleged: 'since its establishment, the commission has never been properly enabled by the Government to fulfil satisfactorily the functions conferred on it by the

Oireachtas.'[54] By the time of Judge Laffoy's resignation in September 2003, 1,957 people had come forward to have their cases investigated by the Investigation Committee, most of them making allegations of abuse against several individuals (under the *CICA Act 2000*, the Investigation Committee had powers to make findings of wrongdoing against individuals and institutions). A further 1,192 survivors had opted for the Confidential Committee hearings (the Confidential Committee was designed for those who did not wish to have their experiences of abuse inquired into but wished to make submissions or recount their experiences in order for the CICA to be in a position to make general proposals and recommendations). Ms Justice Laffoy had lobbied to increase the CICA's resources to enable the creation of a number of divisions that could conduct hearings in parallel and conduct full hearings for all those who wished to have their complaints investigated. Doing so, she claimed, would fulfil the government's promise to survivors to reflect fully the experiences of all who testified and to expose the perpetrators of abuse.[55] Her resignation effectively signalled a significant change in direction.

The government appointed barrister Seán Ryan to succeed Judge Laffoy as the CICA's chair, the same barrister who had conducted the review of the CICA at the behest of the Department of Education. The government also announced that it would appoint Ryan to the High Court, in spite of the fact that the number of judges on that court was limited by law and no vacancies then existed.[56] Chairman Ryan moved quickly to address the problems caused by the Commission's lack of resources. He proposed selecting a limited number of cases for full hearing. Moreover, he decided that investigation of specific institutions would not proceed unless there were twenty or more related allegations of abuse. As a result, some 1,300 victims remained with the investigative process; Judge Ryan promised that each would be interviewed by a solicitor and given the opportunity to provide a written statement that would inform CICA's final report.[57]

A further controversy ensued, however, regarding the naming of the perpetrators responsible for child abuse. Given the hitherto paltry number of convictions related to abuse within the institutions, survivors argued that the CICA provided the last real chance to secure some measure of justice by at least naming those responsible.[58] The religious congregations, most notably the RSM and the Christian Brothers, argued that many of their members were deceased or elderly and infirm, making it impossible for them to mount an effective defence, but the Irish High Court rejected their claim. The Christian Brothers signalled their intention to appeal the decision to the Supreme Court.[59] At this point Chairman Ryan offered a compromise agreeing not to name any perpetrators of abuse who had not already been convicted in a court.[60] The Christian Brothers dropped their challenge. With the CICA no longer naming perpetrators, the Christian Brothers revealed that their archives in Rome held detailed accounts of the Order's awareness of the sexual and physical abuse of children in their Irish institutions over decades.[61] When published in 2009, the *CICA Final Report* did not explicitly state that the anonymized abusers were in fact members of the orders in charge, leaving open the suggestion that abusers were external or lay agents visiting or working at the institutions.

Within a few months of assuming the chairmanship of the CICA, Judge Ryan had espoused revised aims and objectives for the inquiry:

> The vision I have of this inquiry is that it can analyse and understand and explain what happened in the past; it can ascribe responsibility for that – admittedly at a level of some generality – but nevertheless specifying institutions and identifying failures on the part of official bodies where appropriate; it can comment on public and political and social attitudes and on events and policies that underlay those attitudes . . . it can ask how those events can be related to the present; and it can produce recommendations which will have an impact on the treatment of children in care in our modern times.[62]

Ryan thus navigated the CICA away from investigating individual survivors' complaints and holding identifiable perpetrators to account (which are the cornerstones of 'justice' as it is generally understood in society) to a 'vision' of the Commission as a means to understand the abuse as 'history' – albeit as history that might have some bearing on policy regarding the contemporary treatment of children in care in Ireland.[63] With the new objective of merely correcting the general historical record, Judge Ryan might be accused of historicizing crimes that merit legal investigation and the full application of the Irish justice system in the present.[64]

The *CICA Final Report* runs to 2,600 pages and was published in 5 volumes on 20 May 2009, its final conclusions incorporating the evidence of some 1,500 people.[65] Throughout the months of May and June 2009, Irish people lived through global, high-profile, broadcast and print media expressions of shock and condemnation at the treatment of the nation's most vulnerable citizens. The Executive Summary of the *CICA Final Report* confirmed, as *The Irish Times* described it, that 'Abuse was not a failure of the system. It was the system.'[66] Coverage of survivor groups' critical reaction was rather muted in Ireland – most Irish national media outlets, for example, were laudatory of Judge Seán Ryan's chairmanship.[67] International outlets, however, afforded greater prominence to survivors' condemnation. The BBC led with quotes from John Walsh (Irish Survivors of Child Abuse, SOCA) who stated: 'I would have never opened my wounds if I'd known this was going to be the end result. It has devastated me and will devastate most victims because there is no criminal proceedings and no accountability whatsoever.' The BBC also interviewed John Kelly (Irish SOCA) who responded that

> this report's conclusions go very, very, very short of the expectations of the victims. What they wanted was that the courts who sent them, detained them unlawfully in the institutions that were investigated, these courts that violated their constitutional rights weren't even inquired into. And because of that this inquiry is deeply flawed, it's incomplete and many might call it a whitewash.[68]

In 2017, the advocacy group 'Reclaiming Self' highlighted to UNCAT in Geneva that, despite the CICA's finding of 'endemic' sexual abuse and the number of witnesses presenting testimony, only fifteen DPP referrals ensued, resulting in a single prosecution for child sexual abuse. Furthermore, they argued that no evidence exists to suggest that the State or religious authorities did anything to address the issue of abusers (including child sexual abusers) still in their employment.[69] In its defence, the government has claimed that 'the provisions governing the CICA's work precluded the disclosure of the names of persons identified as perpetrators, hence this information was not available to An Garda Síochána for the purposes of initiating criminal investigations'.[70] It is true that the *CICA Act 2000* prohibited disclosure to the Gardaí of information provided to the Confidential Committee unless it concerned a continuing serious offence; however, the information provided to the Investigative Committee does not appear to have been immune to either requests from the Gardaí or orders for discovery.[71] These efforts simply appear not to have been made.

Over a decade on from the publication of the *CICA Final Report* its impact on the historical record of twentieth-century Ireland is almost negligible. The substantial archive of administrative records gathered by the CICA remains inaccessible, thus inhibiting the possibility of rigorous analytical research. The *CICA Act* in fact provides for the deposit of the Commission's archive in the NAI[72] where its contents would be made available according to ordinary rules concerning state records and the protection of personal data.[73] This has never occurred, rendering the records – which remain in the custody of the CICA – in effect secret. The *CICA Act* originally allowed for the operation of the *Freedom of Information Act 1997* in relation to the Commission's archive.[74] In 2014, however, at the very last stage of Dáil debate on the new FOI Bill, the government ('having received a request') exempted the CICA from the definition of a 'public body' to which the rules apply.[75] Then, in February 2019, the minister for education published a Retention of Records Bill which, if passed, would undo the existing archival provisions in legislation and prohibit all access – including by survivors – for at least seventy-five years to the two million documents contained in the archives of the CICA and the RIRB and its Review Committee.[76]

Knowing, not knowing and being respectable

Judge Ryan's team at the CICA hired the international accountancy firm, Mazars, to audit a selection of financial records relating to some of the institutions under investigation. The audit revealed that the Irish Exchequer provided significant sums of money to the institutions in terms of capitation grants per child as well as other grants and subsidies – even as the larger institutions sought to be self-sufficient through the operation of farms, gardens and an array of workshops producing foodstuffs, clothing and other supplies. As Seán Ryan described it in an interview with *The Irish Times*, these residential institutions for children were 'hugely' profitable for the religious orders, and it was 'difficult to see that the money was all spent on the children'.[77] Ryan was asked if monies made by the Christian Brothers in Artane and such places were used to fund their middle-class schools. By way of an answer Ryan explained that the attempt to investigate the monies generated by the institutions was only successful to a degree; it was expected that the Orders would engage with the accountants' reports and when they didn't make any comment, and were not required to answer direct questions on the accounts, the CICA demurred from making clear findings on profitability or where the money was spent.

Novelist John Banville, writing in the *New York Times*, responded to the publication of the *CICA Final Report* with an article entitled 'A Century of Looking the Other Way'.[78] It opens with the phrase: 'Everyone knew'. Banville describes himself as belonging to a 'respectable' family – 'which mainly meant not being poor'. His opinion-editorial asks 'the question of what it means, in this context, to know'. Banville qualifies his assertion that 'Everyone knew, but no one said' to remind us that 'Human beings – human beings everywhere, not just in Ireland – have a remarkable ability to entertain simultaneously any number of contradictory propositions. Perfectly decent people can know a thing and at the same time not know it.' He briefly mentions as cases in point, the genocides of Armenians, Jews, Bosnians, Rwandans and closes his article with the view of Ireland's 'respectable' classes:

> Ireland from 1930 to the late 1990s was a closed state, ruled – the word is not too strong – by an all-powerful Catholic Church with the connivance of politicians and, indeed, the populace as a whole, with some honorable exceptions. The doctrine of original sin was ingrained in us from our earliest years, and we borrowed from Protestantism the concepts of the elect and the unelect. If children were sent to orphanages, industrial schools and reformatories, it must be because they were destined for it, and must belong there. What happened to them within those unscalable walls was no concern of ours. We knew, and did not know. That is our shame today.[79]

The failure of the CICA to fully investigate how the huge profits generated in the residential institutions were used typifies and perpetuates this 'knowing and not knowing' by the respectable classes in Ireland. As Banville reminds us, twentieth-century Ireland was mostly a place where 'The times were harsh, money was scarce and had to be worked hard for'. Respectability, at even the basic requirement of not being poor, was not merely hard won but a rather precarious identity for much of the century. Conforming to the social norms of a rigidly orthodox Catholicism provided the most obvious route to securing respectability's cultural capital and so there were real incentives 'not to know'. Acknowledging how abusive the institutions were would have introduced a profound moral criticism of the Church hierarchy which was the most powerful cultural hegemonic force in the land. In addition, as second-level education was not State-funded until 1967, diligent, dutiful students from respectable families were grateful to the Mercy Order and the Christian Brothers, those orders who also ran the largest and the most infamous residential institutions for poor children, because they operated most of the secondary schools at reasonable prices. *The Irish Times* raised this issue with Seán Ryan:

> You were educated, presumably, by the church, because free education didn't come in until the year after you left school in 1967. So you came out of that system.

> When you were growing up and going through that system, did you suspect this [abuse] was going on? Or the scale of it?

Judge Ryan's response exemplifies Banville's 'knowing' and 'not knowing':

> I was educated by the Christian Brothers. Tom Boland, principal officer I think at the time in the Department of Education, gave evidence at the emergence hearings and he said – and it resonated with me – he said people knew these were not nice places.[80]

When asked if he was shocked at the discovery that sexual abuse was endemic in all boys' institutions, Ryan replied, 'I left school in 1966. There was an awareness, there was a consciousness, but there was no idea . . . there was the story of the few bad apples and that sort of thing.' Ryan's oscillation between knowing and not knowing is hardly unique, and he is the product of his conditioning – the conditioning that Banville illustrates so beautifully. Ryan's queasy knowing and not knowing is perhaps most evident in his expression of surprise at how unfamiliar the order that educated him appeared at the Commission he chaired. Ryan is not able to fully recognize them; he is not able to account for their actions:

> The Christian Brothers' commitment to education was tremendous, in my view. I am a huge admirer of their work in education. But that didn't apply in industrial schools. Here was an opportunity to give kids who had no other chance. It was a way of giving their younger members a real opportunity to teach, to make something extraordinary out of this. That surprised me, I have to say. Leave aside being shocked or anything else. I would have thought with such a commitment the primary focus being on incarceration was strange.[81]

The issue of generating knowledge, a knowledge that everyone can know, was going to be a central part of the JFM campaign: both in terms of demonstrating a knowledge of how the State had always known and interacted with the Magdalene institutions and in terms of bringing survivors' continuing trauma to public awareness.

Abuse in the present

The word 'historical' is frequently used to describe the abuse suffered in Irish institutions. Speaking as recently as 2018 about the treatment of industrial school survivors, Judge Ryan suggested: 'We're looking at this from the 21st century. It's very hard to put ourselves back into the 1960s.' He continued by referring to the CICA in terms that might befit the description of a silent movie, claiming it provided 'pictures of the kind of world we had left behind'.[82] We see the characterization of twentieth-century child abuse as 'historical', too, in the first State apology given by Bertie Ahern in 1999, which initiated the CICA. On the publication of the final report ten years later, then Taoiseach Brian Cowen merely repeated Ahern's words that the State owed a 'long overdue apology to the victims of childhood abuse, for our collective failure to intervene, to detect their pain, to come to their rescue'.[83] In relegating abuse to the 'historical' there is an inference that survivors' and/or family members' ongoing trauma is also a thing of the past, with the resulting logic that these individuals and their advocates are somehow (and merely) anachronistic.[84] On rarer occasions, even the reserve of implication is dropped and survivors are explicitly impugned as lacking the capacity to live in the present; a present, those with power insist, where institutional abuse no longer occurs.[85] And this despite survivors of abuse testifying that they live with the nightmares and daily struggle of their trauma. Some in Ireland's establishment are quick to suggest that the past is a different country and that special historical training and insight is required to interpret properly events in the twentieth century. In doing so, they dismiss survivor testimony as subjective and unreliable and advocates who esteem such evidence as hopelessly naive.

The Executive Summary of the *CICA Final Report* implies that following the *Kennedy Report* in 1970 all was well in the institutional care of children in Ireland; the outlining of the Department of Education's failures concludes with the words: 'it took an independent intervention in the form of the Kennedy Report in 1970 to dismantle a long out-dated system.'[86] However, two more recent Irish governmental reports, one dating from 1980 and the other from 1996, detail systemic abuses in the childcare system that also went unheeded.[87] Moreover, the apology offered to survivors by Bertie Ahern in 1999 is characterized by Jim Smith as a 'pre-emptive strike against revelations in the final episode of the *States of Fear* documentary, broadcast on the very evening of his apology'.[88] This final episode detailed abuses suffered in the 1990s by children and youth particularly those with disabilities and focused on the State's 1996 censorship of the report into abuse at Madonna House, owned and managed by the RSC, who ran Magdalene Laundries in Donnybrook and Peacock Lane in Cork. Censorship in this case excised a chapter entitled 'Management and Operation of Madonna House', which directly linked sexual and other abuses of children to ongoing mismanagement by the religious order. It protected both the State (which had commissioned the report in the first place) and the RSC, the two entities responsible for the abuse of children residing in Madonna House. But these facts were again overlooked ten years later in 2009, when amnesia pervaded media coverage of the publication of the *CICA Final Report*. Irish media reports tacitly accepted the official narrative line that 1970 brought an end to systemic child abuse in Ireland's institutions.[89]

Adding to the devastating continuing impact of perpetrators' criminal impunity, the process adopted by the RIRB pursuant to the 2002 *Residential Institutions Redress Act* was very much a twenty-first-century form of degradation. The 2002 Act required survivors to prove not just that they had been abused in an institution but also that they had suffered injuries which were specifically the result of that abuse.[90] As one survivor, Mary Harney, recalled in November 2019, 'I had to go to a doctor who had to say how my nose was so battered and how my jaw is the way it is. They kept asking if I was sure I was not in a car accident. I was not. I was beaten.'[91] Every person named in a survivor's application for redress, and representatives of every institution named, were entitled to receive a copy of the survivor's documentation and to respond with 'any evidence' in writing that they considered appropriate.[92] These individuals were also entitled to request an opportunity to cross-examine the survivor either directly or through a legal representative 'for the purpose of (i) correcting any mistake of fact or misstatement relating to or affecting the relevant person made in the application, (ii) defending the relevant person in relation to any allegation or defamatory or untrue statement, made in the application, or (iii) protecting and vindicating the personal and other rights of the relevant person'.[93] Such entitlements appear to have been legally entirely unnecessary given the Act's express provisions that any financial award would 'not constitute a finding of fact relating to fault or negligence on the part of the relevant person' and would 'not be construed as a finding of fact that a person who is referred to in an application carried out the acts complained of in the application'.[94] Furthermore, the Act provided that anything said or written to the RIRB would 'not be admissible as evidence against that person, or against any other person who may be liable for the acts or omissions of that person, in any criminal proceedings or in any civil proceedings in a court or other tribunal'.[95]

The words 'personal rights' (referencing Article 40 of the Irish Constitution) appear only once in the 2002 Act – and that is in relation to individuals and representatives of institutions named as abusive in survivors' redress applications. In a two-part documentary for RTÉ Television in March 2020, Dr Mary Lodato recounted how the experience impacted her:

> You had the church's representative, you had the solicitor and a barrister and then you had the judge and a psychiatrist. It was adversarial and you felt like you were on your own. . . . The Church had said that it was a fantasy what had happened to me, that I was sexually abused in that institution. And I had to relive it, so in a way, having to relive it, it's a bit like, you know, you're put on an operating table and you are cut open and you're left there to fester.

Fellow survivor John Prior recalled:

> It took me back into a place like I was behind four walls again and here were the Brothers like a battering ram at me and I had nothing I could do about it. The State gave them full permission that they could say and do whatever they liked. I was in such a bad place for a long time. . . . They absolutely ripped me asunder.[96]

In early 2002, the expert group to advise the government on RIRB payments, chaired by barrister Seán Ryan prior to his appointment to the CICA, had proposed a financial payment scale to match the maximum that would be awarded in an Irish court: a maximum of €300,000, with the possibility to argue for aggravated damages totalling an additional 20 per cent.[97] However, by the time the RIRB concluded its redress process it had made awards to 15,579 people, with each receiving on average €62,250.[98] When asked what he thought of the generally low level of the financial compensation compared to the levels set by the working group he had chaired, Judge Ryan said, 'So it turned out, but that wasn't my business'.[99]

The Caranua fund, established by the *Residential Institutions Statutory Fund Act 2012* to oversee the distribution of cash contributions totalling €110m pledged by the religious congregations to support the needs of survivors and their families, has proven to be a deeply flawed initiative. Survivors and their advocates routinely criticize Caranua for being torturously bureaucratic, for its inequitable treatment of survivors and for its seeming disregard for its own stated policies and procedures.[100] The findings of the *CICA Final Report,* meanwhile, do not substantially differ from Justice Laffoy's damning *Interim Report* published in 2003. And, more than ten years on from that final report, its vaunted recommendations have yet to be fully implemented.[101] Even the public memorial, commissioned to commemorate survivors' experiences and to be located adjacent to Dublin's Garden of Remembrance, fell foul of the State's planning authority, and there seems to be no momentum to find an alternative site.[102]

The public rarely hears testimony from industrial or reformatory school survivors in Ireland. It is, of course, extremely difficult to speak publicly as a survivor of childhood sexual abuse, physical and emotional torture, and extreme neglect. However, survivors also privately point to the fact that they were made to sign a legal undertaking on receipt of financial awards from the RIRB that they would not speak in public about their experience at the board or their application to the board in a way that could identify the individuals who abused them, or even the institution where the abuse occurred. Many survivors interpret this as an injunction prohibiting them from speaking at all about the abuses they endured.[103] A breach of this undertaking (usually referred to by survivors as the 'gagging order') runs the risk of a fine and imprisonment. Survivors tend not to be affluent people, and none of them want to be locked up again. Moreover, many survivors are now elderly. Consequently, it is increasingly unlikely that they will contribute testimony in public.

The lack of access to primary archival material and survivor testimony has led to an eerie silence. There is a dearth of scholarship: there are no academic books analysing the CICA, or the RIRB. There is no sustained attention in the Irish school curriculum to the fact that over 800 (anonymized) abusers tortured thousands of vulnerable children in the State's care. The *CICA Final Report* characterizes abuse in the system as pervasive, chronic, excessive, arbitrary and endemic, but this report appears largely unread: perhaps the content stuns the reader and stymies analysis.[104] The report catalogues atrocious suffering under the cloak of anonymity, and this form makes the report oblique to additional critique. Its sheer scale renders the report a sculptural monument, a tombstone marking the burial of systematic devastation wreaked on generations of impoverished Irish children.

Dealing in indemnity

Following some discussion with cabinet colleagues and senior civil servants (in the caretaker government, during the 2002 election), the minister for education, Dr Michael Woods, signed an indemnity deal on behalf of the Irish State with the Conference of Religious in Ireland (CORI). CORI represents 138 member congregations including the 18 orders that managed Ireland's child residential institutions. The government deal secured the cooperation of CORI members with the CICA and the RIRB in return for an indemnification against costs above €128 million. Transfers to the State of Church property and other assets would constitute the bulk of the €128 million. The deal was neither approved by cabinet nor debated in *Dáil Éireann* (the Irish Parliament) because it was signed by the minister for education on his last day in office. No survivor was present, nor were their views sought. The deal remained a secret to the general public until it was revealed by the media in January 2003. On the publication of the *CICA Final Report* in May 2009, the total cost to the Irish State for the administration of the RIRB and related survivor supports was €1.1 billion, yet both the Taoiseach Brian Cowen and the Minister for Education Batt O'Keeffe were quick to announce that the indemnity deal with the religious orders would not be reopened.[105] The orders, many of whom continued with a campaign of obstruction and denial throughout the CICA, not surprisingly endorsed the government's stand. However, when survivor Michael O'Brien spoke emotionally on live television, on RTÉ's *Questions and Answers*, the government and the orders signalled a willingness to revisit the deal after all:

> Eight of us from the one family, dragged by the ISPCC cruelty man. Put into two cars, brought to the court in Clonmel. Left standing there without food or anything, and the fella in the long black frock and the white collar came along and he put us into a van. . . . And landed us below with 200 other boys. Two nights later I was raped.[106]

All eighteen congregations were asked to increase their contributions beyond the 2002 agreement. Combined they offered what they asserted was an additional €352.61 million in cash and property, but this figure was based on the congregations' presentation of property valuations, some of which appeared inflated.[107] Negotiations continue over the ownership transfer of nine properties. Current costs to the State of the RIRB and related survivor supports are approximately €1.5 billion. And yet, the indemnity deal remains largely in place. Successive governments argue that the Catholic Church has a moral responsibility to pay 50 per cent of redress costs, but to date the religious orders have pledged contributions amounting to 32 per cent (just less than one-third) of the total cost. In reality, they have paid slightly over a half of their agreed amount, and thus have contributed approximately 16 per cent of the total cost.[108]

All four of the orders who ran Magdalene institutions also ran child residential institutions that were the focus of damning indictments in the *CICA Final Report*. They were also accused of abuse at the RIRB. In 2017, two of these congregations were identified as owing money to the Irish Exchequer for outstanding contributions in relation to the RIRB: the RSM owing €24.9 million to the fund and the RSC owing €3 million.[109] Both of these orders run university teaching hospitals, they have been involved in running private hospitals and they also operate hundreds of schools funded by the Irish State.[110] While both orders were founded in nineteenth-century Ireland, they are now international in scope: the RSM operate in nine countries and the RSC in six. The remaining two congregations who ran Magdalene Laundries have since merged and also have a significant international footprint. They continue to receive substantial money from the Irish Exchequer. For example, the SGS received €14.4 million from the Health Services Executive in a five-year period (2006–11). In recent decades, they also sold extensive properties in Cork as well as large campuses in Waterford and Limerick (to the Department of Education for use as Institutes of Technology). Despite this, the SGS announced that they had no assets with which to make additional contributions to the costs of redress for people who had been abused as children in their institutions.[111] When former minister for education Ruairí Quinn wrote to the OLC Sisters in 2012 asking them to sign up to the 50:50 cost sharing principle, the order responded that 'at no point . . . did we make a commitment to a 50-50 cost sharing principle in regard to a response to "the institutional abuse" issue'.[112] In spite of the State's concern that the four orders that ran Magdalene Laundries have not contributed adequately to redress for the abuse of children in their care, it continues to fund their enterprises and has not chosen to re-examine their charitable and tax-exempt status.

The formation of Justice for Magdalenes (JFM)

The government excluded the Magdalene Laundries from the remit of the CICA and subsequently from the jurisdiction of the RIRB.[113] Speaking in Dáil Éireann on 12 February 2002, Dr Michael Woods insisted that 'The laundries differ substantially from the institutions now covered by the Bill in that the residents concerned were for the most part adults and the laundries were entirely private institutions, in respect of which public bodies had no function'.[114] In 2003, Mari Steed, Angela Newsome and Claire McGettrick founded the JFM group. All three were, and are, adoption rights activists. Two are the daughters of women incarcerated in Magdalene Laundries for a combined total of approximately sixty years.[115] Mari's search for her mother was a long and arduous process. Ireland continues to uphold a system of closed and secret adoption, which denies adopted people automatic rights of access to their birth certificate and adoption files while also denying women information about their forcibly disappeared children's fate and whereabouts. The religious and lay religious organizations and individuals that managed Ireland's twentieth-century adoption system are notoriously culpable in preventing mothers and their children from finding each other. Allegations of deliberate falsification of records are routine, including false registration of births (a form of illegal adoption) by State-licenced adoption agencies working in concert with religious orders.[116]

The activists who founded JFM set out by reactivating the MMC along with some of its original members. The MMC was formed in 1993, after significant concerns were raised following the exhumation of a communal Magdalene grave in High Park, Drumcondra. OLC had decided to sell some of their land at High Park to a property developer. They applied to the DoEnv for a licence to exhume 133 bodies from the grave, and they entered an agreement with the developer to split all costs. Contrary to recommended Catholic practice, the nuns cremated the human remains in Ireland's (then) sole crematorium and interred the ashes in a plot they owned at Glasnevin Cemetery.[117] Ten years later in 2003, journalist Mary Raftery broke the story that the undertakers had discovered an additional twenty-two remains during the exhumation process, which necessitated the nuns applying for a supplementary licence. This they obtained from the DoEnv without even needing to identify the additional bodies they sought to exhume and cremate.[118] Traditionally, Irish culture affords significant attention to funerals and the care of burial plots, and Irish people like to think that honouring the dead is something that they do particularly well.[119] The disregard with which the four religious orders have treated the remains of women held in the Magdalene Laundries – often burying them in mass graves, in some cases without a headstone, in other cases with inaccurate information on headstones, exhuming, cremating and reburying them, with little regard for maintaining appropriate records to ensure identification – speaks volumes to the Irish public, who take this lack of respect in death to mirror the treatment these women endured in life.

The MMC in 1993 called for a public funeral for the women buried at the former Magdalene Laundry at High Park. This request was refused. In the years that followed, the group lobbied to have a dedicated plaque affixed to a bench in St Stephen's Green to commemorate all women in the Magdalene Laundries. After a three-year campaign, the MMC was eventually successful. In April 1996, President Mary Robinson unveiled the plaque which reads, 'To the women who worked in the Magdalene laundry institutions and to the children born to some members of those communities – reflect here upon their lives.' Ironically, when MMC began its campaign, it was focused on commemorating the women of the Magdalene institutions, whereas in 1993, many laundries had only recently closed down, and there were still hundreds of women institutionalized behind the walls of religious buildings across Ireland. Indeed, even as President Robinson marked the memorial bench an 'historic' event, another Magdalene Laundry was still in operation less than 2 miles away at Sean McDermott Street in Dublin's city centre. The Sean McDermott Street Laundry did not cease its commercial operations until six months later in October 1996. At the time, there was a population in excess of forty women still in residence, the oldest in her eighties and the youngest in her forties. For those who are active in addressing the ongoing harms caused by Ireland's Magdalene institutions, this propensity to relegate survivors to ancient, opaque history remains a constant challenge.[120]

In 2003, after Mari met film director Peter Mullan at a screening of *The Magdalene Sisters* in Philadelphia, Miramax, the international distributor behind the film approached AdoptionIreland (predecessor organization to ARA) as part of an outreach initiative, offering to fund a postcard campaign calling for justice for the girls and women held in Magdalene institutions. The MMC had disbanded after the installation of the memorial bench in Stephen's Green; however, in August 2003 when Mary Raftery revealed serious discrepancies relating to the High Park exhumations ten years earlier, Mari, Angela, Claire and others from AdoptionIreland contacted former MMC members Margo Kelly, Bláthnaid Ní Chinnéide and Patricia McDonnell with a view to pursuing justice for the High Park women. Bláthnaid's son Ciarán set up the website with Mari, and in October, Angela set up a *Yahoo!* group called Justice for Magdalenes to further mobilize support. In September 2003, the MMC was officially re-formed and took over the postcard campaign from AdoptionIreland. Miramax paid for the printing of 5,000 postcards which called on then Taoiseach Bertie Ahern to establish a State inquiry into the Magdalene Laundries, including the circumstances surrounding the exhumations at High Park. An electronic version of the postcard was made available online, and members of the public both in Ireland and worldwide began sending thousands of hard copy and electronic postcards to the Taoiseach. Although all 5,000 postcards and many hundreds of electronic versions were distributed, the State never responded. Almost a year after re-forming, some of the original MMC members took a step back, and in July 2004, Mari, Angela and Claire relaunched the group as JFM.

In the years that followed the State apology to industrial and reformatory school abuse survivors in 1999, the government repeatedly abdicated responsibility for the Magdalene Laundries. Both government and opposition TDs and senators largely ignored the work of JFM between 2003 and 2009.[121] With no evidence of State involvement in the laundries available to them, JFM members concentrated on raising awareness through media interviews, as well as assisting academics, artists, documentary makers and others interested in the subject. Although JFM characterized itself neither as a survivor support group nor as a representative organization, a number of survivors contacted JFM to share their experiences and seek help in obtaining justice. Some of the women had been trying to access the justice system for many years. Through the generosity and trust of these survivors, JFM members began creating an archive of knowledge of the lived experiences of women and girls confined in the Magdalene Laundries. Some of these survivors also spent their childhood in industrial schools and were subsequently transferred to the laundries. Although section 1(3) of the *Residential Institutions Redress Act, 2002* states that applicants who were transferred from industrial schools to Magdalene Laundries before their eighteenth birthday were entitled to have that abuse considered as part of their RIRB application, many women in this position asserted that the RIRB refused to take their time in the laundries into account.[122] Unfortunately, at the time JFM could do little other than continue to raise awareness, act as a sounding board for survivors and assure the women that they would be kept informed of any developments. All of this would change when Jim Smith, an academic at Boston College, approached JFM with extensive evidence of State involvement in the Magdalene Laundries.

In advance of the publication of his book *Ireland's Magdalen Laundries and the Nation's Architecture of Containment* (2007), Jim had been increasingly public in discussing his research and in collaborating with activists. He met Mari and Claire on the JFM *Yahoo!* group, which he consulted as he wrote his book. He joined JFM when he had the experience of being contacted by a survivor who had read his book. He also recruited Katherine O'Donnell who was then director of the Women's Studies Centre at UCD. Shortly thereafter the group brought Maeve O'Rourke on board after she contacted Jim about his research in the course of her studies for a master's degree in law at Harvard. The reports of the CICA, the muted rumblings of survivors' experiences of the RIRB and Michael O'Brien's contribution on *Questions and Answers* were formative influences on Maeve and Katherine's decision to get involved with JFM. Of the initial three adoption rights activists who had founded JFM, Mari and Claire remained centrally engaged in the campaign, while Angela served on the Advisory Committee and helped to administer the group. Comprised of these five activists, with an advisory group of academics, activists, relatives of women confined in the Magdalene Laundries and survivors of institutional abuse,[123] we at JFM set our sights on securing a State apology for survivors; and a redress and restorative justice scheme that would avoid the adversarial terrors of the RIRB. This effort would become what JFM now calls 'The Political Campaign'.

Of course, none of this happened in a vacuum. We were inspired by the poignant Solidarity March of Survivors of Institutional Abuse in June 2009. We drew additional impetus from Judge Yvonne Murphy's 720-page report on child abuse in the Dublin Archdiocese published at the end of 2009, which stated that it had 'no doubt that clerical child sexual abuse was covered up' and that complaints of parents and their children were ignored. The report concluded that

> The Dublin Archdiocese's pre-occupations in dealing with cases of child sexual abuse, at least until the mid 1990s, were the maintenance of secrecy, the avoidance of scandal, the protection of the reputation of the Church, and the preservation of its assets. All other considerations, including the welfare of children and justice for victims, were subordinated to these priorities. The Archdiocese did not implement its own canon law rules and did its best to avoid any application of the law of the State.[124]

These tactics were familiar to all of us in JFM, and as women increasingly shared their experiences, we keenly felt the obstacles blocking their path to justice. There were other ideological and practical political contexts in which JFM began to form in 2003 that were not auspicious and were to prove decisive in the battles ahead. By then we knew that

- When faced with the CICA and the RIRB the Church/State establishment had operated together to prevent the legal justice system from addressing horrific crimes against Ireland's most vulnerable populations;
- The ruse of presenting such crimes in an outwardly comprehensive narrative but refusing to release the underlying evidence (even in redacted forms to researchers) and closing down all available archives and gagging witnesses ensured that these crimes could be passed off as belonging to a dim and unknowable past, which remained impervious to analysis and hence outside the remit of educators. The information would remain impervious to knowledge-making;
- The religious orders now knew for certain that their extensive financial operations would continue to benefit from State support and protection no matter how heinous their behaviour. The Church would largely run Ireland's State-funded education and health systems. The Church/State establishment would continue;
- The Irish public might be shocked by further revelations of abuse, but the Church/State establishment merely had to withstand that shock as the middle classes, the most empowered section of Irish society and culture, continued in a benign relationship with the Catholic Church and religious orders: sending them their children to be educated and their sick to be cared for; and
- The Irish middle classes would continue to be shocked even after decades of revelations. They would be shocked in being unable to assimilate the knowledge that orders which ran their nice schools and hospitals developed these institutions while being funded by the State to run other institutions for the most vulnerable

> that were grossly abusive. The empowered Irish middle classes would most likely continue to both 'know and not know'.

Yet the five of us who comprised the core working group of JFM were hopeful. We understood our central task, as it was laid out by Fintan O'Toole, that there is a

> propensity for Irish culture to have 'unknown knowns' – things that are known to be true but are treated as if they are outlandish fictions. No honest person seriously doubted that the industrial schools were instruments of terror and torture – why, otherwise, were children threatened with Letterfrack and Daingean, words that induced a numbing chill of fear? Likewise, many of the abusive priests were not secretive but behaved, on the contrary, with a flagrant and swaggering arrogance. Yet, as dramatists have understood since the time of the ancient Greeks, there is often much more power in being forced to confront what you already know than in being amazed by the unexpected.[125]

By the beginning of 2010, we in JFM were in daily contact with each other by Skype and email. Our relationships with Magdalene survivors were strong and deepening, and we felt we owed them an absolute commitment to gaining justice at every level. Bringing the crimes of the Magdalene institutions to the attention of the Irish public and diaspora abroad was a means to creating a more equitable society and, as such, a distinct sense of patriotism informed our endeavour. We understood the abuses of the girls and women in Magdalene institutions as symptomatic of deep misogyny and class prejudice – which we wanted to play our part in uprooting from the Irish State establishment that is still content to delegate, outsource and privatize services and to avoid accountability for abuse.[126] Yet we sometimes trusted, and more generally hoped, that our fellow Irish men and Irish women (at home and abroad) would respond in joining our call for an apology and reparation for Magdalene survivors and their families. By the beginning of 2010, the five of us in JFM trusted each other completely, and we knew that we would never give up.

3

Anatomy of a campaign

The strategies

Introduction: 'What are we going to do about it?'

Sitting in his office at Boston College in October 2008, Jim answered the phone and knew instantly that the halting voice on the line was a survivor. 'Are you the man who wrote the book on the laundries? . . . I just finished reading it. . . . How do you know my story?'[1] Catherine Whelan was in her mid-seventies at the time and living 25 miles north of Boston. She was proud of her Irish heritage. She also knew that what happened to her as a child was wrong. Catherine's mother died when she was seven. At fourteen, she was taken by her father to the Good Shepherd convent in New Ross. For the next four and a half years she washed society's dirty linen and received no pay. Poverty was her only crime. When she refused to work, the nuns cut her hair as punishment. The hair grew back but the loss of her education angered her. To Catherine, it was a prison in all but name. There was no inspector, no child welfare officer. She was abandoned and no one cared. At nineteen, she was sent to work at a Dublin hospital, also run by nuns. She fled to England and onwards to Boston. She felt keenly the stigma attached to her past, protected her privacy at all times, and despite the intervening decades, worried about saying anything that would harm her extended family in Ireland.[2] In 2008, at the end of their initial conversation, she simply asked Jim: 'what are we going to do about it?' This chapter reveals the strategies that JFM developed in the ensuing campaign for justice.

A core ethic: It's about the women

'It's about the women' and 'do no harm': these were the twin tenets which JFM abided by and adopted from the group's co-founders Mari, Claire and Angela. By 2009 they had many years' experience working with Magdalene survivors and adult adopted people searching for their natural mothers – some of whom had been detained in a Magdalene institution. Claire and Mari insisted that JFM involve survivors in the campaign to the extent that they felt comfortable. Concurrently, they pledged to protect the women from the media unless they expressly stated a desire to speak in public. Crucial too was a commitment to keep survivors informed. Jim's ongoing communication with Catherine meant that he – along with Mari in particular, and Maeve, who came to know several survivors living in the UK – ensured that the concerns of women in the Irish Diaspora were always at the forefront of our advocacy.[3] From October 2009 to February 2011, Mari published a series of bi-monthly e-newsletters; we did our best to circulate digital copies to support groups, and we posted hard copies to survivors in touch with JFM. The website also contained an email address, which Mari and Claire administered alongside a private Facebook group. On the basis of increasing correspondence, Claire produced her first 'research guides' for survivors and relatives in 2010; these have been updated regularly and the most recent versions remain available on JFMR's website.[4] The guides seek to empower women and their advocates, and they include template letters and contact information for writing to the religious congregations, various government departments, local government offices and affiliated agencies to seek information and personal records.

Katherine, meanwhile, was in touch with survivors via her work at UCD Women's Studies Centre. Increasingly she was hearing from industrial school survivors, some of who were transferred 'on license' to Magdalene Laundries. Many of these women also endured the adversarial RIRB process and understood themselves to be 'gagged' from speaking publicly about their experiences. Katherine's first JFM meeting also included Rachel Doyle from the NWCI. Thereafter, our campaign reflected the feminist principles of listening to the affected women themselves, ensuring ethical and transparent modes of communication, assisting survivors to speak about their experiences when ready and gathering feedback in relation to our advocacy efforts.

Maeve encountered JFM while a master's student at Harvard Law School, and her studies in human rights gave her an ethical perspective that fit well with the group's twin operating principles. She was encouraged to use her postgraduate research for the practical benefit of the JFM campaign by Professor Catharine MacKinnon, who concluded an office hours conversation about the laundries by asking, 'What are you going to do about it?'[5] Gathering testamentary evidence and taking direct instructions from the women for the purposes of advocacy were legal practice techniques that Maeve both learnt and put to use in the interests of the campaign while training as a barrister in London between 2011 and 2013. By recording JFM's first witness testimonies, Maeve built relationships with numerous survivors with whom she remained in regular contact.

JFM considered itself an advocacy organization not a 'representative' group; that is, we did not seek to create a membership drive to recruit survivors, nor did we insist that survivors join our organization. The campaign was always about opening the door to justice for all women, regardless of group affiliations. Members of our advisory board warned us of the government's attempts to 'divide and conquer' representative groups during the CICA and RIRB processes. We noticed references to JFM as 'an advocacy organization' in our interactions with officials, while government ministers invariably questioned us about the number of survivors we 'represented'. We refused to play the 'numbers game'. We ignored official requests asking us for contact information because many of the women were anxious to protect their privacy. Our advocacy extended to the women who never left a Magdalene Laundry, some still living in the nuns' care, others buried (some exhumed and reburied) with inaccurate, incomplete or no identities noted on gravestones. We also advocated for the sons and daughters of Magdalene women, some of whom had been adopted or 'boarded out'. We maintained good relations with the IWSSN in London, sharing resources and information. We adopted a different approach than that taken by MST, a representative group campaigning for an apology and redress, but we absolutely respected the women involved, their courage in pursing justice and the importance of their testimony.

Clear goals: A plan for redress and restorative justice

JFM's 'Proposed Restorative Justice and Reparations Scheme for Magdalene Survivors' (the Proposal) became the campaign's manifesto. A living document, it went through several iterations between mid-2009 and late 2011. Our advocacy efforts were directed to implementing what the Proposal outlined: (i) a State apology and (ii) elements of redress reflecting the expressed needs of survivors and family members.

We delivered the original Proposal to all TDs and senators on 2 July 2009.[6] It called for an apology recognizing the State's 'failure to protect adequately the constitutional rights of citizens committed to the nation's Magdalen Laundries' and an acknowledgement that these institutions 'were punishing and abusive in nature'.[7] We believed the apology would help neutralize the stigma associated historically with being a Magdalene woman and thereby empower many more survivors to engage with any process that followed. The precedent was Taoiseach Bertie Ahern's apology to survivors of childhood abuse in State residential institutions in May 1999. It came before the CICA and the RIRB and led thousands of survivors to come forward. We were convinced something similar would happen in the context of the laundries. Our initial Proposal further called for

- reparation in lieu of unpaid wages,
- a pension,
- medical assistance and counselling for survivors and their families,
- access to records for survivors and family members,
- sponsorship of an oral history project,
- an appropriate national memorial,
- funding for the upkeep and maintenance of burial plots, and
- a criminal investigation into the exhumation at High Park Magdalene Laundry in Drumcondra.

Days prior to publishing our Proposal, JFM encouraged Ruairí Quinn, the opposition Labour Party's spokesperson for education, to address the laundries on the Dáil floor while introducing his private member's legislation, 'The Institutional Child Abuse Bill, 2009'.[8] The ensuing debate indicated the steep path ahead. Quinn acknowledged that the women's experience was 'horrendous' but pointed to 'technical and legal reasons' for not tackling these abusive institutions in his legislation. Seeking a rationale, he reminded his colleagues that 'it was not just the State and religious teaching orders who were involved' and that 'a culture in some of our families' was also to blame.[9] Quinn's justification aside, Fianna Fáil was vehement in its opposition. Already rumours of a financial bailout were rife. Within a year, Ireland would be forced into a €64 Billion EU-IMF rescue package as Irish banks teetered on failing. In the court of public opinion responsibility lay firmly with the Fianna Fáil government whose policies led to a frenzied overheating of the economy. The last thing politicians wanted to entertain was a call for additional financial compensation and redress for institutional abuse survivors.

JFM submitted its revised 'Restorative Justice and Reparations Scheme' to the new minister for justice, Alan Shatter, in late March 2011.[10] Avoiding an adversarial redress process similar to the RIRB emerged as a priority from our wider consultations in the intervening twenty-one months.[11] We therefore specified that the entitlement to compensation should be 'determined *solely* on the basis of having spent time in a Magdalene Laundry' and that survivors should not be included in any proposed extension of the RIRB 'due to its judicial and adversarial nature' (emphasis in original). In addition, we stipulated that 'The State will not impose a "gag" order on women who receive compensation through the scheme'.[12] And, following conversations with the IWSSN in London, we requested that women living abroad be assisted to return to Ireland and be entitled to housing assistance. Finally, we used the process of redesigning the Proposal to incorporate the human rights language and frameworks we had begun to adopt.

The government's appointment of an IDC, chaired by Senator Martin McAleese, in June 2011 prompted JFM to again revise the Proposal. Our aim now was to make it as precise, comprehensive and practical as possible. At Minister Alan Shatter's request, JFM submitted its third Proposal in as many years on 14 October 2011, having carried out extensive comparative research and consultation with numerous support service providers and legal professionals.[13] We again exchanged drafts with the IWSSN and hosted a meeting in Dublin to discuss our proposals with Irish-based survivors. The women's chief concern – and it was something JFM had encountered before – was the prospect of not being believed, and thus they inquired about the possibility of appearing before any compensation board in groups rather than individually. The Proposal contained four key elements: (1) a State apology, (2) a dedicated unit within the DoJ for survivors of the Magdalene Laundries, (3) a Commission for Financial Reparation and (4) preservation of the historical record and transitional justice measures.

Changing minds: Evidence-based research

The Irish government excluded the Magdalene institutions from the CICA and RIRB in the early 2000s claiming that 'the laundries were entirely private institutions, in respect of which public bodies had no functions'.[14] In his book, Jim had demonstrated otherwise. He showed through archival research that the State used Magdalene Laundries as alternatives to prison for women found guilty of certain crimes, as well as placing other women on remand and on probation in Magdalene convents.[15] He identified official reports confirming the State's awareness of transfers between industrial and reformatory schools and the laundries and other records revealing that it knew about transfers between Mother and Baby Homes and the Magdalenes.[16] Jim uncovered additional evidence indicating that government departments held laundry contracts with the congregations, and that those contracts did not include a 'fair wages' clause.[17]

For the entirety of JFM's campaign, we researched intensely (in the absence of public access to many State and religious archives) and produced mounting evidence of State involvement in the laundries' abuse. And because of Claire's work with the MNP, which was expanding due to her research on Census data, electoral registers and death certificates, we increasingly presented evidence on duration of stay for many women buried in Magdalene plots around the country. At regular intervals we sought formal meetings and presented this evidence, not only with politicians but crucially also with government officials. Doing so underscored the campaign's increasing momentum.

JFM's first meeting with civil servants came in December 2009. The DoJ was managing the State's response, and perhaps tellingly, the section responsible for prisons and the probation service took the lead.[18] During the meeting, and in response to JFM's archival evidence, Assistant Secretary Jimmy Martin acknowledged that after the introduction of *The Criminal Justice Act, 1960*, the DoJ placed women on remand at the Sean McDermott Street Magdalene Laundry and paid a capitation grant to the OLC for each woman.[19] Mr Martin also acknowledged that despite there being no legal basis for doing so, the Irish courts routinely referred women to various Laundry institutions in an arrangement entered into privately by the judiciary and the religious. He further acknowledged that there was no legal basis for An Garda Síochána to capture or return women who escaped – something many survivors pointed to as instilling fear and leading them not to attempt escape.[20]

Just as this first meeting concluded, Mr Martin notified Claire and Jim that an RTÉ camera crew and reporter were downstairs requesting an interview. They opted to leave the building by the rear entrance believing the wiser move was to cultivate credibility with the officials. JFM was in this campaign for the long haul. Walking across St Stephen's Green afterwards, they felt they had somehow passed a test. Both realized a seismic shift had taken place: the DoJ now accepted that the State referred and was complicit in referring women to the laundries, and it was always aware that there was no statutory basis for confining women therein.[21]

Two months later, Claire and Katherine met with the Department of Education.[22] Confronted once again with JFM's evidence, these officials also acknowledged that the department was aware, at least from 1970, that girls leaving industrial and reformatory schools were transferred 'on license' to Magdalene Laundries. Later that spring, then minister for education Mary Coughlan responded to our request for information about such children stating that 'any records which my Department holds could not be relied upon to accurately quantify the numbers involved'.[23] She confirmed, however, that an internal review 'identified 261 references of referrals' of children but that 'the number of laundries involved was unclear as some locations are listed as schools, convents and other laundries'.[24] We found this admission of incomplete records disturbing, especially given that these vulnerable girls were, in a legal sense, the minister's wards. The public had put significant pressure on Brian Cowen's government to request additional financial contributions from the religious orders towards the final cost of the RIRB, at that time in excess of €1.3 billion, and yet elected representatives and the civil service seemed content to leave crucial records untouched in religious archives and unknown to a happily ignorant government.[25]

JFM attended our second meeting with the DoJ on 25 June 2010, hosted once again by Mr Martin who confirmed the department's coordinating role on the laundries.[26] Following a review of the research presented in December, he conceded that the evidence suggested a pattern of State involvement including formal and informal arrangements. He accepted that the *CICA Final Report* established the laundries as abusive institutions and acknowledged that individual survivors' testimonies did likewise, but maintained that without access to appropriate records the abuse was difficult to quantify.[27] This caveat was a now familiar refrain: there was a lack of records, only partial records, or, in one case, a flood had destroyed records. Liability was, Mr Martin contended, strictly a matter for the congregations who operated these institutions. The government would cooperate, would enter into negotiations with the Orders to facilitate access to records and might even consider a contribution to compensation, but the onus for redress would remain squarely with the nuns. Indeed, Mr Martin went so far as to suggest that the government was willing to consider issuing an apology and was prepared to work with JFM on its phrasing, but any such apology could not establish State liability. Mr Martin added that individual survivors were entitled to bring a complaint and pursue justice through the courts. (As we discuss in Chapter 7, this was impracticable.[28]) Not for first time, JFM left a meeting with Irish government officials sensing that the survivors we worked with were right: the State was involved in a policy of 'deny 'til they die!'

Making the Magdalene Laundries a political issue

Three additional tactics fuelled JFM's ambition to make the campaign an issue that politicians could ill afford to ignore.

(i) Parliamentary Questions

We actively involved politicians in our campaign by utilizing the Dáil's PQ function to elicit ministerial responses – mostly written, occasionally for oral delivery – based on a review of departmental records. The responses formed part of the Dáil record. They supplied JFM with additional evidence of State complicity and allowed us to gain maximum impact – in terms of political, media, and public attention – as each newly revealed fact undermined the government's position. Crucially, responses were made available online at the Oireachtas and Kildarestreet websites. We shared responses with key journalists demonstrating a strong interest in our campaign, for example, Patsy McGarry at *The Irish Times*, Conall Ó Fátharta and Claire O'Sullivan at *The Irish Examiner* and Joe Little at *RTÉ*.

This strategy emerged following Minister for Education Batt O'Keeffe's response to JFM's Proposal in September 2009. He insisted the laundries were 'private' and the women and girls were 'employees' who entered 'voluntarily'.[29] JFM objected strenuously through a series of PRs that were picked up by journalists.[30] The media demanded clarification and Minister O'Keeffe finally wrote to Tom Kitt TD who had written to the minister on JFM's behalf, explaining that 'I deeply regret any offense caused by my use of the term "employees." . . . I fully acknowledge that the word "workers" would have been more appropriate.'[31] But when confronted with PQs in the Dáil, O'Keeffe again refused to countenance redress because 'the Magdalen laundries were privately owned and operated establishments which . . . were not subject to State regulation or supervision'.[32] JFM turned to An Taoiseach Brian Cowen, seeking a cross-departmental response on the requested apology and redress.[33] Mr Cowen ignored our letter. But responding to follow-up PQs asked on JFM's behalf, the country's leader redirected calls for information, redress and justice to the four congregations involved and towards the Catholic hierarchy more generally.[34]

Conscious that the nation was entering an era of financial austerity, we used PQs to suggest the government should pursue the congregations for unpaid taxes, especially in light of their failure to submit contributory stamps on the women's behalf. Minister for Social and Family Affairs Mary Hanafin confirmed that the nuns never submitted PRSI contributions for the women despite there being a statutory obligation to do so since 1953.[35] Minister for Finance Brian Lenihan cited 'confidentiality' requirements in refusing to answer whether PAYE and social insurance records existed to indicate that the laundries paid taxes.[36] JFM wrote to Minister Lenihan suggesting that monies owed to the Revenue would go a considerable distance towards funding a survivors' redress scheme.[37] Again, there was no reply. The Department of Enterprise, Trade and Employment was asked whether 'statutory inspections under health and safety were carried out; if proper records existed in respect of working time, holiday time, and accidents at work', but the minister responded with uncertainty as to whether the questions were the remit of his department.[38] Taoiseach Cowen attempted to draw a line under the issue by outright rejecting State responsibility: 'The Government is also conscious that the Magdalene laundries were run by a small number of religious congregations with whom it is understood Magdalene women and their representatives are in contact.'[39] A month later, the minister for justice parroted that response:

> The majority of females who entered or were placed in Magdalen Laundries in the period did so without any direct involvement of the State. Magdalen laundries were not State institutions and their records are a matter for the individual religious congregations concerned.[40]

State and Church constituted Ireland's hegemonic order post-1922, a cosy relationship that continued well into the twenty-first century. The government might, with a nod and a wink, comfortably point the finger of blame at the Church, but it was always understood that Ireland's politicians would not beckon the religious to be accountable for their actions and inaction.

(ii) Oireachtas Ad Hoc Committee

Building on our established relationship with politicians, Tom Kitt invited JFM to speak at the Leinster House 'Media AV' room in December 2009 and proposed that he and Michael Kennedy, a fellow-Fianna Fáil deputy, form an Oireachtas all-party Ad Hoc Committee to address the needs of Magdalene survivors. Tom had been demoted to the back bench as part of Brian Cowen's government and had already announced his intention not to stand at the next general election. He exhibited dogged determination in forcing a written response to JFM's original Proposal from party colleague Batt O'Keeffe. Other politicians took notice. Moreover, they attended the first Ad Hoc Committee Meeting on 16 December at which Claire and Jim spoke. They carefully laid out archival evidence of State complicity across government departments, including justice, health, education, local government, commerce, finance and the Taoiseach's office, and answered questions about JFM's Proposal.[41] Not that we knew how crucial his advice would ultimately prove but Labour Party deputy Michael D. Higgins, now president of Ireland, advised JFM to submit an inquiry application to the IHRC, that the laundries abuse was a human rights issue and that we should explore every forum available to us.

The laundries were front and centre the following day during the Dáil's 'Order of Business' debate. Deputies challenged Taoiseach Cowen to introduce redress measures immediately. Fine Gael's Alan Shatter claimed that 'The Department of Justice . . . now has irrefutable evidence that this State and the courts colluded in sending young women' to the laundries. He added, moreover, that the women were 'treated appallingly' and 'suffered barbaric cruelty'.[42] Fianna Fáil's Michael Kennedy asked whether the State would provide records to relatives of former Magdalene women and to adopted people.[43] But, perhaps most poignantly in the days leading up to Christmas, Labour's Joe Costello revealed the need for urgent action:

> This is a live issue. For example, there are ten women in the Magdalene convent in Sean McDermott Street who will be moved against their will on 1 January to new accommodation. They have been there for between 30 and 50 years. These are extremely elderly women and we have done nothing as a nation to deal with them. It is time we did.[44]

In response, Taoiseach Cowen simply 'noted' what had been said before indicating that he would 'refer it to the relevant Ministers' to determine 'what is the position'. He closed his response with a tellingly honest admission: 'I am not up to date on this matter.'[45]

Politicians continued to ask questions throughout January 2010. Labour's Joan Burton placed the DoJ's recent admission of State involvement on the Dáil record during an Adjournment Debate, before revealing that she herself was adopted and attended school at a convent with a laundry attached. Her remarks were posted to the Labour Party's website, together with a YouTube video clip which, in turn, Mari linked to JFM's Facebook and Twitter pages.[46] We were intent on cultivating political statements about the campaign, disseminating those statements both to survivors and to members of the media, and likewise disseminating ensuing media reports back to all TDs and senators via mass-email chains.[47] Mari and Claire became adept at utilizing social media to 'feed the beast'.

JFM appeared before the Oireachtas Ad Hoc Committee for a second time on 23 June 2010. We updated politicians on additional evidence of State involvement, for example, the fact that the Department of Finance approved the payment of capitation grants for women placed on remand under the 1960 criminal justice legislation, but did so absent any mechanism for inspection and regulation as required by law.[48] Jim challenged those in attendance to balance the evidence of State complicity alongside the government's assertion that the laundries were 'private and charitable' institutions.

(iii) Meetings with politicians and civil servants and the general election agenda

Gathering in Dublin for Ad Hoc Committee presentations enabled JFM to arrange additional meetings over a few days which benefited the campaign by building networks and leveraging the fact that we were speaking to entities from across the spectrum (i.e. politicians, civil servants, the Church, civil society, academics, the public, etc.). We met with members of the Labour Party in December 2009. The Labour Women group had issued a public statement in late September supporting JFM's calls for redress – the first signal from a national political party that our campaign was striking a chord. The Labour Party were most likely going to be a coalition partner in the next government, and we were in the business of laying the groundwork to help move our campaign forward.

Two additional meetings took place over those busy days. Enda Kenny, leader of the Fine Gael party and presumptive Taoiseach in the next government, requested a separate meeting because he was unable to attend the AV Room presentation. Jim happily obliged, as Claire was rushing off to meet with Katherine and Rachel Doyle of the NWCI. Jim shared evidence of the courts' use of the laundries to place women on probation and remand and as places of committal if they accepted suspended sentences. Eventually, Mr Kenny politely interrupted to ask: 'You mean to tell me, these women were criminals?' Jim fumbled for a response, reminding the politician that 'there were no Magdalene Laundries for men'.

JFM's meetings with departmental officials continued throughout early 2010. Claire and Katherine, joined by fellow JFM co-founder and Advisory Board Member Angela Newsome, met with Minister for Health Mary Harney in late March.[49] She appeared sympathetic once presented with evidence of State complicity, acknowledging that the Department of Local Government and Public Health's policy was to transfer women from State-funded Mother and Baby Homes and County Homes to Magdalene Laundries and that the Health Boards later paid capitation grants when placing 'problem girls' in the nuns' care.[50] Minister Harney doubted that the congregations would provide access to their records and floated the idea of opening up National Census records beyond 1911 for the limited purpose of detailing who precisely was resident at Magdalene institutions.

Brian Cowen called a general election in the immediate aftermath of passing the austerity *Finance Act* in January 2011. Political polls augured a collapse in Fianna Fáil's support. JFM entered the election fray, asking voters to consider candidates' record on providing redress for historic and institutional abuses before casting their ballots. On 11 February we posted our programme for the next government, calling for

- an official apology from the Irish State and the Catholic Church,
- the establishment of a redress scheme for Magdalene survivors, and
- a statutory inquiry into human rights violations in the laundries.[51]

Sensitive to the pain austerity was causing to families across Ireland, we still asked the following questions: 'What kind of society do Irish people want? What values do we place on protecting the human rights of all citizens? What is our ongoing obligation (moral, political, and financial) towards survivors of past institutional abuse?' Claire and Mari also designed a flyer, 'Election 2011 and the Magdalene campaign – what you need to know?', that we linked to our website but also distributed online via JFM's Facebook and Twitter accounts. By this time, we were also utilizing mass-emails targeting all TDs and senators, and doing so enabled us to share the flyer with parliamentarians and underline JFM's willingness to hold public representatives accountable for their inaction. We also encouraged the public to register to vote and provided website links for them to follow up.[52]

The new government was in place by early March, a Fine Gael/Labour coalition led by Enda Kenny with Eamon Gilmore serving as Tánaiste. JFM had reason to feel optimistic as key allies in the past were returned to power and others now held ministerial positions. Alan Shatter was appointed Minister for Justice and Equality; he had advocated forcibly for redress in December 2009 and February 2010. Kathleen Lynch was an Oireachtas Ad Hoc Committee convenor and was appointed Minister of State with responsibility for disability, equality and mental health. She would work closely with Minister Shatter and initially at least stayed in regular communication with JFM. Mary Lou McDonald would assume a key role taking over from Caoimhghín Ó Caoláin as Sinn Féin's point of contact on institutional abuse. Likewise, Maureen O'Sullivan (Ind) became one of JFM's go-to representatives for tabling questions and working to facilitate communication across parties. Tom Kitt, who did not run for re-election, introduced us to Dara Calleary (Fianna Fáil) who lent much support. On the issue of the Magdalene Laundries at least, these three deputies exemplified how politics can and should work in a non-partisan manner for the greater good.

JFM wrote to Minister Shatter and Minister of State Lynch on 12 March.[53] We requested that they immediately institute a statutory inquiry into abuse in the laundries and acknowledge that an apology and redress were 'time sensitive' as many survivors were elderly and in poor health. We informed them that JFM was working collaboratively with other representative groups on our revised reparation scheme and that we planned to make submissions to the UNUPR and UNCAT. There was no formal response. Two weeks later, however, and in answer to PQs tabled on JFM's behalf, we learnt that the DoJ had prepared a draft memorandum on the Magdalene Laundries, which was going to be brought to cabinet by Minister Shatter.[54]

Making the Magdalenes a public issue: Press campaign and social media strategy

(i) Public writing

The Sunday Tribune published Jim's first advocacy opinion-editorial on 12 July 2009, which began by relaying Catherine's phone call and concluded by challenging Irish society to rationalize its compartmentalized responses to abuse suffered by children in residential institutions and that suffered by women and young girls in the laundries.[55] Over the course of the campaign JFM made use of opinion editorials, letters to the editor and PRs to increase public awareness of the campaign and the shifting political position.

Throughout these early months, every time we gathered additional evidence we wrote to the relevant minister. By the end of January 2010, their responses were cause for alarm. Minister for Justice Dermot Ahern, for example, acknowledged that the State sent girls and women on probation, on remand or on suspended prison sentences into the Magdalene institutions, but blandly asserted that his department held no records for the citizens so confined.[56] Minister for Education Batt O'Keeffe similarly asserted that 'the position remains that the laundries were privately owned and . . . were not regulated or inspected'.[57] JFM was intent on holding politicians to account for such prevarication and did so by way of 'Letters to the Editor', signalling our willingness to bring such tactics to the attention of society.[58]

JFM also issued over sixty PRs between 2009 and early 2013. The primary motivation, of course, was to cultivate media interest. But as a group, we were also intent on being transparent in all aspects of our work and were committed to building public awareness about the laundries. This began on 3 July 2009 when we issued a release announcing the circulation of our Proposal to Oireachtas members – in the early years of JFM, Claire had already established a media list with contact details, which was to expand as the campaign progressed. Fortune proved kind as the PR was picked up by Patsy McGarry, *The Irish Times*' Religious Affairs' correspondent, who reported our proposals in a front-page story the following Monday.[59]

(ii) Relationships: Building trust, cultivating awareness

JFM's public writing meant that members of the media increasingly turned to us for updates, context and to fact-check their stories. When gathered in Dublin for our Ad Hoc Committee meetings, we availed of BCI's facilities on St Stephen's Green to welcome interested journalists for previews of planned presentations and also shared 'embargoed' PRs. Similarly, we invited journalists to each of our public meetings, held at BCI, UCD and University College Cork. At the time, Mari was based in Philadelphia and took on the task of forwarding media requests, overseeing drafts and then issuing PRs, and organizing interviews. We made it a goal to follow up on every email, text or phone message to underscore that JFM was professional and responsive.

The Public Forum at UCD on 5 July 2011 began a very busy day for JFM. Before a packed room, Katherine, Maeve, Claire and Jim laid out our narrative of State interaction with the laundries and the MNP. We were joined by Paddy Doyle, an industrial school survivor and author of the memoir *The God Squad*, who posted all campaign-related reporting to his online blog where we knew many survivors followed developments.[60] Patsy McGarry also attended and reported on the event.[61] In the early afternoon, the scene moved to Leinster House where in a meeting arranged by Tom Kitt, now out of politics, we met with Fianna Fáil's justice spokesperson Dara Calleary and party leader Micheál Martin. Mr Martin acknowledged that the party had 'come late to the issue of the Magdalenes', but we nonetheless valued the important role that opposition parties play in challenging government policy. JFM insisted that politicians of all parties and none had failed the women in the laundries down the years, and thus we continued to meet, speak and work with everyone in the Oireachtas.[62]

This all-party approach was on display a few hours later during our third Ad Hoc Committee presentation in Leinster House. Notably, Jim's recently compiled evidence of continued State funding for the four congregations who operated Magdalene Laundries hit a nerve.[63] Senator Rónán Mullen (Ind.) objected to JFM drawing attention to Departments of Justice and Health funding for the Ruhama organization. He informed those gathered that JFM lost his support by not recognizing 'the good work done by [nuns] in the present'. Senator Mullen was intent on claiming the moral high ground but remained silent when asked whether delivering State funding to a private, third-party service provider was appropriate if said party refused to account for historic human rights violations.

(iii) Learning to work (with) the media

Although Mari and Claire had media experience from the earlier campaigns, no one on the team came from a communications background – we knew how to write an editorial, a letter, a PR, and a few of us had been on radio and television. Consequently, campaign successes resulted in some of our most stressful days, when our commitment to maintaining the focus on the women sometimes came into tension with the opportunity to maximize exposure, maintain pressure and protect our reputation as professional. A number of stand-out moments prove instructive in this regard.

As discussed in greater detail in Chapter 4, the IHRC in November 2010 called on the government to conduct a statutory investigation into abuses in the Magdalene Laundries based on evidence submitted by JFM. The announcement was followed by a media event where all of the major national outlets sought interviews. The sheer scale of media interest was unprecedented territory for our small crew of volunteer members. RTÉ correspondent Joe Little interviewed Maeve and Jim, and the segment ran on both the six and nine television news programmes;[64] Katherine and Claire did radio interviews for most of the early afternoon, including RTÉ's *News at One* and BBC Northern Ireland's 'Evening Extra' program; and Claire did a number of local radio stations the following morning. Thanks to Mari, who was coordinating media requests from Philadelphia, JFM's PR circulated around the world. The story was reported widely, including by event-attendees Patsy McGarry and Claire O'Sullivan, by many UK outlets, and thanks to the AP's Shawn Pogatchnik as far away as Boston, Los Angeles, Atlanta, San Francisco and Washington, DC.[65]

Six months later, Maeve travelled to Geneva to appear before UNCAT as part of Ireland's first examination after making a written submission on JFM's behalf. We signalled our intent in a PR issued in late March and began hearing from journalists shortly thereafter.[66] 'What's the line?' became a JFM refrain as media interest swelled and we prepared a response. We spoke with journalists who had stayed in touch since the IHRC event, parsed JFM's UNCAT submission and shared an embargoed copy of Maeve's planned 'Statement' in Geneva.[67] Katherine and Maeve did a round of follow-up phone calls to answer questions and draw out the implications of a potential UNCAT recommendation on the laundries. Jim was working to cultivate engagement from a number of freelance journalists working overseas. Carol Ryan pitched a piece to the *New York Times* in the run-up to the hearings and worked closely with JFM to check facts. Her article, 'Irish Church's Forgotten Victims Take Case to the UN', provided unprecedented international exposure, and we shared the piece with all TDs and senators. More importantly, JFM's critique of the government's inaction lay at its centre. It rehearsed Maeve's twin arguments to UNCAT – that the State was legally obliged to investigate the apparent torture and ill-treatment of girls and women in Magdalene Laundries, and that failing to do so was a continuing form of degrading treatment – before cataloguing JFM's evidence of involvement. Ryan finished by foregrounding precisely what was at stake in Geneva:

> 'I have always described them as Ireland's disappeared,' [Smith] said. 'They were edited out in the past and unfortunately the government seems to want to forget them in the present. But we won't let that happen.'[68]

This run-in to Geneva was just a prevue of things to come. UNCAT's 'Concluding Observations' following Ireland's examination were due to be made public on 6 June 2011 at 10.00 am, CET. In one of the better strokes of good fortune to befall JFM, Jim downloaded an advance copy posted online late the night before, at 10.00 pm in Boston. UNCAT expressed 'grave concern at the failure of the State party to protect girls and women who were involuntarily confined between 1922 and 1996 in the Magdalene Laundries'.[69] And the recommendation (discussed in Chapter 4) was unequivocal. JFM members were already working long hours at the time, but given Mari and Jim's location on the US Atlantic coast, it meant that we had sixteen hours-plus of daily coverage. Jim immediately called Mari in Philadelphia, sent a text and woke Claire in Ireland, and together we wrote JFM's PR and issued it before midnight Boston time. It called on the Irish State to act on foot of UNCAT's recommendation, issue a formal apology to survivors and immediately establish a statutory inquiry into these abuses. The release was waiting in every news editor's inbox when they opened email the following morning and it had the desired effect. All Irish media began their early morning reports with the Magdalene Laundries, including the requirement that the State provide information within twelve months on measures taken to give effect to the recommendation.[70] A media blitz ensued: Katherine had already done a pre-record with Joe Little at RTÉ; Maeve appeared on RTÉ's 'Morning Ireland' and Jim spoke with Mary Wilson on RTÉ's

'Drivetime' later that afternoon. Claire and Mari spoke to numerous radio stations and handled international media requests, including from Al Jazeera.

At the time, no other Irish voluntary advocacy group had brought witness statements of abuse to UNCAT and asked it to adjudicate their issues with the State. The 'Concluding Observations' were covered by all major Irish news and many international outlets, including the *New York Times*, the *BBC*, *The Times* (UK), *Time Magazine* and *The Guardian*, and this further galvanized public support for JFM's campaign at home and abroad.[71] Over the days that followed, several politicians made public calls for Dáil and Seanad debates, for an immediate apology, for a statutory inquiry and engaged the government through PQ and Leaders' Questions time.[72]

(iv) Social media campaigning

Building on our work with traditional media, JFM also engaged a series of social media strategies at key junctures throughout the campaign focused on bringing people power to bear on establishment politics. Mari and Claire, especially, were instrumental in this regard.

In the early years of JFM, the organization's social media presence consisted of a *Yahoo!* group. In July 2009, JFM migrated to a Facebook members-only group, and in March 2010 we established a Twitter account. While JFM was by no means the first organization to use social media to further a campaign, we were among the earliest groups to do so in Ireland. Social media platforms, being free of charge, are invaluable to an unfunded organization. For JFM, social media was not merely a way of networking and disseminating information – it became a formidable tool in holding the State to account.

By mid-2010 we began to detect a template-like 'sameness' in ministerial responses to PQs asked on JFM's behalf, an attempt perhaps to block our tactic of placing evidence of State complicity on the Dáil record. Not to be out-manoeuvred, we launched an online petition addressed to the Taoiseach. Doing so signalled that JFM was prepared to mobilize support beyond the survivor community and their families. The petition called for an immediate apology and redress scheme.[73] Mari and Claire deployed JFM's social media platforms to draw attention to the petition, with many people sharing and adding their calls for support. Arranging to meet on the steps of Leinster House on 21 June, Katherine, Claire and Jim handed Tom Kitt and Michael Kennedy the first 1,000 signatures and comments from the online site. As Fianna Fáil backbenchers, they had access to the office of the Taoiseach and personally hand-delivered the signatures to Mr Cowen.[74] Though not publicized, the petition remained online and attracted more signatures over the years, with many coming from overseas. One woman, writing from the United States, underscored the connections between Ireland's array of institutions and their continuing legacies for survivors:

> My mom was transferred to Sundays Well stayed doing laundry for 35 years from Bessboro Sacred Heart where mom stayed for 4 years after I was stripped away from her at birth. I remained at the home for almost 5 years. Mum unable to read or write was instructed to place x on paper and I became a ward of Ireland. Sold off and sent to USA. . . . My mom suffered from respiratory illness for almost 30 years from

> toxins she breathed working endless hours with little nourishment and medical care and she stopped breathing just over four years ago. . . . We did not deserve this.[75]

This would prove JFM's sole experiment with online petitions, but it gave us a sense of its capacity to channel public pressure into the halls of political power.

A year later and building on the significant media attention following UNCAT's recommendation, Mari and Claire again solicited the Irish public's support, calling on people via our social media platforms to participate in an email letter-sending campaign asking politicians to do three things: (i) review the Felice Gaer video clip challenging the State's assertion that women entered the laundries voluntarily, (ii) review copies of JFM's 'Restorative Justice and Reparations Scheme' and (iii) read Jim's recent opinion editorial which underscored the need for immediate government action given survivors' age.[76] The cabinet was due to discuss the DoJ's memorandum on the laundries in the coming weeks, and JFM wanted each minister to feel public pressure to do the right thing.[77] But perhaps the pressure proved too great? At his office desk in Boston College in early June, Jim received a phone call from Minister of State Kathleen Lynch signalling additional delays brought about by the fact that an earlier draft memorandum was so unacceptable to ministers that they demanded it be revised.[78]

Movement building: Civil society alliances

Because JFM was an all-volunteer organization with little institutional support and no guaranteed funding, we worked to build alliances with more established civil society organizations. Over the course of 2010 we developed relationships with key social justice groups, opening lines of communication with Colm O'Gorman, the executive director of AII; with Susan McKay, then CEO of the NWCI; and with Mark Kelly, the director of the ICCL. And, in the year ahead, we received advice and supports from the FLACs, PILA and the IPRT. We also made sure that each of these organizations received copies of our PRs and ensuing media reportage, and we also shared copies of JFM's submissions to the Irish government, the IHRC and various UN bodies. We understood that JFM's campaign benefited when civil society understood our cause.

We actively cultivated a key partnership with the women's council. At its 2010 AGM, the NWCI passed a motion to support JFM's campaign. Shortly thereafter Susan McKay wrote to all women TDs, senators and local councillors urging them to support our call for justice.[79] Following up on the letter, the NWCI's Rachel Doyle coordinated a campaign to get women county/city/urban district councillors to table a motion at their next group meeting:

> That _________ (County/City/Borough/Town) Council calls on the Government and the Catholic Church to (a) issue formal apologies for the abuse inflicted on women and young girls in Magdalene Laundries and (b) establish a distinct redress scheme for all survivors. We further resolve that a copy of this motion be forwarded to the Minister for Local Government.

With each council motion passed, Rachel informed JFM who in turn contacted the elected Oireachtas members from that constituency, who in turn forwarded the motion of support to the minister for environment and local government. The initiative paid rich dividends in terms of building bottom-up political support for our objectives. And, a number of the same local councillors that tabled motions were elected to the Dáil in the 2011 general election and remained steadfast in their support for the women.

A year later, when Maeve was navigating the UNCAT hearings in Geneva, Fiona Crowley (AII), Jane Mulcahy (IPRT) and Deirdre Duffy (ICCL) showed extraordinary support to the newcomer in the room. For example, Amnesty arranged for someone based at their secretariat in Geneva to attend prior to the NGO briefing and provide photocopied pictures of committee members and their interests. A year on, Mark Kelly at the ICCL invited JFM to participate in an event to mark the UNCAT one-year follow-up process at which Felice Gaer, UNCAT's deputy chairperson, also spoke. As discussed in Chapter 4, Maeve's presentation on the day garnered significant attention, in no small part attributable to JFM's well-oiled media operation.

Lobbying the Church

JFM understood that States not religious organizations provide justice. However, we also acknowledged that the Catholic Church was essential to providing a restorative justice response for abuses in the Magdalene Laundries. Starting in November 2009, Jim wrote a series of letters reaching out to Cardinal Sean Brady in Armagh, Archbishop Diarmuid Martin in Dublin and the leaders of the four relevant religious congregations – the RSM, the RSC, the SGS and the OLC. The strategic goal was to initiate communication, foster conversation and exchange points of view. At a minimum, the congregations were impeding attempts to more fully understand this history because of their blanket refusal to afford access to records, including administrative files. We wanted the invitation to remain open, thus we sent additional letters and compilations of JFM materials in April 2010, April 2011 and June 2011.

Ultimately, only two of the four religious congregations responded to our correspondence, and did so only once. Sr Bernie McNally wrote on 11 June 2010 asserting:

> The Good Shepherd Congregations' commitment to its former residents is manifest every day and we are always available to meet with them. Regretfully, it is not possible to meet with you . . . so will not be able to respond further.[80]

Sr Sheila Murphy, Regional Leader of OLC, wrote on 23 June 2010, stating:

> In the light of matters referred to above I do not wish to have, nor do I see any purpose in having a meeting with you at this time.[81]

On 31 March 2010 Cardinal Sean Brady informed the SOCA organization that 'he personally believed the Pope's pastoral letter and its apology placed a responsibility upon the religious orders to address what had happened in' and 'find a just solution for the victims of the Magdalene Laundries'.[82] Jim wrote immediately and the cardinal invited JFM to meet in June with a delegation from the Irish Bishops' Conference. Cardinal Brady was joined by Bishop of Dromore John McAreavey, Fr Tim Bartlett, assistant to Cardinal Brady, Harry Casey, executive administrator of the Bishops' Conference, and Lucy McCaffrey, lay-liaison between survivors' groups and the Bishop's Conference. The meeting was positive in tone. Cardinal Brady characterized the JFM presentation outlining State complicity as 'fair and balanced'; Bishop McAreavey added that it was broad and inclusive. The cardinal had already spoken with Sr Marianne O'Connor, executive director of the CORI, and was hopeful that communication from JFM would be well received. He emphasized, however, that any approach would need to be 'non-threatening'. Cardinal Brady also directed the conference to work with JFM to 'establish trust' between the parties. Not everyone at the table was impressed though. When Mr Casey signalled his willingness to relay the balanced nature of JFM's presentation to the congregations, Ms McCaffrey was quick to respond, 'that is one option, Harry'.[83]

Meanwhile, the clerics explained that the hierarchy no longer exerted the kinds of cultural and ecclesiastical power it once exercised over convents, going so far as to speculate on the congregations' wealth relative to the dioceses they ran. We detected a sense of relief, almost, that the nuns on this occasion were the focus of scrutiny.[84] Meanwhile, Katherine underscored that the congregations' records were key also to determining State and familial culpability for this historic abuse, and she encouraged all present to work to enable their release in a professional and ethical manner, which would also assist in the restoration of dignity to women buried in unmarked or incorrectly marked graves. In a statement to *The Irish Times* after the two-hour meeting, Cardinal Brady encouraged JFM to 'continue its efforts to establish dialogue and a process of justice and healing for all concerned'.[85]

As instructed, Jim wrote to Sr Marianne O'Connor on behalf of JFM and offered to share our presentation with CORI's executive committee and ultimately to meet with the four congregations. He added that one goal was to 'allay anxieties or concerns regarding the nature of what we are seeking to achieve'.[86] We waited until 1 October for a reply, which came by email and was brief:

> The Executive of CORI considered your request for a meeting but decided that you would best be served by direct contact with the Congregations involved because while CORI is an umbrella organisation for religious Congregations each retains its autonomy and management of its own affairs.[87]

We were and remain disappointed by this response.

Confronted by a blanket refusal to engage despite numerous letters, Jim asked Caoimhghín Ó Caoláin TD to table a series of PQs enquiring of various government departments the level of State funding provided in recent years to the four Magdalene congregations. At the time, a number of journalists were also utilizing FOI data requests and re-examining property sales during the Celtic Tiger boom years to question the congregations' refusal to contribute more equitably to the RIRB fund.[88] The RSM had informed the government that they would make a €20 million additional contribution, the RSC a €5 million additional contribution, the OLC a €1.5 million additional contribution plus some property transfers, and the SGS declined claiming it had 'no more funds with which to offer'.[89] The minister for justice responded to Ó Caoláin's question in early May stating that 'no funding was provided by my Department in the past five years'.[90] The minister for health detailed how between 2006 and 2010 the four orders had received in excess of €87 million from the HSE for the provision of services.[91]

Jim's research also led him to Ruhama, the Dublin-based NGO working with women affected by sexual exploitation, including forced prostitution. Ruhama's website, at the time, stated that the organization was a joint initiative founded by the SGS and OLC, both of whom had 'a long history of involvement with marginalised women'. It listed both congregations as Ruhama Trustees, and named Sr Bernie McNally and Sr Sheila Murphy as leading the organization's board of directors. The website also listed the Departments of Health and Justice among Ruhama's 'Funders', a fact not disclosed by either minister in their responses to Ó Caoláin's PQs. JFM was intent on asking why the State continued to fund two congregations that had yet to account for similarly 'marginalized' women and young girls placed in their care in the recent past.[92] It was important to demonstrate not only the manner in which industrial schools (for which redress was already being paid for by the taxpayer) and Magdalene Laundries were substantially linked – in some cases quite literally part of the same convent campus – but equally the ways in which the Church and State cooperated in the past and in the present, and continued in the present to occlude a mutually benefiting relationship.

This was the backdrop for JFM's first meeting with the Catholic archbishop of Dublin, Diarmuid Martin, on 6 July 2011.[93] Archbishop Martin took the meeting alone, writing his own notes and interrupting at will to ask quick-fire questions. This felt different from our visit to Armagh a year earlier. Jim again presented JFM's narrative of State interaction detailing complicity in the operation and function of the laundries across eight government departments. We indicated our willingness to work alongside the recently appointed IDC in the hopes that it might lead to an official apology and ultimately to redress for the elderly survivors. Archbishop Martin in turn detailed his track record in providing records to the Murphy Commission after 'an order of discovery' helpfully alleviated concerns about potential 'litigation'. Like Cardinal Brady he too signalled his willingness to speak with the four congregations and hoped they too would cooperate with the IDC. JFM meanwhile made five specific requests, asking him to

- help allay concerns the religious congregations had regarding JFM's objectives;
- help convince the religious orders that JFM did not want an adversarial, solicitor-driven process that delayed inquiry, restorative justice and reparation for survivors;
- encourage the religious orders to engage JFM in face-face-face meetings;
- instruct the archdiocesan archivist to review files for evidence of State interaction with the laundries; and
- issue a statement indicating support for the government's process.[94]

Archbishop Martin closed the meeting by stating adamantly that he was against any form of gagging survivors and believed in the power of speaking one's individual truth. The following year, Archbishop Martin chose the occasion of an address to the Magill Summer School to signal that he took JFM's presentation on board:

> Perhaps new forms of research-based investigation might better address such issues as the Magdalene laundries or the quality of care in some mother-and-baby homes and other institutions. It would be less adversarial, somewhat on the level of investigative social history through which the truth could emerge.[95]

The four congregations, meanwhile, never agreed to meet with JFM.

4

Anatomy of a campaign

Developing a human rights and justice agenda

Introduction

Whenever we felt stymied in the face of State denial and Church evasion, JFM tried to refocus on our twin objectives for an apology and redress. Needless to say, we took our inspiration from the resilience of the women themselves: Catherine, Josie, 'Maisie', Martina, 'Beth', 'Kathleen', 'Caitríona', Mary, Gabrielle, Elizabeth, Mary, 'Sara' and the other women that we would be privileged to befriend in the years ahead. And, with our campaign strategies firmly in place, we increasingly turned to the international human rights practices that suggested how best to challenge and circumvent domestic power structures. Nothing would come easy.[1] Ireland's political establishment delayed, deferred and denied our pursuit of justice at every turn. Whether through incompetence or intransigence, politicians and senior civil servants thereby squandered survivors' most precious commodity: time. We learnt in due course how to respond effectively to the State's failure to act, its abject lack of empathy and often-cynical power strategies. We hope other campaigners learn from our experience and the countervailing tactics we deployed in response. We offer them here in that spirit.

'Fresh air is the best disinfectant': Exposing Ireland's political establishment

(i) Irish Human Rights Commission

JFM revisited Michael D. Higgins's advice in spring 2010 and began researching the IHRC's inquiry application process. Doing so coincided with the expanding influence that Maeve began to exert on our campaign. Up to this point, we had focused on asserting the State's failure to protect the women's constitutional rights – basically, we were trying to shame the government into doing the right thing. But we didn't possess the expertise to consider the full range of legal obligations that had been breached and the legal arguments and procedures that could be used – notwithstanding survivors' inability to access the Irish courts.[2] JFM's cover letter to our IHRC submission evinces Maeve's impact on our collective thinking:

> The State . . . failed to fulfil its obligations as a signatory nation to international conventions on slavery, enforced labour, and human rights.[3]

The 50-page submission was accompanied by an additional 100-plus pages of appendices, including copies of Jim's archival research, JFM's Proposal and an array of PRs. Maeve transcribed survivor testimony from several TV and radio programmes demonstrating conditions in the laundries between 1922 and 1996.[4] She argued, in particular, that the women's treatment amounted to slavery, servitude and/or forced labour as defined by international law. On this basis, she maintained that the State had violated its protective obligations under several international treaties,[5] the ECHR[6] and arguably also the Irish Constitution.[7] Crucially, she insisted that it did not matter how women or girls entered the laundries – for example, at the hands of family members rather than the State – because the State's legal duties regarding slavery, servitude and forced labour were designed to ensure the suppression of these forms of exploitation by non-State actors. Furthermore, these obligations dated back to the 1930s. This was not a case, Maeve asserted, of applying today's legal standards to judge past conduct unfairly.[8]

Indications that the IHRC was taking JFM's application seriously came in July when we were asked to submit additional materials. Mari and Claire drafted a supplementary ten-page brief entitled 'Magdalene Laundries/Mother and Baby Homes and the Adoption/Fostering Connection'. They included three case studies bridging Magdalene Laundries, Mother and Baby Homes, and industrial schools, highlighting survivors and family members enduring in the present the legacy of past institutional abuse.

We learnt in late October that the IHRC planned to publish an *Assessment of the Human Rights Issues Arising in Relation to the Magdalen Laundries* on 9 November in response to JFM's application. The *Assessment* remained embargoed but we mobilized in anticipation of positive news. We reached out to survivors to see if any felt comfortable attending the planned launch while explaining that the media would be present. On the morning of the event, we were joined by 'Caitríona', a treasured survivor who travelled by train from the south-west of Ireland. Everyone looked out for and made much of Caitríona – she held pride of place and was tended to with sensitivity by all the IHRC staff. The room was full to capacity including politicians Tom Kitt, Kathleen Lynch and Michael Kennedy. There was an air of expectancy as people took their seats.

Éamon MacAodha, the IHRC's chief executive, announced that the Commission was 'calling on the State to establish a statutory inquiry' into abuses in the Magdalene Laundries.[9] Sinéad Lucey, the senior enquiry and legal officer, outlined the *Assessment*'s specific implications for the State:

- There was clear State involvement through the justice system.
- The State may not have honoured its obligation to guard against arbitrary detention.
- The State may have breached its obligations on forced or compulsory labour.
- The State may also have breached its obligations to ensure that no one is held in servitude.

- Serious questions arise regarding the burial, exhumation and cremation in 1993 of the remains [at] High Park Magdalen Laundry in Drumcondra.

JFM felt affirmed, especially when Lucey asserted something we long believed; the *Assessment* called into question the State's position that the laundries were 'private in nature' and that it 'was not' responsible for the abuse that happened therein. She doubted whether such a view could 'hold water'.[10]

The IHRC used the occasion to challenge Irish society to evaluate its treatment of vulnerable women and children in the present. Maurice Manning, the IHRC's president, reminded attendees that

> when the State allows any group or organisation to care for the vulnerable in our society . . . without proper oversight mechanisms, it is almost inevitable that human rights will be breached.[11]

Commissioner Olive Braiden echoed her colleague's concern by speaking directly to survivors:

> We understand that what happened to you was wrong. As a statutory body we recognise the hurt and the pain you have suffered. And we now call on the State to intervene without delay to redress that which demands redress.[12]

The government did not respond with redress, rather announcing its intention to ask the 'Attorney General . . . to consider the IHRC's report' while also expressing regret 'that relevant departments were not offered an opportunity . . . to facilitate a fully balanced evaluation of the facts'.[13] The DoJ seemed especially displeased.

A day that opened with such promise closed on a sour note. Tom Kitt, Michael Kennedy and Kathleen Lynch successfully petitioned for a Dáil Adjournment Debate to discuss the IHRC's findings. Adjournment debates allow for issues to be raised by house members at each sitting; they require a formal statement from the relevant ministerial department but do not lead to a decision being taken. Katherine and Jim were happy to sit in the visitors' gallery and witness the three parliamentarians urge the government to act on the IHRC's recommendation – Tom Kitt called on 'CORI and the four religious orders . . . to deal with the issue of records', Michael Kennedy asserted his belief that 'the State owes an apology to these women for refusing them their freedom', and Kathleen Lynch in an impassioned speech asked:

> why the agencies of the State which were charged with the responsibility in regard to these women did not go into these institutions and ask 'Are you here of your own free will? How long are you supposed to be here for? Would you like to leave?'

Deputy Lynch ended her comments by asking the minister, on behalf of the State, to 'stand up and say: "We are sorry, it should not have happened and we should not have allowed it to continue."'[14]

Minister for Justice Dermot Ahern chose not to appear in the Dáil chamber to join the debate. His statement was read by party colleague, Minister of State Martin Mansergh. There was no apology. Rather, he issued an expression of 'great sympathy' for women who spent time in the laundries, reminding the chamber that this was part of 'an era when Irish society could be harsh and hostile to . . . those who did not comply with what was perceived as respectable'. Worse would follow. The DoJ took issue with the IHRC's *Assessment*. In the absence of 'consultation' with government departments, the minister expressed concern for the congregations whose 'reputations . . . are at issue'. Such posturing served as the opening salvo before the main critique:

> the Human Rights Commission did not make a definite finding that there were human rights violations. The report discusses allegations and the possibility that there were human rights violations.[15]

There would be no statutory inquiry. The minister identified 'challenges', including whether to examine the laundries alone or also include Mother and Baby Homes, the inadequacy of records to support an investigation, and the 'grave matter' of financing an inquiry. His closing remarks rehearsed a line addressed repeatedly to survivors in the years ahead: 'It is worth noting that no complaints have been received from any of these women.' Justice officials met with former Magdalene women in November 2009, JFM's submission included survivor testimony, and the government acknowledged the laundries were abusive institutions in 2002 and again in 2009, but the State now showed itself ready to turn a deaf ear, content to tell the women they could pursue legal recourse through the courts (an avenue which, as explained in Chapter 7, has always been unavailable not only due to costs barriers but also because of the State's censorship of evidence).

The early promise of the day was now tethered to political intransigence. We felt deflated, but within a week JFM rallied to offer an 'Official Response' to the IHRC *Assessment* and shared our perspective with the wider legal community via the *Human Rights in Ireland* online blog.[16] The Adjournment Debate marked the uphill battle ahead, but we would continue to build alliances and draw on expert knowledge across different sectors at home and abroad.

(ii) UN Committee Against Torture

March 2011 ushered in a new government but still no response to the IHRC *Assessment* from the AG. We were concerned for the women: time was not on their side. Maeve decided to make submissions to UNCAT, which was due to examine Ireland for the first time at the end of May, and to the UNUPR, which was to assess Ireland's human rights record in October.[17] Since moving to the UK, Maeve had met survivors at the London Irish Centre who attended IWSSN meetings. She appreciated the crucial importance of survivor testimony in building human rights law cases, and several weekends that spring travelled to meet women (introduced to her by Sally Mulready) who spent time in different Magdalene Laundries. She obtained informed consent from four witnesses, transcribed and anonymized their testimony, and transformed JFM's UN submissions.[18]

The women insisted they were not free to leave the Magdalene institution; doors were locked and windows barred. They were forced to work for no pay, denied their given identities and subjected to severe physical abuse and psychological neglect. They remembered washing laundry from State-regulated industrial schools and other State-affiliated institutions. They recalled the police returning women who escaped (and one woman explained her own escape attempt), whereupon those women were subsequently punished and/or isolated in solitary confinement.[19]

Maeve relied on UNCAT's 'continuing violations' jurisprudence to argue that since Ireland's ratification of the UN Convention Against Torture in 2002, the State had continued to violate its obligations under articles 12, 13 and 14 to investigate and ensure survivors obtained redress for torture or other cruel, inhuman or degrading treatment.[20] Pointing to the women's testimony, she emphasized their present-day suffering as a result of these continuing violations, including poverty, educational deficits, lack of access to records, psychiatric illness and a deep sense of stigmatization.

JFM's resolve was strengthened in the weeks leading up to the UNCAT hearings. Taoiseach Enda Kenny again proclaimed that 'the Magdalene Laundries were not State institutions', that the DoJ placed a small number of women in one institution where they remained 'for short periods' and that the government had 'not received any complaints' from these women.[21] Meanwhile, Maeve obtained credentials to represent JFM in person and make a five-minute presentation as part of UNCAT's advance NGO briefing session scheduled for 20 May in Geneva.[22] JFM's always modest coffers were empty at the time, so she arranged her own accommodation, and paid out of pocket to copy and FED-EX overnight the ten hard copies of the group's submission required for distribution at the briefing, while Katherine paid for the flight. It proved worthwhile. Maeve instinctively knew her submission struck a chord. Committee members had read it in advance. In the informal meet and greet following the briefing session, key members searched Maeve out to ask additional questions. She emailed the group from the airport on her way back to London knowing that she had been heard.

The hearings proper commenced on 23 May, with an opening statement by the head of the Irish delegation, Mr Sean Aylward, general secretary, DoJ. Not only was this Ireland's first examination before UNCAT, but it was also the first time the treaty body's hearings were recorded live and, thanks to the IPRT, streamed online. Mari and Claire captured video of Mr Aylward's responses to members' questions, edited especially pertinent exchanges and posted clips to our Facebook and Twitter accounts. It was important that the women could watch the proceedings, and especially important for Maeve that we find ways to include the four survivors who provided testimony. It was not an auspicious start for Mr Aylward. His ten-page opening statement nowhere referenced 'Magdalene Laundries', 'industrial schools' or 'institutional abuse'.[23] But, if the State party planned to ignore these issues, committee members had very different ideas.

Myrna Kleopas (Cyprus) immediately asked whether the government intended 'to institute an independent investigation into the allegations of torture'.[24] Nora Sveaass

(Norway), referring to the IHRC's 'clear request' for a statutory inquiry, asked when it would happen and who it would cover. She encouraged the government to make available all relevant records and to look closely at JFM's Proposal. Xuexian Wang (China) insisted 'this is not just an historical wrong. It is an ongoing one.' Acting chairperson Felice Gaer (USA) requested information about the State's failure to inspect the laundries despite incarcerating women and knowing about the institutionalization of young girls. She acknowledged that survivors felt they were imprisoned and that the State neither took measures to protect them nor was it now taking measures to acknowledge what happened. The Irish delegation appeared stunned. Not only was the members' engagement informed, but they agreed with Maeve's arguments. No one seemed more surprised than Mr Aylward. As reported by *The Irish Times*, his initial response was halting: 'Some of the issues . . . in relation to the Magdalene laundries relate to a very distant, far-off time . . . and it would be very difficult for the State to rewrite its history.'[25]

Mr Aylward fared little better on day two. He asserted that the government was taking the issue of abuse in the laundries 'seriously'; indeed, he had personally met a delegation of survivors who had 'sad experiences to recount'.[26] The most serious allegations would, he added, constitute criminal offences under Irish law, but he was unaware of complaints being made to the police. (The Irish government has never acknowledged that the Convention Against Torture requires States to investigate wherever there is 'reasonable ground to believe' that torture or ill-treatment has occurred, even in the absence of an express police complaint.[27] JFM also knows Magdalene survivors who have made police complaints, including prior to 2011.[28]) He then doubled down, consistent with the State's strategy to diminish, deny and delay:

> These alleged events happened in most cases a considerable time ago in privately run institutions and therefore the information available to us all is limited. However, as far as we can establish on the facts available the vast majority of women who went to these institutions went there voluntarily, or if they were minors with the consent of their parents or guardians.

He closed by reminding the members that 'the organizations that are the subject of the allegations' still exist, 'mostly orders of nuns'.[29] This encapsulated the government's stance: the State bears no liability, the Church is responsible for redress and the government is available to mediate.

The committee members roundly rebutted Mr Aylward's remarks in turn.[30] Felice Gaer pointed to UNCAT's successful tackling of similar 'historic' abuses in Japan, Algeria, Cyprus and Canada. She underlined the State's obligation to ensure victims obtain redress, instructing Mr Aylward that Article 14 'doesn't say "seeks" redress, it says "obtains"'. Next, she debunked the State's logic on women entering the laundries voluntarily:

> I think that voluntary means that one makes a choice. I think voluntary means that one is informed. I think that voluntary means that one is then free to leave. I think it means that there is nothing coercive in this context. And, I would like to ask if

you have any information to suggest that the vast majority of persons who went to these laundries . . . were aware of the procedure for withdrawing or leaving, . . . or in the few cases of where the individuals were actually sent there as an alternative sentence from courts, again did they receive relevant information in that instance?

Ms Gaer nullified the distinction regarding the age of entrants, asking whether 'minors' were informed of their rights when they reached a majority, before continuing:

> Otherwise, we have a situation where it seems like there was . . . a question about consent but also a situation where there . . . appeared to have been a restraint on people's freedom of movement. We had testimony about locked doors, about people being captured by the police and returned to the institutions, so there's state involvement as well.

Ultimately, and most ruinous to the government's position, Ms Gaer used its own definition of torture, evoked by Mr Aylward earlier when addressing FGM, to insist that the State, and not the nuns alone, were responsible for the abuse:

> You said that 'an omission is a failure to take action, by broadening the definition to include omissions so that a wider number of possible scenarios are covered. For example, the act of torture may also arise from an act of omission and not only a positive act'. So, this definition appears to include the wilful failure to inspect the place or to regulate a place where acts of torture, or cruel, inhuman treatment occur. Wouldn't this apply to the Magdalene Laundries?[31]

The State's contradictory thinking was laid bare – the Department of Foreign Affairs wanted Ireland to assume a progressive stance on FGM; the DoJ meanwhile disclaimed its duty to prevent torture in the laundries. The government could not have it both ways.

UNCAT's 'Concluding Observations' were published on 6 June and, as discussed in Chapter 3, quickly became international headline news. The recommendation to the government was unambiguous – it affirmed JFM's submission, Maeve's arguments and most importantly the women's testimony:

> The Committee recommends that the State party should institute prompt, independent, and thorough investigations into all allegations of torture, and other cruel, inhuman or degrading treatment or punishment that were allegedly committed in the Magdalene Laundries, and, in appropriate cases, prosecute and punish the perpetrators with penalties commensurate with the gravity of the offences committed, and ensure that all victims obtain redress and have an enforceable right to compensation including the means for as full rehabilitation as possible.[32]

(iii) Memorandum for government

UNCAT's recommendation arrived just as JFM was expecting the cabinet to consider the 'Memorandum to Government', first signalled by Minister Shatter on 23 March

2011. Originally, the meeting was scheduled for early May, at which time we published an open letter to cabinet entitled 'Magdalene survivors need justice now' and arranged for a series of PQs to be tabled in the Dáil.[33] It felt like the campaign was finally gaining traction. Each intimation of progress drove us onward. One such signal came on 11 June when CORI issued a statement on behalf of the four congregations:

> As the religious congregations, who, in good faith, took over and ran 10 Magdalene homes during part or most of that time and as congregations still in relationship with many residents and former residents, we are willing to participate in any inquiry that will bring greater clarity, understanding, healing and justice in the interests of all the women involved.[34]

Within hours journalists reported the cabinet would consider the memorandum on 14 June.[35] JFM did not see the memorandum at the time.[36] Reading it in hindsight (alongside the earlier '3rd draft: March 2011' version that Kathleen Lynch informed Jim was sent back[37]), we remain appalled at the levels of cynicism that we had not fully detected in Ireland's political establishment. The government wanted to be seen to create mechanisms that appeared to address abuse in the laundries, while simultaneously ensuring those very procedures foreclose justice and accountability.

The March memorandum requests cabinet approval to write to the religious congregations 'inviting them to comment' on the IHRC report and 'to make their records public'; and also to establish an IDC comprised of civil servants 'to carry out a full review of the IHRC assessment and to make recommendations as appropriate'.[38] Minister Shatter assures the minister for finance that the IDC would 'strengthen the position of the government in dealing with the ongoing campaign' rather than generate pressure for redress. It also exposes the DoJ's aversion towards the IHRC report:

> The Minister has serious reservations about the methodology, accuracy and conclusions. . . . The IHRC report is effectively based on allegations put forward by JFM and no effort was made to obtain clarification, information or observations from the State or (apparently) the relevant religious orders.

Minister Shatter apparently underwent a volte-face since declaring that women in the laundries were 'treated appallingly' and endured 'barbaric cruelty'.[39]

The June memorandum is substantial, replicating and expanding on the March draft. It asserts that 'no wrong doing' took place at the High Park exhumations, claims it 'is not aware of any facts' that would give rise 'to State liability or responsibility for abuses' and contends that if abuses took place, then 'the religious orders . . . were responsible'.[40] It also reveals that DoJ officials had met with Dr Jacinta Prunty, 'a Senior Lecturer from Maynooth (who is a Religious) . . . doing a history of the Sisters of Our Lady of Charity' to be published that year.[41] Influenced by those conversations perhaps, a new diction now characterizes the nuns as providing 'a place of asylum', that the women 'sought refuge', that they were there to 'receive care' and followed 'the same regime as the sisters'. It continues:

> The records indicate that the majority of women stayed for relatively short periods. . . . In some cases, stays were merely overnight. . . . About 5% (441) stayed until death. A number of women apparently went there when ill with a view to receiving care and a Christian burial.

The June document repeats the department's disdain for the IHRC *Assessment*, now criticizing the Commission for contemplating 'an inquiry outside the courts system' to which 'redress or other relief' would be linked.[42] Above all else, the memorandum is at pains to dampen any action that would signal State culpability or create expectations for redress.[43]

'Observations' from government departments, included in the June memorandum, unanimously refute assertions of State liability and insist that the congregations foot the bill for redress. Minister for Education Ruairí Quinn warns that an investigation may well lead to 'demands for enquiries into other situations . . . [including] mother and baby homes, psychiatric hospitals and foster-care settings'.[44] Minister for Public Expenditure and Reform Brendan Howlin warns 'that it does not have the resources to allow for the establishment of redress measures'.[45] Minister for Jobs, Enterprise and Employment Richard Bruton, addressing the duty to regulate and inspect factories, states that 'the mere fact that statutory regulation exists . . . does not, of itself, impose any duty of care on the State in relation to the employees of that sector' and recommends that 'this fundamental principle not be conceded' on the laundries.[46] The AG identifies the IDC's limitations:

> It will have no power to compel witnesses or procure documents. It will not enjoy any form of privilege. . . . It will not be in a position to make findings in terms of liability, causation, or culpability.[47]

The AG also warned the government to anticipate the nuns taking legal action as they had done in the past 'to protect and vindicate the names of their members and to protect the good names of their congregations as a whole'.[48]

Only the DoH comes close to addressing survivors' needs. They too signal support for the IDC but strongly favour the appointment of an independent chairperson – the original plan had the IDC chaired by the DoJ.[49] Health also proposed that Phil Garland, an HSE official, 'conduct a comprehensive inventory to identify the number of surviving women' and thereby establish the 'likely consequences of any redress scheme'.[50] Minister Shatter dismisses this latter suggestion, insisting that the IDC will strengthen the government's position before concluding:

> there can be no special redress measures established for those who were in Magdalen Laundries and no expectation of such redress should be created. Any question of redress has to be a matter for the religious not the State.[51]

Unaware of the official deceit confronting us, JFM members exchanged emails the night before the anticipated government announcement cautioning 'against getting our hopes up', hoping we might be 'pleasantly surprised' and reminding each other that we were 'in this for the long haul'.[52] When issued the following afternoon, the government statement outlined a 'twin-track' approach: (i) the establishment of an IDC charged with producing a narrative of State involvement with the Magdalene Laundries; and (ii) that Ministers Shatter and Lynch would meet separately with survivors and groups representing them as well as the four congregations with three goals in mind: to discuss the making available of records; to obtain information regarding the number of women still living in the care of the religious orders and to put in place a restorative and reconciliation process.[53] We didn't know it at the time, but the fix was already in.

Working the government's 'twin-track' process

(i) Meeting the ministers

The government's 'twin track' approach fell short of what the IHRC and UNCAT had called for, that is, a 'statutory' or 'prompt, thorough, and independent' investigation, yet JFM committed to engage both policy tracks. Maeve wrote to Minister Shatter acknowledging that we would participate while signalling concerns about the process.[54] She reminded the minister of UNCAT's follow-up deadline and linked JFM's cooperation to an assumption that the IDC's terms of reference would not only focus on the State's direct involvement with the Magdalene Laundries but also 'address the issue of state responsibility for human rights violations by private actors'.

The government announced on 1 July that Senator Martin McAleese, the spouse of the popular Irish president, had agreed to serve as independent chairperson.[55] The media turned to JFM to gauge our reaction. We felt somewhat underwhelmed. Dr McAleese lacked expertise in the legal and human rights arenas. We had hoped the government would appoint an external, international and objectively independent expert. Dr McAleese had, on the face of it, deep ties to Ireland's political and religious establishment – he had only recently been appointed to the Seanad by the sitting Taoiseach.[56] On the other hand, his appointment likely alleviated concerns held by the congregations, and from that perspective alone Minister Shatter helped secure their cooperation with an investigation lacking the statutory powers to compel participation. Aware of these facts, JFM cautiously welcomed his appointment realizing that time was not on the women's side.[57]

Minister Shatter wrote on 20 June inviting JFM to meet with him and Minister of State Kathleen Lynch.[58] On a beautiful sunny July morning, we turned up at DoJ headquarters having stopped briefly at the Magdalene memorial park bench while crossing St Stephen's Green to reflect and gather inspiration. Claire, Katherine, Maeve and Jim were joined by Councillor Sally Mulready and Phyllis Morgan from the IWSSN, who we had worked alongside for over a year at this point. Mari Skyped into the meeting from Philadelphia at 5.15 am her time. We presented both ministers with copies of Jim's 'Narrative of State Interaction with the Magdalene Laundries', now a 50-page document accompanied by approximately 400 pages of appendices. Claire also submitted new research from the MNP including comparative analysis data detailing lengthy durations of stay for many women.[59] We also left copies for delivery to Senator McAleese.

Mr Shatter set an informal tone, insisting that he wanted to 'assist' the religious orders and 'former residents' in a restorative and reconciliation process.[60] He was anxious that 'privacy issues . . . be respected' so as to avoid causing 'unnecessary stress' to the women 'who still lived in the care' of the nuns. Claire countered by addressing the difficulties she faced in obtaining access to records and the discrepancies she discovered between names on gravestones and those recorded on death certificates, including for some of the exhumed human remains at High Park in Drumcondra in 1993. She suggested that voter registration records would prove helpful and inquired whether census records post-1911 would be made available to the IDC. Katherine urged Minster Shatter – who was meeting the four congregations that afternoon – to inquire whether the nuns would agree to deposit their records in an archive, where they would be preserved, redacted appropriately and made available to the public. Mr Shatter cited data protection concerns reminding us that the 'records relate to persons who are deceased, persons who do not wish to have access to their personal records, and those who are still alive and don't want to revisit their past'.

The meeting turned slightly fractious when the conversation addressed the IDC's powers, and at this point the two groups diverged in opinion. Both ministers pounced on the fact that Sally and Phyllis representing the women in their group advocated for 'practical' solutions. JFM did not disagree. But, we insisted as a matter of principle that the IDC not only create a fact-finding narrative; it must also investigate human rights abuses. Maeve asked, would the committee's terms of reference be made public and would it have powers to compel evidence? Minister Shatter replied that he would 'not pre-judge the outcome and will not interfere with the committee but if Senator McAleese needs assistance he will be given that assistance'.

Maeve was not satisfied. She pointed to UNCAT's language around prosecutions. Mr Shatter countered that the power to prosecute in the Irish jurisdiction 'rests solely' with An Garda Síochána, before adding that 'UNCAT assumes that there are criminal issues to be prosecuted'. Not backing down, Maeve next asked whether the IDC would investigate beyond direct State involvement to also address 'its failure to establish regulation' and have it enforced in relation to arbitrary detention, forced and compulsory labour, indeed its failure to create 'criminal penalties for slavery'. Minister Shatter was not pleased. A meeting that opened with talk of reconciliation between survivors and the religious was now focused – thanks largely to Maeve – on State culpability. The minister declared himself the person in the room seeking to 'address the issues that are important to those women who felt a sense of grievance, who want access to their records and/or to engage in the restorative and reconciliation process', before posing a question to JFM: 'Do you want to assist in that process or do you want to prosecute the State?' The lines were drawn.

The meeting concluded with a presentation on mediation by Anna Connolly, identified as working with the probation service. She detailed a four-phase process to include taking time to build trust between the parties and storytelling. The DoJ records Sally's response to what was outlined as 'perfect' for IWSSN members. Katherine, in turn, detailed JFM's Proposal, which had met with favour in Geneva and among the survivors in contact with us, stressing the need for an apology, truth-telling and access to records, supports in securing housing and counselling, pensions and compensation for lost wages. On this final point, again according to the DoJ, 'Cllr. Mulready stated that on the financial aspect, the women she represented were "more interested in pensions and would look for a lump sum payment of €10,000"'.[61]

(ii) Meeting the senator

JFM also wrote to Senator McAleese in mid-July assuring him of the group's willingness to contribute to the IDC process.[62] He responded and invited us to a meeting in early September. Notably, the letterhead underscored his specific mandate: 'Inter-Departmental Committee *to establish the facts of State involvement with the Magdalen Laundries*'.[63] This directive was underlined when Jim spoke by phone with Ms Nuala Ní Mhuircheartaigh, appointed adviser to the chairperson and seconded from the Department of Foreign Affairs where her work focused on human rights.

JFM's meeting with the IDC took place on 9 September 2011.[64] We submitted an expanded version of Jim's 'Narrative of State Interaction' with an additional 500 pages of archival evidence.[65] Dr McAleese informed us he was consulting widely, that the committee's terms of reference would evolve over time, that each of the departments represented at the table had been charged with identifying relevant records, and he assured us that an Interim Report would be published on 20 October.[66] He also relayed that the religious orders 'have been very cooperative'. Both he and Ms Ní Mhuircheartaigh had already viewed numerous records in the nuns' possession, and these would be available to the IDC after 'certain comforts' were put in place by way of assurances regarding confidentiality. The senator acknowledged JFM's significant contribution to date before asking for 'steers' in terms of locating additional records. Claire suggested post-1911 Census data and electoral registers as a place to start.

The civil servants, meanwhile, were anxious to ascertain how many women JFM 'represented'. While JFM had been in touch with numerous survivors since 2003, we responded honestly: at that point thirty-six survivors were in contact across various platforms. The senator asked whether our assertions could be proved 'based on thirty-six reports'. When the discussion turned to acts of omission, especially the State's failure to adequately regulate the laundries, Mr Rochford responded that he would be checking his files for evidence of inspections. Mr Martin disputed JFM's assertion that An Grianán – the so-called Training Centre for young girls on the grounds of the OLC's High Park institution – was a Magdalene, suggesting instead that it was a 'home for problem girls'.[67] Mr O'Sullivan wanted to know whether 'babies were born in the laundries'. We suggested he examine department files to ascertain the level of transfers between Mother and Baby Homes and the Magdalene institutions and pointed him to examples of both.

JFM was told not to expect too much from October's Interim Report. Senator McAleese dispelled any notion of an apology being offered: that 'would not be possible' under the IDC's terms of reference. Jim and Claire stressed that survivors were less likely to engage until State and Church acknowledged they were wrong and the women wronged. We were then asked to help circulate an informal questionnaire to survivors, but we had significant reservations – it was informal, it had the potential to re-traumatize survivors, and it would heighten expectations. Senator McAleese reminded us of our status as an advocacy group. He remained non-committal when Maeve pointed to additional issues the IDC should investigate, namely legal issues regarding direct involvement with and State awareness of conditions in the laundries, and failures to protect all girls and women who were incarcerated and forced to work for no pay. He replied that the IDC's 'main thrust was factual'. Ms Ní Mhuircheartaigh added that JFM's submission would be 'checked and verified'.

Katherine welcomed the senator's progress in terms of accessing the congregations' records. She referred to Claire's work with the MNP and JFM's plan to conduct an oral history project before asking the senator to propose to the nuns that they deposit copies of their records with a suitable repository, for example, the National Archives or a university archive. This, she explained, would ensure preservation, appropriate redaction and access for survivors, family members and the public. Senator McAleese hoped that the process would have a positive impact in that direction while reminding everyone of the importance of 'nursing these things along'.[68]

JFM decided not to issue a PR on the day. Rather, we posted a brief summary paragraph to our website and Facebook page providing an overview of the conversation. And, we looked to limit expectations with regard to the Interim Report, which we characterized as unlikely 'to draw any conclusions' and 'merely indicate progress to date'. Many survivors were expecting an apology upfront followed by a period of investigation leading to redress as the CICA/RIRB precedent established. We now knew this was unlikely. We also identified two 'take-aways' from this first encounter: Senator McAleese appeared anxious to preserve good working relations with the religious congregations; and survivor testimony would prove increasingly significant as the campaign progressed.[69]

(iii) 'Deny 'til they die': Mandates, advocacy and the Interim Report

JFM understood we were being challenged on our mandate to represent survivors and on our attention to accessing records – Minister Shatter and Senator McAleese attempted to monopolize the high moral ground in terms of protecting survivors still living in the nuns' 'care' and their right to privacy. Doing so ignored JFM's advocacy work on both these fronts, including concerns we brought to the attention of the 'ministerial-track' that summer. First, we forwarded allegations of precarious living situations involving survivors in different care settings operated by the religious. Second, we lobbied for survivor- and family-member access to records held by the congregations.[70] In this context, JFM drew the ministers' attention to the fact that a recent HIQA report stated of the Beechlawn Nursing Home on the site of the former Magdalene at High Park in which we knew a significant number of survivors resided:

> some institutional practices were observed which require to be reviewed these include empowering residents to make decisions and choices in their daily lives, reviewing forms of address used and ensuring the confidentiality of residents [*sic*] information.[71]

The HIQA report, to our eye, signalled continuing State involvement with former Magdalene women, fifteen years (at that point) after the last institution closed its doors in October 1996. Given that her ministerial brief included treatment of the elderly, JFM also wrote to Minister of State Lynch on 18 August 2011.[72] She indicated by telephone that the issue was seen as part of the work of the IDC and a meeting would therefore be inappropriate.

When contacted by survivors looking to access records, JFM invariably directed them to the research guides posted on our website – we knew they helped as an initial resource.[73] However, survivors increasingly reported back that they rarely received more than a one-page photocopy of their specific single-line entry in the convent register, typically indicating a name, date of entry, referral information, given name while in the institution, a date of release and sometimes onward destination. When Minister Shatter maintained that the nuns provided personal records to individual survivors, it amounted to a copy of this single-line entry.[74] From JFM's perspective, such practice constitutes an ongoing violation of the woman's human rights and evinces a continuing form of harm.

Relatives also sought our assistance in accessing records. Family members looking for information, once they verified their relationship, typically received the same scant record. For those affected by Ireland's secret adoption system, obstacles were often insurmountable. Under Irish law, the Adoption Order removes all trace of the individual's prior identity, and though Irish birth certificates are public documents freely available in the GRO, those responsible for arranging and authorizing adoptions routinely refuse to allow adopted people to know their name at birth.[75] Even if the adopted person overcomes this bar, they then confront the secretive Magdalene system where the changing of women's names was routine. Adopted people were invariably horrified at discovering their natural mother endured ongoing incarceration in a Laundry. If still 'residing' with the nuns, they oftentimes met a woman bearing the debilitating scars of institutionalization.[76] In cases where the woman died behind convent walls, they often had to navigate unmarked or incorrectly marked graves. So-called closure was illusive either way. Both ministers ignored JFM's advocacy on these important issues.

The IDC's October 2011 *Interim Report* revealed that the committee had entered into an 'arrangement' permitting it access to the congregations' records while also 'respecting the privacy of former residents and the legal obligations of the orders'.[77] Minister Shatter facilitated the pact by issuing a Statutory Instrument authorizing the committee to process 'sensitive personal data . . . for reasons of substantial public interest'.[78] This 'mutual understanding of confidence' agreement served as the basis upon which the congregations made their records available to the IDC. Reading the *Interim Report* recalled for us the deference – 'comforts' – extended towards the nuns at our September meeting. The *Report* to our eye contained no equivalent expressions of concern towards survivors. On the contrary, the subsection entitled 'Terminology' stated that 'to avoid distress to any party' the committee will 'use the terms "resident" and "former resident" throughout its work', thereby conferring a degree of agency that few women in the institutions enjoyed.[79] For JFM, 'resident' resonated with the State's use of the term 'voluntary' in Geneva; moreover, it was identical to the language used by the religious orders.[80]

The *Interim Report* also outlined plans for the IDC's archive of materials. Official papers, reports and archival files compiled from government departments, State agencies and other bodies would be 'stored centrally'.[81] But, the archive would not include data disclosed to it by the religious orders: 'All such records will be destroyed and/or returned to the relevant Religious Order upon conclusion of the Committee's work.'[82] Minister Shatter prevaricated on this very issue in the Dáil on 2 November, claiming: 'The religious congregations have also indicated their willingness to discuss the general question of long term retention of and access to records.'[83] The *Interim Report* had already stipulated the return or destruction of all such material two weeks earlier.[84] There would be no transparency or accountability because no one – not survivors, not family members, not researchers – would gain access to the nuns' archives. Although we did not know it then, no one would gain access to the IDC's archive of State papers and administration files 'stored centrally', either.

Between October 2011 and March 2012, JFM endured five months of non-communication. Ministers Shatter and Lynch ignored our advocacy. By this time, we had, at Minister Shatter's request, also submitted our revised restorative justice scheme on 14 October, again greeted with resolute silence. In March, we turned to Deputy Maureen O'Sullivan (Ind.) who agreed to use a 'Priority Question' to compel a Dáil statement. She asked Mr Shatter 'to offer a commitment that the twin-tracks of the Government's investigation are ongoing simultaneously' and that 'he does not envisage them as consecutive'.[85] In his response, Mr Shatter closed with the following:

> I am pleased to say that meetings with all concerned took place some time ago. Progress has been made on the various issues including the question of a restorative and reconciliation process between individuals who had been in such institutions and the orders which ran the institutions in question.

JFM found it difficult to take this seriously. For starters, the congregations refused JFM's numerous invitations to discuss restorative justice. Moreover, Minister Shatter was ignoring the State's legal obligation to ensure the women obtained redress. When pushed on the impact of delays, he resorted to a phrase JFM was already intimately familiar with: 'I am not going to prejudge what is in the report.'

Writing a shadow report, shaping the narrative

(i) Enter Raymond Hill

By February 2012, and confronted with what increasingly felt like official obduracy, JFM started to be guided by Raymond Hill, a London-based tax barrister who generously offered pro bono legal help and worked with Maeve on an ongoing basis over the coming months.[86] Raymond's late mother had been a social worker for much of her career, and he donated his time in her memory. Raymond brought to our campaign twenty-plus-years of experience representing both the UK government and claimants, including in inquiries similar to the McAleese process. He helped us decipher and better understand the IDC as a vehicle of investigation, identify its flaws and recognize its limitations. Those limitations were significant.

The IDC was neither impartial nor transparent.[87] As such, it did not meet the State's human rights obligation to investigate the Magdalene abuses. The 'independent chair' was a government-nominated senator.[88] The other members were senior civil servants from six government departments which referred women to and/or conducted business with the laundries in the past. There were no independent members, no international experts and no survivor representation. The IDC did not have a mandate to investigate allegations of abuse or make determinations about allegations of torture or any criminal offence. It had no power to receive individual complaints, no power to investigate them and no powers to compel witnesses, to subpoena documents or to make recommendations.[89] There was no public invitation to submit evidence. There were no published terms of reference.[90] The IDC was entirely dependent on the bona fides of the religious congregations with respect to accessing documents.[91] There was no way to verify the production of documentation from congregational and diocesan archives.[92] And, as discussed earlier, the IDC agreed to return and/or destroy copies of religious records at the conclusion of its work – conduct contrary to UNCAT's guidelines.[93] For these reasons the UN does not accept that Ireland conducted an independent and thorough investigation as required by international law.

Guided by Raymond's influence, JFM pursued three key countervailing strategies throughout 2012. First, we compiled additional archival evidence documenting State involvement with the laundries. Second, we gathered survivor testimony, transcribed it and integrated it alongside the archival evidence. And third, we lobbied politicians to apply pressure on the government to introduce redress, while simultaneously engaging with the UNCAT one-year follow-up process to maintain international pressure. All three efforts culminated in JFM making its 'Principal Submission' to the IDC in mid-August.

(ii) Sharing evidence with the IDC

Building on JFM's practice of sharing information with government departments for over two years, we began making submissions to the IDC in the days immediately following our first meeting on 9 September 2011.[94] They already possessed copies of our earlier submissions to both ministers in July. And, we alerted them to the witness testimonies of the four women whose evidence Maeve had submitted to the UN.

Jim spent the spring of 2012 on leave in Ireland, which afforded him the opportunity to conduct additional research at the National Archives, the DoH Data Management Centre, the Dublin Diocesan Archives and the Galway Diocesan Archives. He made over a dozen email submissions to the IDC, typically attaching images of archival documents and narrative analysis demonstrating State involvement.[95] His research demonstrated, for example, that so-called problem women routinely ended up in Magdalene Laundries, in the custody of the Good Shepherds, through a series of ad hoc arrangements entered into by public officials.[96] Jim forwarded evidence of persistent traffic between Mother and Baby Homes and Magdalene institutions: when unmarried mothers were transferred to the laundries, some children were 'boarded-out', others sent to State-licensed industrial schools and others still sent for adoption via an array of State-licensed adoption agencies, in some cases adopted overseas to America.[97] This constituted State involvement with the laundries on many different fronts.[98] Given that the IDC had unfettered access to DoH records, which included the mothers' and children's names and registration numbers, and also had access to the religious congregations' records, Jim challenged Senator McAleese to demonstrate conclusively what happened to women transferred from these institutions.[99]

Based on Maeve's legal analysis we argued to the IDC that its investigation must account for the State's failure to protect the rights of the women working for no pay in the laundries. In June 2011, we had arranged for Caoimhghín Ó Caoláin to table a PQ for the minister of jobs, enterprise and innovation on whether 'Ireland's Magdalene laundries were considered factories' under the *Factory Acts, 1955*. Richard Bruton's (and his department officials') response was alarming:

> The mere fact that the State has a right to inspect particular premises does not mean that it has an obligation to do so – there neither was nor is any obligation on the State to inspect every workplace.[100]

To counteract the civil servant doublespeak, JFM set out to demonstrate that the State was indeed required by health and safety legislation in force at the time to inspect the institutions and prosecute for breaches in health and safety regulations.[101] Jim pointed out to the IDC in May 2012 that in debates on the *Factories Act 1955*, the minister for industry and commerce, William Norton, was unambiguous on the inclusion of Magdalene Laundries:

> Once you wash clothes in the institution, not for the institution, then that is a factory. In other words, you have a right to wash clothes for the institution, but if you start to wash other people's clothes it is a factory, for the purpose of Section 84.[102]

This statute and its subsequent secondary regulations required all young persons under the age of eighteen to be 'certified fit' by a State-appointed doctor within ten days of starting work. Working from a list contained in the State's own archives, Jim informed the IDC that there were 420 State-certified doctors fulfilling this function by the late 1960s. Thinking about Catherine in particular, Jim asked if the IDC can demonstrate that each young girl working in a Magdalene Laundry was certified fit by a State-appointed doctor. And if not, why not?[103] Maeve found Hansard records and documents in the law library at Lincoln's Inn and the Westminster Reference Library clarifying that, in fact, Magdalene Laundries had been subject to regulation under the *Factory and Workshop Acts* from 1907 onwards (albeit, as discussed in Chapter 1, subject to sweeping exemptions obtained by the nuns).[104] Jim demonstrated moreover that during the 1940s and early 1950s, a high percentage of all factories in Ireland were visited each year (routinely between 45 and 60 per cent), and, this being the case, 'one must assume that over the nine year period in question at least one of the 10 Magdalene Laundries should have been inspected'.[105] He forwarded to the IDC summaries of five prosecutions following accidents in commercial laundries and, pointing to the fact that survivor testimony spoke to loss of limbs, hair caught in machines, burns, etc., asked the IDC to ascertain whether accidents in the laundries were reported in accordance with statutory requirements.[106]

(iii) Survivor testimony

Survivor testimony proved critical to JFM's 'Principal Submission'. We understood that the women were more likely to be forthcoming in oral rather than written testimony. Consequently, we agreed to bring them together, obtain full and informed consent, record and transcribe their testimony, review and revise it with the women, and submit transcripts to the IDC. It was a daunting prospect, but we were committed to empowering survivors to contribute to the process. Katherine had already applied to the Irish Research Council for what would become the UCD-sponsored project, 'Magdalene Institutions: Recording an Oral and Archival History'.[107] Her project procedures fulfilled UCD's ethical human-subject criteria, and she had already developed an interview guide, consent forms and a questionnaire, all of which were amended for the purpose at hand.[108] Our plan was to use the IDC testimony-gathering as a pilot for the MOHP, which would not commence properly until later in 2012.[109]

JFM met with Senator McAleese and Ms Ní Mhuircheartaigh for a second time on 16 February 2012.[110] Ten days earlier, we inquired as to whether they planned to speak directly with survivors. We pointed to the potential for the appearance of a double standard given that the *Interim Report* put on the record their in-person meeting with the religious congregations. We were still somewhat surprised when they initially resisted face-to-face discussions with the women. They explained that they were concerned not to raise expectations, and they were anxious (understandably so) given that neither had the appropriate training. Claire shared that meetings with the women were invariably uplifting occasions and that with sufficient notice and clear procedures JFM was prepared to help manage expectations. Senator McAleese seemed convinced and insisted that while the *IDC Report* would focus on fact-finding, it should not be 'cold' and speaking to survivors would 'add value' in terms of signalling directions the government might take.[111] JFM understood that we would submit written survivor testimony and thereafter arrange a face-to-face meeting.

Claire contacted the women we knew by letter, explaining our goals for submitting survivor testimony as part of the IDC process and sharing some sample questions so they would know what to expect when we met at BCI on 20 March. Katherine meanwhile worked on amending the consent form for this specific use, stipulating that JFM could use redacted and anonymized excerpts for our 'Principal Submission'. In the same vein, Maeve and Raymond developed a set of questions to elicit testimony that spoke to each woman's individual experience while also focusing attention on various forms of State involvement and responsibility. Seven women turned up at BCI on the day, and after cups of tea and careful explanation of what we were about to undertake, JFM conducted its first interviews with five survivors and two daughters of Magdalene women.

In the weeks that followed, we all carried out additional interviews working to the same template; Claire travelling to Cork and Dublin, Maeve gathering testimony from survivors, relatives and other witnesses in England, Cork and Dublin, Katherine speaking to women in Dublin, and Jim based in Galway interviewing a survivor and a former Laundry manager. Thanks to Evelyn Glynn, we were also able to include in our submissions to the IDC an additional seven testimonies relating to the Good Shepherd Laundry in Limerick.[112] Not long into the transcription process, Maeve inquired as to whether we should arrange to have the testimony sworn – not something we had contemplated to that point. JFM's primary concern in posing the question to both Senator McAleese and the ministers was to protect survivors from having to retell their account on multiple occasions, and thus we asked whether the testimony if sworn would also serve in any ensuing redress scheme.[113] Two days later, Ms Ní Mhuircheartaigh responded by welcoming 'former residents' who wished 'to share their stories', but added:

> There is no need for input submitted in this way to be sworn or witnessed – this is not a legal forum and the Committee does not have a mandate to consider individual complaints. We would not like any excessive formality in the process to risk altering this perception among the women.[114]

In hindsight, we assumed that the IDC was acting in good faith and would weigh survivors' testimony appropriately, reading and treating equally written testimony and that provided face to face. Regrettably, that proved not to be the case.

JFM considers itself privileged to have been trusted with the women's testimony. Their accounts speak to a diverse range of experiences. For example, some of the survivors were transferred to Laundries from industrial schools in their early teens. One woman told us that a nun beat her on the first night, while another lady who, as a teenager was put in by the Legion of Mary, shared that upon arrival she was given a number and told she had no name. In many cases these survivors had attended the RIRB where, without exception, they were barred from speaking about their time in the laundries.

Other survivors spoke about being transferred to the Magdalene from a Mother and Baby Home after being forcibly separated from their baby. One survivor was proud to tell us she eventually managed to get her son back and raise him. Another told us how proud she felt after a reunion with her son because he had become a paramedic – she would have loved to train as a nurse but lost her opportunity after being denied an education upon entering the Laundry at eleven years old. The majority of women were of limited means, and they pointed to their lost education and the lack of skills that resulted directly from their incarceration. One survivor told us that her widower father sent her to what he thought was a school, but she never attended one class.

In some cases, children of Magdalene women were growing up in adjacent industrial schools (e.g. at High Park, Sundays Well, Waterford, New Ross and Limerick). One lady spent much of her childhood on the same convent campus as her mother without ever knowing her. She spoke to her sense of being deprived of family and the chance to meet her mother. Other survivors recounted escape attempts and how both nuns and Gardaí were involved in their capture and return. One survivor shared how after escape she managed to get a job but the nun arrived at her place of work and brought her to two waiting Gardaí who escorted her to a different Magdalene institution.

The majority of survivors in contact with JFM had physical ailments directly attributable to their time in the laundries. One woman communicated how she was always anxious to leave hospital because it reminded her of not being able to escape the Laundry. Stigma was prevalent in these women's lives; it was a recurring trope across all testimonies. In the absence of an official apology the sense of shame had not diminished. One elderly survivor told us her primary concern was to protect her children from this stigma. Another woman relayed her greatest fear was that her family back in Ireland would be shamed if her story became known.

JFM submitted its first tranche of testimonies at the end of May 2012 – 13 separate accounts comprising 519 pages of text, including copies of original documents survivors asked us to include as supporting evidence. In her cover letter to Senator McAleese, Claire explained: 'We . . . set out to ensure that the women's testimony was collected in an ethical manner that conformed to the highest human-subject research standards.'[115]

JFM accompanied a delegation of survivors into Leinster House to meet Senator McAleese face to face on 6 June 2012. Claire wrote to the women in advance, assuring them that no media would attend, and detailing the plan to first meet at BCI before travelling by taxi-mini-bus entering via the 'heads of State' gate off Merrion Square. Six survivors and two daughters attended, some travelling from the south and west of Ireland. There was a real sense of anticipation – the women were conscious that they were finally going to speak their truth. And, that the occasion was taking place in Leinster House did not go unnoticed – one of the ladies took an extra embossed serviette from the Oireachtas catering service as a memento, others treasured copies of the proclamation that were kindly provided.

Senator McAleese and Nuala Ní Mhuircheartaigh were gracious in putting the women at ease – the senator greeted each individually, asked where they had travelled from, listened in turn as they relayed their experience. It was emotionally taxing for all concerned – a few women needed to take a break. They all spoke to recurring themes of being locked in, a daily routine of work and prayer, and the stigma they faced later in life. Each of these survivors had already submitted their testimony as part of JFM's first tranche, and according to Claire, who was present throughout, the verbal and written accounts were consistent.[116] Afterwards, the women felt vindicated – one lady (now deceased) told Claire that she 'felt like a weight had been lifted'.

(iv) Maintaining political pressure: UNCAT's follow-up process

JFM's third strategy was to continue our engagement with UN human rights bodies, thereby ensuring political pressure at home and abroad.[117] We arranged a series of events to coincide with UNCAT's one-year follow-up process in late May 2012, including a fourth presentation to the Oireachtas Ad Hoc Committee and a workshop jointly sponsored with the ICCL at which Felice Gaer, UNCAT's vice-chair and designated rapporteur for follow-up in Ireland's case, presented remarks (speaking in a personal capacity). Her presence in Dublin at the time was no small matter. Since the previous year's formal UNCAT recommendation for an effective investigation, prosecutions and redress, we had worked to this follow-up deadline, and Maeve spent much of April and May drafting our follow-up written submission.[118]

The Irish government also submitted its follow-up report on measures taken to implement the recommendation.[119] It posited that 'any person may initiate a civil action before the courts seeking recompense for any wrongdoing they have suffered'.[120] Maeve anticipated this line of argument and pointed out that survivors had already complained about their abuse through direct letters to government ministers, through testimony submitted to the CICA, UNCAT and UNUPR, and on radio, television and film. In this context, she argued that the government must be aware of its obligation to investigate all reports of torture even in the absence of an express complaint to the police. In a similar vein, she pointed to the lack of prosecutions for child abuse in State residential institutions – also an UNCAT follow-up issue. As such, she suggested that even if Magdalene complaints were forthcoming, it was unlikely that the State would contemplate prosecutions. Likewise, she pointed out that the minister for justice had failed to provide information on how survivors might overcome bars to civil litigation (e.g. the *Statute of Limitations, 1957*) or likely punitive costs.

We rehearsed these same arguments when JFM presented before the Ad Hoc Committee on 24 May, where again we called for an immediate apology and the introduction of redress. Katherine began the event by underscoring the urgency of our campaign: three survivors known to JFM were dying of cancer. JFM was cooperating with the IDC, but Maeve informed the TDs and senators that we also reserved the right 'to call for an investigation with statutory powers'.[121] Jim pointed out that the *CICA Final Report* and survivor testimony established that women's labour in the laundries had been 'forced and wholly unpaid' and that they 'were completely deprived of their liberty and suffered both physical and emotional abuse'.[122] Presenting evidence had become second nature to JFM by this time, but the Media/AV Room was moved to silence when Senator Marie-Louise O'Donnell read anonymized excerpts of survivor testimony conveying what a State apology would mean to their lives:

> Well it would be a sort of a closure. That at least they had the good rights to apologise. If somebody goes out of their way to apologise, that they were in the wrong, well then that would alleviate you.
>
> I think that an apology from the State would be, it wouldn't block out the memories but, it would go half-way towards healing us a bit, give us a bit of relief before we die.

As we often witnessed, the women, when they found a respectful forum, were their own best advocates.

Four days later, JFM presented a courtesy copy of our follow-up report to Felice Gaer.[123] It was a significant day on a number of fronts – we emailed our follow-up submission to Geneva, hand-delivered the first tranche of survivor testimonies to the IDC and made public the evidence Jim had gathered of transfers between Mother and Baby Homes and the laundries.[124] But, the afternoon belonged to Maeve. She spoke before a packed ICCL event and began by repeating a number of times what survivors repeatedly had asked her: 'Is anyone listening? Is anyone listening?' She proceeded to read testimony from a number of survivors, including an escapee returned by An Garda Síochána.[125] Turning to the follow-up submission, Maeve asserted that the government had failed to implement UNCAT's recommendation, specifically its obligation to ensure that survivors obtained redress. She acknowledged the IDC's work, relayed JFM's position that it should not impede women's access to an apology and redress and concluded by asserting JFM's right to call for a fully independent inquiry with statutory powers to compel evidence.[126]

Near the end of her keynote remarks, Felice Gaer turned to the issue of the Magdalene Laundries and recalled JFM's evidence a year earlier as 'dramatic . . . detailed . . . documented' before stating:

> We asked for a full and prompt, effective investigation into these claims. . . . And, that's one of the follow-up issues we are looking forward to hearing about. A lot happened right after our review, but I am not so sure that that much has happened since then, but perhaps I am wrong because we haven't received a report yet.[127]

Senior journalists in the national media attending the event read between the lines of Ms Gaer's remarks. The UN believed the women.[128]

A month later validation also came from Dr Geoffrey Shannon, Ireland's Special Rapporteur on Child Protection, when his Annual Report highlighted how women and young girls in the laundries 'were forced to work in difficult conditions, for long hours, with no payment' and stated that their 'detention amount to "forced labour" under the 1930 Forced Labour Convention of the International Labour Organisation'. He concluded with a forceful assertion: 'It appears from the reports provided by these women and girls that their treatment constituted slavery.'[129]

(v) JFM's 'Principal submission'

Just over three years into the JFM campaign, we made our 'Principal Submission' to the IDC in mid-August, 2012.[130] It was a massive undertaking, arising from our commitment to shape the narrative to reflect survivors' testimony and the historical record. It would not have been possible without Raymond Hill's guiding hand; his hundreds of hours spent reading, drafting, revising and rewriting steered our project. Just before we were due to submit, and after spending days indexing the evidence in London with Maeve, Raymond worked through the night to produce a penultimate draft of the submission before going on holiday with his wife and children. Maeve flew to Dublin and once there, she and Claire took over the draft and spent two days in BCI compiling and indexing additional materials, and finalizing the folders of evidence that Raymond had sent by FED-EX. The submission comprised a 145-page argument on State involvement, supported by 796 pages of survivor testimony in turn corroborated by 3,707 pages of archival and legislative documentation.[131] It encompassed all of JFM's work to date.[132] We distilled our arguments into three main categories of State involvement with, and legal responsibility for, systematic abuse in the Magdalene Laundries:

- That the State sent women and girls to the laundries and ensured they remained there;
- That the State provided the congregations with direct and indirect financial support; and
- That the State failed to supervise the congregations' operation of the laundries.[133]

Ultimately, JFM argued that its submission alone constituted irrefutable evidence of State complicity in myriad violations of rights enshrined in the Irish Constitution and international and European law. That being the case, we again called for an immediate apology and the provision of redress along the lines of the Proposal we had submitted to the government in October 2011 to deafening silence.

We didn't know it at the time, but our submission overwhelmed the IDC's ability to stay on deadline, despite the fact that it received a tranche of survivor testimony in May and archival evidence via email submissions from Jim spread out over ten months.[134] Minister Shatter announced in early September 2012 that the *IDC Report* would now be delayed – for a second time – until the end of the year.[135] We called on Mr Shatter again to acknowledge a threshold of State involvement short of the final report so that an apology could be issued and compensation provided immediately.[136] In what became a JFM tagline over the coming months, we asked whether the government's 'all too familiar policy of "deny til they die"' would now become '"delay til they die"'?[137]

Winning hearts: The Magdalene Laundries as an issue of public morality

(i) Private Members debate: An apology and redress now

Faced with inaction JFM decided to intensify public and political pressure: the women needed help urgently. With their permission, we released a redacted copy of our 'Principal Submission' to members of the Oireachtas in September 2012. We called on all TDs and senators to read the submission and press Minister Shatter to act on an apology and redress.[138] The same week, we also wrote to Minster of State Lynch referring her to our Proposal, which included a call for a 'Dedicated Unit' to provide services to survivors.[139] We asked as an interim measure that she make available a dedicated phone helpline as soon as possible. Our PR ended by laying down a marker: 'the Fine Gael and Labour government continues to fail survivors of the Magdalene Laundries.'[140]

Within days Mary Lou McDonald announced that Sinn Féin planned to table a Private Member's Motion for debate in the Dáil. She requested JFM's assistance in drafting the language to reflect survivors' needs. She also reached out to Dara Calleary in Fianna Fáil, who arranged his party's full support. Maureen O'Sullivan worked with independent members to ensure support across opposition benches. JFM found itself deploying tactics from the campaign's early days: appealing to the public, trying to win minds, making the laundries a moral issue.

The days leading up to the debate brought additional encouragement from unexpected quarters. JFM had been assisting RTÉ on the production of a documentary for *Prime Time Investigates*.[141] As luck would have it, the programme aired on the first night of the debate and featured several survivors in touch with JFM. It also featured Felice Gaer, who was critical of government inaction: 'there hasn't been a response to the victims . . . to provide an apology or assist them.' The documentary also included interviews with Maeve who detailed JFM's human rights arguments and Jim who discussed State complicity alongside footage of archival evidence. Fintan O'Toole published a blistering opinion-editorial in *The Irish Times* the same day, claiming that Magdalene survivors are 'among those who are still waiting for a simple acknowledgement of a nasty truth: that this State imprisoned and enslaved astonishing numbers of its own citizens'.[142] The government's failure to act, O'Toole added, was nothing less than 'cruel, nasty and cynically evasive'. The following day, the same paper published Jim's opinion-editorial asking politicians (and the public) to consider two facts:

> First, the indisputable fact that [after] three years . . . the women . . . find themselves in exactly the same position. No apology, no pension, no lost wages, no redress and no acknowledgement that what happened to them was wrong. Second, there is overwhelming evidence of State involvement in the Magdalene laundries.[143]

Jim criticized Minister Shatter directly for repeatedly refusing to countenance restorative justice measures prior to the publication of the *IDC Report*.

Mary Lou McDonald introduced the Private Members Motion on 25 September 2012.[144] Over two evenings thirty-four Dáil representatives – from all parties – addressed the motion. The debate was extensive, with near unanimous support for survivors. Numerous speakers evoked our call for a 'dignified debate on the motion', which JFM endorsed as 'reasonable and driven by survivors' pressing needs'.[145] There was one noticeable absence: Minister Shatter did not appear in the chamber either evening.

The government's response to the Sinn Féin motion was precisely as Fintan O'Toole described earlier in the day: 'cynically evasive'.[146] Minister of State Kathleen Lynch, deputizing for Mr Shatter, tabled an amendment gutting the motion of any commitment to providing an apology or redress prior to the *IDC Report*. Notably, the government amendment also omitted all reference to UNCAT's recommendation and international laws prohibiting forced labour, arbitrary detention and slavery.[147]

It was demoralizing to witness Kathleen Lynch, at one time a strident advocate, assert that 'allegations of abuse in Magdalen laundries have never been the subject of scrutiny by the courts . . . so the facts remain undetermined'.[148] And, it was disheartening that rather than addressing survivors' immediate needs, she insisted that the debate was 'premature'.[149] When Deputy McDonald spoke the following evening, she excoriated Minister of State Lynch's evasion:

> It is a fact that committal to and residence in the laundries was not voluntary. It is a fact the State interacted actively with the laundries. It is a fact these laundries, although private institutions, enjoyed considerable financial State support while women and girls were enslaved to work without pay. It is a fact the State deliberately failed to inspect these laundries. The trauma and the stigma endured by detainees which lives with them to this day is also a fact.[150]

Ultimately, the government's amendment won the day – a face-saving measure to avoid voting down a motion to help the women. It passed with all seventy-five members of Fine Gael and their coalition Labour Party partners voting in favour.[151] Forty-three TDs, across Sinn Féin, Fianna Fáil and the independents, voted as a bloc against the amendment.

In hindsight, the debate and the associated media coverage benefited JFM's campaign in significant ways. It cultivated an unprecedented level of awareness among Ireland's politicians about the laundries. Even more significantly, survivors' truth was acknowledged and their rights as citizens recognized. If still no apology and no redress, at least they were believed.[152]

(ii) Breach of trust

JFM was asked to arrange a second meeting between survivors and Senator McAleese in early December 2012. In June, Claire had worked alongside Ms Ní Mhuircheartaigh to ensure the women were given adequate notice, felt informed on what to expect and were made to feel comfortable. By comparison, the December meeting was rushed and poorly executed, and from JFM's perspective at least it bordered on adversarial. To our mind, the women were treated without fair procedures and rather as if they were suspects in a criminal investigation who should not be told of any of the evidence being considered against them. Much to survivors' surprise, Senator McAleese revisited and challenged the women's prior testimony; the senator gave no advance notice of the questions he wished to put to the women, why he was asking them or what contradictory position or claims he might be considering and from whom. JFM continues to be concerned by this behaviour – it is decidedly *not* how survivors of serious and systematic abuse, involving the State, should be treated.[153]

Ms Ní Mhuircheartaigh emailed JFM on 27 November 2012 asking to be put in direct contact with survivors. We did not have the women's permission to share contact information so we offered to forward letters instead. This was not acceptable; Ms Ní Mhuircheartaigh responded that any delay 'could leave us in the position of running out of time'.[154] Mari conveyed JFM's disquiet but assured Ms Ní Mhuircheartaigh we would try to make the meeting happen on the IDC's timeline. On 2 December, JFM was asked to notify the women that 'we wish to meet them again this week'.[155] Such urgency disregarded elderly women asked at the last minute to travel in early December with little detail as to the meeting's purpose. Mari travelled from Philadelphia to help Claire coordinate the event, which was scheduled for 6 December – she would take the opportunity to speak to Senator McAleese in person as a daughter of a Magdalene woman. Then word came that 'the structure of the meeting will be a little different this time too – but we will go through this with the women on Thursday'.[156]

The meeting confirmed our worst suspicions. In the end, three survivors were able to attend and two daughters, now also joined by Mari. Senator McAleese was running late due to traffic diversions – Hillary Clinton was visiting Dublin City University where McAleese served as chancellor, and her remarks included the assertion that respecting the human rights of woman and girls 'is the unfinished work of the 21st century'.[157] On arrival, he asked that each woman go one by one to a room 'to clarify' things.[158] The women cooperated as a matter of courtesy, but they were neither given time to process nor consult each other before making an informed decision. This felt different from the June meeting.

Each of the three survivors emerged subdued. They were asked to relay their 'story' again and were surprised that the senator had not read their testimonies. They did not understand why they were asked to repeat how they 'were put into' the laundries, were they 'abused' and if so how, and was their 'hair cut'?[159] None was particularly skilled in expressing what was or was not 'abuse', especially since neither the senator nor his assistant defined the term as they were using it.[160] The daughters reported similar concerns: one was told by the senator that he wanted to 'solidify details', but she got 'the distinct impression' he had not read her testimony.[161] Senator McAleese cautioned another daughter that 'memories fade' with age, before telling her that 'if your mother was sitting here she probably wouldn't remember everything'. These reports left all of us in JFM questioning our role in facilitating the meeting.

(iii) Preparing for the Report

The *IDC Report* did not materialize before Christmas despite a series of commitments to that effect.[162] The new year saw Minister Shatter announce that he expected to receive the report within ten days and after reading would bring it to cabinet, anticipating publication within four weeks.[163] Two weeks later, long-time allies Maureen O'Sullivan, Mary Lou McDonald and Dara Calleary asked the Taoiseach whether the report was indeed finalized, was it in the minister's possession and would it be published.[164] Deputies O'Sullivan and McDonald informed JFM on 24 January 2013 that the *IDC Report* was being forwarded to the minister on a section-by-section basis due to last-minute revisions. We expressed concern as to whether this undermined its independence but were genuinely relieved that the wait was almost over. Finally, Taoiseach Enda Kenny confirmed on 29 January that the report was finalized, that it would come before cabinet on 5 February and that it would be published.[165]

JFM committed to making an unprecedented effort to create an environment whereby it would be politically untenable not to issue an apology and introduce redress immediately upon publication. The women had waited long enough. Claire immediately wrote to the survivors and daughters in touch with JFM: she confirmed that the *IDC Report* was going to cabinet, cautioned them to 'keep your expectations in check', and prepared them for lots of 'media coverage'.[166]

This was an 'all hands on deck moment'. Mari and Claire devised a public pressure campaign, using social media to urge the public to lobby politicians *in person*; we provided their office phone numbers, email addresses and Facebook and Twitter account details. We also activated a new hashtag, posting it across all platforms. Mari uploaded the following 'Call to Action' on Facebook a few days before the report was due:

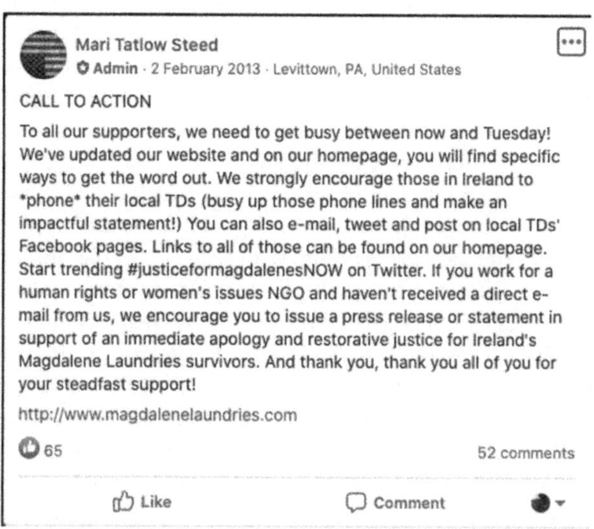

Within hours the impact was felt: #justiceformagdalenesNOW was trending in Ireland.

We emailed NGOs, Trade Unions, Students' Unions, women's groups and other civil society organizations, asking them to issue press releases, write open letters or otherwise call on the State to initiate a comprehensive redress and restorative justice scheme. We also contacted journalists who had written about the laundries in the previous three years, attaching copies of our 'Summary' document, offering to answer questions. A number of prominent stories appeared two weekends running before the report's publication, featuring survivors and JFM members detailing precisely what was at stake on 5 February – we in turn circulated links to these stories on our social media channels and forwarded them to Oireachtas members.[167] Everything was geared to building momentum.

The most poignant intervention came from Samantha Long who posted a series of tweets about Margaret Bullen, her much-loved natural mother, who lived and died at the Sean McDermott Street Magdalene Laundry:

My mother was Magdalene No. 322. Real name Margaret.

Margaret was committed to industrial school in 1954. She was 2 yrs 4 mths old. She left 49 years later in a coffin.

Margaret never went on a date. Never had a boyfriend. Never fell in love. But she was impregnated in care.

> Margaret's twin daughters were taken from her 7 weeks after she gave birth. When she saw us again we were 23.
>
> Margaret died in July 2003, one day before her 51st birthday. She died of her slave related injuries.[168]

Sam's tweets went viral. They were subsequently published in full by Sinead O'Carroll at thejournal.ie and shortly thereafter became international headline news.[169] The five of us in JFM had done as much as it was possible to do – now more than ever our email inboxes were full, our phones were buzzing, and we were failing miserably to keep up with messages.

One phone call Jim did answer on 30 January came from Senator McAleese who wanted to update JFM on his plan for the following Tuesday. He intended to brief the cabinet at its meeting midday. The report itself would be released on the DoJ's website mid-afternoon. He requested the opportunity to brief JFM earlier in the day when we would also receive a printed copy of the *IDC Report*. A cordial conversation ended with Senator McAleese stating that for him 'it is the women who came through those institutions that have to remain front and centre' before asking with emotion that we 'prioritize' what this means to them.[170] Jim assured him that the women remained JFM's first priority. Two days later, on 1 February the media announced that Dr. McAleese had submitted his letter of resignation from the Seanad and was returning to private life.[171]

We finalized our plans over the intervening days. Jim was unable to travel to Dublin due to his mid-semester teaching obligations. His request to Skype into the briefing was refused. Mari issued JFM's Press Advisory before flying from Philadelphia, ensuring it was in journalists' inboxes first thing Monday morning. The advisory offered four brief quotes from survivors, reproduced from the hashtag #justiceformagdalenesNOW. It informed the press that JFM would be available in Dublin on Tuesday afternoon. And, it concluded with a moment of advocacy distilling a decade-long campaign:

> JFM is calling on the government to issue an immediate apology to all survivors of the Magdalene Laundries on Tuesday. Moreover, we are calling on the government to establish a transparent and non-adversarial compensation process, that includes the provision of pensions, lost wages, health and housing services, as well as redress, and that is open to all survivors, putting their welfare at the forefront.[172]

Conclusion

Jim was up early on Tuesday morning, 5 February 2013. He was due to speak live from Boston on RTÉ's *Today with Pat Kenny* radio programme at 10.00 am Irish time. He was conscious as he listened through his phone to the morning's newscast that his JFM colleagues were already at Iveagh House, the home of Ireland's Department of Foreign Affairs. Their scheduled briefing with the senator was in progress. As the minutes passed, he answered a quick email from Raymond: 'No word yet. If I get the Introduction and Executive Summary as promised I will send.'[173] Suddenly Pat Kenny's voice down the phone line was reading Jim's opinion-editorial published that morning in *The Irish Times*. The day began with Catherine Whelan's story – the survivor who ignited JFM's political campaign:

> She remains anonymous by choice. She values her privacy above all. She lives alone and never married. She attends daily Mass. She will never again live in Ireland. She celebrated her 78th birthday recently. She is a survivor of the Magdalene laundries . . . abused in the past, abandoned in the present. . . .
>
> Time is of the essence. It is the one commodity many of these women can ill afford. They have waited for justice too long already. The wait must end today.[174]

5

Publication of the *IDC Report*

The campaign within the campaign

'Inefficient units of production': A private briefing with Dr McAleese

On the morning of 5 February 2013, four of us from JFM, Claire, Mari, Maeve and Katherine, went to meet Dr Martin McAleese for a briefing on the *IDC Report*. The *IDC Report* was due to be published later that day, at 4.00 pm. Jim's teaching duties at Boston College made it impossible for him to attend, but he was on hand for long conversations with the group the night before. Raymond Hill had talked Maeve through possible scenarios that might be presented in the *Report* and how best to rebut them, as well as lines of questioning to pursue with Dr McAleese.

Before she went to bed on 4 February, Katherine spoke with Martina Keogh, a survivor of the Sean McDermott Street Magdalene. Martina, at age sixteen, had been sentenced to two years for involvement in an attempted mugging. She always protested her innocence. Martina had been selling newspapers on a street corner and had been picked up by the Gardaí. Her mother kept petitioning the nuns for her release, and Martina was eventually thrown out when she got into a fight with another inmate. Katherine and Claire always referred to Martina as 'Marvellous Martina' for it seemed to them that she needed a grander title than her surname and Martina was indeed a Marvel. She would often say: 'Kathy, they should take a scan of my brain. I know if other people could have a head like mine they would be able to recover from anything. Maybe if they took a picture of it they could help people.' Martina was justly proud of her intellect. She was intelligent and wise, and had not merely survived atrocious levels of violence and deprivation; she had actually learnt how to thrive and had made a good and happy life for herself. She was generous, humorous and entirely free from shame. She was justly proud of her daughter, Sam, and she delighted in her four grandchildren. Martina Keogh was famous in inner-city Dublin as the go-to person if your pet (dog, cat, rodent, horse, bird) was sick. She would often say: 'Animals are so much nicer than humans, Kathy. They know how to love.' Martina had spent most of her childhood in State residential care managed by nuns and had never been adequately taught how to read and write. Her phone texts were inventive and poetic – the words were spelled by using the dominant consonants as they sounded to Martina; she didn't bother much with vowels. Yet, the word she used most often in her texts was always spelled perfectly: Love.

During their conversation Martina again reminded Katherine of her assessment of the McAleese investigation: 'He's not going to do anything for the women Kathy.' Katherine was to have plenty of reason to reflect on Martina's judgement. She spent a restless night, woke early and began drafting a PR warmly welcoming that the Irish State admitted it was intimately and systematically involved in facilitating the Magdalene institutions. Whatever else the *Report* might say, it would not be able to deny the evidence of State involvement presented in JFM's 146-page *Principal Submission*.[1]

Before meeting with Dr McAleese, JFM gathered at the BCI premises on St Stephen's Green which was to be our HQ for the day. As was our ritual, we also visited the bench commemorating the Magdalenes and paused for reflection before heading to the nearby Department of Foreign Affairs. Entering the building, Katherine announced to the rest of us that she had begun a PR warmly welcoming the State's admission that it was systematically involved with the Magdalene Laundries. 'But we don't know what the report will say!' replied Maeve. Claire looked puzzled before adding, 'JFM doesn't do knee-jerk reactions, we'll have to read it before we do a PR.' Mari smiled as Katherine announced: 'We've achieved our aim of the public fully expecting that the State will apologise if they are shown to have been complicit. We've proved that they are complicit. That's all we need to say: that we welcome their admission.'

Dr McAleese would hold private briefings with JFM, other advocates for the women, members of the opposition and a small number of journalists that morning. Survivors and relatives were excluded from all briefings.[2] JFM's meeting was held in a boardroom with blond wood panelling to half the height of the walls which were painted a tasteful mustard colour. Dr McAleese was smiling and genial as usual; there was just one civil servant in attendance, Nuala Ní Mhuircheartaigh, legal adviser to the IDC. Dr McAleese thanked JFM for our work with the women. 'It was a privilege,' replied Claire. Mindful of Dr McAleese's recent resignation, Maeve asked: 'Who will answer any questions we might have about the *Report*?' Her question remained unanswered.

Once seated, Dr McAleese tapped four large spiral-coil bound volumes and announced them as the 1,000-page *IDC Report*. He added that JFM would receive a single copy after the briefing. He said that JFM might be surprised by some of the findings; the duration of stay, for example, was less than a year for 61 per cent of the women. That was a shock rather than a surprise as it did not tally with any of the archival evidence we had gathered, nor with Claire's MNP research. Most importantly it did not concur with the women's testimonies.

'How do you arrive at that figure?' asked Mari, 'where is that in the *Report*?'

'Did you start the clock each time when a girl or woman was moved from one laundry to another?' asked Katherine.

'Are you including the women who were put into Sean McDermott Street for a night or weekend while on remand for a court hearing?' Maeve asked, 'Is that how you arrived at that figure?'

'Are you discounting the women who died there?' asked Claire. Dr McAleese and Ms Ní Mhuircheartaigh said that these women represented a small minority. Claire shook her head, baffled.

'What about the women who are still institutionalised?' asked Mari. 'Are you counting them?'

'How many women were held in the Magdalenes?' asked Katherine. Dr McAleese responded that there were approximately 10,000 women who spent time in the laundries. An exact figure was not possible as not all of the records were complete.[3]

Dr McAleese said the religious orders had clarified to the IDC that the women were given religious names to protect their privacy.[4] He and Ms Ní Mhuircheartaigh explained that two of the orders had a rule of enclosure, hence the lack of communication with the outside world. 'But two of the orders weren't enclosed,' said Katherine, feeling that she shouldn't even engage with the illogic. 'Vows of enclosure are beside the point that the women and girls were locked up against their will, they had no religious vocation for enclosure. The nuns had the keys,' she added rather desperately.

'What about deprivation of liberty, forced hard labour? This amounts to torture,' said Maeve. 'What is the State's response?' 'The women didn't understand that the orders were enclosed,' responded the senator. 'Is that the State's official response?' asked Maeve.

Claire and Mari were silent. Claire normally takes copious notes, but by now she had stopped.

Katherine continued to take notes, and she continued to argue: 'But the last laundry closed in 1996, the rule of enclosure, they were changed after Vatican II, in 1965, the rule of enclosure has nothing to do with how and why the women were locked up and put to hard labour.'

Maeve asked: 'What is the State's response to the call for apology and restorative justice?'

Dr McAleese replied that as the committee felt they were pursuing issues of public interest, he thought it advisable to step outside his remit and address these issues.[5] Dr McAleese then stated that the majority of women who shared their 'stories' with the IDC had said there was no physical abuse in the laundries.[6]

Claire sagged in her chair.

'What do you mean, there was no physical abuse?' asked Katherine. Dr McAleese said that the women had made a distinction; the physical abuse that was prevalent in the industrial schools was not a feature of the Magdalene Laundries.[7]

'What about Sr Stan's book?' asked Katherine.

Dr McAleese and Ms Ní Mhuircheartaigh responded that Patricia Burke Brogan was just a novice and spent only a week in the laundry.

Katherine countered: 'I didn't mention Patricia Burke Brogan. I said Sr Stan, we sent you a PDF of her book chapter where it mentions physical punishment in the Magdalene Laundries and the effects of institutionalisation.'

Again came the response that Patricia Burke Brogan was just a novice and spent only a week in the laundry.

'Deprivation of liberty, forced hard labour, forced disappearance, amounts to torture – that's abuse. A failure to provide an effective response amounts to continuing ill-treatment,' said Maeve.

Dr McAleese said the IDC also stepped outside its remit to pay attention to the claim that the laundries were highly profitable and that this was not the case.[8] He said the laundries operated for the most part on a subsistence or close to break-even basis, rather than on a commercial or highly profitable basis.

Dr McAleese added that a contributing factor was the women were not 'efficient units of production', that they were not very good workers.

All four JFM members sat stunned, in silence.

We were then told that the committee identified policies which stipulated that a girl who had been in an industrial school might be sent to a Magdalene until she was twenty-one if a member of the public was worried about her safety. 'But what was the legal basis?' asked Maeve, 'what about their constitutional rights?' Dr McAleese said the details about the regulations could be found in the *Report*, and that factory inspectors did make inspections.

'That's good', said Katherine, 'they inspected for health and safety on the factory floor but didn't check on the living quarters or conditions of the forced and unpaid labourers. So we can say that the State was involved then in the Magdalene institutions and it clearly states that in this *Report*.'

Dr McAleese said that that was clear, but that the picture was not at all what has been popularly imagined. Katherine stopped taking notes at this stage.[9] It was clear what her work was going to be for the next few hours.

Claire and Mari were shell-shocked leaving the building. They had been campaigning far longer than Maeve or Katherine, and it was personal. Mari's mother Josie had been held for ten years in Sundays Well. Claire felt she had a number of extra grandmothers through her long campaigning on their behalf. She tried to put some of the volumes of the report into her bag. 'It is going to be impossible to read all of this and respond to the media!' Blindly reacting to a report of this magnitude was not 'the JFM way'.

'No physical abuse! No physical abuse!' Maeve kept repeating. 'Do they think we are mad?!' 'He said that the State admits it was involved in the Magdalenes', said Mari. 'Exactly!', said Katherine, adding,

> We'll get to BC, have a quick scan, see what liabilities are admitted and then run immediately with a PR, saying that we are delighted with the report, that it admits full State involvement with the Magdalene Institutions and that we expect that the Taoiseach will issue an apology later in the day when he comes into the Dáil. That it's an historic day and we have some worries about some of the details and claims in the *Report*, but the most important thing is that the State admits its involvement.

'But we never break embargoes', said Claire.

Katherine said,

> We have a narrow window here, we have to catch mid-morning and lunchtime news and dominate it. Make it impossible in the public mind that there will not be an apology. We have to put a roasting fire of public support for the Magdalenes under Enda Kenny. If we don't do it right now we will lose everything, they will actually insist that the work was occupational therapy for a few months for

lackadaisical women who were free to come and go and no money was made and there was no abuse.

Jim was on the phone and Claire was trying to brief him; the phone was passed around and each of us tried to recount the inexplicable. Maeve was on the phone to Raymond.

Journalists started arriving to BCI; our phones were ringing non-stop and our email inboxes were inundated. Maeve told Katherine that someone was needed to talk to TV cameras which were set up around the corner, at the back of the Dáil on Merrion Square, and so Katherine put on her coat and headed off, even as she was beginning to have qualms about her approach: the activist had taken over and she was neglecting her academic duties which would have meant finding seclusion and time to parse the *Report*.[10] But JFM had been buried in a thousand pages of paper: the digital (searchable) copy of the *Report* would not be available until after the embargo at 4.00 pm. BCI's Thea Gillen scanned the Introduction and Executive Summary to send to Jim and Raymond. All we could do was focus on those two sections – a skim through the rest of the *Report* left us aghast at the mounds of obfuscation. It was impossible to make any sense of the voluminous, badly bound printout, with no index and multiple appendices that seemed to prioritize selected documents that had been found in an archival trawl.

JFM decided on a two-pronged strategy: we would immediately issue a PR, but place it under an embargo until 4.00 pm when the *Report* was released. Meanwhile, Katherine would bend the rules in her television interviews; she would speak to camera and leave it to the news organizations whether or not they would respect the embargo. On Merrion Square, Katherine was taken aback to see just how many Outside Broadcasting (OB) units were set up. The BBC alone had two OB vans as well as a range of teams representing the various regional BBC news channels. First, she gave an interview to Al Jazeera, next it was CNN and then it was over to all of the BBC units. In each interview, Katherine said JFM welcomed the State's admission that it was deeply involved in perpetuating the Magdalene system, and she said that JFM expected Mr Kenny would offer a State apology in the Dáil later that afternoon. She was standing near one of the OB vans trying to get some shelter from the biting wind while giving an interview when she overheard a conversation with one of the journalists she had spoken to. His editor was asking him if he had got an interview. 'Yes, but with all due respect to the JFM representative who is standing right here, I don't yet have a response from Irish officials. They say the report is embargoed until 4pm.' The journalist agreed to send his interview with JFM to his editor, who seemed very anxious to get on with it. So, the Magdalenes were breaking news at lunchtime. Katherine spent over four hours giving TV interviews. A friend emailed her to say an interview with her was on the night-time news in Japan, another friend texted her to say that he was in a hotel in China watching her interview and 'well done on getting the apology!' 'Too soon, my friend,' she thought, but at least it was going to be extremely uncomfortable for Mr Kenny.

Once JFM's embargoed PR issued just after 2.30 pm, Mari and Claire made their way towards Leinster House for the Order of Business.[11] Mary Lou McDonald had tabled a 'Topical Issue' on the need for the State to provide an apology and redress scheme for Magdalene survivors. Maeve stayed in BCI, continuing to read the *IDC Report* in preparation for the RTÉ *Prime Time* slot later that night. Still on Merrion Square, Katherine asked the conscientious journalist if she could sit inside his OB van and watch the debate. In the Dáil, McDonald welcomed the publication of the *IDC Report*, said that the women had been vindicated as the IDC had established State involvement and called on the Taoiseach Enda Kenny to offer a full apology. Mr Kenny rose from his seat and thanked Dr McAleese and Ms Ní Mhuircheartaigh for their work. Then his tone changed: 'Clearly, Deputy McDonald has not yet had an opportunity to read this report. The 1,000-page report deals with the facts, as was the mandate given to Senator McAleese and his group. It deals with them in a way that is very different from the impression that many people might have of what happened.' Refusing to apologize, the Taoiseach alleged that because of the *Report*, 'the truth and reality' had been 'uncovered and laid out for everyone to read and to understand'. He emphasized strongly that there was no sexual abuse perpetrated by nuns on the women, though this was never an issue raised by survivors and their advocates, and in any case, it was difficult to see by what methods the IDC explored this issue. Mari and Claire sat bewildered in the public gallery. They were directly opposite the Taoiseach, who was flanked by his coalition partners, some of whom were staunch supporters of the women when serving in the opposition in the previous Dáil. According to Mr Kenny, 'Far from jumping to conclusions, everybody should read this report carefully and reflect on it deeply. . . . We should return in two weeks to debate it in the Oireachtas.'[12]

The previous day, Maeve had thought to book a room in the Shelbourne Hotel for a press conference at 4.45 pm. When Katherine arrived at the hotel just before 4.00 pm, the place was already frenetic with journalists, and they were being directed to JFM's room upstairs. The room wasn't big enough to hold everyone; journalists decided between themselves to give priority to broadcast crews while their many print colleagues thronged the corridor and stairwells.

Katherine sent urgent texts to the others: 'Press here. More bodies needed. Quick!' Claire and Mari were on their way from Leinster House, doing interviews with radio stations as they walked up Kildare Street. When JFM convened at the Shelbourne, we quickly decided on 'the line': we were very disappointed that the Taoiseach had not apologized as the *IDC Report* clearly stated that the State was systematically involved with the religious orders in running the Magdalene institutions. The women had waited long enough; it was awful to have them wait another fortnight for an apology.

Mari, Maeve, Katherine and Claire took their seats at the press conference, and Claire called Jim on Skype so he could listen in. The journalists wanted to know what we thought of the claim in the *Report*'s Executive Summary that the women's and girls' average 'duration of stay' was 3.22 years and the median only 27.6 weeks; didn't that seem very low?[13] Not only did those figures seem low – the discrepancy between the average and median was quite striking, and because the *Report* didn't disclose what figures it was working with, we could only surmise that it was including girls and women who were placed in Sean McDermott Street on remand, waiting there anytime from a few hours to a few weeks for a court trial. We wondered, too, if the *Report* treated the transfers of girls and women between Laundries as beginning a new period of detention.[14] What did we think of the fact that only 26.5 per cent of 'referrals' (to use the preferred term of the *Report*) to Magdalene Laundries were made or 'facilitated by' the State? That seemed to us a very significant amount of direct committals to Magdalene institutions, and the *Report* also showed the State to have provided lucrative contracts without requiring 'fair wages' to be paid. The State had been derelict in its duty to protect every woman's rights – a duty established by contemporaneous legislation, the Constitution and European and international human rights treaties. One of the final questions concerned the finding that the nuns made no money from the Magdalenes. Katherine replied:

> How can the religious sisters seem to have been such poor managers? They had an unpaid workforce, they had lucrative contracts, and they made no money? So we'll be coming back to that and looking in some more detail at our archive . . . as well as the issue of the utter minimising, to put it mildly, of the physical abuse that these women suffered within the laundry system.[15]

Claire left the press conference early to go to RTÉ for an interview on the *Six One News*. As she travelled in the taxi to the studios, Katherine texted: 'International press running with story that there is an apology. We need one-line press release stating that was no apology.' When Claire arrived at RTÉ, she went straight to the staff canteen to write and issue the PR:

> JFM . . . wishes to dispute reports that An Taoiseach Enda Kenny apologised to Magdalene survivors. The Taoiseach's statement falls far short of the full and sincere apology deserved by the women who were incarcerated against their will in Ireland's Magdalene Laundries. Further statements will follow when JFM has the opportunity to review the report in full.[16]

The usual JFM method of checking drafts and approving the PR with at least one other person had to be dispensed with. There was simply no time. A short time later in the newsroom, as Claire was interviewed by RTÉ's Bryan Dobson, she realized the hardest task facing us in the coming days: 'this needs to come back to . . . the women . . . we don't know how we're going to tell them about what Enda Kenny did or didn't do today . . . because frankly, their country has failed them yet again.'[17]

Back at the Shelbourne, Katherine, Maeve and Mari were still speaking to journalists, while Maeve's mother, Caroline Murphy, was putting final touches to Maeve's op-ed for the *Irish Examiner*.[18] When the media dispersed, there was barely time to quickly find some food before moving on to the next set of commitments. Maeve was to appear on RTÉ's *Prime Time* (which she had never done before), and once the op-ed was filed, Caroline rushed to Dunnes Stores for a strong-coloured jacket for her to wear. Meanwhile, Maeve's father and broadcaster, Sean O'Rourke, made plans to meet them both in RTÉ with some moral support and energy bars to keep Maeve going.

Claire would do TV3's *Tonight with Vincent Browne* show later on. Mari was exhausted, having travelled from the United States overnight; Katherine too was feeling the impact, still cold from hours spent outside on Merrion Square. Along with Jim in

Boston, Mari and Katherine continued to field media calls while the others prepared for the late evening's engagements.

Minister of State Kathleen Lynch represented the government on *Prime Time*. Maeve challenged her, saying:

> I do not understand the hold up with the apology today. . . . It has been accepted for a long time that these were abusive institutions, and the idea that they were not physically abusive . . . is an outrage. Martin McAleese did not refute that the women earned no money and that they were locked in. If unpaid labour behind locked doors is not physical abuse, I do not know what is. And this Committee was given one job. It had been accepted that these were abusive institutions . . . and the only thing that was left to establish was whether the State was responsible. It has been firmly established now that the State was responsible. . . . The State oversaw the system and didn't do anything to stop it.[19]

Minister Lynch responded that a 'knee-jerk reaction at this stage is not what we want'. Presenter Miriam O'Callaghan asked the minister, would she go to the Taoiseach and say: 'Frankly, Taoiseach, I really think we should give an apology'? After initially replying that she could not (this brought heckles from the audience), Minister Lynch said, 'Of course you can ask, but we have agreed that it is to be a more fulsome approach in two weeks' time.'

We were exhausted. We had worked non-stop for four years, and now we had to face into another phase of campaigning to wrest a modicum of justice for the women. We knew we had an uphill battle ahead of us. In a pre-recorded interview on *Prime Time*, Professor Eoin O'Sullivan of Trinity College Dublin, co-author with the late Mary Raftery of *Suffer the Little Children*, seemed to have accepted the *IDC Report*'s conclusions.[20] He said the 'assumption' that 'these were extraordinarily punitive institutions, places where women were incarcerated for very significant periods of time . . . certainly does not seem to be borne out by the evidence in the McAleese Report'. TV3 journalist Ursula Halligan had not been at the Shelbourne Hotel for JFM's press conference. Her report for the 5.30 pm news that evening declared that the *IDC Report*

> certainly shatters the popular image that these places were hell holes of sadistic practices with slave like conditions where the residents were systematically exploited for commercial profit. And the report does this by systematically setting out the cold facts as Martin McAleese found them over the last eighteen months. . . . It found that the laundries weren't run for profit, they didn't make profits, they just about broke even. It found that physical torture was not a feature of the laundries and that no allegation of sexual abuse was made against any nun. So all in all, this report was a complete turnabout from what we were led to believe that the Magdalene Laundries were all about.[21]

We were worn out but we knew we needed to stay in the battle. If we didn't, there would be no apology or redress for the women, and the flawed findings of the *IDC Report* would become the final official word on the matter.

6 February 2013: Labour revolt

JFM members were up early the following morning. Maeve had to return to London but continued to do media interviews while in transit. Mari, Katherine and Claire were scattered in various parts of Katherine's house doing one interview after another. Jim was holding the fort in Boston, doing a series of interviews by phone. On her way home to Cavan later that day, Claire phoned some of the women in touch with JFM to let them know what had transpired in the Dáil (it being the first available opportunity to do so). As is typical of Magdalene survivors, instead of getting angry they told Claire not to worry, and that they knew we were doing our best for them.

A welcome breakthrough came that evening, when Jim emailed a statement that had been issued from the Labour Parliamentary Party. The statement stopped short of advocating for a redress scheme, but the party called for a formal apology, services for survivors, measures to deal with the stigma and a process of engagement with survivors and family members.[22] John Drennan of the *Sunday Independent* would report a week later that the party hierarchy 'barely prevented an unprecedented walkout by its TDs. . . as a gesture of protest over the failure of the Taoiseach Enda Kenny to issue a public apology to the Magdalene women'.[23] Although Minister Kathleen Lynch had robustly defended the government's position during *Prime Time* on 5 February, Drennan reported that 'sharp exchanges' had occurred between Enda Kenny and Minister Lynch during the Cabinet briefing the same day. Minister Lynch allegedly said, 'you would be better off being seen to apologise of your own volition rather than having it forced out of you.'

'Laundry Survivors Snub the Taoiseach'

On 8 February, Nuala Ní Mhuircheartaigh sent Claire an email:

> I've been trying to reach you by phone today, I need to speak to you urgently to arrange a meeting for a small number of women from all groups with the Taoiseach. I have already made the arrangements with the two representative groups. I would appreciate it if you could call me back as soon as possible.[24]

Mindful of our experience during the December meeting with Senator McAleese, and in line with our ethos, JFM was determined to ensure that survivors could make an informed decision regarding their attendance at the meeting. We responded to Ms Ní Mhuircheartaigh the same day, requesting a letter from the Taoiseach's office setting out the purpose of the meeting, the format of the meeting, the agenda for the meeting, who would be present, and whether it would be open to all survivors who wished to attend.[25] We also asked what guarantees could be given that survivors would be protected from the media. No response came from the Taoiseach's office, and therefore, survivors in contact with JFM did not meet with Enda Kenny during this time. That weekend, an article on the front page of the *Sunday Times* (Ireland edition) bore the headline: 'Laundry Survivors Snub the Taoiseach'.[26]

Chapter Nineteen of the IDC Report

In the days after the *IDC Report*'s publication, JFM carefully examined Chapter Nineteen, which dealt with 'Living and Working Conditions' in the laundries. This chapter revealed the logic behind the second meetings Senator McAleese held with survivors. The *Report* claimed that the first meetings with survivors 'consisted of an opportunity for the women concerned to tell their story in a natural and unprompted way'.[27] However, the second meetings 'afforded the Committee an opportunity to seek clarifications on areas of particular interest'. The *IDC Report* explained that 'this process enabled it to gain a greater understanding of a number of significant issues' and that these 'included a clear distinction between some of the practices in industrial and reformatory schools and the Magdalen Laundries, in particular in relation to practices of physical punishment and abuse'.[28] According to the *Report*, the second meetings 'enabled the Committee to express this distinction, where up to now there may have been confusion in public analysis'. Our fears about the December meeting had been validated.

The Taoiseach met with Ms Ní Mhuircheartaigh to discuss the *IDC Report* on 11 February.[29] On the same day, he also met with a group of Magdalene survivors.[30] Also that day, Claire analysed the quotations from survivor testimonies in the *IDC Report*. That afternoon she emailed the other members of JFM, feeling sick. She told them that none of the written testimonies that JFM submitted had been cited in Chapter Nineteen of the *IDC Report*. JFM had gathered the testimonies using strict ethical protocols; we had gone to great lengths to ensure the women had given informed consent. Not one of the quotations in the chapter comes from the almost 800 pages of written testimony submitted by JFM, and although the *IDC Report* cites what appeared to be direct quotations from the women, it offers no explanation of how these were recorded. Claire was present for both meetings with survivors and does not recall seeing any recording devices, or permission being asked to tape what the survivors were saying. Written testimony from survivors in contact with JFM had been ignored for the purposes of the *IDC Report*; however, the committee had accepted written statements from doctors, priests, former laundry managers and others quoted in the same chapter.[31] The testimony of nuns was quoted without question.[32]

12 to 13 February: Meetings in Leinster House and Fianna Fáil Private Members Motion

On 12 February, Claire had a series of meetings in Leinster House, the first of which was with Labour backbenchers, Anne Ferris, Ged Nash and Aodhán O Riordáin. She was joined by her Adoption Rights Alliance colleague Susan Lohan. During the meeting a text came through from survivor 'Kathleen R', who had been given a copy of the *IDC Report* by Minister Kathleen Lynch's constituency office (to our knowledge, Kathleen R is the only survivor to have received a hard copy of the *Report*):

> Rang u clair but I ges ur very buisy its just that im on page 90 ov de report I havent com across any ov our stories what pages are they on clair thank u.

It was devastating to have to explain that none of the submitted testimony had been included. Later that day, Claire also met with Fianna Fáil TD Dara Calleary to discuss a Private Members Motion that the party was due to put forward that night. Deputy Calleary told Claire he had been telling politicians to ensure they read the *IDC Report* along with JFM's Principal Submission. At the final meeting of the day, Sinn Féin's Mary Lou McDonald told Claire that the one thing that resonated with the public whenever she spoke about the Magdalene Laundries was the simple statement, 'I believe the women.' This idea sparked a plan to quickly email TDs to ask them to read survivor testimonies into the record during the Private Members debate and state 'I believe the women.'

Later that evening, Dara Calleary proposed the Private Members' Motion calling for an apology to the women and for the establishment of a dedicated unit to coordinate a redress scheme. In his speech, Deputy Calleary recalled his words from the Sinn Féin Private Members debate the previous September. They turned out to be prophetic:

> I have no doubt of the commitment of those in government who are working on this issue. However, I doubt the institutions of the State. When I hear reference to cross-departmental committees, I become worried because I am aware that the defensive mechanism which is in-built in the institutions of the State will kick in. There is some sort of innate inability to acknowledge the State's role in respect of this matter.[33]

Deputy Calleary urged people to read the survivors' testimonies, before reading an excerpt into the Dáil record: 'I believe Maisie. I believe Attracta. I believe all the women.' Minister Kathleen Lynch proposed an amendment to the motion on behalf of the government. It deleted the proposal for an apology and instead commended Dr McAleese for his 'authoritative' *Report* and praised the government's action on the Magdalene Laundry issue. It acknowledged the suffering of survivors but insisted that the *Report* would be debated in the Dáil the following week. Minister Lynch's party colleague Dominic Hannigan read an excerpt from Maisie K.'s testimony, who was watching the debate live from her home: 'I believe Maisie as well as the testimonies I have read in the report and seen in the documentaries. It was not the women's fault that they were there.' Ged Nash read from the testimony of a daughter of a Magdalene woman about their first meeting: 'We could not believe she was only 42. . . . She had the face of hard work, the face that one sees in so many women who have just had to work too hard and never had anyone to take care of them. . . . It was the first time she ever had coffee . . . and she had not seen brown sugar before.' Mary Lou McDonald read from Kate's testimony: 'I believe Kate's story as well as all those of the Kates, the Marys and the other women who were incarcerated and brutalised in Magdalen laundries.' The debate resumed on the evening of 13 February. Catherine Murphy (Ind) read from the testimony of a former paid hand at the Galway Magdalene: 'It is important that these testimonies are heard. . . . I believe these women.' Anne Ferris read from Kathleen

R.'s testimony and informed the Dáil of Kathleen's text to Claire the previous day: 'I believe the women.'[34] Despite these allies' best efforts, the government amendment to the motion was passed.

16 February: Public release of JFM's Principal Submission

On 14 February, the Taoiseach held a meeting at Beechlawn Nursing Home, which also serves as the headquarters of the OLC.[35] We do not know the purpose of this meeting or who was in attendance. On 16 February, Mr Kenny travelled to London to meet some of the Magdalene survivors who had emigrated to the UK.[36] On the same day, and having obtained permission from survivors and other witnesses, JFM published the redacted version of our Principal Submission to the IDC. We wanted to ensure that the public would have an opportunity to read the women's testimony in the Submission before the Dáil debate on 19 February. At this point it was widely anticipated that the Taoiseach would deliver an apology, but JFM was leaving nothing to chance in light of the *IDC Report*'s minimization of the women's experiences of abuse. In our PR we also encouraged politicians and the general public to read our 'Reparations and Restorative Justice Scheme' submitted to the DoJ on 14 October 2011. On the morning of 16 February, Jim had emailed politicians with a copy of Maeve's opinion piece in the *Irish Independent*.[37] To his surprise, the email could not be delivered to one of the recipients – something that had never happened before in our experience so soon after politicians left office:

> User martin.mcaleese (martin.mcaleese@oireachtas.ie) not listed in Domino Directory. (The e-mail address to which you sent your mail is invalid. There is no one with that address on the Oireachtas network.)

19 February 2013: Official State apology

At noon on 19 February 2013, in advance of the much-anticipated State apology, JFM along with AII and the ICCL conducted a briefing on the *IDC Report* for all Oireachtas members in the A/V Room at Leinster House. That afternoon JFM and survivors congregated at BCI, and we arranged taxis for the women to make their way to the Dáil. JFM also invited Patricia Burke Brogan to join us. At 5.00 pm, JFM and the NWCI held a candlelit vigil in support of Magdalene survivors and their families outside Dáil Éireann. In the days leading up to the apology, JFM had worked with Mary Lou McDonald, Maureen O'Sullivan and Dara Calleary to ensure that survivors and relatives in contact with us could gain entry to the Dáil gallery. The women who did not want to attend the vigil were brought to the side entrance of Leinster House by Sinéad Pembroke, Katherine and Claire's colleague on the MOHP. At the vigil, the atmosphere was quiet and respectful as survivors, relatives and allies joined together in solidarity with living survivors and in remembrance of the dead. Although it was rush hour, Kildare Street seemed to be in complete silence as Mary Coughlan sang

'Magdalene Laundry'.[38] Claire remembers looking over to Gabrielle O'Gorman, a consummate survivor, and seeing a single tear fall down her face.

When JFM arrived at the gallery, we noticed that the government had reserved seats for the IWSSN and MST groups, but not for survivors in contact with JFM. Thanks to the kindness and respect shown by Mary Lou, Maureen and Dara, the women did not detect the slight. As it happened, they now had the best seats in the house, directly opposite where the Taoiseach and other members of Cabinet were sitting. They would have a front row seat for the apology. Fearful of being exposed to the media, they had spent the afternoon being treated like royalty by the three TDs, as well as Sinéad Ní Bhroin and Sarah Clarkin, whom we would later get to know through the NWCI but then working as an intern for McDonald. Many survivors were listening to the broadcast of the event, including Catherine Whelan in the United States. Now that they were gathered in the gallery, excitement was building, with a few survivors laughing and waving at Minister Shatter, who could not help but wave and smile back.

At last the Taoiseach took to his feet and delivered an eighteen-minute apology to the survivors of Ireland's Magdalene Laundries 'for the hurt that was done to them, and for any stigma they suffered'.[39] Enda Kenny also announced that he had asked Mr Justice John Quirke to make recommendations to government on a redress scheme for Magdalene Laundry survivors. Some of the women sat in silence, while others cried quietly. Vindicated at last! When the Taoiseach resumed his seat, the survivors in the gallery applauded. In response all members of the Dáil spontaneously rose to a standing ovation looking towards the women in the gallery and applauding them. It was unprecedented and the impact was profound. As Maisie wrote to Claire a few days later, 'It meant so much to hear a Taoiseach admit the wrongs done to us.'

JFM members in the gallery were, on the one hand, deeply honoured to witness this moment with the women, but on the other, we exchanged worried looks, knowing that, apology aside, the official State record insisted that no abuse took place in the laundries. We took solace in Tánaiste Eamonn Gilmore's mention of human rights: 'The principles of human rights, personal freedom and personal dignity should not only underpin the State's relationship with its citizens, but also the relationship between citizens and powerful institutions.'[40] Minister Shatter's speech included an announcement that the government would provide funding of €250,000 to the IWSSN for survivors based in Britain, once they had established a legal basis for their organization. Katherine and Maeve looked at each other – what of the women in Ireland? And Jim later asked about women in the Diaspora beyond the UK.

Claire had left the debate early to eat quickly before going to RTÉ studios for *Prime Time*. She Skyped Jim and Mari and exchanged emails with Katherine and Maeve who were still in the gallery to discuss our approach. We were in a difficult position: this was the survivors' day, so how were we meant to hold the line while not taking away from their joy? On *Prime Time*, Claire was joined by survivor Mary Merritt and Minister Shatter. Presenter Miriam O'Callaghan asked Claire for JFM's views on the proposed redress measures: 'today is about [the women], and I don't want to take away from that because . . . they come first, okay. What we do need to bear in mind though is that this [redress] process must be open, it must be transparent . . . compensation . . . needs to happen fast.'[41] Mary Merritt wanted to know how to apply to the scheme. Minister

Shatter said the scheme's details would go up on the DoJ website. (Many survivors do not own computers.) Claire asked if there would be an appeals process. The minister ignored the question and continued that there would be other supports, including health and psychological services. Just as Claire noticed a Post-It Note in the minister's hand bearing the names of the two directors of the IWSSN, the minister repeated his earlier announcement of €250,000 in funding for the London group. Claire interrupted: 'But Minister . . . [supports for survivors] can't be based on membership of a group!' At that point, time had run out and there was no further opportunity for debate.

As Claire finished on *Prime Time*, Katherine participated in RTÉ's *Late Debate* radio show while Maeve returned once again to London. Our collective energies were drained, and we deeply appreciated the fact that after the Dáil debate, Mary Lou, Dara and Maureen arranged for the women to leave Leinster House protected from the media glare.

6

Never tell, never acknowledge (. . . everyone knew, but no one said)

Throughout JFM's campaign we committed ourselves to generating public knowledge of what happened in Ireland's Magdalene Laundries. We aimed to bring survivors' ongoing trauma to public awareness and to demonstrate for Irish politicians and civil servants – from the State's own archives – how the State had facilitated and interacted with these institutions and in doing so had broken domestic law and violated the Irish Constitution and European and international human rights treaties (also giving rise to ongoing violations of the right to a remedy). Our research, teaching and activist skills equipped us to take on those tasks. Yet these same skills created a naive and significant blind spot where we assumed that all we had to do was scrupulously collect the evidence, rigorously construct compelling arguments and disseminate information so that the public might support the apology and restorative redress scheme that we proposed. We did not appreciate that those with power are adept at maintaining their power by a belligerent ignorance. We did not fully realize the import of John Banville's *New York Times* article in response to the *CICA Final Report* that catalogued endemic sexual, physical abuse and systemic neglect of children in religious-run residential institutions. Banville had written:

> Never tell, never acknowledge, that was the unspoken watchword. Everyone knew, but no one said.
>
> Amid all the reaction to these terrible revelations, I have heard no one address the question of what it means, in this context, to know. Human beings – human beings everywhere, not just in Ireland – have a remarkable ability to entertain simultaneously any number of contradictory propositions. Perfectly decent people can know a thing and at the same time not know it.[1]

We failed to grasp that Ireland's respectable classes were willing to maintain their supremacy over those they designate 'unrespectable' by deploying ignorance as a strategy. This all changed after February 2013. With the benefit of hindsight, we now discern the distinct strategies by which the Irish establishment supresses 'unsettling knowledge'. By unsettling knowledge we mean the kind of knowledge that challenges the status quo of those who govern, and the foundations of respectability and control of knowledge on which they assume and enact their superior power.

We were to learn the hard way that even though the vast majority in the Republic might warmly support a call for justice for Magdalene women, those charged with the administration of justice regularly felt affronted at the idea. The knowledge produced by the women's testimony, along with the knowledge produced by our archival research and the knowledge produced by our legal arguments, would all be routinely and systematically 'unknown'. We began to realize that the religious/State, those respectable people in power, would insist on preserving their ignorance and prejudice which had rendered null and void the rights of the citizens incarcerated in Magdalene institutions and marred their lives. Ireland's establishment would deploy strategies of ignorance to render justice unimaginable and therefore unattainable.

How to read the *IDC Report* (or how the *IDC Report* uses strategies of 'not knowing' to assert knowledge and maintain ignorance)

The *IDC Report* is an exemplary document of how governing classes exert power through strategies of ignorance. Such modes of ignorance often include the following:

- Appearing to not know and also deftly 'unknowing' something they might have once been forced to accept as truthful, reliable, real;
- Ignoring correspondence and reports and failing to engage in communication;
- Miscounting, misapprehending, equivocation and mis-defining;
- Declaring that what they, the powerful and respectable, know is all there is to know. Nothing further needs to be known if it is not already known by the powerful. If it needed to be known, it would be known by them;
- Assuming their own supremacy in matters of morality and being the sole arbiters of what counts as tasteful, refined, mannerly and respectable;
- Winning uncontentious arguments that are not being debated and showering reams of irrelevant information as forms of decoy (look over there at the strawman!);[2]
- Censoring and hoarding information, and denying access to archives and documents on which their claims are (apparently) based;
- Magical thinking about temporalities – insisting that the past is an entirely different and unknowable country: the bad things happened back there because it was 'then' but here now everything is 'fine'. Also insisting that the good things that were supposed to happen did happen, merely because they were claimed and supposed to have happened (although there is proof that they did not happen);
- Patronizing, denigrating and punishing those who challenge the narrative of those in power and hence their claims to supremacy and the enjoyment of their positive self-regard. Patronizing, deriding and punishing those who have the temerity to point to the governing classes' errors, their failures, their exploitation, violence and lies;

- Creating divisions and confusion among spokespeople for oppressed and marginalized groups;
- Declaring that what appears as wrongdoing is merely a misunderstanding. Misinterpretations are nobody's fault or everybody's fault, hence everybody and so nobody is accountable, and there are, in fact, no faults to be found (*it was back then after all*);
- Ignoring and hence being ignorant of those who have suffered the trauma enacted by the governing class. Dictionaries remind us that roots of the words ignore and ignorant are entwined.

All of these rhetorical devices are to be found in the *IDC Report*. Below we give a brief sketch of some of the more prominent examples of these strategies of ignorance.

Miscounting and not counting: So lives do not count

The Executive Summary of the *IDC Report* claims that '10,012 or fewer women are known to have entered the Magdalen Laundries between 1922 and 1996'.[3] The startling assertion that there may be *fewer* than the 10,012 incarcerated revealed in the religious records remains unexplained. But perhaps even more damning is that this figure appears to be a significant underestimate given that it excludes women who spent time in the RSM Magdalene Laundries in Galway and Dún Laoghaire, due to 'the absence of records'.[4] The IDC's claim that '10,012 or fewer *women* entered the Magdalen Laundries' does not give due significance to its own admission that girls as young as nine were held in those institutions, and its use of the word 'entered' is typical of how the Irish State continues to foster the impression that these institutions were somehow popular destinations of choice for Irish girls and women, that is, that women entered 'voluntarily'. Furthermore, this official figure of 10,012 is manifestly unsupported in that the religious records relied upon were returned to the nuns and are unavailable for corroboration: an arrangement put in place prior to the nuns agreeing to cooperate with the IDC's inquiry.[5] The figure of 10,012 girls and women excludes those who entered before 1922 and remained thereafter – the State occludes these girls and women who total at least 762, nominating them as 'legacy' cases.[6] Neither does it include girls detained in 'voluntary' (unregulated but funded by the State) residential children's and teenage institutions known as 'Training Centres', sometimes on the same grounds as Magdalene Laundries, who were forced by the nuns to enter and work in the laundries for some or all of their days.

The IDC asserts that the State placed 26.5 per cent of the women and girls affected into Magdalene Laundries using a variety of means to do so, including by way of the courts, the Gardaí, local authority health and social services, industrial and reformatory Schools, and Mother and Baby Homes.[7] However, this figure of 26.5 per cent is based on only 55 per cent of the records available to the *IDC Report* since the remaining 45 per cent did not state a route of entry.[8] Other women and girls were placed in Magdalene Laundries by priests, family members and NGOs that received State support (and often acted on behalf of the State) such as the National Society for the Prevention of Cruelty to Children (NSPCC) and the Legion of Mary (accounting for 7.1 per cent of known entry routes). Most tellingly, the *IDC Report* does not know whether to count these organizations as 'State or non-State actors' and admits that these organizations were working both in the capacity of agents of the State and as charitable concerns 'in unknown proportions'.[9] The practice of the State funding 'voluntary' denominational organizations rather than developing full State welfare and probation services is underscored in this admission.[10]

Perhaps the most egregious figures asserted by the IDC are those on the length of time women and girls spent incarcerated in the Magdalene institutions. The *IDC Report* claims that women's and girls' 'duration of stay' was on average 3.22 years, and the median was 27.6 weeks.[11] The average and median durations of stay figures are arrived at by treating transfers between Laundries and repeat entries as beginning a new period of detention.[12] It is also unclear if girls and women held in the Sean McDermott Street Magdalene on remand for a few hours or days while awaiting a court trial are also included in the computations, leading to significantly lower figures for the total length of time girls and women actually spent in the laundries. The IDC also entirely disregards for the purpose of its calculations the detentions of women who had entered Magdalene Laundries before 1922 and remained thereafter, many of whom died behind the convent walls having lived almost all their lives confined therein.[13] The *IDC Report*, in calculating 'duration of stay', further disregards that time in which women remained in the *care* of the nuns after each institution closed down – hundreds of women continued to live under the nuns' jurisdiction, some for decades, before ultimately dying. Indeed, at the time of the *IDC Report*'s publication at least 117 former Magdalene women were still living at a number of nursing home locations around Ireland operated by the religious congregations.[14] The IDC also disregarded these women in its 'list of deaths': 'Deaths occurring in nursing homes after the closure of the Magdalen Laundries, of women who had in their earlier lives been admitted to a Magdalen Laundry, were not included.'[15]

The *IDC Report*'s presentation of its statistics on 'duration of stay' features prominently in the Executive Summary (which circulated quickly among the media on 5 February 2013), yet its figures are arrived at only by dismissing 58 per cent of the 14,607 available entry records on the basis that they do not disclose a duration of stay.[16] The Executive Summary contains no reference to this fact, which only becomes clear in Chapter Eight. The IDC does not acknowledge that the absence of an exit date in a record might denote that a woman never left the institution. In fact, the *IDC Report* asserts that 'because the distribution of length of stay is skewed by the small number of women who remained in the Magdalen Laundries for life, the average length of stay is a biased estimate of central tendency'.[17] The unsupported claim by the IDC that only a 'small number of women remained in the Magdalen Laundries for life' is contradicted in Claire's MNP research, which indicates that for at least two institutions (High Park and Donnybrook in Dublin), over half of the girls and women who were registered in the electoral roll for these laundries between 1954 and 1964 died behind convent walls. In the case of the Limerick Magdalene, an average of 60.4 per cent of women on the electoral register between 1961 and 1983 died at the institution.[18]

Ignoring and ignorance of those who have suffered and suffer

The *IDC Report* starts out with five pages of acknowledgements: bishops, archbishops, accountants, doctors, historians, academics, State agencies, civil servants, advocacy and representative groups are listed and thanked. At the bottom of page 5, the last line of the acknowledgements reads: 'And finally a special thanks to all the women who shared the story of their time in the Magdalen Laundries with the Committee.'[19] The women's testimony of the abuses they suffered is described as 'the story of their time in the Magdalen Laundries'. They are thanked for 'sharing'.

The *IDC Report* is voluminous yet the first mention that the women were not paid for their work comes obliquely on page 774 where it states that the women working in Magdalene laundries did not qualify for social insurance 'as they would not have been in receipt of payment'. The second and final mention of a lack of wages occurs in the penultimate Chapter Nineteen where just one former Magdalene is noted as saying that she received no pay. Otherwise forced labour is simply not addressed.

The *IDC Report*'s Introduction asserts that 'the majority of the small number of women who engaged with the Committee had been admitted to the laundries either by a non-state route of referral, or most common of all, following time in an Industrial school'. Leaving aside the difficulty of parsing the 'majority of a small number' (*how many?*), this sentence is unfortunately typical of many in the *IDC Report* in that it creates confusion rather than clarity or certainty. Did the majority of the small number of women who engaged with the committee enter Magdalene Laundries from industrial schools (which surely must be a 'State route') or did the majority of the small number of women who engaged with the committee enter by 'non-State routes'? The *IDC Report*'s Introduction continues with the observation that 'The vast majority told the Committee that the ill-treatment, physical punishment and abuse that was prevalent in the Industrial School system was not something that they experienced in the Magdalen Laundries'.[20] Does this 'vast majority' relate to the total of 'the small number of women who engaged with the Committee' or does this 'vast majority' number relate to the women who came to the Magdalenes from industrial schools? Does the IDC mean to suggest that the physical punishment and abuse prevalent in the industrial schools was different to the kind of physical abuse they experienced in the Magdalene institutions or that there was no physical punishment and abuse in the laundries? This unclear statement is followed by other assertions that seem to suggest that the punishment and abuse of the Magdalenes was merely different: we are told that the women who talked to Senator McAleese spoke of an 'uncompromising regime of physically demanding work and prayer', of the 'deep hurt they felt' arising from 'their loss of freedom, the fact that they were not informed why they were there, lack of information on when they would be allowed to leave, and denial of contact with the outside world, particularly family and friends'.[21] We are not given any discussion of what questions were asked, how these answers were recorded, what were the mechanisms used to ensure informed consent by the 'small number' of women who engaged with the committee or even how they were invited or selected to participate. We are expected to take the IDC's pronouncements as authoritative without any evidence that protocols were put in place to ensure that the data on which they base their statements is robust. We are expected to take the IDC's pronouncements as authoritative even without any evidence being produced. We are expected to take the IDC's pronouncements as authoritative even when what they announce is unclear and confusing.

Chapter Nineteen (entitled 'Living and Working Conditions') seems to offer further elaboration on this issue raised in the 'Introduction'. Chapter Nineteen alleges that survivors who engaged with the IDC expressed a 'clear distinction between some of the practices in industrial and reformatory schools and the Magdalen Laundries, in particular in relation to practices of physical punishment and abuse', which 'enabled' the IDC to clarify the 'confusion in public analysis'.[22] What is meant by the phrase 'confusion in public analysis' remains unclear. Does there have to be a hierarchy between the ill-treatment, physical punishment and abuse associated with being locked up indefinitely and without reason except to slave at hard labour, and the horrific physical, sexual and psychological abuse suffered by children in the industrial schools? The *IDC Report* invests a significant amount of space in this pursuit of ranking one form of torture over another. As Anne Enright describes it, the voices of the former Magdalenes are relegated to the form of a 'chorus'; their voices are disembodied, not related to any name or discreet identity (e.g. through a pseudonym), and they are recorded as fragmentary refrains on the fringes of the *Report*.[23] While survivors remain nameless, other individuals are identified: the directors of the IWSSN and many identified men, including doctors, priests and laundry managers.[24] These people's perspectives are recorded in detail through their interviews and letters to the IDC.

Throughout the *IDC Report*, survivor testimonies of the abuses they suffered are routinely described as 'stories'. The first mention of the word 'stories' appears on page 1:

> the Committee was conscious that the operation of the Magdalen Laundries since the foundation of the State has, prior to this process, not been fully understood, as many State records were neither readily available nor easily accessible and the records of the Religious Congregations were not available for inspection or analysis. It is understandable that – fuelled by this absence of information – stories grew to fill these gaps.[25]

The *IDC Report* claims to give 'information' to dispel 'stories' while the women are almost invariably described as 'sharing their stories'.[26] The 'stories' of the women in Chapter Nineteen include being made to wear the bed sheets one had wet during the night, being forced to wear a cup one had broken around one's neck, being made to stand on a stool while stripped naked and beaten by auxiliaries. There is mention of the isolation punishment cells where girls and women were kept and denied food for breaches of discipline such as refusing to work, trying to escape and breaking the many rules around prayer and silence. There are allusions to the humiliation punishment of lying on the ground and kissing the floor, or kneeling on the floor for hours as a spectacle before the nuns and other girls and women. The *IDC Report* considers these punishments as 'non-physical'. In Chapter Nineteen we learn how the women describe their hair being cut and kept short which many found humiliating, and the *IDC Report* also relates that hair-cutting was used as a specific punishment. The punishment of denying food to a non-cooperative 'penitent' is described as routine in accounts by both the religious sisters and the women. The section on survivor testimony is immediately followed by a new section entitled 'Comments by the Religious Congregations *in Response*'.[27] Survivors were not given an opportunity to respond to the Orders' assertions, and there is no discussion of any ethical issues that this might have raised for the committee.

The *IDC Report* also reproduces extracts from a letter from two directors of the IWSSN in London, 'Ms Mulready and Ms Morgan' as the *Report* calls them, better known as Sally and Phyllis to JFM. Both women self-identify as survivors of residential schools. Their letter acknowledges that girls and women in Magdalene institutions were imprisoned behind iron bars without being told if or when their detention might end and forced to work at heavy labour constantly with the use of solitary confinement as punishment. However, the letter also argues: 'As both authors of this submission spent our childhoods and young adulthood in institutions, we are both fully aware from personal experience and observations that violence of all kinds was common place in children's institutions. However, we do not believe such violence took place in the laundries.'[28] Yet, the letter continues: 'Women have often described getting a "thump in the back" or their hair pulled in retaliation for answering back but physical violence from the nuns does not seem to have gone beyond this in most cases.' The IDC says that 'Ms Mulready and Ms Morgan express the view that "this was a different, not a lesser, form of assault"'.[29] The committee then contradicts the careful distinctions made by Ms Mulready and Ms Morgan to declare that the IWSSN submission 'suggests that instead of physical punishment, the laundries were places of hard labour and "psychological cruelty and isolation"'. We remain unclear what motivated the letter writers and whether they were invited to comment on the IDC's hypothesis explored in the second meeting with Dr McAleese that the women were 'confused' about 'abuse'. What is clear in the morass of obfuscation and contradiction is that the IDC wants us to 'unknow' physical punishment: hard labour, being thumped, having our hair pulled is not physical punishment and 'psychological cruelty and isolation' is never enacted on bodies nor felt by bodies.

The IDC at no point made a public call for testimony, yet its *Report* says that 118 women 'came forward and engaged with the Committee' including 58 Magdalene women living in the care of the religious orders.[30] It is unclear under what conditions these fifty-eight survivors, just one of whom is cited, gave their 'stories'.[31] Chapter Nineteen is also difficult to read when we know that the IDC ignored some 800 pages of survivor testimony, gathered under strict ethical human-subject criteria and submitted by JFM. It is also unnerving to see the committee's omission of a range of reports (most notably perhaps the November 2010 report of the IHRC on this issue) and the neglect of academic research on the Magdalenes such as that conducted by Sr Stanislaus Kennedy, which we had brought to the attention of the committee.[32] In 1985, Sr Stan referred not only to the physical punishments meted out in the laundries but wrote astutely about the traumatic effects of the system on the 241 women who remained still working in the laundries at the time of her survey – their trauma being most evident in their 'institutionalisation'.[33] This chapter of the *IDC Report* on the living and working conditions of the Magdalene women privileges the perspective of the Religious Congregations, who are offered the opportunity to respond to the IDC's summary of what it thinks necessary to record from 'the small number of women who engaged with the Committee'. The *IDC Report* presents the views of the nuns without comment or analysis, leaving them in effect with the final word on the living and working conditions of the Magdalenes. 'In the words of one Sister, "There were a lot of things you would do differently if you had it again. But sure, we were institutionalised too."'[34]

Wrongdoing is merely a misunderstanding

Chapter Nine, entitled 'Routes of Entry to the Magdalen Laundries (A) Criminal Justice System', offers a pithy example of how the *IDC Report* creates 'unknowing' – that is, a sense of doubt about what we know to be correct and confusion about how to assess information presented to us.[35] This part of the *IDC Report* focuses on the Garda practice of arresting girls and women who had escaped from the Magdalene institutions and returning them to their places of imprisonment. The IDC tells us that there was a standing order in the 1923 Garda Handbook which read: 'persons in institution uniform – if persons are noticed to be wandering about in the uniform of institutions, e.g. workhouse inmates, they should be questioned and if they cannot give a satisfactory account of themselves they should be arrested'.[36] Having asked Garda headquarters what was the legal basis for this instruction and its implementation, the IDC did not question nor comment on the response that [it] 'may refer to the power of arrest at common law for the larceny of the uniform. This was a regular incident that Gardaí had to deal with and indeed some Garda records show that people have received convictions for "larceny of apparel"'.[37] We are supposed to accept that the girls and women who were arrested while trying to escape from the Magdalenes were guilty of wearing the uniform or clothes assigned to them.

Later in the same chapter, there is an astonishing explanation offered of the famous photograph of the women from Sean McDermott Street Laundry walking in a religious procession with a file of Gardaí on either side policing their participation. The committee managed to contact the priest and a Garda depicted in the photograph and accepts that it was merely coincidental that the two lines of Gardaí on either side of the Magdalene women just happened to be marching, at the same time in the same procession, 'in veneration of Our Lady and for no other reason'.[38] The IDC Committee does not appear to have made any attempt to find any of the women pictured and ask them whether they thought they were under police surveillance.

Chapter Five of the *IDC Report* presents what it refers to as the 'large range of legislation underpinning State involvement with the Magdalen Laundries'.[39] The *Report* asserts: 'It is possible that a lack of modern awareness of these Acts may have contributed to confusion or a mistaken sense that the Magdalen Laundries were unregulated or that State referrals of girls and women to the laundries occurred in all cases without any legal basis.'[40] In fact, the entirety of the *IDC Report* provides copious evidence that both these modern 'confusions' are not 'mistaken' and are in fact accurate in many cases and in general terms.[41] Chapter Five lists statutory provisions which, for example, permitted criminal justice detention in approved institutions for a specifically defined period; and the 'recall' of a young person released from industrial schools for up to three months' further detention in the industrial school (note: not in a Magdalene Laundry) – only if 'necessary' for their 'protection' and only with authorization of the minister for education if aged over eighteen. The statutory provisions also empowered the State to pay grants under the Health and Public Assistance Acts to private institutions for the maintenance of individuals in need of care. At no point does the IDC analyse or indicate whether these statutes were complied with bearing in mind the conditions in Magdalene Laundries. At no point, either, does the IDC mention the relevance or contents of that overarching and overriding piece of Irish legislation, the Irish Constitution. An outstanding instance of where the report's authors find themselves resorting to wilfully dismissing expert evidence and asserting an unsubstantiated counterclaim can be found in Chapter Eighteen where the report attempts to summarize academic work that is unrelentingly critical of the Magdalene regime and the pervasive culture of 'coercive confinement' endemic in twentieth-century Ireland. Amid detailed descriptions of the brutal social oppression enacted through mass institutionalization of Ireland's most vulnerable populations, the *IDC Report* insists that 'such institutions could legitimately claim to be a charitable outreach to the marginalised'.[42]

Chapter Twelve, entitled 'The Factories Acts and Regulation of the Workplace', claims to demonstrate that the laundries were under careful monitoring by the State's designated inspectorate of workplaces with the implication that the institutions were therefore compliant with their legal obligations: 'Records of inspections carried out indicate that on many occasions, no contraventions of the standards then in force were identified during these inspections of the Magdalen Laundries'.[43] The IDC does not question what the content of its report as a whole – including the finding that girls as young as nine were in Magdalene Laundries – suggests about the quality of the inspections that occurred. The chapter contains evidence from the Department of Industry, the religious orders, retired inspectors and, in one case, a man who was the paid manager of the Limerick Magdalene Laundry. Two former Magdalene women (who refer to the factory inspectors as 'the suits') give an account of the process for inspections. The women report all work in the laundry ceasing, with the girls and women lining up outside the factory area while the inspectors carried out their duties of checking the workplace and the machines.[44] In other words, no State official enquired about the welfare of those locked up in that institution and forced to compulsory labour in the laundry. The *Report* relays without comment that 'All of these retired Inspectors also confirmed that inspections of institutional laundries (including Magdalen Laundries) were conducted in precisely the same way as inspections of commercial or non-institutional laundries'.[45] A former manager of the Limerick Magdalene Laundry said that he knew of three bad industrial accidents in the institution, and the *Report* records his anecdote that 'The one in which the lady lost her forearm in the callender (large roller iron), I am reliably told by a Resident, was completely her own fault'.[46]

'Close to break-even basis'[47]

Chapter Fifteen, entitled 'Financial (C): Taxation, Commercial Rates and Social Insurance', asserts, on the one hand, that all of the profits of the Magdalene institutions which were the result of unpaid labour were deemed tax exempt, and on the other, that any work done by paid workers for the same orders was not exempt from tax.[48] This discussion is followed by a report on whether or not Magdalene Laundries paid commercial rates to local authorities and the assiduous efforts made by Magdalene Laundries to legally challenge having to pay such rates.[49] It is not until page 763 that we come to the question of whether the girls and women held in the Magdalene Laundries were forced to work without pay, and the level of connivance or knowledge by the State of that fact. As noted earlier the *IDC Report* approaches the matter obliquely, through a discussion of whether or not social insurance was paid by their 'employers', the religious orders.[50] This section of the chapter considers the 'employment status' of the women and girls, 'in particular whether work in the Magdalen Laundries qualified as insurable employment'.[51] The IDC admits that under Irish law those put to work in a Magdalene would be expected to be in insurable employment. Yet according to the IDC, a file once existed in the Department of Social Welfare detailing an issued decision, which stated that a girl or woman working in a Magdalene Laundry was not engaged in insurable employment. This file no longer exists and is presumed to have been destroyed.[52] In spite of, or indeed inspired by, the non-existence of this file the *IDC Report* constructs possible 'legislative bases' for the Department of Social Welfare's supposed decision and offers these suppositions to current departmental officials who in turn accept this rationale rather than admit the department's role in depriving Magdalene girls and women of their rights and colluding with extracting their unpaid hard labour.[53] The *IDC Report* finally asserts that 'after 1979, it is likely that the women working in the Magdalen Laundries did not qualify as being in insurable employment, as they would not have been in receipt of payment of greater than the threshold amount of £6 per week'.[54] So the IDC ultimately confirms the fact that girls and women worked without pay and uses this fact to exonerate the nuns for not paying social insurance.

The *IDC Report* closes with Chapter Twenty ('Financial Viability of the Magdalen Laundries'). The committee claims that in examining the records of the four Magdalene orders it was 'aware' of the 'significant public interest in relation to the question of the profitability of the Magdalen Laundries during their years of operation. A common perception has been that the laundries were highly profitable.'[55] The *Report* goes on to say that 'Although the Committee was not required to do so, it decided, in the public interest, to conduct an analysis of the available financial records of the Magdalen Laundries in order to more accurately assess their financial viability.'[56] On the basis of scant one-page financial statements prepared by the religious orders' accountants, the IDC concluded that 'in general, the Magdalen Laundries operated on a subsistence or close to break-even basis, rather than on a commercial or highly profitable basis and would have found it difficult to survive financially without other sources of income – donations, bequests and financial support from the State'.[57] The closing lines of the *IDC Report* provide an explanation for the Irish State's involvement with the Magdalene institutions: if the State had not given financial support, the nuns would have found it difficult to have their institutions 'survive'. The strangeness of this explanation entirely ignores that the Magdalenes were an abusive regime and the State should not merely have *not* colluded in perpetuating abuses but should have protected the girls and women held in these institutions from the manifold harms they suffered. Moreover, even the figures compiled by the nuns' own accountants seriously challenge the blithe assertion by the IDC that they operated 'on a subsistence or close to break-even basis' (it is unclear what the difference is supposed to be between these two terms). Taking the account presented for the Limerick laundry as an example, the laundry expenditure (excluding capital items) is given as €411,624 (in the value of 2011). Yet this figure seems very high, given that laundry expenditure must represent power, fuel and detergent, yet it is well over ten times the amount of €29,547 spent on capital items of laundry plant, equipment and vehicles.[58] Furthermore, the IDC openly attributes the living costs of the nuns in the Convent as costs of the Laundry since 'to ignore their work contribution would distort the laundry costs'.[59] The copious amounts of oral histories, witness statements and journalistic documentary accounts cohere on the view that only a few nuns were involved in running the Magdalenes, as supervisors and enforcers of discipline. Even assuming that the nuns did significant work, it is questionable whether charging the Convent costs to the Magdalene Laundries is valid. The nuns were not specifically recruited to supervise the laundry. They were there because of a vocation. To offset the cost of the nuns' expenses, which they would have required anyway, against the laundry profits and hence to declare that the laundries were not profitable does not appear to be justifiable. Finally, the costs to maintain the girls and women in the Magdalenes were also deducted from the laundry profits. As Raymond Hill has pointed out, 'To deduct for the expense of imprisoning them amounts to a suggestion that the women should be forced to work to pay for their own imprisonment.'[60]

'No factual evidence to support allegations of systematic torture or ill treatment of a criminal nature'

The Irish government continues to cite the *IDC Report* as if it is reliable and accurate, reasoned and impartial, when called to account by UN bodies for the State's failure to conduct a prompt, thorough and independent investigation and refusal to allow public access to administrative records of the wrongs perpetuated on the girls and women held in the Magdalenes and forced to work there. The central defence of the Irish State runs along the following lines: we would investigate criminal abuse if there was any to find and there is no criminal abuse to find as is evident in the fact that we are not investigating criminal abuse. Three months after the *IDC Report*'s publication, in May 2013, Felice Gaer wrote on behalf of UNCAT to Ireland's Permanent Representative to the UN in Geneva, Ambassador Gerard Corr. Gaer stated that while UNCAT was 'pleased' at the IDC's establishment, from an international human rights law perspective the committee and its resulting *IDC Report* lacked many elements of 'a prompt, independent and thorough investigation'.[61] She asked:

> Please clarify whether the State party intends to set up an inquiry body that is independent, with definite terms of reference, and statutory powers to compel evidence, and retain evidence obtained from relevant religious bodies? Would such an inquiry be empowered with the capacity to hold public hearings or

obtain access to evidence for survivors or representative groups? Would such an inquiry have the authority to conduct a full-scale investigation into the abuses, and issue a public invitation to submit evidence? Given the nature and duration of institutionalized abuse, as well as the advanced age (and possible geographical remoteness) of some survivors, what steps does the State party intend to take to encourage survivors to lodge complaints?

The government's response was a resounding rejection of UNCAT's premise: 'in absence [*sic*] of any credible evidence of systematic torture or criminal abuse being committed in the Magdalen laundries, the Irish Government does not propose to set up a specific Magdalen inquiry body.' Corr's letter explained: 'The Committee had no remit to investigate or make determinations about allegations of torture or any other criminal offence. . . . No factual evidence to support allegations of systematic torture or ill treatment of a criminal nature in these institutions was found.' The State's defence concluded: 'If the Committee or any party has knowledge of a person with direct knowledge of an alleged criminal offence and forwards it to us, we shall request the appropriate authorities to carry out a criminal investigation into such allegations.'[62]

Since that letter in 2013, the Irish government has repeated that the *IDC Report* discloses 'no factual evidence to support allegations of systematic torture or ill treatment of a criminal nature' to UNCAT in 2015, 2018 and 2019; to the UN Human Rights Committee in 2014 and 2017; and to the UN Committee on the Elimination of Discrimination Against Women in 2015 and 2016.[63] The government progressed to claiming that there is an 'absence of any *credible* [emphasis added] evidence of systematic torture or criminal abuse' to the Human Rights Committee four years running (in 2014, 2015, 2016 and 2017) and to UNCAT in 2018.[64] In 2014 came the legal argument that the evidence available to the State does 'not support the allegations that women were systematically detained unlawfully in these institutions or kept for long periods against their will.'[65] The State's 2015 report to UNCAT supplied the interpretation that '[t]he majority of entrants into Magdalen Laundries were not "confined" there in any legal sense.'[66]

Even more emboldened and factually erroneous statements have appeared in recent years to the effect that the State had no meaningful involvement in the Magdalene Laundries at all. The government insisted in 2015 to UNCAT: 'No Government Department was involved in the running of a Magdalen Laundry. These were private institutions under the sole ownership and control of the religious congregations concerned and had no special statutory recognition or status.'[67] In defence of Elizabeth Coppin's individual case before UNCAT, the State has recently characterized the laundries as 'refuges' where women 'were mainly engaged in work in the laundry, which may have included sewing', and which 'were operated on a private basis by religious congregations with no statutory basis for either admitting a person to or confining a person to a Magdalen Laundry'.[68]

Startlingly, several high-ranking politicians have repeated these arguments on the Dáil record *since* Enda Kenny's February 2013 apology. In November 2013, Finian McGrath TD asked Minister for Justice Alan Shatter 'if the State downplayed the abuse suffered by the Magdalen women at the United Nations'.[69] The minister responded:

> The McAleese report provides an independent, comprehensive, factual account of the Magdalen institutions. . . . In particular nothing was discovered to suggest there was systematic torture or other criminal behaviour that would warrant a comprehensive criminal investigation with a view to multiple criminal prosecutions. This is not to down play the harsh conditions endured by the women in question.[70]

In 2015, Minister for Justice Frances Fitzgerald TD answered a Parliamentary Question from Micheál Martin TD about 'whether she or her Department believe there will be any prosecutions made following the McAleese report' with the statement:

> It may be helpful to the Deputy to indicate that while not specifically part of the terms of reference of the McAleese Committee, the Committee did take the opportunity to record evidence and testimony that might throw light on allegations of systematic abuse. In this context 118 women who had been in these institutions agreed to complete a questionnaire on conditions (food, punishment etc.) in these institutions and/or to meet with and discuss these issues with the independent Chair. No factual evidence to support allegations of systematic torture or ill treatment of a criminal nature in these institutions was found. The majority of women did report verbal abuse but not of a nature that would constitute a criminal offence.[71]

Going a step further by denying that the State had 'any liability' for the Magdalene Laundries at all, Fitzgerald again responded in February 2017 to PQs from Clare Daly TD, Jim O'Callaghan TD and Catherine Connolly TD about the management of the ex gratia 'restorative justice' scheme by noting: 'Although there was no finding in the McAleese Report which indicated that the State had any liability in the matter, following the report's publication the Taoiseach issued a State apology to the women.'[72] Richard Bruton, minister for education and skills, repeated this assertion in a written answer to Catherine Murphy TD in October 2017.[73]

In May 2013, the report by Mr Justice John Quirke (president of the Irish Law Reform Commission and former High Court judge) acknowledged that forced unpaid labour, involuntary detention, degradation and denial of education were systemic features of the Magdalene Laundries.[74] The IHRC, similarly, reached a dramatically different conclusion to the government about the contents of the *IDC Report*. Conducting a provisional human rights analysis of the *IDC Report*'s contents in June 2013 '[i]n the absence of a more thorough investigation, as recommended by the IHRC and the United Nations Committee Against Torture', it concluded that[75]

- 'Magdalen Laundries clearly operated as a *discriminatory regime* in respect of girls and women in the state. The State itself had knowledge of the regime and actively engaged with it, indeed financially benefitting from it in some cases. Society at large accepted the regime, and also supported it by placing sisters, daughters and mothers behind the walls of the laundries. . . . *the State appears to have taken no cognisance of the women's right to equality* when it engaged with, and permitted the laundries to operate';[76]

- '[W]omen were *deprived of their liberty* while in the laundries. The *lawfulness of such detention is questionable* in a number of respects';[77]
- 'The placement of children in Magdalen Laundries, either by the State or others, may have given rise to a *breach of the right to education* under the Constitution and the right of access to education under the ECHR' [European Convention on Human Rights];[78]
- 'The *State's culpability in regard to forced or compulsory labour and/or servitude appears to be threefold* . . . it failed to outlaw and police against such practices . . . the State or its agents placed girls and women in the laundries knowing that such girls and women would be obliged to provide their labour in those institutions . . . the State further supported these practices by benefitting from commercial contracts with the laundries';[79]
- 'from the testimonies of survivors it appears that a certain level of *ill-treatment occurred*';[80] and
- inadequate recording of the identities and burial sites of deceased Magdalene women 'could potentially have impacted on the *Article 8 [ECHR] rights of living relatives* of the deceased women to information about their origins'.[81]

The Irish State still insists on unknowing the Magdalene Laundries and its ignorance of the abuses suffered by girls and women there, in spite of their testimony and the vast amount of corroborating evidence and supported argument generated over the past decade of campaigning.

7

Ex gratia 'redress'

Denial of rights through the 'redress' process

In the course of his apology to Magdalene survivors on 19 February 2013, Taoiseach Enda Kenny revealed the government's plan for redress: Mr Justice John Quirke, president of the Law Reform Commission of Ireland, would consider and report within three months on 'the help that the Government can provide in the areas of payments and other supports, including medical cards, psychological and counselling services and other welfare needs'.[1] Minister for Justice Alan Shatter began his remarks following the Taoiseach's speech by recognizing the historic occasion as 'the day the State is finally opening its heart and accepting its moral duty to those who felt abandoned and lost and believed they had no future'. The minister's avoidance of any mention of 'rights' or legal responsibility forewarned that the government's Terms of Reference (ToR) for Mr Justice Quirke, sent in the post the next day, would instruct the judge to 'advise on the establishment of an ex gratia Scheme (to operate on a non-adversarial basis)'.[2]

An 'ex gratia payment' is 'one that is given as a favour or gift and not because it is legally necessary'.[3] Judge Quirke explained in his ensuing *Quirke Report* that payments under the ex gratia Scheme would be significantly reduced by comparison to court-ordered damages and would not 'reflect or include a calculation of loss of earnings sustained by the women'.[4] The *Quirke Report* proffered the explanation that because redress payments had *not* been ordered by a court, they would constitute 'an important and sincere . . . recognition of past State failures'. It added: 'by avoiding any adversarial process, the needs and interests of the Magdalen women and of Irish society generally are also met, because the voluntary nature of the offer of payments would contribute to the process of on-going reconciliation.'[5]

According to Judge Quirke's *Report*, it would not be possible for the government to offer 'full and complete damages to compensate the Magdalen women for injury and loss caused by the wrongdoing of the State' without the women undergoing the ordinary, court-based 'detailed (and usually lengthy) adversarial process'.[6] On the contrary, it had appeared to us in researching our October 2011 Restorative Justice and Reparations Proposal that the government could accept State liability for constitutional and human rights violations either voluntarily on an administrative basis or through legislation establishing a redress scheme. Several senior Irish practising lawyers assisted us in drafting our proposal, which recommended a non-adversarial approach to providing redress on the very basis that it 'will be an accepted fact that the Magdalene Laundries were by their nature abusive, punitive institutions, in which girls and women were routinely subjected to forced unpaid labour and unlawful and false imprisonment'.[7] JFM believed that any redress process must attempt to transform the denial of human dignity at the root of the Magdalene Laundries abuse by expressly recognizing the women's status as rights-holders. We also knew that the legislation creating the highly traumatizing and degrading proceedings of the RIRB had specified that payments to industrial and reformatory school survivors were ex gratia.[8] Therefore, 'ex gratia', in the context of Irish 'historical' abuse redress schemes, did not necessarily mean 'non-adversarial'.

Our proposal contended that every woman who spent time in a Magdalene Laundry should be entitled automatically to a sum of money in recognition of an accepted threshold of abuse and injury; that each woman if she wished to demonstrate specific abuse and injuries could make an application to an independent, non-adversarial body to claim further payment; and that the usual civil court causation rules (requiring specific injuries to be tied to particular incidents of abuse) would be altered to allow for a general congruence of damage and abuse bearing in mind what was known about the system. We argued further that survivors should be supported by lawyers, and other research and advocacy assistants where necessary, to prepare a written Victim Impact Statement that would form 'the core of the claim' for evidentiary purposes, with a non-adversarial oral hearing being available but not compulsory. We insisted that the religious congregations should not be allowed to participate in the assessment process because payments would not involve findings against a named person. Our proposal did not countenance women being denied their right to access court if they wished to seek further recompense or other forms of justice.

The Quirke recommendations

Thirty-three female barristers volunteered to help Judge Quirke gather information from 337 survivors between March and May 2013 (almost 3 times as many survivors as had met with Senator McAleese, demonstrating the impact of the Taoiseach's apology). In addition, Judge Quirke met with 'a number of senior members of the Religious Orders who now accommodate and care for a further 117 of those women'.[9] To assist survivors to inform Judge Quirke and these barristers of their needs and experiences, Claire published online and distributed widely in Ireland and abroad a 'Survivor Guide to the Magdalen Commission'.[10] It contained tick boxes and space for women to provide information and recommendations covering all aspects of well-being and personal autonomy potentially impacted by their abuse. Claire created a second guide to encourage relatives of deceased women to communicate with Judge Quirke also.[11] The Magdalen Commission undertook an impressively in-depth evaluation of survivors' welfare needs. Most survivors are uncomfortable asking for what they need, and the guides had empowered many in this regard.

It is clear that Judge Quirke was moved by the rights violations that girls and women suffered. His *Report* specifically noted that all of the women with whom he spoke were 'entirely credible' in informing him of their unpaid labour, incarceration and 'traumatic incidents such as escape from the laundries and subsequent recapture and return', experiences of being 'degraded, humiliated, stigmatised and exploited (sometimes in a calculated manner)' and deprivation of education.[12] Numerous women remarked to us that they felt validated and dignified by the opportunity to meet personally with Judge Quirke. Elizabeth Coppin recalls:

> Justice Quirke was the only person who was good – he was very professional and wasn't patronising. He was just listening to us. I felt he not just listened to us, but he believed what we had to say. He took me at face value, he wasn't giving me crocodile tears or apologies. . . . But still, he had to follow what he was told to do, which was not to bother with our human rights.[13]

The oral history transcript of Pippa Flanagan, speaking with Claire, conveys a similar sentiment: 'Judge Quirke . . . he was a *lovely* man, and he was so understanding . . . you know then, people are starting to take notice and believe you.'[14] In another oral history, Kathleen recalls: 'I found him very pleasant . . . it was very easy to understand him, he assured me that I would be okay for the rest of my life and I was never to be ashamed of my time in the Magdalene Laundries. He assured me it wasn't my fault.'[15]

However, Judge Quirke recommended that the women should sign a waiver giving up their legal rights against the State in order to gain access to the ex gratia Scheme. On the one hand, therefore, the Scheme would operate as if the State had no legal obligations towards the women and committed no wrongdoing. On the other hand, the Scheme would recognize the women's rights in order to remove them. The recommendation of a legal waiver by the *Quirke Report* was a mistake, we believe, with enormous consequences. The waiver copper-fastened the notion that the State was 'not liable' for the Magdalene Laundries abuse. It ensured that survivors participating in the Scheme would not ever be permitted to seek a court judgment to set the record straight.

Judge Quirke's Commission produced several recommendations that promised, should they be fully implemented, to make a positive impact on many women's lives. His *Report* recounts that he and the barristers who assisted him pro bono sought to 'give a coherent voice and a degree of "self determination" to a cohort of women . . . who have told me that they have for a very long time felt forgotten, denied and disbelieved'.[16] The *Quirke Report* was delivered to government at the end of May 2013. Minister Shatter published it on 26 June 2013, stating that the government intended 'in principle to implement these recommendations in full' and estimated that the Scheme would cost between €34.5 and €58 million.[17]

The key recommendations were for (1) extensive health and social care services equivalent to those provided to people infected by the State with Hepatitis C in the 1990s through a Health Amendment Act card, known the 'HAA card'; (2) financial payments calculated according to each woman's duration of time spent in a Magdalene institution; and (3) funding for an independent Dedicated Unit, to provide general advocacy assistance to the women and to facilitate the women to meet each other and to consult on memorialization measures which the Dedicated Unit would then oversee. The government announced that it would include in the Scheme survivors of two institutions for teenage girls in addition to the ten Magdalene Laundries.

Justifying his health and social care recommendation, Judge Quirke noted some aspects of the women's state of well-being. Of the 386 women whose age was known to the Commission, their average was 68 years of age.[18] Only half of 292 women described their mobility as 'good'. Two-thirds of 282 women stated that they were experiencing 'serious health issues'. Notably, even though 91 per cent of 231 women already had a public medical card or GP visit card, they still had substantial 'complaints and worries' regarding their ability to access health and social care services. The *Quirke Report* explained:

> Many women indicated that they wished to be provided with access to counselling. Some wished to have access to a medical card and to be given an opportunity to see their GP on a more regular basis. Others described how they were currently on waiting lists awaiting surgery and how their scheduled surgery has been delayed or cancelled. Some women described how they struggled with mobility issues and a number of women stated that they believed that their lives would be greatly improved were they to be provided with walking frames or stair-lifts. Some described how they required improvements and alterations to be made to their homes to accommodate their health conditions.[19]

The *Quirke Report* recommended two payments for each woman under the Scheme, both of which should be exempt from tax and means-testing in relation to existing and future social welfare supports. The first payment was characterized as a pension top-up for women over sixty-six years of age: to put them in the position they would have occupied had sufficient social insurance contributions been paid on their behalf for a contributory State pension of €230.30 per week. Until reaching sixty-six, younger women would receive a weekly payment to bring them up to a State-provided income of €100 per week. The second payment was a lump sum of between €11,500 and €100,000, calculated according to duration of time spent in a Magdalene Laundry. Any ex gratia payments in excess of €50,000, however, were not to be paid as a lump but as an actuarially calculated weekly income for the remainder of the woman's life with any unpaid money reverting to the State upon her death.

Explaining the reasoning behind these payments, Judge Quirke noted that 90 per cent of 231 women who spoke with the Commission about their education had received only primary-level schooling.[20] The *Report* highlighted that many survivors lived in poverty:

> Many of the women stated that they found it hard to make ends meet and to pay household bills. . . . Many of the women wished to improve their living conditions; a number of women spoke of having no hot water and no central heating. . . . Some women described being worried about security and wished to be in a position to replace the doors and the windows of their homes.

Judge Quirke further stated that his payment recommendations related to the women's unpaid 'harsh and physically demanding work', and 'the traumatic, ongoing effects which incarceration within the laundries has had upon their security, their confidence and their self-esteem'.[21]

Limited though they are, the financial aspects of the Scheme have provided comfort to many survivors – although in our experience the women, true to form, have frequently used their money for others' benefit. However, for a large number of other women, engaging with the DoJ's administration of the scheme was arduous and deeply traumatizing. In this chapter we demonstrate that

- The DoJ effectively appointed the religious congregations as arbiters of women's applications. Whenever there was a conflict between what a survivor told the department and what the nuns told the department, the religious congregation was believed. Where the nuns had lost or destroyed records, the survivor's evidence was deemed insufficient to ground her application;
- Hundreds of women were paid less money than they claimed for;
- The DoJ refused to accept the applications of dozens of women who were registered in industrial schools or 'training centres' annexed to the Magdalene Laundries and – the DoJ and nuns acknowledged – were forced to work as child labourers in the Laundries;
- The DoJ deemed dozens of women to lack sufficient financial decision-making capacity to apply to the scheme and then abandoned them as the government failed (and at the time of writing continues to fail) to bring into operation a scheme for Assisted Decision-Making which was legislated for in 2015;
- Fearful of setting a precedent, the government never provided the extensive health and social care entitlements that Judge Quirke recommended; and
- The government failed to fund the independent Dedicated Unit, which Judge Quirke recommended for the purposes of providing the women with advocacy services and undertaking the women's recommended forms of memorialization.

The campaign is retired and JFMR is born

Claire and Katherine met Judge Quirke in March 2013 and provided him with our proposal and additional written submissions.[22] Nuala Ní Mhuircheartaigh was in attendance and she did not hide her irritation with us. As Katherine recalls, Judge Quirke, for his part, seemed rather wary and non-committal in response to our questions about how the Scheme's decision-making process would actually work in practice, and Ms Ní Mhuircheartaigh was swift in dismissing our concerns. When we pointed out that according to the *IDC Report* the Mercy Order had no registers for their two Magdalene Laundries and said that we hoped survivors would be enabled to swear an affidavit to support their claim, Ms Ní Mhuircheartaigh declared to Judge Quirke that there were 'six different ways' to find records that would demonstrate a woman's length of stay in a Magdalene institution.[23] Katherine sensed that she should query why, then, *IDC Report* had failed to draw on these sources but all she could feel was her own and Claire's exhaustion. All of us in JFM had at this point worked for four years voluntarily at full tilt, incurring several hospitalizations between us.

After the meeting Katherine and Claire Skyped the other JFM members. It seemed we had achieved all we could by way of political advocacy. We would need to focus on empowering the women and their own personal advocates to engage with Judge Quirke in his deliberations on how to deliver a restorative justice scheme, so we immediately began drawing up our 'Survivor Guide to the Magdalen Commission'. We decided to retire the JFM political campaign and re-form as JFMR, with a focus on research, public education, curriculum development and active memorialization through truth-telling, the MOHP and the MNP.[24] We agreed that we would continue to maintain contact with survivors in a personal capacity, providing advocacy and assistance when needed.

In the period leading up to the end of the JFM campaign, we took several steps to empower the general public to hold the State accountable in future. In addition to publishing Survivor Guides and communicating with Judge Quirke, we circulated to Oireachtas members a list of outstanding questions and concerns relating to the proposed scheme, and we made a submission to UNCAT requesting that the committee 'monitor the design and implementation of the forthcoming Magdalene Laundries reparation process and . . . make recommendations to, and engage in dialogue with, the Irish government as it deems appropriate'.[25]

Our personal contact with Magdalene survivors led us back before long, however, into the political arena with regard to the ex gratia Scheme. We found the advocacy required from late 2013 onwards to be more challenging in some ways than our previous campaigning. Every woman's circumstances were different and the government's opaque methods of administering the ex gratia Scheme therefore had disparate and complex impacts. Intensive efforts sometimes advanced one woman's or a few women's struggle for fairer treatment by the State, but the effect was not necessarily shared by others. The government refused to provide independent advocacy or legal assistance to survivors who applied to the Scheme apart from €500, at the tail end of the process, for a solicitor to witness the woman signing away her legal rights in exchange for payment. In the absence of coordinated representation, officials and government ministers were in a position constantly to meet our and others' arguments with the (un-evidenced) assertion that the concerns we raised did not relate to the majority of the women.

JFMR's wide-ranging advocacy since 2013 (conducted in addition to the research agenda we set ourselves) has focused on combatting the government's maladministration of the ex gratia Scheme and the State's continued denial of legal responsibility for the Magdalene Laundries abuse. This advocacy was waged on many fronts, including enabling survivors to engage with broadcast media and newspapers, continuing to gather Magdalene Oral History testimonies, writing in academic publications and organizing the Dublin Honours Magdalenes Listening Exercise Event.[26] We have also written opinion editorials and PRs, participated in radio and television broadcasts, asked TDs to submit PQs, made presentations in Leinster House, compiled Briefing Notes to TDs and senators and had meetings with government ministers and their officials and with backbench and opposition politicians and their advisers.[27] We have written letters to government ministers and officials, made observations on planning applications regarding former Magdalene convent sites and made submissions to the Ombudsman on the Scheme's administration in 2017 and 2019.[28] When survivors needed legal advice, we referred them to sympathetic solicitors and barristers specializing in human rights, and we have continued our engagement with several international human rights bodies (which also functioned as correspondence with the State).[29] We have continued to work with national statutory bodies and NGOs who have joined in the effort to advocate for former Magdalene women.[30] We have also supported, with Maeve as a lead lawyer, the case of *Elizabeth Coppin v. Ireland*, which is currently proceeding before UNCAT.[31]

Structural barriers to a full and fair implementation of Judge Quirke's recommendations

Officials' attitudes

Records released under FOI reveal a distinct belief on the part of some senior civil servants that Judge Quirke's recommendations were overly generous. In August 2013, one Department of Finance official opined:

> The proposed Scheme appears very generous and moreso [*sic*] than others out there, such as the Redress one (and in those cases, the level of award to be given was 'tested'). In relation to lump sums, there is no indication or, it seems, rationale for how these are calculated. €11,500 for 3 months spent in a laundry seems very high, including if it is compared with the amount to be allowed in relation to a 10 year period spent.[32]

DoJ assistant secretary general Jimmy Martin was responsible for coordinating all departments' preparations for implementing the Scheme. In September 2013, an Inter Departmental Group (IDG) of civil servants convened by Mr Martin delivered a report (*IDG Report*) to Cabinet on how the Scheme should operate. The *IDG Report* advised rejecting Judge Quirke's pension/weekly payment recommendation for women incarcerated for less than three months because it 'would seem to be inconsistent with the intent behind the scheme and standard practice for pension schemes if for example an applicant who spent only a few days in an institution would gain entitlement to a life-long pension over and above any other entitlements'.[33] (The government, thankfully, did not take up this suggestion.) The IDG successfully proposed that the commencement date for pension payments should be 'the date of the Government Decision on the issues raised in this Report', rather than backdating to when a woman reached pensionable age.[34] The *IDG Report* also disregarded out of hand the need for a Dedicated Unit, asserting:

> Judge Quirke seems to envisage the establishment of a dedicated unit with an advisory committee outside the normal services provided by Departments which would assist the women on a wide variety of issues outside the direct scope of the scheme. Such a unit would require staff and premises. There is a doubt as to whether there would be sufficient demand to justify establishing a new unit of this type even without taking into account the costs involved.[35]

Thus, the Dedicated Unit – a crucial component of the redress scheme – has never come to pass. The IDG further declined to estimate the cost of any memorial. The officials noted Judge Quirke's suggestion that a memorial garden could be created at the site of the former Magdalene Laundry at Sean McDermott Street and simply conveyed what they said was the view of officials in DCC: 'This may pose difficulties as there is extensive use of the Area as a car park for Dublin City Council staff, Housing Maintenance and Waste Management trucks and people from the adjoining Sisters of Our Lady of Charity Building. There would be no difficulty in having a garden there whenever the area is redeveloped.'[36] Parking for refuse lorries, council staff and nuns was therefore prioritized over a memorial.

The Ombudsman concluded in a lengthy investigation report in 2017 that civil servants' desire to prevent 'fraudulent claims' by Magdalene survivors was a major factor contributing to the unfair administration of the scheme.[37] A prolonged dispute between Mr Martin and the Office of the Ombudsman between 2016 and 2018 revealed the vehemence of the government's position that Magdalene survivors were not victims of forced labour or criminal abuse, accordingly deserving of reparation, but were rather recipients of the State's grace and favour.

The manipulation of access to legal assistance

The government limited the legal assistance available through the ex gratia Scheme to €500 + VAT for each woman to seek advice and a solicitor's signature on her legal waiver form once an offer of payment had been made – that is, after the woman had navigated the Scheme alone.[38] In his speech on 19 February 2013, Minister Shatter promised that the response to Magdalene survivors' needs would be both 'non-adversarial' and lawyer-free. Judge Quirke's ToR required him to devise a system for administering redress claims 'in an effective and timely manner that ensures the monies . . . are directed only to the benefit of eligible applicants and not on legal fees and expenses'. In a later speech, the minister referred to the 'many concerns about the approach taken in the *Residential Institutions Redress Act 2002*'; he noted that 'many victims of institutional abuse thought that the system was very legalistic and traumatic and that too much money went to the lawyers rather than to the victims themselves'.[39]

Minister Shatter's stated desire not to repeat the previous RIRB-related abuses was laudable. However, his construction of a false equivalence between the women's interests and the total absence of legal help camouflaged the reality that (1) the denial of legal assistance to the women would not inexorably lead to them being treated fairly by the Scheme's administrators and would undermine their ability to challenge unfairness if and when it arose; (2) legal representation of survivors, in itself, was not the cause of the RIRB's re-traumatization of so many people who interacted with it (rather, the court-like procedures adopted and rights afforded to alleged abusers despite RIRB payments not reflecting any fault were the primary problems); (3) while Magdalene survivors would not have access to lawyers to assist them in interacting with the Scheme, the State and religious congregations would remain legally represented at all times; and (4) the State would nonetheless pay for lawyers to witness survivors signing away their legal rights against the State in relation to their abuse.

Correspondence in the summer of 2013 between the DoJ and the LAB shows that the government knew that survivors' potential legal needs went far beyond the signature of a solicitor on their waiver form, and that it was not prepared to meet all of these needs. LAB Chief Executive Moling Ryan wrote to Jimmy Martin that if the board were to provide a service under the Scheme, its funding would need to account for 'the urgency and frailty of some of the applicants and potential other issues such as wardship that might arise', as well as the fact that '[i]ndividual circumstances could give rise to advices not to accept the scheme on offer and the Board may then be faced with the costs of pursuing court action'. Mr Ryan continued: 'There is always the possibility of connected claims, in particular Judicial Review, by dissatisfied claimants. While it is appreciated that the proposed service is specifically with regard to advice on the waiver, that limited service is subject to complicating factors and the prospect of a more protracted and expensive process must be anticipated.'[40] The *IDG Report* to Cabinet in September 2013 advised against using the LAB. Recommending a payment of €500 + VAT for a private solicitor to advise each survivor in relation to the waiver, the officials noted without any comment on the implications for the women's ability to access justice: 'While for some applicants, the legal issues will be straightforward (e.g. taking into account the Statute of Limitations, evidence of personal injuries etc.) in the case of others matters may be more complex and solicitors may legitimately seek a level of remuneration from their client above the "cap" established under the Scheme.'[41]

Thus, the government denied Magdalene survivors not only the legal assistance that they would need to challenge the denial of fair procedures within the Scheme's administration but also the means to have a realistic choice between the Scheme and litigation in court. A further, crucial, consequence of the government's misleading insistence that the Scheme would not involve any 'legalistic' procedure was that the DoJ refused to assist survivors to swear an affidavit as a way of evidencing their 'duration of stay' in a Magdalene Laundry.[42] Given that documentary records of women's detention were sparse, difficult to access and not always accurate, the government's denial of legal assistance to enable the women to prove their own case had appalling consequences.

A continuing mutual relationship of control

The DoJ and the religious congregations assumed joint control of the process of assessing survivors' applications to the Scheme: the DoJ as the Scheme's administrator and the nuns as 'verifiers' of the women's 'duration of stay'.[43] The government's designation of the Scheme as 'ex gratia' effectively functioned as a declaration that neither State departments nor the religious congregations were to be treated as wrongdoers who might be inclined to treat survivors with a lack of respect. As a corollary, the women were portrayed not to require any independent advocacy or other assistance that would help undo the effects of their previous subordination.

We made an overarching request to Judge Quirke in March 2013, as his report records, that the Scheme would be administered independently and on a statutory footing.[44] We believed that legislation was necessary to compel the nuns to hand over the women's records to a 'properly resourced, suitable data protection agency' that would employ 'a competent, independent archivist' to ensure survivors' access to their own information. We were greatly concerned by Minister Shatter's announcement on 6 March 2013 that the government had no plans to intervene in the religious orders' custody of records. In response to a PQ by Catherine Murphy TD asking whether he would consider establishing 'a thorough and comprehensive record facility' as a measure of redress, Minister Shatter claimed:

> I have no control over records held by the religious congregations or other non-State bodies. . . . It is not within my power to establish a facility that would allow the women who were admitted to the Magdalen Laundries and their families access to all genealogical and other records necessary to locate their families and reconstruct their family identities.[45]

It is clear from the overall tenor of Judge Quirke's *Report* that he intended his recommendation that payments would be calculated solely according to time spent in a Magdalene Laundry to ensure a swift and non-adversarial response to all women's applications for redress. However, the *Quirke Report* did not address whether the religious congregations could or should be relied upon to support survivors' applications, or whether the Scheme should be administered by an independent person or entity capable of assessing the women's own testimony as the primary form of evidence.

Our hope for an independent decision-making process disappeared upon Minister Shatter's publication of the *Quirke Report* on 26 June 2013.[46] The minister explained that his department had already established a Restorative Justice Implementation Team 'to validate and to process applications'. He said that the religious congregations would be 'providing crucial help with regard to the records of those former residents who apply under the scheme'. His references to the nuns were conciliatory: 'The Religious Congregations have assured me that they will cooperate fully with the process. I want to publicly thank them for their continued cooperation and assistance.' He echoed the orders' own justification for refusing to contribute financially to the Scheme: 'It is not widely understood that the religious congregations are still caring for over 100 elderly women who originally resided in the Magdalen Laundries.' Minister Shatter continued: 'Together with Kathleen Lynch I met on Tuesday of last week with the congregations and discussed with them their making of a contribution to the ex gratia fund and I know this is an issue on which they are presently reflecting.' The RSC had, however, the day before already penned their letter clarifying that they would not make any financial donation. Indeed, a string of letters between the DoJ and the four religious congregations in late June and early July 2013 conveyed the orders' position that they had no legal or moral obligation to pay into the Scheme and that allowing the women to access their own personal data would be a sufficiently generous contribution.[47]

Lack of access to ordinary democratic accountability mechanisms

The larger context for all of the above was – and remains – a deficit of ordinary civil and criminal legal accountability for the Magdalene Laundries abuse. During

Ireland's examination in 2014, chair of the UN Human Rights Committee Sir Professor Nigel Rodley commented to Minister Frances Fitzgerald that he did not 'want to pour cold water on' efforts to provide financial redress for various 'historical' abuses, but that

> In all of these cases, the issue that remains for the state party is to consider what it is going to do about accountability. Accountability for its own responsibilities, accountability for its failures to monitor what others have been doing, and the accountability of others for committing abuses that the State might well be able to think of as crimes. The accountability that I mention is missing in everything that we've heard so far.[48]

The government has claimed repeatedly in the past decade that any survivor of the Magdalene Laundries may complain to the Gardaí and her complaint will be investigated. At the same time, however, the government has vociferously asserted that the incarceration and forced unpaid labour generally characterizing the Magdalene Laundries was not criminal. Unsurprisingly, the Gardaí have never announced a systematic investigation into the Magdalenes. The IDC's archive has not been turned over to the Gardaí. The CICA did not allow Gardaí to access its archive in the 2000s.[49] The legislation which underpinned the MBHCOI states that all information gathered (whether documentary or testamentary) is 'inadmissible as evidence against a person in any criminal or other proceedings'.[50]

The civil courts have proved impossible for Magdalene survivors to access, leaving aside the impact and explaining the uptake of the ex gratia Scheme's legal waiver. Ireland's Statute of Limitations is far stricter than in England and presents an almost total bar to 'historical' claims against State and non-State Defendants.[51] Furthermore, as barristers Colin Smith and April Duff note, 'religious orders and State agencies are vigorous in seeking costs against litigants whose claims against them have failed.' Smith and Duff point out that 'victims of historic institutional abuse receiving legal advice will receive a stark warning from their lawyers that if their proceedings fail, they will face financial ruin'.[52] Moreover, legal aid is extremely difficult to obtain.[53] Other obstacles identified by Smith and Duff are the narrow understanding of vicarious liability in Irish tort law such that abuse in privately managed, State-funded social care services will not necessarily give rise to State responsibility, and the difficulty of determining which defendant(s) to sue because religious congregations in Ireland, remarkably, have no independent legal personality and so cannot be sued as an entity. Furthermore, there is a lack of legislation that would allow for class actions, and the absence of modern judicial case management procedures in the Irish High Court means that defendants can cause inordinate delays to the progress of proceedings.[54]

Censorship of information, even that recorded on official files, by the State and religious congregations adds to the prevailing impunity as it hampers survivors' ability to press for effective criminal and civil justice while also denying other forms of personal and collective redress. The *FOI Act 2014* establishes a right of access only to information created after October 1998 (or 2008 for some public bodies), with few exceptions,[55] and civil servants have managed to avoid implementing even the limited law that *is* on the books.

The DoT currently possesses the archive of all State records gathered by the IDC. Although the IDC decided that 'maintenance of these copies together in a single location will be a concrete outcome to the Committee's work and may be a resource for future research', the DoT has repeatedly rejected requests under the *FOI Act 2014* for access to material in the archive.[56] The DoT asserts that 'these records are stored in this Department for the purpose of safe keeping in a central location and are not held nor within the control of the Department for the purposes of the *FOI Act*. They cannot therefore be released by this Department.'[57] It seems that the State understands 'safe keeping' to mean ensuring no access is given. The department will not even release the archive's index.[58] In February 2017, Minister Fitzgerald stated in response to a PQ from Maureen O'Sullivan TD that '[i]n relation to the State archive there are no plans to make it available publicly at this time'.[59] In January 2020, one survivor obtained a ruling from the information commissioner that the department's decision that it did not hold the records for the purposes of the *FOI Act* was wrong.[60] The department did not appeal but public access to the records has yet to be granted. Meanwhile, the AG has asserted in response to Elizabeth Coppin's case before UNCAT that if Mrs Coppin wishes to access the IDC's archive, she should attempt to recreate it herself by making requests of each original source of the records gathered by the IDC.[61]

For the entirety of its investigation into Mother and Baby Homes, including the transfer of girls and women to Magdalene Laundries, the MBHCOI refused to conduct public hearings or publish evidence, despite survivors' requests. It refused to disclose to survivors any personal information of theirs that it had gathered, even after the introduction in 2018 of the EU GDPR, which is supreme over any conflicting Irish law and prohibits blanket bars to personal data access. The MBHCOI would not give relatives of the deceased any records that it had gathered about the fate or whereabouts of their next of kin. It further refused to give witnesses a copy of their own transcript of evidence.[62] Additionally, although the Oireachtas inserted into the *CICA Act 2000* a requirement that the eventual archive of the CICA would be preserved and made available in the NAI, in 2019 the Department of Education published a Retention of Records Bill which proposed to prohibit all access (including by survivors) to every document contained in the archives of the CICA, and the RIRB and its Review Committee, for seventy-five years.[63]

The NAI should in theory contain a great deal of information about government departments' interactions with Magdalene Laundries and related abuses. However, the chronic lack of funding to the NAI makes a mockery of its statutory role. In August 2019 the archivists' branch of the Fórsa trade union published a report showing the NAI to have 'about 40% of the staff per capita compared to Scotland and only 25% compared to Northern Ireland or Denmark'.[64] The Fórsa report stated that 'the NAI is only able to say it provides a comprehensive service to four departments'. It added: 'There is a perception among some departments that their obligations under the *National Archives Act* do not need to be met due to the inability of the National Archives to accept transfers of records.'[65] Over one-third of the NAI's limited collection has not yet even been catalogued for public access.[66]

The *National Archives Act 1986* does not designate health or social care institutions or providers as sources of records that must be preserved and deposited in the NAI for public access.[67] The list of State entities other than government departments to which the 1986 Act applies is also now thirty-four years out of date. Fórsa's report on the NAI in 2019 noted that Ireland is unique among the four national archives studied in failing to hold or collect the archives of 'non-official bodies (e.g., businesses, religious organisations)'.[68] In 2018 the DoJ claimed to UNCAT that because 'records relating to the institutions the subject of the Magdalen ex-gratia scheme are in the ownership of the religious congregations', the State 'does not have the authority to instruct them on their operation'.[69] In actual fact, the government chose not to provide statutory powers of compellability to the IDC, with the result that the IDC returned all records voluntarily disclosed by the nuns to them upon the conclusion of the IDC's work. It is patently false to claim that the State has no way of legally forcing the production of privately held records. The government's *Adoption (Information and Tracing) Bill 2016*, while not passed, proposed vast powers to compel the production of records to the Adoption Authority of Ireland from any 'person who the Minister reasonably believes has, at any time, made or attempted to make arrangements for the adoption of a child'.[70] Statutory inquiries into Church-related abuses have also had legal powers to force production of religious congregations' records.

Amid all of the above, apart from a small number of exceptions (perhaps most notably, the Dublin Diocesan Archives), the religious congregations and dioceses generally have not allowed public access to their private archives. They claim, and the State asserts, that they provide survivors with all personal data upon request.[71] Yet, the experiences of women seeking to prove their duration of detention in a Magdalene Laundry for the ex gratia Scheme show this not always to be the case. Jim's interactions with the Galway Diocesan Archive demonstrate some of the difficulties that academic researchers face. In May 2012, Jim was given permission to access the Bishop Browne Archive. He found material concerning the Galway Magdalene Laundry including financial records, contemporaneous documentation demonstrating the nuns' practice of calling the Gardaí to prevent family members reclaiming women, and evidence of physical abuse and medical neglect. Jim informed the IDC of this archive's contents at the time. In 2013, he requested permission to write about the records. The archivist instructed him that he should submit his academic work, once completed, to the Galway Diocesan Trustees for approval. In May 2014, the archivist wrote again to state that the entire archive was now 'embargoed until such time as it is definitively, absolutely, entirely, totally and objectively established that "personal data" within the *Data Protection Act* no longer arises'. The archivist added: 'permission has not been given by the diocese, or its agents, to you to publish or otherwise reproduce, the material.'[72]

The government has made no concerted attempt to guide all of the controllers of 'historical' abuse information to respect the provisions of the GDPR: including that it establishes a strong right of access to personal data which cannot be restricted on a blanket basis or without legislative authority, that its definition of 'personal data' includes information that relates to more than one person at the same time, and that it authorizes archiving in the public interest. The government's failure to legislate to guarantee access to records of 'historical' abuses for survivors, and to researchers and the general public (while protecting survivors' privacy), has allowed the flourishing of ad hoc legally dubious decision making that can only be described as additional and ongoing abuse.[73]

Maladministration of the ex gratia scheme

Duration of stay/eligibility assessment

Minister Shatter's speech upon publishing the *Quirke Report* gave the impression that the Scheme's single eligibility criterion was enough, in itself, to guarantee a simple and non-adversarial process of assessing survivors' applications.[74] The minister gave no indication of his department's awareness since May 2013 on the basis of over 500 expressions of interest received: 'Records are not easily available and in some cases not available at all. We can therefore expect major problems to arise.'[75]

The DoJ's Restorative Justice Implementation Team sent a letter in late June 2013 to the women who had expressed a preliminary interest, explaining that they should attach to their application '[p]hotocopies of records or other evidence' of their 'residence' in the institutions covered by the scheme. The letter stated: 'If you don't have records or evidence of your residence in one of the relevant institutions you will need to contact the religious order to request a copy of whatever documents they hold in relation to your time in residence with them.' The DoJ did not clarify what its decision-making procedure would be in the inevitable cases where the nuns could not produce supporting evidence, noting merely that if this happened, 'We will then be in touch with you to see how we can best confirm that you resided and worked in the designated institution in question.'[76]

We first raised the alarm in a PR on 28 November 2013 that the department had offered 'compensation payments reflecting much shorter lengths of stay than the women endured' to numerous survivors without clearly explaining why.[77] On 19 February 2014 we wrote in the *Irish Examiner* that we were receiving phone calls from women 'paralysed in the face of confusing paperwork and fretful when asked to contact members of the religious congregations to help resolve disputed claims'.[78]

One of these survivors was known to Jim. 'Joan' (pseudonym) had escaped from a RSM Magdalene Laundry in the early 1950s. In May 2014, Jim asked Maureen O'Sullivan TD to see if she could find out why the department had not yet made a decision on Joan's application submitted in late 2013. The RSM were unable to produce any records for the relevant time period; however, Joan had obtained a record from the HSE demonstrating the date of her placement by a State official. She had also informed the department that a friend would be able to formally confirm her date of escape, and her lengthy oral history transcript served as further evidence of her detention and credibility. On 12 May 2014 Maureen O'Sullivan contacted us to say that the officials had not devised a way of dealing with applications for which the nuns could not provide ledger entries. Our email correspondence demonstrates our frustration and worry, Jim remarking: 'Imagine what it must be like for the other ladies? Where would

[Joan] be without Maureen? This is just disgraceful . . . talk about the tail wagging the dog! It still comes down to the nuns and their records!' Katherine too had been hearing anecdotal reports from survivors: 'I'm finding this – and the other cases I'm coming across very depressing – so many – So very many – of the women are being cut short their monies.'[79]

We wrote to Minister Frances Fitzgerald in September 2014 requesting a meeting to discuss our concern that the department 'may not be implementing fair procedures in determining duration of stay'.[80] We suggested: 'Possible solutions to the current problems may include enabling an applicant to swear an affidavit or inviting an applicant for a meeting. Both of these routes would, naturally, require legal representation.' Our letter highlighted not only the apparent stalemate in cases where the nuns could not produce any records but also the problems facing women who disputed information that the nuns had conveyed. We referred to a July 2014 news article in the London-based *Irish Post*, which reported Phyllis Morgan of the IWSSN saying that 'although most of her forty clients who have received redress so far are "extremely happy" with the speed of the service, most have received less than they think they deserve because the records kept by nuns do not reflect accurately how long they were in a laundry'.[81] Our letter further described to Minister Fitzgerald the experiences of two women who had contacted us after giving up their efforts to demonstrate that the nuns' documentation was incorrect. Both had gone as far as the department's internal review but had decided not to appeal further to the Ombudsman. This was because 'One of the women was in debt and was being pursued by loan sharks daily. The other woman had suffered a stroke, which she believes was brought on by the stress of not being believed, as she saw it, by DoJ officials who preferred without question the religious congregation's version of events.'[82]

JFMR met with Minister Fitzgerald on 20 October 2014, along with officials including Mr Martin and Janet Lacey. Journalist Kathy Sheridan was also present, unexpectedly, profiling the minister for *The Irish Times*.[83] Our notes record that the minister questioned intently at the outset of the meeting whether we represented survivors and how many women we had contact with. Mr Martin disagreed with our argument that the Scheme's procedures seemed unfair. Our notes record:

> James Martin said he had to defend his staff . . . [he] said (repeatedly) that the women were 'confused', that they 'think' they were there for a certain length of time, but when they are presented with 'the facts' they agree they were mistaken . . . [he] said there had to be 'safeguards' in the process – meaning they didn't want someone to come in and just claim they were in the laundry and 'get €50k'.[84]

Minister Fitzgerald told us that the department was about to introduce an interview process for cases where an offer of payment had not yet been made. She emphasized that it was 'not a legal procedure' and that the purpose was 'to give women the opportunity to tell their story'. We asked for a written explanation of the procedure and pressed for a commitment that the department would allow women who had already accepted payments for shorter lengths of time than claimed to attend for interview if they wished.[85] The minister said that this was unlikely to be allowed. She did offer, however, that anyone with 'new evidence' could contact the department and ask for it to be considered. Our meeting notes record: 'Maeve pointed out that testimony was evidence.'[86]

By January 2015, during Dáil debates on the Bill to provide healthcare under the ex gratia scheme, TDs were continuing to highlight the harmful impact that the department's method of assessing 'duration of stay' was having on some survivors.[87] Minister Fitzgerald stated simply in response: 'All that has to be established is that a woman was admitted to and worked in a relevant institution. For this reason, it should be recognised that the scheme represents an appropriate and caring provision by the State to the women in respect of what was inevitably a traumatic experience in their lives.'[88] In the Seanad two months later, Minister Fitzgerald claimed that '[w]e have, obviously, erred totally on the side of believing the women concerned in the first instance.'[89]

Litigation by a number of survivors prompted the Ombudsman in December 2016 to investigate the Scheme's administration, leading to a substantial and scathing report published in November 2017 entitled *Opportunity Lost*. The Ombudsman found that the department had 'maladministered' the Scheme, largely because officials refused to treat survivors' own testimony as having evidentiary value while relying heavily on documents and testimony from the nuns in order to establish the women's duration of stay. As the Ombudsman described it, 'There was an over reliance on the records of the congregations and it is not apparent what weight if any was afforded to the testimony of the women and/or their relatives.'[90]

The Ombudsman found that officials had accorded 'supremacy' to the religious orders' accounts even, remarkably, where the nuns could not produce supporting contemporaneous documentation.[91] His *Report* notes, for example: 'in one case the congregation advised (and without providing a copy of the original register) that while the "*discharge date is not recorded in the register*", they were nevertheless "satisfied" that she was in their care for a certain period of time. The Department made no further enquiries of the congregation as to why they were "satisfied".'[92]

The report gives another example regarding Stanhope Street Training Centre – an institution for which the RSC have been unable to produce any records dating from 17 August 1952 to the institution's closure in 1967.[93] The woman in question explained that she had been detained in Stanhope Street for four years. The Ombudsman found that the 'evidence in support of the applicant, for example, having been taken off the primary school roll and her account (subsequently verified by the congregation) of another girl giving birth in Stanhope Street while she was there was seemingly not given any credence and therefore not followed up.'[94] The explanation for this was an internal departmental memo which 'noted that, as the Religious Sisters of Charity confirmed that the applicant would have completed a two year training course "*we make an offer of a 2 year stay (even in some cases where the applicant has said they were there longer)*"'.[95]

The Ombudsman's report also revealed that for the first year of the Scheme's administration the department left it up to the women to find any records which might displace the nuns' account of their experience. According to the Ombudsman, it was not until September 2014, when prompted by his office, that the department began to search for survivors' primary school records (by which time over 600 decisions had issued). The report notes, for example, that one woman's 'advocate sourced and provided copies of electoral records' after the department issued an offer for three years' stay based on the nuns' account. This resulted in the department offering the woman an extra year's payment. The Ombudsman observes: 'there is nothing to suggest that the possibility of consulting electoral records was previously considered by the Department and there is nothing to suggest that earlier applications were revisited in light of this possible new source of evidence.'[96] A major criticism by the Ombudsman was that the department failed to put in place any mechanism to consider the women's own testimony or that of their family members or friends until late 2014, by which time it had decided upon most applications.[97]

Following the Ombudsman's report the next minister for justice, Charlie Flanagan, appointed a Senior Counsel in April 2018 to review all cases where the department had made or offered a payment reflecting less time than a woman claimed for.[98] By June 2020 Mary O'Toole SC was still investigating 48 of the 215 cases identified, and she had recommended that the department pay an additional amount to 104 women.[99] The department's website states that twenty-three women 'withdrew from the process'; it is unclear whether some or all of these women died. We have continued to recommend to the DoJ that survivors should be enabled to swear an affidavit and that a presumption in favour of accepting the women's sworn testimony should apply with a view to speeding up the process.[100] Given the refusal of the State and religious orders to open their administrative archives, we argue, survivors should be spared the anxiety and powerlessness imposed by the department's insistence on endlessly searching for and attempting to piece together documentary records that may be incomplete or inaccurate.

Most startling is the acknowledgement by Ms O'Toole that some records produced by the religious congregations are false. In September 2019, she found in the case of 'Caitríona', whom JFMR had been assisting along with Caitríona's friend and three solicitors acting pro bono at different times since 2013, that both a ledger entry produced by the nuns and a primary school record produced by a Parish Priest were inaccurate. Ms O'Toole accepted that Caitríona had (as she had stated consistently and in numerous contexts over two decades) been detained from the age of eleven for seven years following repeated rape by a family member, rather than from the age of fifteen for two years as the nuns claimed. Factors relevant to Ms O'Toole's decision included the detail and consistency of Caitríona's account, the testimony of Caitríona's former classmates, the existence of non-contemporaneous markings in both the Magdalene and primary school records, a period of two years in which the documents produced by the State and Church placed Caitríona nowhere, and written correspondence from some of the congregation. Ms O'Toole's twenty-four-page decision, responding to JFMR's 254 pages of written submissions and exhibits, concluded that Caitríona's account was consistent with the approach of church authorities to child sexual abuse during the 1950s. She stated:

> It is known that during that era the view was taken that a child who had been sexually abused posed a risk to other children and was potentially a corrupting

> influence. . . . McAleese recounts that this became a phenomenon in industrial schools, where a number of young girls were sexually abused by a male member of staff there. When this came to light, the children concerned were removed. . . . It appears that the Good Shepherd Order were willing to take such children.

Ms O'Toole's decision continued:

> It may have been considered that it was necessary to continue the fiction that Ms — was in school because she was of school age but could not be permitted to stay in school in the company of other children . . . it is conceivable that it was regarded as charitable in all the circumstances to continue the fiction of Ms — being in school for the sake of her family.

Strikingly, Ms O'Toole's decision revealed: 'There is another case in the Review where similar circumstances arise in respect of the written records of an applicant who was the victim of sexual abuse.'[101]

High Court action

Between 2015 and 2017, High Court judicial review proceedings brought to light the DoJ's additional practice of refusing to allow survivors to see or comment on information from the nuns, upon which officials were relying to reject the women's applications to the Scheme. The women who decided to litigate had been forced to work as children in Magdalene Laundries while registered on the rolls of adjacent 'educational' institutions also operated by the nuns. Both the department and the religious congregations accepted that these girls had worked in the laundries; however, the nuns asserted that the institutions in which the girls were registered were 'separate'. The department rejected the women's applications on the ground that the Scheme was for women who both were 'admitted to and worked in' the laundries and the nuns had not 'admitted' them.

In May 2014 JFMR started receiving communications from women who had been forced to work as children in the OLC Magdalene Laundry at High Park while registered at An Grianán Training Centre for teenage girls, located in the same building. Some had already written to the Ombudsman to appeal the department's rejection of their applications. Several of the women said that they received no schooling and were forced to work all day, every day in the laundry. Others had received lessons in the mornings before being sent through a door into the laundry each afternoon. One woman recalled sharing a cubicle with another teenager in the large dormitory where older women in the Magdalene Laundry also slept.

The department's rejection letters asserted that, according to the OLC Sisters, An Grianán 'was recognised as a separate and specific institution in itself' and was covered under the RIRB.[102] The women's refutations fell on deaf ears. They argued that, clearly, the institutions were not in fact separate despite the nuns' characterization of them. Due to a lack of information, not all survivors had applied to the previous RIRB within

Plates

Figure 1 Corpus Christi religious procession leaving Sean McDermott Street Magdalene in the mid-1960s.

Figure 2 Representatives of the Sisters of Our Lady of Charity of Refuge and Fr Tony Coote at the reburial of the cremated remains of the women exhumed from High Park, 11 September 1993.

Figure 3 Mari Steed, Claire McGettrick, Katherine O'Donnell and Maeve O'Rourke, press conference on the release of the *IDC Report*, 5 February 2013.

Figure 4 The vigil outside the Dáil on 19 February 2013.

Figure 5 Dublin Honours Magdalenes event, 5 June 2018.

Figure 6 Mari Steed, Maeve O'Rourke, Jim Smith and Katherine O'Donnell outside the Mansion House at Dublin Honours Magdalenes event, 5 June 2018.

Figure 7 Margaret Joyce and Pauline Goggin at the Garden Party at Áras an Úachtaráin as part of the Dublin Honours Magdalenes event, 5 June 2018.

the requisite timeframe. Additionally, they made the point that the RIRB had not provided any payments for forced labour but rather was concerned with other forms of abuse (this is borne out by the RIRB's assessment matrix and the lack of any reference in the *CICA Final Report* to the transfer of children on a daily basis to Magdalene Laundries).[103] The women highlighted that Judge Quirke specifically stated in his eleventh recommendation that the Magdalene Scheme should not take into account any RIRB payments. They further argued that girls forced to work in Magdalene Laundries were doubly victimized because they had been denied their right to education at the same time. The Ombudsman's decision-maker affirmed the department's approach, however, finding that although the State and nuns agreed that girls registered in An Grianán had worked in the Magdalene Laundry, OLC's characterization of An Grianán demonstrated that it was not one of the twelve specified in the terms of the ex gratia scheme.[104]

On 12 May 2014, Maeve travelled from Durham to Dublin to meet with some of the women in this position who had contacted us. The following day Jim emailed Maureen O'Sullivan asking her to raise the issue with Minister Fitzgerald and suggesting a list of PQs.[105] This led to more women contacting Deputy O'Sullivan, and Mary Lou McDonald among others, and they continued to advocate on individual women's behalf through correspondence with the minister. Maeve started to collect the women's information, calling them and visiting to gather documentation and create summaries of the legal issues arising. Soon afterwards, she struck up a relationship with Gareth Noble, Partner at KOD Lyons human rights solicitors, and his colleague and solicitor Wendy Lyon. Both were willing to help the women pro bono.

Over the next year, Gareth, Wendy, Susie Kiely (also at KOD Lyons) and Maeve worked with Colin Smith BL and Michael Lynn SC to gather and prepare statements, and to assist women in making fresh applications with robust legal arguments to the department and the Ombudsman. More women, including those registered in children's educational institutions other than An Grianán but similarly forced to work in an adjacent or adjoining Magdalene Laundry, and those with other problems concerning the scheme, came to KOD Lyons's and JFMR's attention.[106] On 4 June 2015, Conall Ó Fátharta wrote in the *Irish Examiner* that the DoJ had been in possession since 2012 of a HSE memorandum written for the IDC which explained that historical records gathered by HSE personnel showed 'quite categorically' that An Grianán and St Mary's (the laundry) were 'one and the same thing'.[107] We issued a statement calling for the An Grianán survivors to be included immediately in the scheme; in response, the department simply reiterated that An Grianán 'served a different purpose' to the Magdalene Laundry.[108]

KOD Lyons filed several judicial review applications against the Ombudsman in late 2015, and lodged two actions against the minister for justice, in September 2015 and January 2016 respectively.[109] At least one other solicitor brought an application for judicial review on behalf of a woman similarly rejected from the scheme due to the nuns' listing of her in a children's educational institution while forcing her to work in a Magdalene Laundry. The Ombudsman settled the judicial review proceedings against him in the spring of 2016 by agreeing to take the decisions afresh. However, no change to the position of either the Ombudsman or the minister and her department was apparent by the time the two cases against the minister came before Mr Justice White in the Four Courts in January 2017.[110]

Opening the trial on 25 January 2017, Michael Lynn argued that the department had interpreted the phrase 'admitted to and worked in', contained in the Terms of the Scheme, irrationally by incorporating a requirement of total residence in the Magdalene Laundry. He and Colin Smith contended that, surely, the nuns had 'admitted' the girls according to the plain meaning of the word: permitting them to enter the laundry each day. (As one of the women supporting her friends in the back bench quipped to Maeve and Donnchadh Ó Laoghaire TD and his adviser Stephen Todd, who attended the proceedings, 'we didn't break the windows to get in.') The women's lawyers further argued that the department had breached its obligations of natural and constitutional justice and fair procedures by relying on information from the religious orders which was not in the public domain and which the department had not disclosed to the two women for comment prior to making a decision on their application, despite their express requests. Not only had the department kept general information about the institutions' administration from the women, but officials had also withheld *personal* documentation concerning them, disclosing it only as part of its affidavits in advance of the court hearing. Finally, the women's lawyers contended that it was irrelevant that An Grianán was a listed institution for the purposes of the RIRB; one of the women had not applied to the RIRB but, regardless, the applications to the Magdalene ex gratia scheme were concerned with the women's experiences in two laundries rather than the educational institutions which they were listed as attending.

The minister's first defence was that the survivors' application to court was premature because they should have appealed to the Ombudsman, as other women had. Making this argument on the first day of trial David Hardiman SC read from an affidavit by DoJ civil servant Janet Lacey, in which she gave sworn testimony that the minister considered herself bound by the Ombudsman's recommendations. Sitting at the back of the courtroom, however, was a legal adviser to the Ombudsman undertaking a 'watching brief' to keep her office informed of proceedings. That evening she emailed the Chief State Solicitor's Office to say that 'as one practising solicitor to another' she was 'uncomfortable with' a number of the officials' sworn statements read out earlier in the day.[111] The Ombudsman's legal adviser continued by explaining that, as the department was well aware, the Ombudsman had commenced a formal investigation into the Scheme's administration – which was at that very moment ongoing – because the DoJ had been refusing for many months to comply with the Ombudsman's decisions on several survivors' cases.[112]

The High Court hearing was thus brought to an abrupt pause, and only re-commenced on 21 February 2017. Having been caught misleading the court, and having caused further delay and stress for the women concerned, the minister dropped her first defence but no apology was offered, and the minister did not concede the case. The department now acknowledged that, since April 2016, it had been in an ongoing dispute with the Ombudsman over his recommendation that several women forced to work in Magdalene Laundries while registered in An Grianán and other adjacent educational institutions be included in the scheme.[113] Jimmy Martin's February 2017 High Court affidavit included copies of correspondence with Tom

Morgan in the Office of the Ombudsman over several months in 2016 regarding An Grianán.[114] This correspondence reveals two key lines of argument used by the DoJ to deny forced labour and other constitutional or human rights abuses in the Magdalene Laundries.

The DoJ's first method of argument was to ignore the survivors entirely, focusing instead on what it termed the 'status' of the An Grianán institution. Aptly, Conrad Bryan of the Association of Mixed Race Irish has observed that in order to limit its exposure to liability for 'historical' abuses in Ireland, 'tragically, the State investigates buildings rather than people and their experiences of human rights violations'.[115] Mr Martin argued that 'post 1971, it is clear that An Grianan Training Centre was completely separate to St Mary's Refuge. It had a separate legal status and served a different purpose to St Mary's Refuge.' (In fact, the State never assigned a legal status or purpose to either institution, failing to regulate their operations despite the 1970 *Kennedy Report*'s warnings.[116]) Mr Martin pointed to documentation from the nuns – which Mr Morgan had to request to see since it was not on the women's case files – stating that An Grianán had its 'own entrance' and that 'facilities such as dormitories, recreation, bathrooms and dining were also separate to that of the Refuge'. Mr Martin also referred to An Grianán's registration as a remand institution in 1972 under Part V of the *Children Act* 1908; Mr Morgan noted in response that the 'Order certifying it as a remand centre certifies it for four girls but there were fifteen girls there at any one time'.

The DoJ's second strategy was to deny that the known treatment of girls and women in Magdalene Laundries met any legal definition of abuse. Mr Morgan, in the women's favour, asserted that whatever the nuns said about the status of An Grianán it was the Ombudsman's view 'that any individual who underwent forced labour at the behest of the State without pay should be entitled to redress under the Scheme'. Mr Martin responded: 'It is clear that our interpretation of the purpose of the scheme does differ from that of the Ombudsman.... The purpose of the Magdalen Scheme introduced was never intended to provide redress to persons for "loss of liberty" and "forced labour" "at the behest of the State"'. Mr Martin argued that 'the facts' found by the IDC 'did not support the popular media accounts of Magdalen laundries' and that 'the evidence suggests such women were free to leave if they wished'. He added: 'There has been no court ruling that the State has any liability for women who entered such institutions, nor have we ever seen any legal advice or factual evidence that would give rise to the belief that the State has any legal liability. We are also not aware of any successful legal action taken against the religious orders concerned.'[117]

Learning in February 2017 of the vehemence of the DoJ's position caused further anxiety and upset to the women who were litigating and others in a similar position, several of whom came to court each day of the hearing. Politicians took up their cause in the Dáil, but Mr Martin's rejection of the Ombudsman's recommendations and denial of State liability for the Magdalene Laundries had Minister Fitzgerald's imprimatur.[118]

Mr Justice White issued his decision in June 2017. He found in the women's favour, adjudicating that the minister had violated the women's 'right to natural and constitutional justice and fair procedures' by not handing over all material received from the nuns. The judge ordered the minister to reconsider the women's applications 'in the context of the other matters which are under review between the respondent and the Ombudsman's office'.[119] The published judgment criticizes the DoJ for providing 'incorrect' information in sworn evidence, while not using the term 'perjury'.[120]

The Ombudsman's November 2017 report, *Opportunity Lost*, recommended that the DoJ include in the Scheme every woman who 'worked in one of the listed laundries but was officially recorded as having been "admitted to" a training centre or industrial school located in the same building, attached to or located on the grounds of one of the laundries'.[121] This was still not the end of the matter. Minister Charlie Flanagan responded to the Ombudsman's recommendation in November and December 2017 in an equivocal manner.[122] The Joint Oireachtas Committee on Justice and Equality then invited both the Ombudsman and Jimmy Martin to appear before it on 31 January 2018. Pressed by Donnchadh Ó Laoghaire to clarify whether the department accepted any State liability for the Magdalene Laundries abuse, Mr Martin explained: 'The State does not admit liability, but it is not necessarily denying it either as that is a matter for the Attorney General and the Government to decide.' The Ombudsman, Peter Tyndall, was clearly emotional as he told the committee that in his ten years in the role, four in Ireland and six elsewhere, 'I have never reached the point where a Department has, prior to the publication of a report, absolutely and categorically refused to engage with the process around accepting and implementing the recommendations.' He explained:

> We are talking about women who went down the same stairs every day with women who accessed the scheme and in some instances slept in the next room to women who had access to the scheme. They worked in the laundries that are part of the scheme. We have been clear from the outset that we were not seeking to extend the institutions covered by the scheme but we were saying the criteria being used to determine whether the women concerned were admitted to and worked in those laundries were being interpreted too narrowly.[123]

Eventually, in mid-April 2018 after many more public advocacy efforts by the women and on our part with the support of Colin Smith BL and Lewis Mooney BL, and following significant interventions by senior opposition politicians Jim O'Callaghan and Mary Lou McDonald among others, Taoiseach Leo Varadkar announced that he and Minister Flanagan had met with the Ombudsman 'to resolve the matter'.[124] Another half year then went by as DoJ officials refused to back down from their original argument that including women registered by the nuns in what they alleged to be 'separate' institutions would require Cabinet to change the Terms of the Scheme.[125] In November 2018 the government published an 'Addendum to the Terms of the Magdalen Restorative Justice *Ex Gratia* Scheme', extending the Scheme to a further fourteen institutions and applying new calculations to women falling under this extension: they would receive distinct amounts for '(a) the length of time the applicant resided in the adjoining institution and (b) the length of time she worked in the laundry of the Magdalen institution'.[126] Further political advocacy was needed to counteract continuing procedural unfairness even after this point: the DoJ's 'Addendum' stated that payments would be calculated 'on the basis that no child under twelve years of age worked in a Magdalen Laundry, unless an applicant provides evidence of such work before they reached the age of twelve years'; the department's application for women falling under the 'Addendum' required them to specify the number of weekly hours worked without explaining why; and by April 2019 the department still had not made an offer of payment to women registered in An Grianán after 1980, stating (without showing the relevant evidence to the women for comment) that the nuns had confirmed that no girls worked in the Magdalene Laundry at High Park after 1980.[127]

Denial of personal support and care services

Decision-making assistance

The Ombudsman found the DoJ guilty of maladministering the Scheme for an additional reason: officials had deemed dozens of survivors whose applications were made by people close to them to lack capacity, and then failed to ensure that the women received the necessary decision-making assistance to accept and benefit from the Scheme. The Ombudsman concluded that placing women in this legal limbo was 'inexcusable' and 'the result of negligence and carelessness, improperly discriminatory and otherwise contrary to fair or sound administration'.[128] According to the Ombudsman's report, the department treated approximately forty women this way from 2013. Eighteen women remained in this situation in November 2017.[129]

A number of these women were still institutionalized, living under the auspices of the religious congregations.[130] Senator Jillian Van Turnhout spoke to their experience in March 2015 when she told the Seanad of

> two separate cases of women . . . who, because our capacity legislation is not in place, cannot sign to get the amount of money of which they are so deserving. . . . These women are in a nursing home and are paying out of their own money for mattress protectors and walkers, products that should be provided by the HSE. . . . These are women who do not have that money, who have been institutionalised for thirty to forty years and who do not necessarily have an extended family because they have been institutionalised by the State.[131]

Minister Fitzgerald acknowledged in February 2017 that seventeen women deemed to lack capacity had qualified for the maximum payment under the Scheme and that eight had died since their application was made. In accordance with Judge Quirke's recommendations, half of these women's payments would now accrue to their estates, the other half remaining with the State.[132] In April 2019 at the Oireachtas Public Accounts Committee, the department's secretary general acknowledged in response to Catherine Connolly TD's questioning of a budget surplus regarding the ex gratia Scheme: 'The *saving* is due mainly to a delay that occurred in commencing the Assisted Decision-Making (Capacity) Act 2015. Those payments could not be made in a number of cases.'[133]

Judge Quirke's *Report* stated that no Magdalene survivor should be made a Ward of Court under the *Lunacy Regulation (Ireland) Act 1871* for the purpose of applying to the Scheme. He referred to his own Law Reform Commission's 2006 report recommending the abolition of the wardship system due to its 'paternalistic' nature and the failure of its procedures to respect and protect constitutional and human rights.[134] However, wardship under the 1871 *Act* still remains the law regulating legal capacity in Ireland. The archaic procedure strips a person of all legal autonomy as the High Court takes on the responsibility of making decisions about the person's life based on their 'best interests'. The *Quirke Report* noted that the government planned in 2013 to publish draft legislation proposing the replacement of the wardship system. However, Judge Quirke did not recommend waiting for the *Assisted Decision-Making (Capacity) Bill* to come into force. His view of the likely delays in enacting the legislation was shared by the officials writing in the *IDG Report* in September 2013. They noted: 'it is a large Bill . . . and it is not clear that it will be enacted and commenced within a time frame that would facilitate its use in the implementation of the Quirke Scheme.'[135] Instead, Judge Quirke recommended an amendment to the *Nursing Homes Support Scheme Act 2009* (NHSS), which regulates the 'Fair Deal' system of joint self- and State funding of nursing home care. Under the 2009 *Act*, the Circuit Court has the power to appoint a person's relative, friend, legal representative or health or social care practitioner as their 'care representative' for the purpose of applying to the Fair Deal scheme. Judge Quirke proposed that the 'care representative' provisions should be extended to enable applications to the ex gratia scheme, as an extraordinary measure.

On 24 June 2014, Minister Fitzgerald announced that she had obtained Cabinet approval for the publication of draft legislation to provide for healthcare under the scheme and a system of appointing personal representatives to apply on behalf of women deemed to lack sufficient decision-making capacity.[136] The department duly published its *General Scheme of the Redress for Women Who Were in Certain Institutions Bill* on 8 August 2014.[137] Rather than following Judge Quirke's recommendation precisely, the General Scheme of Bill proposed a bespoke procedure modelled on a combination of the *NHSS Act 2009* and the provisions of the *Assisted Decision Making (Capacity) Bill 2013*.

Inexplicably, however, at the next legislative stage when the government published the *RWRCI Act* proper in December 2014, the provision for decision-making assistance had been deleted.[138] We issued a briefing note to politicians and held a press conference with the NWCI, the ICCL and AII – also in reaction to the healthcare provisions in the Bill.[139] Introducing the Bill to the Dáil on 28 January 2015, Minister Fitzgerald was adamant that there was no problem. The minister revealed that the department had decided that Magdalene survivors should wait for the *Assisted Decision Making (Capacity) Bill 2013* to come into operation, rather than benefiting from bespoke legislation.[140] Having received several PQs in response to our briefing note and press conference, the minister stated publicly on the Dáil floor that our advocacy was misguided:

> There has been some comment suggesting that no provision is being made for women entitled to these supports who do not have the capacity to make the necessary applications or arrangements. This is simply incorrect. . . . I do understand the role of advocacy groups. I have met those working with the women who were resident in the Magdalen laundries and I want to recognise their work.

> I have laid out clearly today, however, how in fact the Government is meeting Mr Justice Quirke's recommendations in full. I hope this is now clear and that no further misunderstandings will be created on this important issue for the women concerned.[141]

TDs and senators from all parties and none voiced their concern during Dáil and Seanad debates in January and February 2015, but their declarations came to nought.

The *Assisted Decision Making (Capacity) Act 2015* still is not operational at the time of writing as the government has not yet 'commenced' most sections of the legislation. Journalist Kitty Holland reported in January 2020 that this is primarily because the DoJ has failed to provide sufficient funding for the new national Decision Support Service required under the act. The Mental Health Commission, whose responsibility it is to establish the Decision Support Service, had received only one-third of the funding sought from the DoJ in 2018 and 2019. By early 2020, this Commission's view was that 'the repeated failure to open the service puts Ireland in breach of international human rights obligations, raises safeguarding issues and denies thousands of vulnerable adults a say in basic aspects of their lives'.[142]

Numerous survivors have now been made Wards of Court, contrary to Judge Quirke's explicit recommendation. The Ombudsman concluded in November 2017 that it was 'with the greatest reluctance that I must accept that the Department's current proposal (to request that the women who lack capacity be made Wards of Court) is at this stage the most realistic option . . . despite the informed comments of Mr. Justice Quirke in May 2013 about the unsuitability of the Wards of Court system'.[143] A solicitor has alerted us that in at least one case of a survivor living in a nursing home under the custody of the same nuns who detained her in a Magdalene Laundry, the nuns' solicitors applied for the woman to be made a Ward of Court and were appointed as the survivor's decision-making committee – despite the survivor having living relatives who were not notified.[144]

Independent advocates

Bearing in mind the extreme vulnerability which the absence of an assisted decision-making service caused, we called repeatedly for the DoJ to offer independent personal advocacy assistance to every survivor whom it had deemed to lack capacity. The past two decades have seen a growing movement in Ireland demanding statutory rights to independent advocacy where and when people depend on others for personal assistance or care.[145] The Law Reform Commission recognizes the evidence that, in addition to helping people to understand and act on the choices of daily living, '[i]ndependent advocates can act as a safety net for at risk adults in relation to capacity assessments; advocates could challenge a process if they believed that decisions were made that an individual could have made themselves'.[146]

A significant number of the women 'deemed' by the DoJ to lack capacity were and still are living in the custody of the religious congregations.[147] These women, we believed, were particularly in need of independent representation regarding any wardship proceedings, including the proposal of individuals to serve as the woman's decision-making committee. In fact, our personal contacts with survivors led us to the view that *every* survivor still living in institutions run by nuns should have access to independent advocacy services.[148]

An oral history interview that Claire conducted with 'Sara W.' in March 2012 encapsulates some of the many reasons for our concern about the independence and well-being of women still living in religious-run institutions. Sara had been detained in Magdalene Laundries in both Donnybrook and Peacock Lane between 1954 and 1958, from the age of fifteen. She described to Claire her experience of continuing to visit some of the women who had never left the nuns' custody, explaining: 'now, "Mairéad" works down in the refectory and . . . she cleans all that place and she gets €30 a week now, that's what she gets, and her keep I suppose. . . . She's sixty-four now. . . . She's working every day, seven days a week.'[149]

'Bridget Flynn', who provided weekly services for over a decade from the mid-1990s to a group of women still in the nuns' care, also spoke to the MOHP. She recalled the disempowerment caused by a lifetime's institutionalization:

> There was a fear, most definitely a fear that the right thing be said or done and you know, not to rock the boat anyway, you know. . . . I often remarked to myself that there would never be the newspaper there or, yeah, reading and writing were a problem. Some of them were going to lessons and all of that in later life anyway . . . so they were trying to learn to read and write, but that would have been in their late fifties and a very small number.

Bridget claimed that 'certainly there would have been happenings to me as an outsider going in that I would perceive as being absolutely wrong in happening and this would have been in relatively recent years'. Regarding the women's choice of home, she said: 'there was no real consultation on major moves that I was aware of, you know, or if some of them had reached the stage, and perhaps I'm sure it does happen right across society, that they had to move to a different location because of illness or whatever, you know, it just happened, you know.'

When asked whether she would recommend any particular measures for these women as part of the ex gratia scheme since she was still in contact with several survivors now in a nursing home owned by the nuns, Bridget responded: 'Is each of those women going to have an outside advocate . . .? I think they should. Somebody from the outside, not within the system at the minute, I mean not from within the convent . . . I'd be very definite about that, that they would need an advocate from outside to put their case forward.'[150]

In October 2013 Claire made a confidential report to both the HSE regional older adult social work team and Minister of State Kathleen Lynch about the seemingly forced re-institutionalization of 'Patty', who was a close friend of a survivor whom we knew well, 'Maisie K.'. Patty and Maisie were incarcerated together as young teenagers in the late 1940s. Patty never left the Magdalene Laundry – unlike Maisie, who managed to escape. Born in a Mother and Baby Home, Patty had been transferred to the Magdalene following abuse by her foster family. The nuns in the Magdalene Laundry told her that her mother was dead. However, in the summer of 2013, through the efforts of a voluntary day service for older people that wanted to help trace Patty's family, she discovered that her mother in fact lived until 2001. Her mother, in turn, went to her grave believing what *she* had been told by the nuns in the Mother and Baby Home after giving birth: that Patty died as a baby.

Maisie contacted JFMR in September 2013 to say that Patty had recently been put into a nursing home by a nun formerly of the Magdalene Laundry, following the death of another, kinder, nun who had looked out for Patty in later life and arranged for her to live in a 'sheltered' apartment. In a subsequent letter to Jim, Maisie recalled what led her to contact JFMR:

> Sr B died . . . six months later enter Sister D in charge of her, announcing to the staff in care of the elderly: 'I am in charge of Patty now and am next of kin.' She took over. First she took Patty's money from her including the pension book. She stopped her going to town. She claimed Patty's money was being mishandled and that Patty was not taking her tablets right etc.[151]

In September 2013 Maisie explained to Claire that the previous month Patty had gone from her apartment into hospital for two weeks due to a flare-up of her diabetes. Claire's complaint to the HSE and Minister Lynch noted: 'Sr D arranged for Patty to go to a nursing home after her release from hospital. Maisie says that Patty did not wish to go to a nursing home but seemed unable to articulate this in front of Sr D.' In her letter to Jim, Maisie recalled:

> I went to see Patty one day in the hospital and she told me that D got her to sign a form to say she agreed to go into St — 's Nursing Home. I asked her, 'How do you feel about it Patty?' She said after a while 'Maisie, I don't want to be locked up in a nursing home for the rest of my life.'

Maisie insisted that Patty's re-institutionalization was both unnecessary and harmful. In her oral history interview in 2016, Maisie explained:

> I have no objection to Patty having to go into a nursing home if her health was gone, but it wasn't then when she was put in. . . . She was well able to look after herself, from what I saw anyway, because any time I went in, she'd make the tea . . . and she'd tell me all about sport and what she saw on the television, such and such won such a match. . . . As much as they'd like to produce that she was, she was not stupid.
>
> . . . She used to get up and go into the neighbours in the flats. She'd go into the other place where they had had the daily cups of tea and the jazz and she'd sing songs, and all that kind of thing. But . . . by putting her into the nursing home, it was putting her back into institutionalisation where she would be never again able to take down a coat, put it on her, walk out of her own free will to the door to visit a neighbour. . . . That's what brought it, and that's what she remembered with the Magdalene. She couldn't do it. That was gone back to the old days.[152]

Claire never received a reply to her complaint from either the HSE or the Minister of State. With the help of her mother's friends, Patty was made a Ward of Court before her death. In April 2018 Maisie wrote to Jim, telling him:

> My little friend I told you about, Patty, passed away in the nursing home last month. . . . But we ourselves buried Patty with dignity and respect. Good people, friends of Patty's mother (RIP) gave the nun no choice in that in any way. She was not nice about it. One thing I did Jim with few close friends is we went over that nun's head, and got Patty buried with her mother. Social workers found her mother's grave in — and the priest there agreed to let it be done.

In February 2015, we pressed for an amendment to the *RWRCI Act* to require the provision of personal advocacy services under the ex gratia Scheme to women deemed to lack capacity and all women still living in the care or custody of the nuns.[153] Opposition TDs and senators tabled several permutations of such an amendment at four stages during the course of the Dáil and Seanad debates on the Bill, to no avail.[154] Repeatedly, when TDs raised the question of independent advocacy for women deemed to lack capacity, Minister Fitzgerald conflated it with the need for a legislative framework for assisted decision making - without acknowledging that the continuing *absence* of such a framework made advocacy all the more urgent and important.[155]

In response to further questioning from TDs and senators in March 2015, Minister Fitzgerald suggested that those calling for independent advocacy (spurred on by JFMR) misunderstood its role: 'It is important to note that a personal advocate has very limited powers with regard to a person who lacks capacity. A personal advocate does not have power of attorney, to make a decision or otherwise to manage the affairs of the person.'[156] The minister's reference to advocates' 'limited powers' is striking because the government has for a decade and a half refused to commence the part of the *Citizens Information Act 2007* which legislated for a national advocacy service and gave statutory powers to professional independent advocates.[157] The government's failure to commence these enacted legislative provisions, as with the failure to commence most of the *Assisted Decision-Making (Capacity) Act 2015*, is a spectacular undermining of the democratic process at the expense of our society's least powerful.

Healthcare

A 'fundamental element of the Scheme', according to Judge Quirke, was his very first recommendation concerning health and social care, which responded to survivors' 'principal' concerns expressed during the consultation in early 2013.[158] Judge Quirke recommended that 'Magdalen women should have access to the full range of services currently enjoyed by holders of the *Health (Amendment) Act 1996* Card ("the HAA card")'. The text of this recommendation specifies that '[d]etails of the range, extent and diversity of the community services to be provided to the women are described within Appendix G'.[159] Appendix G of Judge Quirke's *Report* explains that it is largely a reproduction of the information guide provided to current holders of the HAA card – who are, as explained earlier, those infected by the State with Hepatitis C in the 1990s.

The services set out in Appendix G include

- access to a Liaison Officer who arranges and pays for all services, either in advance or upon the production of receipts;
- chiropody and podiatry services, provided by any qualified professional as frequently as needed without any requirement to obtain prior approval or a doctor's referral;
- complementary therapies such as massage, reflexology, acupuncture, aromatherapy, hydrotherapy, chiropractic services and osteopathy, provided by a registered medical practitioner such as a GP, registered nurse or physiotherapist, following an initial doctor's referral;
- counselling, psychological and psychotherapy services, for cardholders and their immediate relatives provided by an accredited professional, without any requirement to obtain prior approval or a doctor's referral;
- all necessary dental services, provided either by dentists participating in the State's Dental Treatment Services Scheme or by another dentist with prior approval;
- hearing tests and aids, without limitation;
- ophthalmic services, without any requirement to obtain prior approval or a doctor's referral;
- a specialist home nursing service, involving a clinical nurse-led home care plan that is 'individualised, client focused, flexible and easily accessible . . . which meets the assessed needs at any given time of each client and which is reviewed on a regular basis to reflect changing needs', the aim being 'to provide and support client focused care in the community to enable the individual to be cared for at home and to reduce unnecessary admissions to hospital';
- a home support service to assist with household chores, either provided by the State or through direct employment by the cardholder which is reimbursed;
- all necessary aids and appliances as prescribed by a GP, Consultant, Occupational Therapist or Public Health Nurse (e.g. walking sticks and frames, wheelchairs, grab rails, shower seats, and bath and bed hoists);
- physiotherapy services, provided by any chartered professional, following a doctor's referral;
- GP services from any licenced professional without limitation;
- no charge for any prescription by a GP; and
- referrals to a consultant doctor by a GP to be facilitated within two weeks.

As the first anniversary of Enda Kenny's apology approached, Maeve and Jim published an opinion piece in *The Irish Times* criticizing the government's failure to table legislation providing for Judge Quirke's recommended health and social care.[160] They noted that the December 2013 Terms of the Scheme described in only one sentence the healthcare that would in future be available and contained no mention of any access to private service providers or care for women living abroad.[161]

Minister Shatter issued a forceful riposte in a letter to the editor of *The Irish Times* a week later, 'to set the record straight'.[162] He denied that there was any 'opaqueness' to the Scheme, arguing: 'There is a team of nine people in my department whose sole task is to help the women with their applications and answer their queries. This includes, I should add, reassuring women who telephoned subsequent to the February 6th piece, unnecessarily worried, having read it, that they would not receive money due to them under the scheme.' He defended the decision to require survivors to sign a waiver before knowing exactly what health and social care services they would receive, stating: 'The authors of the Opinion piece seem also to suggest that it is unfair that each woman has to sign a waiver before acceptance into the Scheme but do not mention that it was Judge Quirke himself who recommended that such waiver should form part of the scheme.' The minister concluded by characterizing the forthcoming healthcare as something over which his department ultimately had no control:

> With regard to the provision of medical services, Judge Quirke does not state that the women should receive private health care. He recommended they should have access to the same range of services as enjoyed by holders of the Health (Amendment) Act 1996 card. The necessary legislation is included on the priority list of the Government Legislation Programme for the spring/summer 2014. Details of exactly what services will be provided, and where and how they will be provided is being determined by the Department of Health.

The Redress for Women Resident in Certain Institutions (RWRCI) Bill gave no cause for comfort when published on 12 December 2014.[163] The Bill set out a list of services that would be available without charge to Magdalene survivors under the Scheme and stated in relation to most of them that they would be of the nature 'specified' in the *Health Act 1970* – the legislation that creates the public medical card, thereby relegating the women's entitlements to that level.

The RWRCI Bill further stated that the drugs, medicines and medical and surgical appliances available to the women would be those provided to public medical card holders under the 'Reimbursement List' stemming from the *Health (Pricing and Supply of Medical Goods) Act 2013* and section 59 of the *Health Act 1970*. A counselling service, meanwhile, would be available to the women following a referral by a registered medical practitioner, but not to their immediate family members. The Bill made no mention of complementary therapies or of aids and appliances.

We knew and accepted that the previous legislation establishing the HAA card in 1996 did not list every *single* service, or the extent of each service, that was thereafter made available to cardholders. The 1996 *Health (Amendment) Act* instead provided the minister for health with discretion to 'prescribe' any further services that should be available and any further classes of person to whom they should apply. Crucially, however, the RWRCI Bill for Magdalene survivors contained no such discretion, meaning that the services set out in writing in the draft legislation were the full extent of what the women would receive. Another key difference on the face of the two pieces of legislation was that the 1996 *Health Amendment Act* did not attach the 1970 *Health Act*'s 'specification' to services to the same extent as the RWRCI Bill. Given our faltering trust in the government's respect for Magdalene survivors' rights and the DoJ's insistence that it had no control over DoH policy, JFMR did not see how the RWRCI Bill would ensure the delivery of services equivalent to the HAA card – even were we to disregard the indications in the Bill's text that it would *not*.

'Unacceptable, unfair and full of broken promises to survivors' was how we characterized the RWRCI Bill in our press conference on 19 January 2015.[164] We contended that 'the Bill promises little more than the regular medical card, which most of the women already have'. This assessment was borne out by a phone call which Claire received on 23 December 2014 from 'Kathleen R', now deceased. Claire knew Kathleen well. Kathleen's family were Travellers, and she had been detained in an Industrial School for most of her childhood and was confined in three different Magdalene Laundries from the age of sixteen until her early twenties.[165] Kathleen's spirit was strong; she rebelled against her confinement to the extent that the nuns transferred her multiple times before eventually throwing her out, forcing her to walk for miles to safety in three inches of snow. Just before Christmas, Kathleen had opened a letter from the DoJ explaining the healthcare arrangements under the Scheme. She told Claire that many survivors were very upset about the healthcare card and that some had returned their letters in anger. Claire recorded in an email to JFMR: 'as Kathleen said herself, survivors aren't stupid, they can read the letters and they know that what's there can already be obtained via the regular medical card.'[166]

The debate on the RWRCI Bill was fraught.[167] On 25 January 2015, Sarah Clancy and Mark Conroy from the contact.ie website launched an email campaign on behalf of the women, imploring the government to provide the full extent of the healthcare recommended by Judge Quirke. Members of the public sent over 400 emails to TDs.[168] Numerous TDs and senators proposed amendments to replace subsections of the RWRCI Bill with wording from the *HAA 1996*, but all were ruled out of order in the Dáil pursuant to procedural rules prohibiting opposition amendments that 'could have the effect of imposing or increasing a charge upon the revenue'.[169] Minister Fitzgerald and Minister of State Aodhán Ó Ríordáin TD repeatedly refused to reckon with the fact that Judge Quirke's recommendation referred explicitly to the ten-page Appendix G, which described entitlements far beyond what was ordinarily available to public medical card holders.

In the Seanad, Minister Ó Ríordáin was asked to provide a line-by-line explanation of how the wording of the RWRCI Bill would guarantee HAA-standard services. The following brief excerpt illustrates the exchange, as Senator John Gilroy read points from JFMR's briefing note about what the Bill failed to guarantee and his colleague responded:

> SENATOR JOHN GILROY: Point No. 3: 'Any and all chiropody/podiatry services from any qualified (including private) chiropodist/podiatrist, without the need for a GP's referral.'
>
> DEPUTY AODHÁN Ó RÍORDÁIN: That is absolutely incorrect.
>
> SENATOR JOHN GILROY: That is provided for under the HAA card.
>
> DEPUTY AODHÁN Ó RÍORDÁIN: It is in black and white in the Bill.
>
> . . .

SENATOR JOHN GILROY: Point No. 6: 'Comprehensive dental care, including access to private dentists not within the Dental Treatment Services Scheme.'
DEPUTY AODHÁN Ó RÍORDÁIN: Absolutely incorrect. It is in the Bill.
SENATOR JOHN GILROY: I hope there is no ambiguity with regard to any of these points.
DEPUTY AODHÁN Ó RÍORDÁIN: No.[170]

The government ministers argued that where any divergences between the HAA and RWRCI schemes might occur, it was because not all HAA services were appropriate for Magdalene survivors. Regarding counselling for immediate family members and 'open access to specialist hospital treatment', for example, Minister Ó Ríordáin asserted: 'it would make no sense whatsoever to include these specific provisions in this Bill. The Magdalen women do not have this illness and would not need or benefit in any way from the specific treatments for hepatitis C.'[171] Of the HAA entitlement to be seen by a hospital consultant within two weeks of a GP's referral, Minister Fitzgerald stated: 'The reference to a period of "two weeks" relates to urgent treatment for hepatitis C patients and does not apply in the same way to the women we are discussing who were in Magdalen homes.'[172] During the Dáil debates, Minister Fitzgerald agreed to amend the Bill to include private GP services – the Minister argued, to 'confirm that we were acting in good faith in implementing the Quirke recommendations'.[173] In our view, this rather confirmed that private services generally were excluded.

Justifying the exclusion of therapies such as massage, reflexology, acupuncture and hydrotherapy provided by a registered medical practitioner from the Bill's wording, Minister Fitzgerald claimed that Judge Quirke 'did not comment one way or another on complementary therapies'.[174] The minister added: 'homeopathy, angel healing and aromatherapy . . . have no proven medical benefits'.[175] In response to several TDs' arguments that complementary therapies were relevant to stress relief[176] – and indeed to Maureen O'Sullivan's observation that Minister of State Kathleen Lynch was poised to 'next week launch Acupuncture Awareness Week, the theme of which will be the benefits of acupuncture in the treatment and management of stress'[177] – Minister Fitzgerald agreed to 'come up with proposals for a separate, carefully laid out scheme – an administrative rather than a statutory scheme' to provide complementary therapies.[178] This never happened.

Increasingly frustrated with questioning from TDs and senators, both ministers criticized JFMR's advocacy.[179] Aodhán Ó Ríordáin was particularly vociferous:

> If people are going to send out statements on what is and is not in the Bill, I wish they would stick to the facts because it is easy to make a statement understanding how passionate and emotional people feel about this issue . . . of course it will upset people.

Ó Ríordáin continued:

> I do not want anybody who has gone through this lifetime abuse, if one wants to call it that, to have that situation compounded by misinformation. . . . There comes

> a stage when the campaigning ends and the winning begins. That is the same in every single campaign that anybody has ever been involved in. There comes a stage when the winning begins. This Bill is where the winning begins in terms of what Mr. Justice Quirke has asked for.[180]

Two months later, the DoJ wrote to scheme participants to provide 'an update on . . . the enhanced medical card as there has been some misinformation concerning the issue in the media'.[181]

Internal notes released under FOI show that before Judge Quirke's *Report* and recommendations had reached the DoJ at the end of May 2013, Mr Martin had discussed with the DoH the cost of providing only the ordinary public medical card to survivors who did not already have one.[182] Other documentation demonstrates that, upon receiving the *Quirke Report*, the DoH resisted the idea of providing HAA-standard care. An email from Jimmy Martin to a colleague on 4 July 2013 relayed that the 'observations of the Department of Health' on the *Quirke Report* were as follows:

> The notion of an 'enhanced' medical card is unclear. However, health legislation could be prepared to deem a person that has received a cash payment relating to her stay in a Magdalen laundry from the Minister of Justice and Equality to have full eligibility regardless of her means/income. Full eligibility entitles a person resident in Ireland to a range of public health and the public acute hospital services. The cost of this would be in the region of €3m per year. If the legislation was changed for the Magdalen women there will be an expectation by other groups (e.g. symphysiotomy, thalidomide, narcolepsy etc.) who are receiving medical card type services through the HSE that a similar legislative provision would apply to them. This precedent would require further detailed analysis.[183]

The DoJ did not force the issue, informing health officials that the extent of the services provided was their prerogative. A note of a meeting on 8 July 2013 between Mr Martin and DoH officials records: '[DoH] has concerns re giving medical cards over and above the norm or providing them to people living outside the State. [Mr] Martin indicated that the Government had already agreed to provide the Magdalen women with medical cards. What these would cover was a matter for the Department of Health. Counselling had been mentioned repeatedly.'[184]

Four months after the *RWRCI Act*'s enactment, as the DoH began to notify survivors and care practitioners of the legislation's provisions, it became obvious in practice, as well as on paper, that survivors were being given little more than ordinary public medical card services. On 13 July 2015 Katherine received an email from the chief executive of the Irish Dental Association to say that

> Members of the dental profession have been contacted by the HSE recently and notified of the limited dental care and treatment being made available to former Magdalene residents by the state. . . . This has been met with great disappointment by dentists for such a vulnerable and wronged group, and a sense of a distinctly

ungenerous approach by the state especially in contrast to other groups wronged during their stay in state-funded institutions.[185]

We issued a PR characterizing as 'an insult' the five-page guide to services which survivors received in July 2015, our Notes to Editors comparing the guide's paltry provisions against the detail of the HSE's forty-eight-page guide to HAA services.[186] The next month, three dentists published a letter to the editor of the *Journal of the Irish Dental Association* noting that the RWRCI card entitles Magdalene survivors 'to the limited and incomplete treatment that the DTSS [Dental Treatment Services Scheme] provides for most medical card holders'. The dentists 'urge[d] the Council of the Irish Dental Association to publicly disassociate itself from this act by the Government and to speak out publicly on behalf of its members who do not accept the injustice we are expected to support'.[187] On 16 July 2015, contact.ie set up another email campaign for us calling on TDs and senators to urgently provide the women with adequate healthcare. Over 200 people emailed TDs and senators, amounting to over 60,000 emails being sent from the contact.ie server.[188]

In August 2015, Kathleen R. told Claire she felt 'hoodwinked' by the State.[189] Kathleen's HSE 'home help' hours had been reduced and she was completely distraught. Having been confined in institutions for most of her first twenty-three years, Kathleen had fought hard for her independence, and she could not face the thought of re-institutionalization in adulthood. Kathleen phoned the HSE Contact Person in her area, and that person told her bluntly that she was not entitled to extra hours and that the RWRCI card was merely there to provide free medicine.[190]

Claire's experience of attempting to obtain mobility aids and counselling for a survivor of both a Magdalene Laundry and a Mother and Baby Home, 'Beth', who is also now deceased, further illustrates the problems that arose immediately for survivors. In August 2015 Claire emailed the HSE regional Contact Person for the RWRCI scheme to say that Beth 'has difficulty getting up and down the stairs at her home due to ongoing medical issues which severely affect her mobility' and that she 'would like to apply for a stair lift under the RWRCI Card'. The reply stated: 'Unfortunately the Health Service Executive do not provide stair lifts.' Claire asked if the RWRCI card might help Beth to obtain specially designed walking sticks, as she had arthritis in both hands. The reply stated: 'Unfortunately, there is no priority given to holders of the RWRCI Cards.'[191]

In late September 2015, Claire again emailed the RWRCI Contact Person to ask if it was possible for Beth to be prioritized for counselling. Beth had been experiencing suicidal thoughts and self-harm, and she had been placed on a waiting list by the HSE National Counselling Service in early August following a GP's referral several months previously. A response from the RWRCI Contact Person in mid-October conveyed a message from the National Counselling Service that 'they do not prioritise their waiting list at all. They adhere strictly to this policy. Seemingly they receive numerous requests from G.P.'s.'[192]

It was only following letters from pro bono lawyers, with the support of a pro bono expert psychological report, that Beth began to receive counselling in late February 2016.[193] Responding to Beth's solicitor's letter, and while agreeing that the National Counselling Service would clinically review Beth's GP's referral, the HSE national director of primary care clarified that RWRCI cardholders were not entitled to HAA-standard psychological care. The letter said: 'The terms of the Redress for Women Resident in Certain Institutions Act 2015 (Section 2(1)(f)) states [*sic*] that the "*HSE shall make available without charge to relevant participants a counselling service, following a referral made in that regard by a registered medical practitioner*." Please note that the act does not make specific mention of payment for private counselling services.'[194] Beth died just over a year later.

Our repeated efforts since 2015 to have the Scheme's health and social care provision match what was recommended by Judge Quirke and formally accepted by the government have been unsuccessful.[195] In addition to the problems faced by survivors living in Ireland, women residing abroad have to rely on an opaque reimbursement process operated on an administrative basis, which prevents survivors from accessing care because they cannot afford to pay upfront.[196]

In June 2019, the government introduced an RWRCI (Amendment) Bill to include within the Scheme survivors who were forced to work in Magdalene Laundries while registered on the rolls of adjacent children's institutions. We briefed TDs and senators that this was an opportunity to fix the health and social care problems created in 2015.[197] Bearing in mind the government's practice of rejecting all opposition amendments deemed to incur a cost, Senator Lynn Ruane proposed an amendment to the 2019 Bill to require the minister for justice to produce a report within three months on any differences between the services available under the Magdalene Scheme and those available to HAA cardholders.[198] Minister Flanagan rejected the amendment, rehearsing the familiar argument that 'The arrangements in respect of the HAA are clearly based on a person having been infected with hepatitis C' and that differences between the two schemes are 'individually focused to meet the health needs of what I might describe as somewhat or indeed very different cohorts of persons requiring access to packages of targeted health supports'. Senator Ruane then proposed a more limited version of her amendment. The minister rejected it, stating, however: 'I will give a commitment to examine the issues. . . . I would be happy to convey any concerns to other Ministers who may have responsibility in that area.'[199] No longer minister for justice since mid-2020, Charlie Flanagan TD has called from government back benches for the current minister for health to explain 'the reason the health card, as recommended in the Magdalen commission report and agreed to in full by the then Government, has not been fulfilled or honoured' and for survivors to be given what they were promised in return for waiving their legal rights.[200]

8

Bringing up the dead

Burials and land deals at High Park

The Magdalene Names Project

Affording dignity to the women who died behind convent walls has been a central aim of JFM(R)'s work since it began in 2003 following Mary Raftery's investigation into the exhumation of 155 human remains from the OLC Magdalene Laundry at High Park ten years earlier. Days after reading Raftery's article in *The Irish Times*, Claire and Angela Newsome visited Glasnevin Cemetery to photograph the grave in which the remains of the women exhumed from High Park were now interred.[1] From these photographs Claire and Angela transcribed the name and date of death stated for each woman. They posted the list online in a private adoption forum as a way of honouring the women's memories.[2] This work marked the establishment of the MNP, which Claire continues to lead.[3] Honouring the Magdalene dead and understanding the lessons we need to learn from these women's treatment are continuing motivations of survivors and their allies.

The MNP uses available data such as gravestones, digitized census records, electoral records, graveyard registers, death certificates, inquest records and newspaper archives to ascertain the identities and whereabouts of women who died while incarcerated behind convent walls. To date, the MNP has recorded the details of 1,837 women who died in Magdalene institutions across the Republic of Ireland.[4] The majority (62.7 per cent) died after the foundation of the State in 1922. The total number may be greater. Our research is hampered by a lack of access to the religious orders' records and also because of the OLC Sisters' practice of recording numerous women's deaths using 'Magdalene' names (e.g. 'Magdalene of Bernadine' or 'Magdalene of St John'). Because of such obstacles, there are an additional 121 women known to have died in a Magdalene institution for whom the MNP has been unable to establish a legal identity.[5]

Traditionally, Irish culture reveres the rituals accompanying death, including wakes, funerals and burials. 'Cemetery Sunday', with its annual blessing of the graves, is celebrated to this day and families tend not only to their own plot but oftentimes also to that of a deceased neighbour with no one left to care for it. Set against Ireland's history of colonial dispossession on the one hand and of emigration on the other, it is hardly surprising that the family plot has become 'a treasured piece of land'.[6] And yet, not all Irish graves are respected equally. Writing in response to revelations regarding Ireland's 'dishonoured' dead – including the 796 infants presumed buried in a disused 'septic' tank on the grounds of the former Tuam Baby Home and the 155 human remains exhumed at the High Park Magdalene institution in 1993 – Anne Enright insists that 'the dead do not lie', that these discarded bodies and disturbed human remains constitute 'indelible' evidence of the wrongs committed against them in life. Irish society has, over the last decade, finally begun to honour these women and children's existence; annual vigils now take place at 'angel plots' on the grounds of former Mother and Baby Homes, and locally organized 'Flowers for Magdalenes' ceremonies take place in cemeteries all across Ireland.[7] However, the High Park exhumations continue to disturb those of us committed to a more just society precisely because the Irish State- and Catholic Church-establishment repeatedly buries the truth of what happened in the recent past and, in so doing, denies these women, and their families, the dignity and respect they are due.[8]

The MNP provides essential information to family members and dignifies deceased women by acknowledging their identities and existence. It has also raised the consciousness of the general public and those directly involved in property planning and development, encouraging them to consider the implications of decisions to destroy or 'repurpose' Magdalene buildings and grounds which are the material evidence of a national history that is not yet adequately acknowledged. In addition, the MNP is a citizen-led archiving initiative that enables holding the State and Church to account. The MNP's research formed a significant part of JFM's Principal Submissions to the IDC. We used the MNP's findings to make factual submissions regarding the length of many women's detention, and legal submissions concerning the State's apparent failure to require the registration of all deaths and its continuing failure to guarantee relatives access to information about the fate and whereabouts of their loved ones. We highlighted the fact that the identities of many of the women exhumed at High Park remained unknown, and several of the Magdalene Laundry graves around the country did not have gravestones and/or displayed discrepancies such as duplicated names. We also pointed out that the location of some Magdalene gravesites was altogether unknown. Despite the IDC having unparalleled access to the nuns' records, cemetery records and assistance from the Office of the Register General (GRO) to examine death certificates, its *Report* raises more questions than it answered.[9]

The MNP is all the more crucial due to the secrecy that the DoT has imposed over the entire IDC archive, and because the religious orders refuse to open their Magdalene Laundry records.[10] This is illustrated by the following account of what the MNP tells us about the High Park exhumations in 1993, thought to be the largest exhumation in the history of the State. Using the State's own documents (retrieved via numerous FOI requests) and other records, this case study paints a very different picture to the findings in the 'official' record (i.e. the *IDC Report*).[11] It demonstrates that

- It was clear to DCC observers supervising the 1993 exhumations that the overwhelming majority of names provided by OLC (to the extent that names were provided) did not match the identities of the bodies being exhumed;[12]

- These discrepancies should have been clear to the DoEnv, which issued the licence, as DCC's supervision was a condition mandated by that department;[13]
- The DoEnv demonstrated alarming levels of deference to OLC during the licence application process and a complete lack of follow-up after the exhumations;
- The Gardaí repeatedly failed to conduct an adequate investigation into the High Park exhumations;
- The IDC relied on deeply flawed research commissioned by OLC and directed by Dr Jacinta Prunty, then senior lecturer in history at Maynooth University and a Holy Faith nun;[14]
- The motivation for the sale of the cemetery and the manner of exhumation and cremation was guided by OLC's financial concerns;
- OLC's characterization of their care for the women they exhumed is untenable; and
- The *IDC Report*'s assertion that all 155 exhumed women have been accounted for is simply untrue.[15]

The IDC's narrative of the High Park exhumations

Chapter Sixteen of the *IDC Report*, 'Death Registration, Burial and Exhumation', asserts that there is no reason for continuing concern about OLC's disinterment and subsequent cremation (of all but one) of 155 Magdalene women at High Park in 1993. The IDC investigation accessed 'all relevant records' of the OLC Sisters and the DoEnv, as well as records of previous 'examinations' of the matter by the Dublin City Coroner and An Garda Síochána.[16] It did not examine DCC's records on the High Park exhumations. The committee returned all of OLC's documentation to them at the conclusion of its work, and the Order refuses to allow public access to their records. Chapter Sixteen of the *IDC Report* refers repeatedly in its footnotes to documents that the IDC did not make publicly available in its *Report*'s appendices. Meanwhile, the DoT has embargoed the entire IDC archive. It was therefore impossible to go behind the IDC's 'findings' at the time of the *Report*'s publication.

The *IDC Report* claims there is no longer any reason to be alarmed about unidentified remains at High Park because, following a 'research and cataloguing exercise' on OLC's records, 'all 155 women whose remains were exhumed . . . were identified and matched to their names and dates of death'.[17] In defence of the lack of accurate and full inscription of these names on a headstone in the grave where the cremated remains lie in Glasnevin Cemetery, the *IDC Report* relays that 'the Congregation is now at an advanced stage in making arrangements for the full and accurate details relating to these women (birth names and dates of death) to be recorded'.[18]

The *IDC Report* finds no impropriety in the DoEnv's actions. It suggests that the department's decision to issue two licences for exhumation and cremation (in the absence of death certificates for 80 of 155 exhumed women) complied with the department's guidance to all local authorities.[19] (Yet, as we explain later, the 133 names which OLC did provide for the licence do not all relate to women who were exhumed.

This has never been acknowledged by OLC or the State.) While a 1989 DoEnv Circular stated that exhumation applications under the relevant legislation should be accompanied by death certificates, a subsequent departmental Circular created an exception to this rule 'where a death certificate would be inordinately difficult to obtain'.[20] The *IDC Report* concludes, simply: 'The fact that death certificates were not available for all women in respect of whom the original application was made was not therefore in itself a bar to issuance of an exhumation licence by the Department.'[21]

There is no suggestion in the *IDC Report* that the OLC Sisters acted unlawfully, either. The *Report* notes the existence since 1863 of a statutory requirement to register deaths.[22] However, the IDC claims that an 'administrative reason, namely the absence at that time of archived or catalogued records' explained OLC's inability to identify all women.[23] Satisfied that all 155 women exhumed from High Park in 1993 are now accounted for, the IDC closes Chapter Sixteen by referring to the Garda position that no criminal wrongdoing occurred:

> An Garda Síochána also carried out enquiries in relation to this matter, both in 2003 and again in 2012 at the request of the Committee. . . . These enquiries concluded without any suggestion of criminal action or wrongdoing and, on the basis of those records, no further action on the matter was deemed necessary by the Gardaí.[24]

JFM was not convinced by the IDC's conclusions. Neither was Sheila Ahern, researcher for the *States of Fear* documentaries, who phoned Claire upon reading the *IDC Report* and offered her access to Mary Raftery's archive. Two years later, realizing that FOI requests were newly free to make and could be submitted easily by email (crucial factors for a voluntary unfunded organization), Claire began applying under FOI to the original departments for copies of documents cited in the *IDC Report*'s footnotes and more records besides.[25] She also obtained death certificates for 370 of the women who died while confined at High Park.[26]

A tale of two cemeteries

The burial ground where the exhumations took place was officially called St Mary's Graveyard. It held the remains of the 'consecrated Magdalenes' of High Park. Consecrated Magdalenes (also known as 'auxiliaries') were women and girls who, in exchange for taking what the nuns describe as a 'quasi-religious status' and a vow to spend the rest of their lives at the Magdalene Laundry, would be guaranteed a burial in their own graveyard on the convent grounds, set apart from the other women and girls who were buried in public graveyards.[27] St Mary's was not the only graveyard at High Park; there was also the Convent Community Cemetery which was reserved for the Sisters themselves. St Mary's was situated on the extreme south-western side of High Park, while the Community Cemetery was located at the upper north-east border of the campus. By 1993, St Mary's Graveyard was thoroughly neglected and had been used as a dumping ground by vandals who destroyed many crosses marking the graves.[28] Meanwhile the Sisters' Community Cemetery was pristine. As Ann Kelly, an employee at High Park during the 1980s, describes,

> I'd go into the women's graveyard and it was just a mass of weeds and overgrown grass, and then I'd walk into the nuns' graveyards, perfect graves with perfect white crosses . . . it would have been so easy for them to make it as nice as the nuns' one. . . . So even in death there was discrimination.[29]

Although the High Park campus has been developed numerous times since 1993, the Community Cemetery remains undisturbed. Over 120 white crosses mark individual plots, and the grass surrounding the graves is well maintained. The presence of two garden gazebos on either side of the cemetery suggests that visitors are welcome to sit and remember the dead. The Celtic cross erected in 1900 to commemorate Sr Mary of the Sacred Heart Kelly, founder of High Park, remains intact.[30] Meanwhile, after the exhumations, the St Mary's Celtic cross, which bore the inscription 'St Mary's High Park: They Had Loved Much', was left lying on its side, broken into several pieces.[31]

Even today the Community Cemetery is reserved for religious sisters only; the Magdalene survivors who die in the Beechlawn Nursing Home are interred in Glasnevin Cemetery. In a letter to the *Irish Independent* just after the exhumations in 1993, Sr Angela Fahy, then provincial superior of OLC, said of the survivors at Beechlawn: 'The reality is that these women have made their home with us; we know them; we want them and we care for them.'[32] Yet, when survivors die at Beechlawn, the death notices are often minimal:

> The death has occurred of [name, location]. Peacefully. Reposing in [location] today, Monday, from 4pm. Funeral Mass tomorrow, Tuesday, at 11.45am followed by burial in Glasnevin Cemetery.[33]

In contrast, the Sisters' death notices state how much the deceased will be missed, the work they did in life and their age at death:

> The death has occurred of Sr [name, location] Formerly of [location] In her [age] year. A woman of wisdom, love and integrity. A great loss and very sadly missed by her community, nephews, nieces, grandnephews, grandnieces, family, relatives and a large circle of friends. Rest in Peace. Reposing in [location, time]. Removal on Tuesday morning from [location] to the [church location], arriving at 11.15am for funeral Mass at 11.30am. Burial afterwards in the Community Cemetery, Beechlawn.[34]

Carelessness with the women's identities

OLC's first application for an exhumation licence in July 1992 requested permission to exhume 140 remains: a fact unacknowledged by the IDC.[35] This application did not include death certificates for the deceased; the DoEnv asked for these to be produced.[36] In response, OLC submitted a revised application in January 1993 for a licence to exhume 133 bodies.[37] Enclosed with the application were seventy-five death certificates, thirty-four GRO 'no trace forms' (indicating that a search for the named person had returned no record of death), and a letter from the GRO stating that it was not possible to conduct a search for twenty-three women with Magdalene names.[38] One woman on the application had a first name with no surname.

Internal notes show that the DoEnv's legal adviser was concerned by the high number of 'no trace' forms submitted.[39] This was relayed to OLC's solicitors, Eugene F. Collins, who informed the department that the exhumations had to be completed by September.[40] The DoEnv went so far as to draft a letter notifying OLC that they must retrospectively register the fifty-eight deaths for which certificates had not been produced.[41] The draft letter also asked why the number of proposed exhumations had decreased from 140 to 133. Departmental records indicate that this letter was never sent, however. Instead, a file note records a decision that OLC seemed 'to have gone as far as could reasonably be asked' in their attempts to produce death certificates.[42] The January 1993 application, which included an individual application form for each woman, is no longer in the DoEnv file.[43] Internal notes make clear that the DoEnv permitted Eugene F. Collins to physically remove it before submitting a fresh application in May 1993.[44]

The OLC Sisters thereafter submitted a new application, on 12 May 1993, for a licence to exhume and cremate or rebury 133 remains. This time OLC did not provide individual application forms for each woman; rather, they enclosed with a covering letter seventy-five death certificates, thirty-four 'no trace' letters, the January letter from the GRO and three appendices purporting to demonstrate their efforts to identify all remains. These appendices contained largely the same information provided in January save that cause of death information was added for the seventy-five women in relation to whom death certificates had already been produced. The solicitors 'certified' that the contents of their application were 'true in all respects'.[45] Death certificates remained outstanding for fifty-eight women. Nonetheless, on 25 May 1993 an assistant secretary in the DoEnv, John Cullen, signed a Ministerial Order on behalf of the Minister for the Environment Michael Smith TD permitting the OLC Sisters to exhume 133 bodies from St Mary's Graveyard and to cremate or rebury the remains intact.[46]

Cutting costs: 'Simple coffins with no embellishments . . .'

Once the exhumation licence was issued, Mary Lee, an EHO with the Environmental Health Section of DCC wrote to Eugene F. Collins setting out a list of conditions and stressing that 'due care and decency' and public safety were paramount in order to proceed with the disinterment.[47] In a letter seeking costings for exhumation and reburial versus exhumation and cremation from Patrick Massey Funeral Directors, OLC's solicitors raised the issue of costs no less than five times; yet, there is not a single mention of the women, other than a reference to '133 remains'.[48] Regarding the decision whether to cremate or rebury the women, the Massey firm responded that '[t]he difference in cost between earth burial for all and cremation is so great that, bearing in mind that your clients wish to keep costs to a minimum, the former is not really on the cards'. Masseys quoted a total of £30,000 to exhume and cremate the women and inter the urns of ashes in Glasnevin.[49] They suggested that the coffins would be 'simple with no embellishments and suitable for cremation'. The Sisters accepted the tender on condition that no further costs would be incurred.[50]

Until 1983, cremation was forbidden by the Catholic Church. Canon Law 1176 (3) 'earnestly recommends' the burial of remains, and states that cremation is not forbidden 'unless this is chosen for reasons which are contrary to Christian teaching'.[51] When Mary Raftery wrote to the Sisters asking why they decided to cremate, whether they were aware of Canon Law 1176, and if they had a comment on their decision in this context, OLC did not reply to her questions.[52]

Oversight of the exhumations

The licence granted on 25 May 1993 required the exhumations to be supervised by DCC. Council records show that of the several observers attending the seven-day exhumation process between 23 August and 2 September 1993, Mary Lee, the EHO, was present throughout and paid careful attention to the details.[53] A crucial function of the EHO during an exhumation is to monitor for correspondence between the name plate on the coffin as it emerges from the ground and the name stated on the schedule to the exhumation licence.[54] As each woman's remains were exhumed, Ms Lee noted the name and date of death stated on the iron cross which marked the grave and/or on the coffin plate. As Ms Lee recorded, some of the graves were not marked by a cross and in some instances the details on a cross did not match those on the coffin plate.[55] Ms Lee also referred to a map of the graveyard, created by OLC in the summer of 1993, to mark the location of each grave.[56] In addition, Ms Lee recorded the number of each new coffin into which remains were placed in preparation for cremation (forty coffins had two women in each). Ms Lee's handwritten database '*List One: Exhumation Records – In Order of Date and Grave No*' (hereafter *List One*) is the most accurate available record of what transpired during the exhumations.[57]

List One shows that, of the 155 women whose remains were exhumed (including the additional 22 women disinterred on the final day), the names stated on the crosses and/or coffin plates matched the exhumation licence in only 32 instances. Twenty-two women were simply marked as 'unknown' on *List One*; without a coffin plate or a name on the cross, there was no way to identify them or attempt to correspond their remains with a name on the exhumation licence.[58] Contrary to what is commonly believed, the twenty-two unidentifiable bodies were not all disinterred on the final day of exhumations: *List One* makes clear that the undertakers were exhuming 'unknown' remains from the outset. Of the 155 exhumed women, 19 appear on *List One* under their legal names, while 110 have Magdalene names only. In the case of four women, only their first or second name could be found. Although OLC told the DoEnv that it had created its list of 133 names by counting the crosses in the graveyard as well as by consulting its records, Ms Lee's *List One* shows that she counted 14 more crosses than the nuns did.[59]

The MNP has located sixteen of the nineteen women with legal names on *List One* in census and electoral records. These women spent considerable lengths of time in the institution, ranging from at least twelve to thirty-two years. The first woman exhumed was Magdalene of St Bernadine, also known as Charlotte K., who died in 1946 from heart disease.[60] Magdalene of Faith died in 1899; when she was exhumed on 25 August, no skull could be found. The final woman exhumed was Magdalene of St Peter, also known as Alice B. who, at the age of twenty-six, was sent to High Park from the North Dublin Union workhouse in November 1889.[61] She died on 30 April 1948 at eighty-nine from senility and cardiac failure, having spent over fifty-eight years in High Park. Alice's name is engraved on a headstone in Glasnevin, but for many years after reinterment her date of death was erroneously inscribed as 31 April 1948.

The exhumations were stopped twice over the seven days: first, on 24 August to allow for cremation; the DoEnv licence required exhumed remains to be reburied or cremated within forty-eight hours and the number of bodies exhumed at that point exceeded the capacity of Glasnevin Crematorium. The DCC observers halted proceedings for a second time on 28 August because the maximum number of exhumations provided for by the licence had been reached.[62] The undertakers had found further remains in the cemetery, beyond 133, but they did not know how many more existed.[63]

The OLC Sisters applied on 30 August for 'a further licence for the exhumation of remains of deceased persons'. In the application Eugene F. Collins stated that 'right up until Thursday, 26 August 1993, our clients . . . and ourselves believed that 133 remains represented the total amount of interred bodies in the grave ground'. The solicitors said that on 26 August the undertakers had become aware that there were 'a number of remains interred in the grave ground not included in the original Exhumation Licence or accounted for in the convent records' and that 'so far' fourteen 'extra remains' had been located.[64] In fact, from day one the undertakers had found remains that did not match the exhumation licence list and further remains that had no name whatsoever.[65] By 26 August, the cross and/or coffin details of a mere seventeen bodies, out of a total of ninety-six exhumed so far, matched the exhumation licence. Nonetheless, the solicitors certified that the particulars provided were 'true in all respects'.[66]

DoEnv officials assisted Eugene F. Collins to finesse their application for the supplementary exhumation and cremation licence. A draft version of the application in the DoEnv file, sent on 27 August, shows handwritten notes by the officials, suggesting edits (predominantly deletions of whole lines of text).[67] All suggested changes were implemented in OLC's formal letter of application dated 30 August. The DoEnv did not query the discrepancies between the May exhumation licence and the bodies exhumed thus far, nor OLC's inability to state how many further remains were buried and whose remains they were. It did not initiate an investigation or refer the matter to the Gardaí. On the contrary, it expedited the nuns' application for a supplementary exhumation and cremation licence.

The second Ministerial Order was signed on 31 August 1993, a mere twenty-four hours after OLC submitted their request.[68] The licence allowed for the exhumation and cremation not of specified remains, nor even a specified number of bodies, but of 'all human remains' left in the cemetery. The exhumations resumed on 2 September, when the final 22 women were disinterred and cremated, bringing the total to 155.[69] Eight of the names stated on the crosses and/or coffin plates matched the first exhumation licence schedule.

Financial matters: The St Mary's land deal

The OLC Sisters were £2 million in debt from the construction of the Beechlawn Nursing Home on their campus.[70] They had failed to get permission to build the housing development originally planned to fund the project.[71] The Sisters had spent over a year trying to dispose of the land for which they had entered a contract of sale, and the clock was ticking on the deal. The exhumations needed to be completed by September 1993.[72] Then, on 30 August 1993 it emerged that Tony Ryan had stepped aside as chair of Guinness Peat Aviation – unwelcome news for the OLC Sisters, who had in 1991 purchased $110,000 worth of shares in a company that was now in its dying days.[73] Meanwhile, media coverage of the exhumations was intensifying.[74] Costs were also mounting with the discovery of additional women's bodies which added an extra £9,350 to the undertakers' fee.[75] The undertakers stipulated that the new tender was based on a maximum of twenty-four additional remains, and if further bodies were discovered, there would be a charge of £380 each. The original plan was that all women who died before 1948 would be cremated with three in each coffin, and 'that they could manage two per coffin from 1948 to 1965'. However, according to the undertakers, 'this was not achieved in practice due to the attending Dublin Corporation observers insisting on more coffins being used'. In the end, 115 coffins were required, with 75 women in individual coffins, and 40 coffins with 2 women in each.[76] Glasnevin Crematorium wanted another £4,500 to cremate the extra coffins, but the undertakers negotiated it down to £2,000. In total, the cost of exhuming, cremating and interring the 155 women from St Mary's Graveyard came to £41,350.[77] The exhumation costs were split evenly between OLC and Regan Developments, who purchased the site.

St Mary's Graveyard was a relatively small portion (2 per cent according to OLC) of the eleven and a half acres on the market in 1993.[78] The entire plot of land was sold for a sum estimated between £1.2 and £1.5 million.[79] Based on OLC's estimate of the size of the graveyard, as a proportion of the sale St Mary's was worth between £24,000 and £30,000.[80] Why then would the developer agree to pay an additional sum of £20,850 (half the exhumations costs) to close the deal? The answer seems clearly to lie in the location: owning the burial site unencumbered of remains was crucial to the overall plans of Regan Developments, who owned the Regency Airport Hotel (now the Bonnington Hotel) which bordered the OLC property. Regans wanted to build houses but planning restrictions prevented all but pedestrian and service vehicle access to the site from Grace Park Road, which was to the east of their hotel.[81] Thus, to develop the lands, Regans had to provide vehicular access to their proposed housing project from the Swords Road on the western side, via a newly constructed road through the grounds of their hotel. St Mary's was walled in and situated on the eastern boundary of the hotel. The area where the graveyard was once located now comprises a car park to the rear of the hotel, and the road providing access to the housing development runs alongside it. Had St Mary's remained intact, developing the land for housing would have been deeply problematic, so it appears for the deal to go through the graveyard had to be cleared: the women were in the way. Today, all that remains of St Mary's Graveyard are two mature cedar trees which were protected under planning conditions.[82]

The official OLC explanation for why the graves had to be disinterred did not prominently feature mention of their land deal. Sr Angela Fahy explained to the *Irish Independent* newspaper that

> We released the cemetery for the very serious reason that we were convinced of the inevitability that in due course it would become isolated and inaccessible. The preferable choice, therefore, was to have the remains exhumed and reinterred in a public place which would be well maintained and readily accessible to visitors. . . . The names of those interred in Glasnevin will be engraved on a headstone at the grave.[83]

The OLC Sisters did not act on this stated concern about visitors' accessibility to the former Magdalene women's graves. Generally, women from High Park are buried in at least seven separate locations in Glasnevin Cemetery.[84] Just three of these burial plots have headstones, and the other four graves remain unmarked. Where there are headstones, there are significant errors and discrepancies. If a family member, friend or a member of the public wishes to pay their respects, it is a significant challenge to navigate the graves and ensure that the correct location has been found.

Relatives and truth: 'There was nobody to inform . . .that's the truth'

Amid the haggling around costs, it does not seem to have occurred to OLC, the undertakers, Glasnevin or any State official that placing two or more women in a coffin and then cremating them would make it impossible for family members to claim their relative's remains. In their exhumation licence application, the Order alleged that women buried at St Mary's had been 'left with' the Sisters 'by families who chose to ignore their very existence'. For this reason, they did 'not believe that any relatives of the deceased would object to the exhumation of the remains of the deceased'.[85] However, there is clear evidence that where a family sought contact, in many instances they were discouraged. In 1993, Elizabeth H.'s family read about the exhumations in the newspapers and managed to intervene and stop her cremation with just ten minutes to spare.[86] When Elizabeth had died ten years previously, her family was told she was a Ward of Court and relatives were denied access to her remains. Moreover, Elizabeth's family did not ignore her existence; they visited her at High Park regularly, bringing gifts and clothes. After the near-exhumation, Elizabeth was buried in the family plot in Glasnevin. When another relative, Anthony O'B., read of the exhumations, he contacted OLC as he was concerned that his aunt, Mary H., was about to be disinterred; however, the Order denied all knowledge of her existence.[87] The MNP investigated and found Mary's death certificate, which establishes that she died in 1958. An examination of Glasnevin's genealogy records reveals that Mary H. was buried in Glasnevin at the time of her death. Furthermore, the

1954–6 electoral registers show that Mary was present in High Park at that time, and, Mary H.'s death certificate confirms that she was 'late of High Park'. Yet, OLC claimed no knowledge of her existence. Mary Brehany died in High Park in 1972 having been confined for forty years. Her grandson Frank informed JFMR he would like to reclaim his grandmother's remains: 'when the enormity of what happened . . . came into focus . . . I had to find a way to bring Mary home.'[88] But with no record of Mary Brehany on the exhumation licence, and no clear entry for her on *List One* generated by the EHO, there is no paper trail to show what became of her remains. And, because OLC were allowed to cremate, it is impossible to carry out DNA testing to ascertain whether she is one of the 155 women exhumed. The Sisters allege that the women were effectively abandoned by their families, yet the Catholic Press Office said that 'anyone who knew the women would have been informed' about their exhumation.[89] All the evidence suggests that this did not happen. Shortly after the exhumations concluded, Sr Angela Fahy appeared in the audience of RTÉ's *Kenny Live* television programme, her patience clearly wearing thin:

> About five years ago, we made a decision that we wanted to build a modern complex for our ladies to give them proper living conditions . . . we did that to the tune of £2 million and a lovely red brick [building] for those who are sick and all the rest, okay, right. Beside the institution was the graveyard. We needed to pay . . . we were in a lot of debt. . . . That graveyard, the impression would be given . . . that people were visiting. . . . Nobody, apart from the Sisters and the ladies, would have visited that graveyard in years . . . when you say why not inform people, there was nobody to inform. . . . That's the truth.[90]

'On the occasion of their exhumation': Reburial ceremony at Glasnevin

The reburial ceremony on 11 September was a private affair, attended only by a group of around twenty-five nuns and a small number of lay people, none of whom were relatives of the women.[91] The Sisters travelled to Glasnevin in limousines, while the urns containing the ashes of the exhumed women were transported to the graveside in the back of a jeep.[92] A spokesperson for the Catholic Press Office claimed that 'all those connected with the women' had been invited to the ceremony.[93] Relatives and friends of the women disputed this at the time and argued that OLC had conducted the ceremony in secret 'to avoid controversy'.[94] Sr Frances Robinson, then manager of an OLC 'teenage unit', admitted that no relatives were invited to the ceremony.[95] When asked why the forty institutionalized survivors at High Park were not invited, she said, '[w]e did not want them to be abused by the press and photographers. We didn't want them stigmatised, photographed with the Magdalen crest over their heads.' Sr Fahy told the *Irish Independent* that a 'special liturgy' was also celebrated at High Park for the women 'on the occasion of their exhumation', and it appears this service was also closed to relatives and friends of the women.[96]

Three weeks prior to the reburial ceremony, Margo Kelly and Bláthnaid Ní Chinneide first learnt about the exhumations in a newspaper article. They felt compelled to act and so the first seeds of the MMC were sown.[97] Margo and Bláthnaid made contact with OLC and initially established a good relationship with Sr Fahy. However, the week before the women were reinterred, High Park cut off all communication. Realizing they had been shut out, Margo and Bláthnaid tried desperately to learn the details of the reburial ceremony, to no avail. Days before the service the Dublin Archdiocese refused MMC's request to fund a memorial. A church spokesperson told the *Irish Press* 'he could see no reason for the memorial'.[98]

Despite their best efforts, Margo and Bláthnaid remained in the dark about the details of the ceremony, and no friends or relatives of the women attended. The invited guests were led in prayer by Fr Tony Coote, the now-deceased social justice campaigner, in his capacity as then chaplain to High Park. As the urns were placed into the grave, the group sang 'Jesus remember me, when you come into your kingdom'.[99] While the service was underway, Margo and Bláthnaid received a phone call from the journalist Susan McKay to tip them off about the ceremony.[100] The women rushed to Glasnevin on Margo's Honda 50 motorcycle and arrived just in time to see the OLC Sisters' cortege of limousines emerging through the cemetery gates. They sped up and down Glasnevin's paths looking for mounds of clay and eventually found their way to the open grave, just in time to look in at the urns before the plot was filled in.

The night after the reburial ceremony, the MMC held a public meeting in the Ormonde Hotel.[101] Many relatives were in attendance, including one woman who traced her mother to High Park, but was told her mother's name had been changed. When the woman's mother died, she was not notified by OLC. At this point, there was significant media coverage of the exhumations, and members of the public were expressing their views in letters to the editors of national newspapers. One correspondent wrote: 'Even in death, they seem to be in the way. There's no doubt that these graves wouldn't be exhumed if the dead were not female, poor and dependent.'[102] Two days after the exhumed women were reinterred at Glasnevin, Sr Fahy and other OLC representatives signed company incorporation documents for their work with another marginalized population: the Ruhama Women's Project.[103]

No accountability

Ms Lee's report on what transpired during the exhumations appears to have been of no consequence to the DoEnv. Once the department had issued the supplementary licence permitting the disposal of 'all human remains', it washed its hands of the matter. Internally, DoEnv officials took an imperious tone when Mary Raftery asked in 2003 how OLC had responded to the question on each exhumation licence application form regarding the location of the deceased's grave.[104] A file note reads: 'Entire burial ground was covered by the licence – identification of individual plots was hardly necessary for the purpose of the licence.'[105] Other departmental notes on Raftery's queries defer completely to OLC's successful licence application in May 1993.[106] After Raftery's article appeared in *The Irish Times*, Finian McGrath, TD, asked then minister for the environment Martin Cullen in a parliamentary question why the DoEnv raised no objection when it was revealed that twenty-two further remains had been found.

The minister's response consists almost exclusively of extracts copied from OLC's supplementary licence application in August 1993.[107]

The publicity surrounding Mary Raftery's article prompted a Garda investigation in September 2003.[108] The Gardaí conducted their enquiries in private without issuing a public call for evidence; relatives and members of the public were therefore unable to participate. The investigation lasted for about a month as Gardaí obtained information from the DoEnv, met with Dublin City Coroner Dr Brian Farrell and surveyed records held by OLC.[109] The Garda investigation appears not to have included DCC.

The Gardaí found no evidence of wrongdoing in 2003, according to a DoJ 2011 memorandum to government.[110] In 2009, after a meeting with a group of Magdalene survivors (and subsequently JFM), the secretary general of the DoJ, Sean Aylward, wrote to the Garda Commissioner, Fachtna Murphy, to ask for a review of the previous investigation.[111] The Commissioner responded with a report in May 2010.[112] There is a notable similarity (at times, word-for-word) between this report's account of what was said at a meeting between Gardaí and OLC in September 2003, and the May 1993 letter to the DoEnv from Eugene F. Collins enclosing OLC's successful application for the first exhumation licence.[113] Commissioner Murphy's report further advised that 'an archivist' had provided Gardaí with a preliminary summary of findings regarding OLC's records which, according to the DoJ, 'suggest that the Religious Order followed all the appropriate steps in registering the deaths of their residents'.[114] The DoJ's June 2011 memorandum to government clarifies that the unnamed 'archivist' upon whom the Gardaí relied is Dr Jacinta Prunty.[115] (OLC gave Dr Prunty exclusive access to their archive so that she could write a commissioned history of their institutions in Ireland, published in 2017.[116] The Order refuses to allow public access to the documentation upon which the book relies.[117])

DoEnv records show that in August 2010, the department (finally) wrote to OLC expressing concern about differences between the first exhumation licence issued in 1993 and the names on the headstones of the women's grave in Glasnevin.[118] Dr Prunty responded on behalf of OLC, providing a research summary and a database that she claimed demonstrated 'burial details' for the 133 women named on the original exhumation licence.[119] Dr Prunty told the DoEnv: 'as a professional academic with a long-standing involvement in historical research . . . I must state that the research in this matter has been pursued in so far as the records will allow.' She added that she was in the process of writing 'an independent, scholarly history' of OLC's work in Ireland, in which she would address 'legitimate queries' about the Order's Magdalene Laundries. Dr Prunty added that her project had been delayed because of the 'slow work' of compiling the *High Park database*, and that she looked forward to 'being able to progress it without any further interruptions'.[120]

In November 2010 the DoJ again raised the exhumations with the Garda Commissioner after the IHRC published its *Assessment of the Human Rights Issues Arising in relation to the 'Magdalen Laundries'*.[121] The IHRC's *Assessment* contended that the State may have breached Article 8 of the ECHR, which requires respect for private and family life, by failing to ensure that the identities of deceased Magdalene women were established such that their relatives would know their fate and whereabouts.[122] The DoJ asked the Garda Commissioner for an update on Dr Prunty's research.[123] The

DoJ redacted Dr Prunty's name from correspondence released to JFMR under FOI. On 2 February 2011, the newly appointed Garda Commissioner Martin Callinan informed the department that a detective inspector had met with Dr Prunty in January 2011. Dr Prunty informed the inspector that after ten years examining the available records, her 'research does not disclose any finding that would warrant further Garda investigation'. Commissioner Callinan concluded: 'In light of the results of [redacted's] research, there appear to be no further avenues of investigation available to pursue.'[124]

On 16 October 2012, Assistant Garda Commissioner Derek Byrne made a submission to the DoJ to assist the IDC's work.[125] The *IDC Report* asserts that the Gardaí carried out fresh enquiries in 2012; however, their 2012 report is almost identical to the May 2010 submission to the DoJ by Garda Commissioner Fachtna Murphy.[126]

155 women accounted for? Flaws in the IDC Report and Dr Prunty's research

The *IDC Report* does not name the 'researchers' who worked on a 'research and cataloguing' project at High Park between 2003 and 2005, which it claims had 'identified and matched' the names and dates of death of 'all 155 women whose remains were exhumed'.[127] Nor does the IDC name 'the researcher' who informed the DoEnv in 2010 that OLC had commissioned a memorial for Glasnevin Cemetery 'which will correct the discrepancies on the earlier memorial and in addition will add the individual names, and dates, of all those women who were buried from High Park in Glasnevin Cemetery'.[128] However, when the date of the researcher's letter to the DoEnv, as cited in the *IDC Report*, is compared to Dr Prunty's letter and to the DoJ's Memorandum in June 2011, it is possible to discern that Dr Jacinta Prunty is said researcher and the person who led the team working on OLC's records between 2003 and 2005. The IDC did not publish Dr Prunty's report to the DoEnv in August 2010 as an appendix to its *Report*; however, it is contained in the department file released to JFMR through FOI.

The OLC Sisters have refused JFMR access to their records of deceased Magdalene women. In the absence of this information, Claire has used the MNP archive and methodologies to analyse to the best of her ability Dr Prunty's database of who she claims the exhumed women to be. Dr Prunty's research contains myriad deficiencies and inaccuracies – to the extent that the first exhumation licence schedule is more accurate than the database she provided to the DoEnv. What follows are a number of examples of the glaring inaccuracies in Dr Prunty's report, and in the aforementioned State bodies' interpretations of its import. The first is that the report provides details for only 133 women, whereas 155 bodies were exhumed and 154 cremated in 1993.[129] The second problem on its face is that Dr Prunty acknowledged in her letter to the DoEnv that she had only 'managed to resolve *most* cases where there was a discrepancy'.[130] A third obvious mistake is that Dr Prunty's database contains duplications in two instances, creating gaps where missing women should be identified. For example, Dr Prunty notes that the May 1993 exhumation licence listed Alice B. (who was the last woman exhumed) both by her legal name and as 'Magdalen of St Peter', but the database retains the duplication.[131] (The second duplication, Mary Groves, is discussed later in the chapter). Thus, Dr Prunty's database merely accounts for 131 women. Both the IDC and the Gardaí appear to have missed these obvious flaws in Dr Prunty's research.

A far more fundamental error that lies in Dr Prunty's research is her stated methodology, as outlined in her letter to the DoEnv:

> To return to the question of the licence issued by your Department for the exhumation of 133 individuals from St. Mary's graveyard, High Park, Drumcondra, in 1993, I have extracted from the High Park database the burial details of all the persons listed on that schedule. From this you will see how we have managed to resolve most cases where there was a discrepancy.[132]

The primary purpose of Dr Prunty's *High Park database* was to facilitate the erection of accurate headstones at Glasnevin. The matter of resolving discrepancies between the exhumation licence and the headstones only seems to have arisen when the DoEnv wrote to OLC: Dr Prunty told the department their enquiry was 'timely' because she had just completed work on the *High Park database* for the purposes of the Glasnevin memorial.[133] However, Victoria Perry, a member of Dr Prunty's research team, claimed in 2007 that there was a list of 155 names known as 'St Mary's Database' in OLC's archives at Beechlawn.[134] It is puzzling therefore that Dr Prunty supplied a list of only 133 names to the DoEnv. It is also perplexing that although Dr Prunty had numerous sources available to her, she opted to use the first exhumation licence schedule as a template for compiling a database for the DoEnv, to the extent that the names in her database are set out in precisely the same order as that schedule. Crucially, as we know from Ms Lee's report, the licence schedule is a deeply flawed document: only thirty-two crosses and/or coffin plates relating to women exhumed in 1993 corresponded to the names on the licence.[135] Moreover, the licence schedule is merely a list of names; without dates or causes of death, the task of accurately verifying the identity of each woman is impossible.

Mary Lee's *List One* remains the more reliable source to cross reference OLC's records and the names of women exhumed.[136] Yet, there is no reference in Dr Prunty's report to *List One*. Dr Prunty offers legal names and dates of death only for the twenty-three Magdalene names given to the DoEnv in the exhumation licence application (rather than the 110 Magdalene names recorded by Ms Lee during the exhumations). Dr Prunty's database also does not refer to or include names from the cremation forms that OLC signed for each woman's remains (generated from *List One*).[137] Furthermore, Dr Prunty's report does not refer to OLC's handwritten list of *Names of other women buried in St Mary's*, which was given to Masseys Undertakers at the time of the exhumations.[138] This list is not contained in either the DCC or DoEnv file. Four of the women on this list are also named on Ms Lee's *List One* (and were therefore exhumed); however, they are not listed on the exhumation licence schedule or Dr Prunty's database.[139] Although these and numerous other sources were available to Dr Prunty, she nonetheless told the DoEnv that the research had been 'pursued *in so far as the records will allow*'.[140]

Dr Prunty's database includes a 'source' column, but there are twenty-five entries where it remains blank. Furthermore, Dr Prunty told the DoEnv that a member of her team 'worked in the records office of Glasnevin Cemetery on their interment registers'.[141] There are seven entries on Dr Prunty's database for which she cites Glasnevin Cemetery as her source. Glasnevin's interment registers provide the date of burial, and in the case of these seven women, the records clearly indicate that they were buried in Glasnevin when they died, between 1893 and 1967.[142] Dr Prunty and her team had access to Glasnevin registers on a level beyond that afforded to members of the public (who cannot view the ledgers and must pay to search online using specific names). Yet, Dr Prunty appears to be under the impression that these seven women were exhumed from St Mary's Graveyard in 1993.

Dr Prunty told the DoEnv she also viewed other sources, including

> death certificates, invoices and receipts for purchase of coffins and other burial expenses, obituaries, certificates or 'grants of right of burial' to numbered plots in Prospect (Glasnevin) Cemetery (with notes on who was buried in that particular plot), and correspondence with various parties (including the cemetery committee, the archbishop, benefactors, and within OLC).[143]

Nonetheless, Dr Prunty signals no awareness that at least nine of the women named on the first licence schedule were never exhumed: seven of these were buried in Glasnevin at the time of their deaths, and two others (Edith D. and Mary Morgan, who is discussed later) were buried in other cemeteries directly after death.[144] Edith D. was buried three days after she died in her family's plot in a cemetery 100 kilometres away from High Park. Yet, as demonstrated by a note in Dr Prunty's database, she seems under the misconception that Edith's remains were claimed after exhumation from St Mary's: 'Taken to family plot for *reburial*. NB name not to appear on new headstone'.[145]

Dr Prunty erroneously substitutes different names for 11 of the 133 entries on the first exhumation licence schedule. For instance, Dr Prunty created a duplication by changing two names from the first exhumation licence (Mary Grimes and Mary Graves) to the same identity, Mary Groves who died on 21 May 1938. Seven of the eleven new identities relate to women who could never have been exhumed as they were always buried in Glasnevin. One case warranted further investigation by the MNP. The first exhumation licence names Mary Morgan, whose date of death, according to OLC's May application and the enclosed death certificate, was 12 January 1933.[146] Dr Prunty contends that the licence should have instead listed Mary Anne Morgan (d.o.d. 13/2/1919). That cannot be correct, however, because Glasnevin records show that Mary Anne Morgan (d.o.d. 13/2/1919) was buried in Glasnevin when she died and thus was never exhumed. The fact that the DoEnv accepted a death certificate in January 1993 for Mary Morgan (d.o.d. 12/1/1933) is alarming because her death certificate makes no reference to High Park and states that she died of 'asphyxia'. Public inquest records show that Mary Morgan (d.o.d. 12/1/1933) lived in Phibsborough in Dublin and that her body was found in the Royal Canal near Broombridge in January 1933.[147] Her son Michael, who played for Dublin's Bohemian Football Club, saw her the day before her death.[148] Mary is buried with her husband in Ballymaglassan Church

Cemetery in Batterstown, County Meath.[149] A search of the *Register of Deaths* confirms that only one Mary Morgan died in Dublin in 1933.[150] OLC inputted the name of a woman with no connection to High Park on their exhumation licence application and nobody seems to have noticed.

Dr Prunty's database also provides names and dates of death purporting to be the legal identities of the twenty-three Magdalene names and the woman with only a first name on the licence schedule. A check against Glasnevin Cemetery records reveals that two of the new identities provided by Dr Prunty relate to women who were interred in Glasnevin and never buried in St Mary's Cemetery. A comparison with *List One* reveals five further erroneous substitutions – for example, Dr Prunty contends that Magdalene of Lourdes (d.o.d. 1943) is Annie B (d.o.d. 1972). However, *List One* reveals that two women known as Magdalene of Lourdes were exhumed. One died in 1943 and the other in 1972 (the latter was not named on the licence). Therefore Annie B. is not Magdalene of Lourdes (d.o.d. 1943).

Dr Prunty's report – the 'authority' upon which Chapter Sixteen of the *IDC Report* depends – is flawed, incomplete, misleading, inaccurate and unverifiable in part. Yet, nobody seems to have interrogated Dr Prunty's findings. Instead, Dr Prunty's report offered the Gardaí, the DoJ and IDC 'cover' to conceal their inaction by refusing to investigate the exhumation and cremation of 155 vulnerable women in an independent and objective manner.

What is the current situation?

In 2015, JFMR revealed significant discrepancies between the headstones at Glasnevin and the locations where the women are in fact interred in the cemetery.[151] Both OLC and the State failed to respond to our concerns. On 17 August 2010, Dr Prunty had sent OLC a 'final list' of names and dates to be engraved on the new memorial.[152] Today, the discrepancies JFMR raised remain on public view.

As for family members enquiring about deceased Magdalene women, Frank Brehany's correspondence with OLC raises significant concerns about how the Order responds to such enquiries. The Sisters told Frank that Mary was buried 'in the OLC plot' at Glasnevin.[153] While OLC gave Frank a location reference for Mary's burial place, it relates to a range of plots in the same grave, suggesting that the Order does not know precisely where Mary is buried. As Frank's grandmother Mary was a consecrate, she would almost certainly have been buried at St Mary's Graveyard. Yet, her name does not appear on the exhumation licence. Moreover, Mary is named on OLC's handwritten list of 'other women' purportedly buried at St Mary's, but the Sisters told Frank nothing of the exhumations.

The site where St Mary's once stood is now a car park at the rear of the Bonnington Hotel in Dublin and currently, there are a number of planned developments on this site. Both DCC and the planning authority, An Bord Pleanála (ABP) have raised concerns about the possibility of additional human remains at the site. On 28 November 2019, the City Archaeologist's Office recommended a 'test excavation of the site . . . to ensure that no further undocumented burials are present'.[154] On 21 September 2020,

ABP granted permission for one development but stipulated that the developer must 'facilitate the preservation, recording and protection of archaeological materials . . . to secure the preservation and protection of any remains that may exist within the site'.[155]

Is it possible that additional bodies remain at the site where St Mary's once stood? Mary Lee's report reveals that 'a trench was dug across the length of the *unmarked ground* to the front of the graveyard' to ensure there were no further unmarked burials.[156] This suggests that the undertakers dug a trench along the unmarked ground, but not the entire graveyard. It is also possible that there were more than 155 consecrated Magdalenes who died at High Park. According to one author writing in the *Irish Rosary* in 1897, there were forty-eight consecrates and ninety-eight 'Children of Mary' in High Park at that time.[157] Forty-eight consecrates in 1897, and potentially others from the Child of Mary ranks, is a high number if we are meant to believe that only 155 consecrated women were buried at St Mary's over its lifetime. Moreover, the MNP has not yet been able to establish the burial place of 146 women whose death certificates signal they died at High Park.[158] We do not suggest that all 146 are still buried at the former St Mary's site. However, in light of the significant anomalies detailed earlier, the possibility of additional human remains cannot be ruled out.

Today, the Irish State does not have a clear policy requiring death certificates as a prerequisite for exhumation licence applications, even where remains are not identified.[159] When JFMR applied under FOI for all exhumation policy records held by the Department of Rural and Community Development (the current central government department with responsibility for exhumations), the department responded that 'the function of issuing exhumation licences was devolved to the local authorities with effect from 1 July 1994, the Department holds no records relevant to your request'.[160] In response to an FOI request, the HSE, which advises local authorities on exhumation licence applications, asserts it 'has no national policy on exhumation applications for remains, identified or unidentified'.[161] Three decades after the High Park exhumations, nothing has been learnt.

Conclusion

Who do we want to be?

We have seen throughout this book how the State's refusal to search for, listen to, reveal or accept the truth of the Magdalene Laundries abuse continues to degrade and cause concrete harm to survivors and their families. International and European human rights law tells us that truth-telling is foundational for redressing gross and systematic human rights violations.

UNCAT member and psychologist Nora Sveaass has written that organized violence involving torture or other cruel, inhuman or degrading treatment or arbitrary detention persists 'from a psychological point of view' for as long as the facts of it are concealed or denied.[1] Sveaass and others contend that where the 'reality experienced is denied . . . psychological reactions such as feelings of worthlessness and disempowerment, as well as even cognitive distortions, may follow', and there 'may be strong feelings of vulnerability'.[2] Public disclosure of 'the time, place and nature of violent actions' and 'the identity of the perpetrators who executed the actions and/or gave the orders' is frequently 'of the utmost psychological value for surviving victims and their close relatives'.[3] Based on our work with survivors over many years, JFMR concurs with this expert view.

Elizabeth Coppin's case before UNCAT contends that the inhuman and degrading treatment which she experienced continues to this day because impunity prevails.[4] It appears to us that for as long as the State conceals information about the fate and whereabouts of individuals who died while incarcerated in Magdalene Laundries and in other State-supported institutions, its behaviour amounts to a continuing situation of 'enforced disappearances' (a human rights violation which is so serious it is considered a crime against humanity when systematic).[5] Furthermore, in our view the State is infringing survivors' rights to privacy and freedom of expression by withholding evidence of their experiences from them. The government's denial of archival access is also a major obstacle to survivors accessing civil or criminal justice, including proper compensation.

Truth-telling is not only a personal right but also a *collective* societal entitlement under international and emerging European human rights law.[6] In other words, information about gross and systematic human rights violations should be provided not only to those directly affected but also to the general public in a way that protects victims' and survivors' privacy and freedom of expression.

Public truth-telling is directly connected to the idea that redress for torture and other gross abuses must aim to 'guarantee non-repetition'. UNCAT explains that 'guarantees of non-repetition offer an important potential for the transformation of social relations that may be the underlying causes of violence'.[7] In 2013, the IHRC concluded its *Follow-up Report on State involvement with Magdalen Laundries* by recommending changes to current laws and practices to combat 'failures of the State, in terms of protecting the human rights of girls and women in the laundries, [that] are still evident today'.[8] These recommendations – which never received an official response from the government – included the amendment of equality legislation to ensure more comprehensive protection from discrimination; review of regulatory and oversight frameworks to guarantee that rights are fully protected when the State outsources its functions to non-State actors; the creation of a legal framework to suppress and prevent forced or compulsory labour; strengthening of protections against arbitrary detention of people with disabilities including through greater provision of community-based mental health services; the introduction of legislation to provide access to information and identity for adopted people; strengthening of State oversight of exhumations and cremations; and greater compliance by State bodies with their record-keeping duties so that they are 'in a position to properly record State interventions in matters of public and private life, where those interventions and interactions engage the human rights of its citizens'.[9]

To this list we would add that non-repetition of Ireland's so-called 'historical' abuses also requires tackling the non-regulation of deprivation of liberty in nursing homes and other care settings in Ireland, and the coercive institutionalization of individuals and families experiencing homelessness and seeking asylum (injustices that numerous Magdalene survivors have raised with us). Our understanding of the Magdalene Laundries system tells us that we also, urgently, need to create statutory rights to person-centred health, social care and educational needs services, and independent advocacy in these contexts, so that when each of us is in need, we are not simply treated as a 'charity case' and subjected to whatever fate our 'benefactor' may choose. Wholesale review of and investment in access to justice also appear to us to be essential 'guarantees' to prevent similar abuse in future.[10]

This holistic understanding of reparation or 'redress' aligns with the concept of 'transitional justice'. Transitional justice is an internationally recognized approach to facilitating the emergence of peaceful democracy following large-scale conflict and civil rights violations in any given society.[11] Truth-telling is a non-negotiable requirement of transitional justice: it is necessary for the achievement of the process's other essential aspects, namely, accountability, reparation and guarantees of non-recurrence (often described as institutional reform). In our 2011 Restorative Justice and Reparations Proposals and 2012 follow-up report to UNCAT, JFMR argued that Ireland should adopt a transitional justice approach to responding to the Magdalene Laundries abuse.[12] Other scholars in Ireland and internationally have given further consideration in recent years to whether transitional justice is an appropriate framework for addressing non-conflict-related systematic human rights violations, such as institutional abuses. At an international conference which we convened at Boston College in 2018, survivors of many connected forms of institutional, gender-based and care-related abuses in Ireland joined academics, activists and policy makers in unanimously concluding that (1) Ireland has failed in its attempts at truth-telling, and (2) real truth-telling, as defined by those who experienced the abuse, must be at the heart of 'redress'.[13]

JFM/R's work since 2009 has further drawn on and adapted to the Irish context the concepts of 'gender-sensitive' reparations and 'transformative' reparations – conceived of originally by scholars, courts, civil society and United Nations human rights bodies concerned with sexual violence during conflict and/or authoritarianism.[14] We maintain that in order to rebalance power, survivors of Magdalene Laundries and all related institutional, gender-based and social care-related abuses must be invited to define the harms that they have experienced, to explain how those harms persist to the present day and to clarify how they might be remedied. In order to restore dignity, survivors need to be recognized as rights-holders, possessing Constitutional, European and international human rights law entitlements in the course of all attempts to provide redress and reparation – rather than as the undeserving recipients of State and Church 'benevolence'.

Dublin Honours Magdalenes

Judge Quirke's recommendation of a Dedicated Unit within the DoJ to serve Magdalene survivors held great promise as a mechanism to give the women transformative power and control over the State's redress activities. We had been pleased to see the recommendation as we had been proposing such a unit since our 2011 draft of a restorative justice scheme. The *Quirke Report* envisaged the Dedicated Unit assisting survivors to meet with each other and to make their views known through facilitated consultation on the form that national memorialization of the Magdalene Laundries abuse should take. The Dedicated Unit would then create and maintain a 'garden, museum or other form of memorial' according to the women's wishes and under the supervision of a committee of survivors including those living abroad.

On 1 March 2016, however, as the 'decade of centenaries' commemorations of Ireland's path to independence were in full swing, JFMR felt compelled to issue a PR upon discovering that a property developer planned to demolish the former Magdalene Laundry in Donnybrook to make way for luxury apartments.[15] The Magdalene convent in New Ross had been destroyed only two months previously over the Christmas holidays. Our PR highlighted that the government was still failing to implement the Dedicated Unit and memorialization aspects of the ex gratia Scheme. Meanwhile, Magdalene-era machinery, paperwork and other contents remained on the Donnybrook site.[16] More importantly, an archaeological assessment submitted with the planning permission application cautioned that, in the absence of 'clear records as to what happened to some of the women who operated within the laundries once they died', women's remains may be buried there unmarked.[17]

As part of the planning permission process, Claire sent a written submission from JFMR to DCC calling for clarity as to whether women were indeed buried on the grounds and, if so, what were their identities. In addition, our submission insisted that survivors and relatives should be consulted regarding the fate of the site. We argued that expert consultation should happen in particular with the women 'still living in the Donnybrook complex in an institutionalised setting in the custody of the Sisters of Charity'.[18] Subject to survivors' and relatives' wishes, we offered our view that the State should buy the Donnybrook building to preserve it as 'part of the historical record of what happened in Ireland's Magdalene Laundries'. Our submission also noted that DCC owned the large Magdalene convent site at Sean McDermott Street at the heart of Dublin's inner city (which it acquired in an exchange of lands with the OLC Sisters in 2001). In the event of the State refusing to purchase the Donnybrook building and DCC granting permission for its demolition, we suggested, Sean McDermott Street might provide a home for the contents salvaged from Donnybrook.[19]

On 6 February 2017, news broke that DCC officials were now planning to sell that two-acre Sean McDermott Street Magdalene site to a commercial buyer.[20] Maeve contacted politicians to request that they join us in a 'concerted effort' to 'prevent the sale of Sean McDermott Street by DCC, and to ensure that consultation with the women takes place on what should happen to (a) Donnybrook and its contents, and (b) Sean McDermott Street'.[21] Because local councillors' consent is required for the sale of local authority assets, Gary Gannon, then a Social Democrats Dublin City councillor, moved quickly with Sinn Féin councillor Críona Ní Dhálaigh to gather full cross-party support for an emergency motion on 6 March 2017. The councillors' motion requested the DCC public servants to commit to 'convening and consulting with a committee of Magdalene survivors . . . as recommended by the Quirke Commission and promised by the Government as part of the Magdalene restorative justice scheme'.[22]

Gary Gannon then arranged for Katherine, Maeve and Claire to meet with DCC officials in March 2017 to begin devising a concrete plan for a survivor consultation on memorialization.[23] We suggested that the DoJ's ex gratia Scheme budget could easily fund every survivor to travel to Dublin with a companion; the department had spent approximately €25 million by March 2017 whereas the 2013 cost estimate for the scheme was €34–€58 million.[24] By April 2017 our thoughts had evolved into a written proposal for a two-day event entitled 'Dublin Honours Magdalenes' (DHM).[25] We envisaged the historic Round Room at the Mansion House – the venue of the first Dáil Éireann meeting, in 1919 – hosting the consultation and a gala evening of dinner and entertainment to honour the women. The previous year, then Dublin lord mayor Críona Ní Dhálaigh had presented JFMR with a Lord Mayor's Award on behalf of Magdalene Laundry survivors at a ceremony in the Mansion House Round Room.[26] Six survivors and two relatives of deceased women collected the award with us, and that powerful experience of official acknowledgement and national significance was one which we wanted to recreate for all.

Katherine wrote to Minister Fitzgerald on 10 April 2017 to inform her that we were in constructive discussions with DCC, and to request that the minister appoint officials 'to work with us on issuing an invitation to all of the women who have been in contact with the Department in relation to the redress scheme and to arrange for the accommodation and other logistical details in hosting this event'.[27] We sent a similar letter and email to the Taoiseach, cc'ing Minister Fitzgerald, in early May 2017. We reminded Enda Kenny that he had promised during his apology in 2013 'to engage directly' with 'as many of the women as possible to agree on the creation of an appropriate memorial to be financed from the Government separately from the funds that are being set aside for the direct assistance for the women'.[28] A group of Maeve's UCD students and their friends set up a webpage, Facebook page and Twitter account with the aim of building public support for the event. Working alongside Gary Gannon and playwright Grace Dyas and other artists and activists, the students created short films, shared media coverage, arranged a public rally at the Sean McDermott Street site and circulated an online petition.[29] Dyas began to devise her play *We Don't Know What's Buried Here* during this time, particularly in response to a DCC-commissioned Archaeological Assessment of the Sean McDermott Street Magdalene site, which stated (similarly to the Donnybrook assessment) that in light of the nuns' failure to register all women's deaths and 'the lack of transparency and cooperation of the religious orders', it was 'impossible to state with certainty that there are no burials located within the site at present'.[30]

Our letters to both the Taoiseach and Minister Fitzgerald went unanswered. By October 2017 we committed to each other that we would 'pull back completely from campaigning' due to our increasing burnout and our desire to devote time to the MOHP, the MNP and reporting to human rights bodies.[31] Throughout 2017 Claire and Maeve were also voluntarily coordinating the 'Clann Project', which they had created in 2015 in an effort to replicate our previous method of 'shadowing' the IDC – this time in relation to the MBHCOI.

The Clann Project involved fifty lawyers in the global law firm Hogan Lovells providing free assistance to anyone who might wish to make a witness statement to the Commission of Investigation. Maeve and Claire were also working with Hogan Lovells's Rod Baker to coordinate a written submission to the Commission, making factual and legal arguments and recommendations on the basis of the witness evidence gathered and pro bono research by twenty-two members of the Bar of Ireland and others.[32] Claire was busy, too, making submissions to Cork City Council planners in 2017 in response to a developer's proposal to partly demolish and redevelop the Sundays Well Magdalene Laundry and industrial school site.[33] She argued that survivors needed to be consulted on memorialization and requested an independent investigation into the identities of women buried on the site in light of the Good Shepherds Sisters' poor record-keeping, and given that there are significant discrepancies and gaps in the existing headstones marking Good Shepherd graves. Claire also raised JFMR's concern that the auxiliaries' grave on the Sundays Well site is located behind a ten-foot wall which is covered in razor wire and remains inaccessible to the families and friends of these women.

Gary Gannon kept the 'DHM' flame alive. He remained in touch with Maeve, who had by November 2017 taken a job as Senior Research and Policy Officer at the ICCL, giving her more opportunity to advocate. In December Cllr Gannon asked his fellow DCC Central Area Committee councillors to dedicate some of their 'discretionary budget' to DHM; his hope was that such a move 'might shame the Justice department to free up any remaining funds necessary to bring together the women'.[34] The councillors agreed to contribute €30,000 – a move that would prove crucial to DHM becoming a reality. In early January 2018 Maeve drafted a letter which the ICCL, AII, the NWCI, Sage Support and Advocacy Service and JFMR sent to the newly appointed Minister for Justice Charlie Flanagan, asking for his support to fund and invite survivors to attend DHM.[35]

Both DCC and the DoJ acted in early 2018 as if the commercial sale of the Sean McDermott Street Magdalene site was a foregone conclusion. They claimed that the new, private, owner of the land would install a Magdalene memorial. Brendan Kenny, deputy chief executive of DCC, emailed Katherine and Maeve on 23 January asking us to meet to discuss his proposal 'to dispose of the entire property' at Sean McDermott Street while 'ensuring that there is a permanent memorial included in the new development'.[36] Two days later, Minister Flanagan's private secretary responded to the five NGOs' letter with a similar message; the minister's letter made no reference to the DHM proposal and stated that DCC would be pursuing 'a significant commercial redevelopment' at Sean McDermott Street and would 'consult with Magdalen representative groups' regarding a memorial. We replied to Brendan Kenny to state that it was 'absolutely crucial that it is the women themselves who are consulted, and that no women are left out of the invitation to consult'.[37] Jim O'Callaghan TD worked meanwhile to keep our request for support for DHM on Minister Flanagan's agenda.

A golden opportunity arose when Caoimhghín Ó Caoláin TD, chair of the Oireachtas Justice Committee and a previous member of the Ad Hoc Committee on the Magdalene Laundries from 2009, stopped to speak with Maeve in Leinster House following the Ombudsman's presentation regarding his findings of maladministration by the DoJ on 31 January 2018. That evening, Ó Caoláin was to visit the lord mayor of Dublin and he agreed to raise the question of inviting survivors to the Mansion House with his party colleague Mícheál MacDonncha.[38] Within a fortnight, the lord mayor had committed to a two-day event in June 2018. He would announce his invitation during 'Lord Mayor's Business' at the next meeting of DCC, on 5 March.[39] Now the question was how to make DHM happen? Having met her in London years previously and knowing her reputation for philanthropy and supporting feminist causes, Maeve emailed businesswoman Norah Casey to ask if she would meet to discuss 'a creative solution' to the question of bringing survivors together as we had 'run into a wall with the government'.[40] Norah's swift and enthusiastic response rocketed JFMR out of campaign retirement – but what happened next was worth every last ounce of energy that we had.

Norah, Maeve, Katherine and Claire formed as the DHM Organising Committee. On 6 March 2018, with some help and advice from former journalist Miriam Donohue we briefed several members of the press and published a PR announcing a done deal: that 'several hundred survivors of the Magdalene Laundries will be honoured and celebrated by the City of Dublin' on 5 and 6 June 2018 to 'fulfil two of the key recommendations of Mr Justice Quirke's Magdalene Redress Scheme'.[41] Our PR then called on the minister for justice to agree to invite the women and contribute the outstanding funding. Norah spent much of 6 March giving media interviews, and behind the scenes, Senator Marie-Louise O'Donnell played her part in encouraging Charlie Flanagan to consider our proposal. A mere three days later we were able to issue the further statement: 'Minister for Justice marks International Women's Day by confirming that he will invite women to the Dublin event on behalf of JFMR'.[42] The minister, having faced the significant challenge of convincing his officials, insisted that his department would not merely issue invitations, but it would provide the necessary €300,000 to ensure that DHM would happen.

It is not possible here to do justice to the alacrity, altruism and sensitivity with which Norah swung into action after that day, ultimately overseeing a gathering of more than 230 survivors, each with a companion, from all over Ireland as well as the United States, the United Kingdom, several other European countries and Australia. Some women were returning to Ireland for the first time. Minister Flanagan had instructed the DoJ to issue invitations to the more than 700 women whose applications to the scheme were either pending or accepted. Each of our weekly meetings at Norah's office revealed not only the enormity of the task but also its impending impact on the women who planned to attend. Every survivor's individual circumstances were accommodated, down to the taxi fare to get to an airport and any special assistance needed on the plane. In mid-April, once funding from the DoJ had been agreed (with the DCC councillors' seed funding securing venue bookings in the meantime), Norah was able to hire an events team and our excitement grew as artists at the pinnacle of the Irish entertainment world lined up to honour the women.[43] Meanwhile, we helped to compile invitations and welcome packs, gathered a group of thirty-five volunteers and agreed on a method for guaranteeing confidentiality to women who wished to maintain it while affording opportunities to other women to speak publicly during the two days.[44] Crucially, we also devised a plan for the facilitated consultation at the heart of the event. Katherine agreed to lead this 'Listening Exercise' given her experience directing the MOHP. She set about convening twenty-six expert facilitators and twenty-nine scribes for tables of up to ten women. She also composed a ten-minute introductory video script produced by New Decade films so that the women attending would learn about the current state of the institutions that held them and how the Magdalene issue was being engaged with by visual artists, writers and academics. Using the MOHP ethical protocols, Katherine planned for the facilitator at each table to read aloud the information forms and ensure that consent was informed. Participants would not be identified in the report or the transcripts of the Listening Exercise; each woman would be assigned a pseudonym instead.[45]

One of Norah's earliest and most significant efforts was to arrange with President Michael D. Higgins and his staff that the two days' proceedings would begin with a garden party and presidential address at Áras an Úachtaráin. The president's speech on the afternoon of Tuesday 5 June began and ended with an apology to the women, recognizing that they had been 'profoundly failed' by State institutions, governments, religious orders and society as a whole. The president warmly acknowledged the value of the women's decision to share their experiences through the Listening Exercise that would take place the following day. Noting that their generosity in speaking had already broken society's silence and shifted the nation 'from a time of disbelief, denial and even hostility towards your experiences, to a time where we acknowledge that we must deliver . . . a genuine and heartfelt will to hear, to share and to learn from your testimonies', the president emphasized the importance of the women's truth-telling to the protection of human dignity in the future:

> Each of your individual experiences is a critical element of the whole, and all are equally important in enabling us to engage ethically with your stories and to truly understand them. It is only through this remembering and understanding

> that we can hope to learn and apply these lessons to our present and our future circumstances.[46]

Norah also arranged with An Garda Síochána for a fleet of outriders to accompany the eight coaches that would bring the women from venue to venue in order to stop traffic and enable swift journey times. As cars came to a standstill along the Grand Canal, and the buses with their purple 'DHM' dashboard signs drove by on the way from Áras an Úachtaráin to the Mansion House, motorists got out of their vehicles, and passers-by stood, waving and clapping. Further applause awaited at Dawson Street, where hundreds of people – many holding homemade signs – had gathered to greet the Magdalene survivors as they made their way into the gala dinner venue.[47] Numerous women reflected on this during the Listening Exercise the next morning:

> They were sobbing. 'Welcome home', you know.
>
> a girl called me over and shook me hand . . . actually cried because . . . it's after taking a little bit of burden off me.
>
> I don't think anyone in this room will forget them people out there, welcoming us last night.
>
> There was a young little girl there . . . She's the generation that's going to remember this.
>
> It was like we were being welcomed back into society, or whatever . . . Accepted again, that we're humans, yeah.
>
> Did you see that crowd out there yesterday when we were coming in? . . . Those women, they really . . . they were saying, 'you look nice! Welcome home, sisters.'
>
> last night, to see the women, and people to come out and welcome us, it was so emotional. . . . Like, we thought . . . that nobody wanted us.
>
> And we'd also like to thank all these people that supported us.
>
> Like what you basically need is respect and I think it was shown this week to us by the President, which not everybody gets that opportunity, but it was a great opportunity for us. Well deserved, I would say, but in the other way, it was lovely, you know, and I do appreciate what the President did yesterday. And what about them people outside that gate yesterday? They were absolutely tremendous. People we didn't even know. I even get goose bumps . . . even talking about it.[48]

The DHM Listening Exercise was an unprecedented event and uncharted territory in this field of research, and thus the process of transcribing the simultaneous conversations of 146 women was in equal measure challenging, rewarding and deeply moving.[49] The *Listening Exercise Report*, which Katherine and Claire published in June 2020 with an accompanying volume of over 1,000 pages of anonymized transcripts, is testament to the power of the women's voices and the transformative potential of listening to them.[50]

The *Listening Exercise Report* begins with a quote from one participant, 'Charlotte', who explained: 'I'm still there.' She lives in a nursing home on the grounds of the former Magdalene Laundry in which she was forced to work and has been institutionalized on the site for over forty years. It disturbed us that the women living in the OLC nursing home at Beechlawn, Drumcondra, were not in attendance although invitations had been sent and Minister Flanagan was in contact about their non-registration prior to the event.[51] The *Listening Exercise Report* opens with a dedication to all the women who died in the institutions; survivors stated repeatedly during the Listening Exercise that these women should be remembered and 'honoured'.

When asked what lessons should be learnt, the women emphasized that similar abuses must never happen again. They wanted reassurance, in the words of one woman, 'That what happened to us will never again happen to another girl or woman in this lifetime . . . that Ireland will start looking after its children and its women because for a long time they did not do that.' There was general consensus among survivors that younger people need to be educated about the Magdalene Laundries in order to prevent similar abuse in future. As one woman put it,

> I'd like to say that as we're older women, that the younger people that will be studying this and looking at this, that we could be a light or a torch down that path to let them see what's down there . . . so that if they see, when they're old enough and mature enough, if they see an injustice starting to happen, before it gets out of control, they can look at that light and say, 'hold on, hey, stop, this happened before'.

That Irish society should know the 'truth' about the Magdalene Laundries was a recurring recommendation throughout the Listening Exercise. The women want it known, for example, that the Magdalene regime 'punished women for situations that the women had no control over', that the Magdalene Laundries were a system of 'illegal confinement', that 'rape victims were singled out . . . it was all women that was punished, while the guilty walked free', that the abuse was a result of 'collusion . . . the State and the church together', and that societal discrimination meant that the victims of abuse were not believed and therefore had no avenues of complaint or justice available to them. As one woman explained,

> Basically, what people should understand and know, that we were unimportant people, we didn't need to be remembered or mentioned, because they were believed, and that's what I'm saying, no matter what they said they were believed, we weren't, so there was no point, we were wrong, so there was no point in us complaining because nobody listened.

The women expressed various views about what should happen to the physical sites of incarceration and exploitation, and otherwise by way of symbolic memorialization. Several women expressed a wish to see every grave marked. One woman suggested: 'a plaque with *mea culpa, mea culpa* and a few words to say "We will forever make sure that this never happens again'". Many survivors supported the creation of a commemorative space in a prominent location. One woman, for example, shared her vision of 'a garden with a fountain in the middle with water flowing. I'd like a sculpture like the Phoenix or just women in the centre. The women with their hands high up in the sky, with . . . sympathetic [*sic*] . . . ' cause they've been through sadness and they kind of represent light and warmth.'[52] While a few women found no merit in the idea of a monument, several suggested a statute in O'Connell Street in the heart of Dublin City Centre, on the basis that people going about their ordinary business 'would see it and be aware of it. . . . They need to be very aware of what Ireland has done to people like us.' Others added that 'every town' or 'each county' should have a memorial. A commemorative day or event was suggested by numerous survivors.

Some women spoke directly about the two-acre Sean McDermott Street site which, by the time of the Listening Exercise, DCC officials planned to sell to a Japanese budget hotel chain. A few women wanted to see the convent building burned down, while another woman suggested that it should be turned into 'a safe home for women and children'. Numerous others expressed a wish for it to be converted into a museum. As one of these women offered,

> What hardship we all went through. And that's why I think one of them should be left standing as a laundry, as an institution . . . like Kilmainham Gaol. People go into Kilmainham Gaol because they know the history of it. The same way with the laundry.[53]

Preventing the sale of the Sean McDermott Street 'site of conscience'

Galvanized by DHM, Gary Gannon pressed on with his campaign to convince his fellow DCC councillors to veto the proposal for the sale of the Sean McDermott Street site. He convened a public meeting in the Belvedere Youth Club on 28 June 2018; there was standing room only despite it being the hottest day in Ireland in over forty years. Deirdre Cadwell, a survivor of the High Park Magdalene Laundry, explained to those gathered:

> I would like to see a museum or an interactive centre where children can come on school trips and be shown how we lived, how we worked every single day, and listen to our stories. This way they can see that this was part of the Irish history, and it's something that we don't ever, ever want to see happen again.[54]

Sian Muldowney of the Inner City Organisations Network emphasized the local community's need for social housing, while numerous survivors present and local residents stated their agreement that a museum commemorating the range of connected institutional abuses in Ireland alongside social housing was a far more necessary and appropriate use for the 2-acre site than a 350-bed budget hotel. Cllr Gannon summed up the key message emanating from the meeting on the RTÉ *Nine*

O'Clock News that night: 'Keep it in public ownership. Build something enormously special there: a tribute to the surviving women, many of whom are here tonight, and something for the community of the North Inner City.'

Having begun with the Referendum to repeal the Eighth Amendment to the Constitution, summer 2018 ended with Pope Francis's visit to Ireland to participate in the World Meeting of Families on 25 and 26 August (at a cost to the State of approximately €18 million).[55] In his speech of welcome to the Pope the Taoiseach raised the issue of the abuse of children and women in Church-run/State-financed institutions. Not surprisingly, while he implored the Pope 'to listen to the victims' of Church-related abuse in Ireland, the Taoiseach did not acknowledge any State responsibility when he said that there was 'much to be done to bring about justice and truth and healing for victims and survivors'.[56] The Pope, meanwhile, visited the parish church on Sean McDermott Street at the suggestion of Archbishop Diarmuid Martin and failed to pause at or recognize in any way the Magdalene convent standing directly opposite.[57] A brief meeting between abuse survivors and the Pope included no woman who had been detained in a Magdalene Laundry, Mother and Baby Home, or County Home. *The Irish Times* reported clerical abuse survivor Marie Collins stating that the Pope was 'taken aback' and 'shocked' upon hearing about Mother and Baby Homes and that he had 'no idea' what Magdalene Laundries were.[58] In lieu of a public apology to abuse survivors in Ireland, the Pope instead prayed to God for forgiveness during Mass at the Phoenix Park.[59]

Many members of the public, however, joined together in placing a firm focus on the need for truth-telling, and for survivors to be listened to and respected, by the State as well as the Church. Colm O'Gorman, director of AII and a clerical abuse survivor, with a voluntary group of activists and artists arranged a public demonstration under the banner 'Stand for Truth' at Dublin's Garden of Remembrance while the Papal mass was happening in the Phoenix Park.[60] Following a programme of speeches, songs and poems, the 5,000-strong crowd walked silently for 1 kilometre to the Sean McDermott Street Magdalene Laundry site. Survivors offered testimony once everyone was assembled, drawing connections between all forms of institutional, gender-based, clerical and care-related abuses, and between the injustices of the past and the silencing and neglect permeating the present.

In early September Gary Gannon took the opportunity to place a motion before Dublin City councillors to veto the DCC public servants' plan to sell the Sean McDermott Street site.[61] Three days before the vote, Deputy Chief Executive Brendan Kenny produced a brochure describing the global business success of the 'preferred bidder', Japanese budget hotel chain, Toyoko Inn, and acknowledging the work of various State agencies in making Dublin the European headquarters of the company.[62] The brochure further announced that Toyoko were 'very happy to include a memorial garden to commemorate former workers in the Magdalene Laundries here and throughout the country'. Kenny's proposal contained a fierce warning:

> If this proposal from management is rejected then this development/investment opportunity will be lost including the significant disposal proceeds which would have been invested back into the city (and into the NEIC [North East Inner City])

> on much needed capital projects. The site will remain vacant and undeveloped with the risk of ongoing deterioration in the condition of existing buildings and it will take some considerable time to formulate other possible plans for the site. We believe that this type of opportunity may not arise again in this area.[63]

The local community and their representatives refused to be cowed. Their vision, as Gary explained on RTÉ Radio's *Morning Ireland* the morning after a near unanimous vote of councillors succeeded in preventing the sale, is of an inclusive and caring society which will emerge through respect for abuse survivors and mature reckoning with our faults and failings:

> It isn't hotels that will revolutionise the North Inner City . . . give us something that's going to really revitalise the area and don't ask us to sell off the family jewels for this fake promise that we've had on several different occasions that something better will materialise. What we've said is, look at that site, see the opportunity, the asset that we have on our hands at the moment, and let's build with that in mind, a proper memorial and some public housing: that's what the city needs.
>
> . . . We've all sorts of memorials to when we were valiant in this country, but we've nothing to really talk about when we weren't, and I think we need to find the learning space for that. And we believe that that location down there in the heart of the North Inner City could be that location.[64]

The DCC councillors' vote was followed, in December 2018, by South Dublin County councillors' unanimous approval of a motion proposed by their fellow councillor and institutional abuse survivor Francis Timmons: 'support[ing] calls for the last remaining former Magdalene Laundry, that shut in 1996, in Sean McDermot [*sic*] Street not be sold', committing to write to DCC chief executive Owen Keegan to 'stress the importance of this site to many Irish Citizens who were enslaved and worked long hours in this laundry without pay' and 'implor[ing] Dublin City Council not to aid in any cover up and bury what happened here. These people deserve Truth and Justice.'[65]

Open Heart City

Soon after his motion passed in September 2018, Gary Gannon advised JFMR that in view of the DCC officials' resistance to anything other than commercial sale it would be up to us, and him, and any others who wished to participate, to present an alternative professional plan for the Sean McDermott Street site. Within a fortnight of the DCC councillors' vote, Katherine contacted Shelley McNamara and Yvonne Farrell of the internationally multi-award-winning Grafton Architects.[66] Katherine wrote that the 'Councillors overwhelmingly recognise that to take the site of the former Magdalene Laundry (which closed in 1996) out of public ownership would be to lose the opportunity to have a site of public conscience at the heart of the area that has suffered most since the foundation of our State', but that the 'issue now remains as to what should be done with the site'. She explained that JFMR was 'in a budding coalition with many concerned groups and community leaders who are beginning to articulate a shared vision for the site', and asked if Grafton might be in a position to help pro bono to further that process. Katherine's email shared JFMR's thinking so far, influenced by the women's views at DHM and the responses that Gary Gannon's campaign had elicited over the previous two years:

> We hope that a development of the site will include a 'site of conscience', that is an interpretive centre and living archive whereby citizens and visitors can engage in encountering the dark heritage yet also be challenged and empowered to co-create an inclusive collaborative future. We hope that the development will provide beautiful housing for older community members and those who want to make a community of participant citizens.

By January 2019, Katherine and Gary had prepared a comprehensive brief and – thanks to Grafton's help – the group of architects, academics, artists and activists keen to assist in facilitating the emergence of a concrete design for the Sean McDermott Street site had grown significantly. The 'Open Heart City' initiative was born: a collaboration between academics in a range of disciplines (the 'Open Heart City Collective') led by Katherine and Professor Hugh Campbell, Dean of UCD School of Architecture, and an amalgamation of three young international architecture offices, Denise Murray, Dún-na-nTuar and plattenbaustudio, who together form CoLab. The initiative was and remains further supported by Grafton Architects, Louise Lowe and JFMR, among others.[67] The aim of 'Open Heart City' is to facilitate the emergence of a shared design for the Sean McDermott Street site, by paying attention to previous survivor consultation reports and through further consultation with those personally affected by the Magdalene Laundries and the full range of connected institutional, family separation and other 'care'-related abuses, and with local residents, community leaders and the general public.

It is clear that access to information remains high among survivors' present needs. Personal data access was one of Judge Sean Ryan's key recommendations at the conclusion of the CICA in 2009.[68] In October 2018, the *Clann Project Report* made eight recommendations to the MBHCOI on the basis of evidence contained in eighty witness statements. An investigation with the purpose of producing records to those directly affected as well as appropriately anonymized records to the general public was the first recommendation, and information access was an essential aspect of all others.[69] Also in 2018, the 'Collaborative Forum of Former Residents of Mother and Baby Homes and Related Institutions' recommended 'a new One-Stop-Shop to house records from across State, religious orders, county and other sources so as to enable access to identity, personal and institutional information by any person separated from their family of origin, or detained in State funded or regulated Institutions'.[70] An independent consultation with over 100 industrial school survivors in 2019 further revealed a need for 'records and files to be made available to survivors' along with a 'tracing service for individuals wishing to find their families and relatives'.[71]

In November 2019, nine survivors of industrial schools gave evidence regarding the Retention of Records Bill to a special meeting of the Oireachtas Joint Committee on Education and Skills. This meeting was organized in haste through pressure from survivors, activists, academics and several politicians not to allow the Bill (which proposed 'sealing' entirely all records of the CICA and the RIRB and its Review Committee for at least seventy-five years) to proceed to Committee Stage in the Dáil without the Joint Committee hearing directly from those affected.[72] These survivors joined a coalition of seventy-two others, including second-generation survivors, academics, activists and practitioners in calling for the creation of a National Archive of Historical Institutional and Care-Related Records, as an Annex to the NAI, to provide at a minimum:

- Access to full personal files for institutional abuse survivors and those affected by adoption, including women whose children were unlawfully taken from them;
- Access for family members of those who died while in custody or care to information about their relative's fate and whereabouts;
- An opportunity for survivors and others to deposit testimony and other information for public access now or in the future;
- Public access to the (appropriately anonymized) administrative records of the systems of institutionalization and adoption in twentieth-century Ireland, whether currently held by private or State bodies; and
- The extra staffing, training and records management infrastructure (physical and digital) required at the National Archives or appointed body in order to achieve the above.[73]

Along with Máiréad Enright, Sinéad Ring and James Gallen, Maeve convened an initial working group of survivors, academics and practitioners in NUI Galway in December 2019 to discuss with the spokesperson for the Stasi Records Agency, Dagmar Hovestadt, the potential contents of Irish legislation that could provide for such an independent national archive.[74] The German example is particularly useful in light of the constant, erroneous arguments from Irish officialdom and other data controllers that European Union data protection law does not allow abuse survivors to access information that names other people – even where those other people relate to or are recorded as acting in relation to the person seeking their personal data, or where the other person is deceased. Pending the creation of the national archive that survivors seek, there is an urgent need for the State and all non-State bodies that hold survivors' information to properly interpret EU law, as Maeve and others insisted to the Oireachtas Joint Committee on Education and Skills in 2019 and as JFMR and ARA through the Clann Project continue to explain.[75]

At the time of writing, as part of the 'Open Heart City' initiative, CoLab are preparing designs for consultation that include a national archive for truth-telling, a museum and commemorative space, a place for survivors to gather, community social housing and an educational centre at Sean McDermott Street. During the 2019/20 academic year, in preparation for this work, master's students in the UCD School of Architecture researched and recorded the fabric of the site and its social, political and historical significance. They also modelled possible designs, as did master's students at Queen's University School of Architecture in Belfast. Maeve and her postgraduate students at NUI Galway created a website to explain 'Open Heart City' and its progress, and they gathered the records of previous consultations with survivors of industrial schools, Mother and Baby Homes and County Homes, as well as Magdalene Laundries, regarding memorialization.[76] Emerging from all of these consultations are the same messages that women voiced during the DHM Listening Exercise: that remembering the past is vital to honouring the dignity of those who suffered, that exercises in memorialization will only have integrity if accompanied by respect for the current care and educational needs and rights of abuse survivors and their families, and that the purpose and methods of memorialization must be to educate the public (especially younger people) with a view to preventing similar abuses in the future.

Concluding thoughts: Who do we want to be?

JFM was co-founded by Mari Steed, Angela Newsome and Claire McGettrick, motivated not least because of Mari and Angela's mothers, and other personal encounters with Magdalene survivors. Jim was called into advocacy when survivor Catherine Whelan phoned him; Maeve realized that human rights abuses needed to be addressed in Ireland when she heard the testimony of Michael O'Brien; and Katherine felt she was '*faoi geasa*' (put under the most solemn obligation) when having recorded her first oral history a survivor asked her 'Do you think it was wrong? What happened to me? Do you think it was wrong?' Relationships with Magdalene survivors have enriched our lives: we are better critical thinkers, we are more committed citizens, and we are more grateful and appreciative people because we have been befriended by and learnt from Magdalene survivors.

Reflecting on over a decade of research, advocacy and activism, one of the harsher lessons we learnt is that injustices proliferate when concern for commercial profits dominates the provision of social services: when care is first and foremost a commodity, and when the State does not fully develop comprehensive rights-based social welfare systems. We saw how difficult it is to make a State responsible when politicians do not hold civil servants to account. We saw, again and again, how abuses multiply when the perspectives and experiences of those most directly affected by an issue are systemically ignored. We are watching how the Irish State is becoming increasingly adept at shutting down access to archives, denying individuals access to their personal information and foreclosing the possibility for critical analysis and the formation of public knowledge which is crucial to creating a just society. We are also listening as survivors, their friends and concerned health professionals tell us in increasing despair that the opposite of what government ministers repeat from official briefings is true and that survivors face re-institutionalization in their older years because they do not have access to person-centred care.

Among the more positive lessons we learnt is that Irish civil society has a cohesive thirst for justice and will hold leaders to account if given an opportunity. We know that Irish people in the Republic are no longer in an anxious post-colonial mindset; that there is an appetite and aptitude for looking at how and where we have collectively failed. We know that a movement of academics, artists, activists and good neighbours will coalesce to support survivors' call for – and indeed to co-create – truth-telling, recognition of injustices, accountability for harms suffered and ways of ensuring that lessons are learnt and remembered. We know now that these precepts will guide us in being more expert in how we construct and evaluate knowledge. We know that truth-telling, recognition of harm and accountability will help us make better sense of our world, assist in making better policies and lead us collectively into a more equitable, more broadly shared future.

We have learnt from listening to Magdalene survivors tell us how they survived repeated degradation: they found others to care for. They cared for injured animals, mothers in distress, neglected older people and children. There is invariably that moment in the conversation where they will tell you that others had much harder lives than they did. The women we have met, and been befriended by, have cared for us. And for that care, most of all, we thank them.

Notes

Foreword

1 See *Report of the Commission of the Relief of the Sick and Destitute Poor, Including the Insane Poor* (Dublin: Stationery Office, 1928), 68.
2 See June Goulding, *A Light in the Window* (Dublin: Poolbeg, 1999).
3 See Mari Steed, 'Justice for Magdalenes: The Little NGO that could', Plenary Address, SNAP Conference, Dublin, 2013. Technically, JFM was not, nor did it see itself as, an NGO.

Introduction

1 Katherine O'Donnell, Claire McGettrick et al., 'Preface', in *Dublin Honours Magdalenes Listening Exercise Report Vol 1, Report on Key Findings* (Dublin: Justice for Magdalenes Research/Department of Justice, 2020). JFM and JFMR spell Magdalene using the more popular spelling. Most academic and official texts drop the final 'e'.
2 O'Donnell and McGettrick et al. *Dublin Honours Magdalenes Listening Exercise Report, Vol 1*, 21, 33, 38.
3 Máiréad Enright and Sinéad Ring, 'State Legal Responses to Historical Institutional Abuse: Shame, Sovereignty, and Epistemic Injustice', *Éire-Ireland: An Interdisciplinary Journal of Irish Studies*, 55, nos. 1–2 (Spring/Summer 2020): 68–99, 70.
4 Letter, Mr Gerard Corr, Ambassador Extraordinary and Plenipotentiary, Permanent Representative of Ireland, To the United Nations Office in Geneva, to Ms Felice D. Gaer, Rapporteur, Office of the United Nations High Commissioner for Human Rights, Committee Against Torture Secretariat, 8 August 2013.
5 Fintan O'Toole, 'GPA, Magdalen Women and the Underground Connection', *The Irish Times*, 8 September 1993.

Chapter 1

1 For an authoritative overview of this history, see Cormac Ó Gráda, *Ireland: A New Economic History, 1780-1939* (Oxford: Clarendon Press, 1995).
2 Brendan Grimes, 'Funding a Roman Catholic Church in Nineteenth-Century Ireland', *Architectural History*, 52 (2009): 147.
3 Quoted in Grimes, 'Funding a Roman Catholic Church in Nineteenth-Century Ireland', 157.

4 Quoted in Grimes, 'Funding a Roman Catholic Church in Nineteenth-Century Ireland', 157.
5 Niamh NicGhabhann, 'How the Catholic Church Built Its Property Portfolio', RTÉ Brainstorm podcast 27 August 2018.
6 Stuart Henderson, 'Religion and Development in Post-Famine Ireland', *Economic History Review*, 72, no. 4 (2019): 1251–85; Emmet Larkin, 'Economic Growth, Capital Investment, and the Roman Catholic Church in Nineteenth Century Ireland', *The American Historical Review*, 72, no. 3 (1967): 852–84.
7 James M. Smith's *Ireland's Magdalen Laundries and the Nation's Architecture of Containment* (South Bend: Notre Dame Press, 2007), 24.
8 Maria Luddy, '"Possessed of Fine Properties": Power, Authority and the Funding of Convents in Ireland, 1780-1900', in *The Economics of Providence*, eds M. Van Dijck and J. De Maeyer (Leuven: Leuven University Press, 2012), 228.
9 Joanna Bourke, *Husbandry to Housewifery: Women, Economic Change, and Housework in Ireland, 1890-1914* (Oxford: Clarendon, 1993); Cara Delay, *Irish Women and the Creation of Modern Catholicism, 1850-1950* (Manchester: Manchester University Press, 2019).
10 James M. Smith, Maeve O'Rourke, Raymond Hill, Claire McGettrick, with additional input from Katherine O'Donnell and Mari Steed, *State Involvement in the Magdalene Laundries JFM's Principal Submissions to the Inter-departmental Committee to Establish the Facts of State Involvement with the Magdalene Laundries*, 18 August 2012 [hereafter 'Principal Submission'], 111–13.
11 Magdalene institutions, both Catholic and Protestant, continued to operate in Northern Ireland, Leeanne McCormack, *Regulating Sexuality: Women in Twentieth-Century Northern Ireland* (Manchester: Manchester University Press, 2009).
12 Maria Luddy, 'Magdalene Asylums in Ireland, 1880-1930, Welfare, Reform, Incarceration?', in *Armenfürsorge und Wohltätigkeit. Ländliche Gesellschaften in Europa, - Poor Relief and Charity. Rural Societies in Europe, 1850-1930*, eds Inga Brandes and Katrin Marx-Jaskulski (Frankfurt am Main: Peter Lang, 2008), 293.
13 Tom Inglis, *Moral Monopoly: Rise and Fall of the Catholic Church in Modern Ireland*, 2nd edn (Dublin: University College Press, 2019), 15–94; Clair Wills, *That Neutral Island: A Cultural History of Ireland During the Second World War* (London: Faber & Faber, 2007).
14 Don O'Leary, *Vocationalism and Social Catholicism in Twentieth-Century Ireland: The Search for a Christian Social Order* (Dublin: Irish Academic Press, 2000).
15 Gerry McNally, 'Probation in Ireland: A Brief History of the Early Years', *Irish Probation Journal*, 4, no. 1 (2007): 5–24.
16 Lindsey Earner-Byrne, 'Mother and Child Scheme Controversy', History Hub Podcast.
17 Principal Submission, 105 ff, & 123–5.
18 Conditions of Employment Act, 1936, section 62.
19 Department of Justice and Equality, *Report of the Inter-Departmental Committee to Establish the Facts of State Involvement with the Magdalen Laundries* (hereafter *IDC Report*), Chapter 12, pp. 522, 571, 573. Maeve O'Rourke, *Justice for Magdalenes Research NGO Submission to the UN Committee against Torture in respect of IRELAND (for the session)*, July 2017, 13. Also see Principal Submission, 117–31.
20 Principal Submission, 51–6. Smith, *Ireland's Magdalen Laundries and the Nation's Architecture of Containment*, 65.

21 Principal Submission, 58–9. Smith, *Ireland's Magdalen Laundries and the Nation's Architecture of Containment*, 75–6.
22 Carl O'Brien, 'Bruton Faces Fight over Plans to Lift Schools' "Baptism barrier"', *Irish Times*, 3 January 2018.
23 Claire Hogan, 'Catholic Church's Influence over Irish Hospital Medicine Persists', *Irish Times*, 28 April 2016; Paul Cullen, 'Six Catholic Hospitals in Dublin Together Worth over €1bn: Hospitals Owned by Two Religious Orders that have Underpaid Millions in Redress Scheme', *Irish Times*, 20 March 2017; Emer O'Toole, 'The Sisters of Charity Presided over Abuse: They Must not Run a Maternity Hospital', *Guardian*, 20 April 2017.
24 Ronan McGreevy, 'Nuns "haven't gone away" from Maternity Hospital', *Irish Times*, 8 December 2018; Justine McCarthy, 'Sisters Are Not Doing It For the New National Maternity Hospital', *Sunday Times*, 9 June 2019; Paul Cullen, 'National Maternity Hospital: Has Threat of Church Influence Been Removed?', *Irish Times*, 2 June 2020.
25 Joan McCarthy, 'Reproductive Justice in Ireland, A Feminist Analysis of the Neary and Halappanavar Cases', in *Ethical and Legal Debates in Irish Healthcare: Confronting Complexities*, eds Mary Donnelly, Rob Kitchin and Claire Murray (Manchester: Manchester University Press, 2016), 9–23.
26 Mary E. Daly, 'Marriage, Fertility and Women's Lives in Twentieth-Century Ireland (c.1900–c.1970)', *Women's History Review*, 15, no. 4 (2006): 571–85; James M. Smith, 'The Politics of Sexual Knowledge: The Origins of Ireland's Containment Culture and the Carrigan Report (1931)', *Journal of the History of Sexuality*, 13, no. 2 (2004): 208–33.
27 Kitty Holland, Sa*vita: The Tragedy that Shook a Nation* (Dublin: Transworld Ireland, 2013); Peter C. Boylan, *In the Shadow of the Eighth* (Dublin: Penguin Ireland, 2019).
28 Marie O'Connor, *Bodily Harm: Symphysiotomy and Pubiotomy in Ireland 1944–92* (Evertype: Westport 2011). Máiréad Enright, '"No. I Won't Go Back": National Time, Trauma and Legacies of Symphysiotomy in Ireland', in *Law and Time*, eds Sian Beynon-Jones and Emily Grabham (London: Routledge, 2018).
29 June Goulding, *The Light in the Window* (Dublin: Poolbeg Press, 1998). Maeve O'Rourke, Claire McGettrick, Rod Baker, Raymond Hill et al., *CLANN: Ireland's Unmarried Mothers and their Children: Gathering the Data: Principal Submission to the Commission of Investigation into Mother and Baby Homes* (Dublin: Justice for Magdalenes Research, Adoption Rights Alliance, Hogan Lovells, 15 October 2018). [Hereafter, *CLANN Report*] http://clannproject.org/.
30 Maria Luddy, 'Unmarried Mothers in Ireland, 1880–1973', *Women's History Review*, 20, no. 1 (2011): 110.
31 Smith's *Ireland's Magdalen Laundries and the Nation's Architecture of Containment*, 54–7, 55; Maria Luddy's *Prostitution and Irish Society: 1800-1940* (Cambridge: Cambridge University Press, 2007), 109–26; Lindsey Earner-Byrne, *Mother and Child: Maternity and Child Welfare in Dublin, 1922-60* (Manchester: Manchester University Press, 2007), 172–211; Paul Michael Garrett, 'Excavating the Past: Mother and Baby Homes in the Republic of Ireland', *British Journal of Social Work*, 47 (2017): 358–74; Eoin O'Sullivan and Ian O'Donnell, eds, *Coercive Confinement in Post-Independent Ireland: Patients, Prisoners and Penitents* (Manchester: Manchester University Press, 2012).
32 Mike Milotte, *Banished Babies* (Dublin: New Island Books, 2012); *CLANN Report*, 36–43.
33 Earner-Byrne, *Mother and Child*, 207.

34 Hannah McGee, Rebecca Garavan, Mairead de Barra, Joanne Byrne and Ronan Conroy, *The SAVI Report – Sexual Abuse and Violence in Ireland: A National Study of Irish Experiences, Beliefs and Attitudes Concerning Sexual Violence* (Dublin: Liffey Press, 2002).
35 *Bunreacht na hÉireann/Constitution of Ireland* (Dublin: Stationery Office).
36 Maria Luddy, 'The Wrens of the Curragh: An Outcast Community', *Women's History Review*, 1, no. 3 (1992): 341–55.
37 James Joyce, *Ulysses* (Harmondsworth: Penguin, 1986), 266.
38 Ben Novick, *Conceiving Revolution: Irish Nationalist Propaganda during the First World War* (Dublin: Four Courts Press, 2001), 154.
39 Padraig Yeates, *A City in Wartime: Dublin 1914-1918* (Dublin: Gill & Macmillan, 2011), 9–10.
40 Margaret Ó hÓgartaigh, *Kathleen Lynn, Irishwoman, Patriot, Doctor* (Dublin: Irish Academic Press, 2006).
41 See Luddy, *Prostitution and Irish Society*; Clair Wills, 'Joyce, Prostitution, and the Colonial City', *South Atlantic Quarterly*, 95 (1996): 79–95.
42 Philip Howell, 'Venereal Disease and the Politics of Prostitution in the Irish Free State', *Irish Historical Studies*, 33, no. 131 (2003): 325 ff.
43 Smith, *Ireland's Magdalen Laundries and the Nation's Architecture of Containment*, 44–84.
44 O'Sullivan and O'Donnell, *Coercive Confinement in Post-Independent Ireland*, 2012.
45 By 'settled' we mean non-traveller.
46 Bernadette Whelan, 'Women on the Move: A Review of the Historiography of Irish Emigration to the USA, 1750–1900', *Women's History Review*, 24, no. 6 (2015): 900.
47 Joseph J. Lee, *Ireland, 1912-1985, Politics and Society* (Cambridge: Cambridge University Press, 1989), 377.
48 Quoted in Jennifer Redmond, '"Sinful Singleness"? Exploring the Discourses on Irish Single Women's Emigration to England, 1922–1948', *Women's History Review*, 17, no. 3 (2008): 457.
49 Quoted in Lee, *Ireland, 1912-1985*, 377.
50 Mary E. Daly, 'Turn on the Tap: The State, Irish Women and Running Water', in *Women & Irish History: Essays in Honour of Margaret MacCurtain*, eds Maryann Gialanella Valiulis, and Mary O'Dowd (Dublin: Wolfhound Press, 1997), 206–19.
51 Barbara Walsh, 'Lifting the Veil on Entrepreneurial Irishwomen', *History Ireland*, 4, no. 11 (Winter 2003): 27; Mary Peckham Magray, *The Transforming Power of the Nuns: Women, Religion, and Cultural Change in Ireland, 1750-1900* (Oxford: Oxford University Press, 1998).
52 Maureen Fitzgerald, *Habits of Compassion: Irish Catholic Nuns and the Origins of New York's Welfare System, 1830-1920* (Urbana: University of Illinois Press, 2006).
53 Margaret MacCurtain, 'Late in the Field: Catholic Sisters in Twentieth-Century Ireland and the New Religious History', *Journal of Women's History*, 6&7, nos. 4&1 (1995): 59.
54 Deirdre Raftery, 'The "mission" of Nuns in Female Education in Ireland, c.1850–1950', *Paedagogica Historica*, 48, no. 2 (2012): 302.
55 Barbara Walsh, *Roman Catholic Nuns in England and Wales, 1800-1937* (Dublin: Irish Academic Press, 2002), 22–9.
56 Walsh, *Roman Catholic Nuns in England and Wales*, 123.
57 Walsh, *Roman Catholic Nuns in England and Wales*, 115.

58 Walsh, *Roman Catholic Nuns in England and Wales*, 24–5.
59 MacCurtain, 'Late in the Field', 53.
60 'Magdalene Laundries – Margaret MacCurtain in Conversation with Diarmaid Ferriter', Dublin Festival of History, 23 November 2013, 42.07.
61 *Are Nuns Human?* Radharc introduced by Father Peter Lemass, produced by Fr Joe Dunn and Fr Desmond Forristal, with John Wall reporting, aired 19 January 1971, RTÉ. https://www.rte.ie/archives/2016/0118/761035-are-nuns-human/ 4:00ff.
62 MacCurtain, 'Late in the Field', 59.
63 See Gary Culliton, 'Last Days of a Laundry', *Irish Times*, 25 September 1996.
64 These two orders trace their lineage back to a convent founded in Caen, France, by Fr Eudes in 1641. In 2007 both congregations entered formal dialogue, which resulted in a merger decree in 2014 formalizing their unification. For a history of OLC in Ireland, see Jacinta Prunty, *The Monasteries, Magdalen Asylums and Reformatory Schools of Our Lady of Charity in Ireland 1853-1973* (Dublin: The Columba Press, 2017).
65 Katherine O'Donnell, Sinead Pembroke and Claire McGettrick, *Magdalene Institutions: Recording an Oral and Archival History*, Government of Ireland Collaborative Research Project funded by the Irish Research Council, 2012. http://jfmresearch.com/home/oralhistoryproject/.
66 O'Donnell, Pembroke and McGettrick, 'Oral History of Caitríona Hayes' Magdalene Institutions: Recording an Oral and Archival History. Government of Ireland Collaborative Research Project, Irish Research Council; O'Donnell, Pembroke and McGettrick, 'Oral History of Maisie K.(a)'; O'Donnell, Pembroke and McGettrick, 'Oral History of Evelyn'. See also, Principal Submission, 76–80.
67 Principal Submission, 78–9. O'Donnell, Pembroke and McGettrick, 'Oral History of Evelyn'.
68 *Final Report of the Commission to Inquire into Child Abuse* (Dublin: Stationary Office, 20 May 2009) [hereafter *CICA Final Report*], Vol. III, Chapter 18; O'Donnell, Pembroke and McGettrick, Magdalene Institutions: Recording an Oral and Archival History. Government of Ireland Collaborative Research Project, Irish Research Council; Principal Submission; Maeve O'Rourke, *Submission to the United Nations Universal Periodic Review*, Twelfth Session of the Working Group of the UPR Human Rights Council, 6 October 2011.
69 *IDC Report*, 5 February 2013: Chapter 19, Para 63 regarding the imposition of 'house names', Paras 64 and 65 regarding separation from the outside world, Paras 67 and 68 regarding enforced silence, Paras 69–71 regarding incarceration and Paras 73–5 regarding punishments, Para 112 regarding incarceration and unpaid labour, and Para 114 regarding emotional abuse, Para 142 regarding the prohibition on communicating with friends and acquaintances on the outside, Para 144 regarding punishments and Para 147 regarding incarceration and lack of wages.
70 A number of the survivors of the Magdalene institutions object to being described as 'Magdalenes' or 'Magdalene women' (and most object to being called 'Maggies'). In this book we are careful not to refer to survivors as such, to the extent possible. Occasionally, we use the term 'Magdalenes' to refer to how these women and girls were labelled and hence treated as deserving incarceration and forced labour.
71 O'Donnell, Pembroke and McGettrick, Oral history of Maisie K.(a); O'Donnell, Pembroke and McGettrick, Oral History of Kathleen R.; O'Donnell, Pembroke and McGettrick, Oral History of Sara W.; O'Donnell, Pembroke and McGettrick, Oral

History of Kate O'Sullivan; O'Donnell, Pembroke and McGettrick, Oral History of Mary; Oral History of Beth. Principal Submission, 13–16.

72 Frances Finnegan, *Do Penance or Perish* (Piltown, Co. Kilkenny: Congrave Press, 2001), 45, 67 and 69. Finnegan also reveals that the records show that many women remained in the laundries for their entire lives, esp. 40, 65, 68, 108 and 120.

73 O'Donnell, Pembroke and McGettrick, Oral History of Maisie K. (a). See also: *JFM's Principal Submissions to the IDC*, 19–20.

74 Principal Submission, 25.

75 O'Donnell, Pembroke and McGettrick, Oral History of Kate O'Sullivan.

76 Principal Submission, 60. See also: O'Donnell, Pembroke and McGettrick, Oral History of Evelyn.

77 Sr Stanislaus Kennedy, *But Where Can I Go?: Homeless Women in Dublin* (Dublin: Arlen House, 1985), Table 9.9, 132.

78 Ms Justice Mary Laffoy, *Commission to Inquire into Child Abuse Third Interim Report* (Dublin: Stationary Office, 2003) [hereafter *CICA* 2003], 45.

79 *CICA Final Report*, 2009, Vol. III, Chapter 18, Para 105.

80 O'Donnell, Pembroke and McGettrick, Oral History of Kate O'Sullivan.

81 Principal Submission, 31–2. Catherine was identified as 'AB' in the Principal Submission; however, she consented to be identified after her death. See also O'Donnell, Pembroke and McGettrick, Oral History of Catherine Whelan.

82 O'Donnell, Pembroke and McGettrick, Oral History of Sara W. See also Principal Submission, 31–2.

83 Principal Submission, 26. See also O'Donnell, Pembroke and McGettrick, Oral History of Evelyn.

84 O'Donnell, Pembroke and McGettrick, Oral History of Sara W. See also Principal Submission, 26.

85 O'Donnell, Pembroke and McGettrick, Oral History of Mary.

86 O'Donnell, Pembroke and McGettrick, Oral History of Pippa Flanagan.

87 *IDC Report*. Executive Summary XIII.

88 O'Donnell, Pembroke and McGettrick, Oral History of Maisie K. (a).

89 Principal Submission, 136.

90 For survivor accounts of the auxiliary system, see O'Donnell, Pembroke and McGettrick, Oral History of Martha; O'Donnell, Pembroke and McGettrick, Oral History of Philomena; O'Donnell, Pembroke and McGettrick, Oral History of Nora Lynch; O'Donnell, Pembroke and McGettrick, Oral History of Kathleen; O'Donnell, Pembroke and McGettrick, Oral History of Margaret Burke; O'Donnell, Pembroke and McGettrick, Oral History of Kathleen R.

91 From the early 1990s, the religious orders began to erect headstones on a number of the Magdalene graves, many of which have inaccuracies.

92 O'Donnell, Pembroke and McGettrick, Oral History of Kathleen R. See also Principal Submission, 145.

93 O'Donnell, Pembroke and McGettrick, Oral History of Mary Collins (see *Interviews with Key Informants*). See also Principal Submission, 145.

94 Principal Submission, 145. Mary C.'s testimony is corroborated by Galway's Bohermore Cemetery records, which indicate that many women were buried within a day of their deaths. http://jfmresearch.com/home/magdalene-names-project/.

95 Claire McGettrick and JFM, 'Death, Institutionalisation & Duration of Stay: A Critique of Chapter 16 of the Report of the Inter-departmental Committee to

Establish the Facts of State Involvement with the Magdalen Laundries', 19 February 2015, 59–60.

96 Susan McKay, 'Sentenced to a Life of Slavery', *Sunday Tribune*, 5 September 1993.

97 O'Donnell, Pembroke and McGettrick, Oral History of Maisie K. (a); O'Donnell, Pembroke and McGettrick, Oral History of Kate O'Sullivan; O'Donnell, Pembroke and McGettrick, Oral History of Beth; Principal Submission, 83–91.

98 Mary Norris describes how an aunt who had emigrated to the United States came back to Ireland and agitated successfully for her release from Sunday's Well, see Mary Raftery, *States of Fear*, RTÉ, aired April–May 1999.

99 It remains unclear, in a legal sense, whether any girl under sixteen years of age should have been 'detained' in a Magdalene Laundry under the Children's Act, 1941.

100 *IDC Report*, Chapter 5, 70ff. As the Report puts it, 'The effect of this supervision [*sic*] was that until the age of 18 or 19 (until 1941) and until the age of 21 (after 1941), they remained under supervision and liable to recall. Release on licence and recall during post-discharge supervision were the basis in many cases for women [*sic*] being placed in the Magdalene Laundries either directly from or within a number of years of their discharge from an industrial or Reformatory School', 70.

101 O'Donnell, Pembroke and McGettrick, Oral History of Kate O'Sullivan.

102 Lorna Siggins, 'Mass Escape Using Ladder Among Incidents at Galway Magdalene Laundry', *Irish Times*, 5 November 2018.

103 Susan McKay, 'Nuns Silent Over Scandal', *Sunday Tribune*, 5 September 1993.

104 *IDC Report*, Chapter 5 indicates closures as follows: Sean McDermott Street, 1996; Donnybrook, 1992; High Park, 1991; Galway, 1984; Good Shepherd-Limerick, 1982; Good Shepherd-Waterford, 1982; Good Shepherd-Sundays Well, Cork, 1977; Good Shepherd-New Ross, 1967; Dún Laoghaire, 1963; Peacock Lane, unclear.

105 Culliton, 'Last Days of a Laundry'.

106 *IDC Report*, Executive Summary, XIV, the extant registers record that just 10.5 per cent of girls or women who were put in a Magdalene were brought there by family members.

107 For example, the RSC run private schools in Nigeria and hospitals and schools in Zambia; the Mercy Order operates schools and hospitals in Kenya and South Africa. The OLC and SGS have combined to form the Congregation of Our Lady of Charity of the Good Shepherd and have thirty separate provinces in Asia-Pacific, North America, Latin America, Europe, and the Middle East and Africa, http://www.goodshepherdsisters.org.ph/gssw. Currently they work in over thirty-six countries in the Global South, see https://www.gsif.it/our-mission/.

Chapter 2

1 Jacinta Prunty and Frances Finnegan both enjoyed exclusive access to OLC and SGS archives, making it difficult for other scholars to independently evaluate their work. See also Catríona Crowe, 'Valuable Addition to History of Magdalene Laundries Uses "Private" Records', *Irish Times*, 2 September 2017.

2 'Sr Stanislaus Kennedy: Visionary and Social Innovator' (personal website). Updated 2020. https://www.srstan.ie/about/awards.532.html. See also *Being Stan: A Life in Focus*, narrated by Brenda Fricker, aired 13 February 2020, RTÉ.

3 Mary Raftery, 'Child Abuse at St Joseph's: "We Were Not Responsible"', *Magill Magazine*, 12 July 2006.
4 Sr Stanislaus, 62–74.
5 Sr Stanislaus, 62.
6 Sr Stanislaus, 88.
7 Sr Stanislaus, 123.
8 Sr Stanislaus, 75 and 82.
9 Sr Stanislaus, 15–61.
10 Sr Stanislaus, 123.
11 Sr Stanislaus, 124.
12 Sr Stanislaus, 125.
13 Sr Stanislaus, 126.
14 Sr Stanislaus, 126.
15 The truncated quotes are presented exactly as they appear: Sr Stanislaus, 128.
16 Sr Stanislaus, 123.
17 Sr Stanislaus, 130–2.
18 O'Donnell, Pembroke and McGettrick, *Magdalene Institutions: Recording an Oral and Archival History*. Oral History of Kathleen R.
19 Sr Stanislaus, 82 and 123.
20 'Group 1' comprises 241 women (plus 3 other women who were resident in a long-term hostel that catered mainly for men) but analysis is based on information for only 220 of these women, with no explanation as to why that is the case. Sr Stanislaus, Table 9.7, 132.
21 Sr Stanislaus, 129.
22 Sr Stanislaus, 129.
23 McKay, 'Nuns Silent Over Scandal'.
24 Sr Stanislaus, 82.
25 Sr Stanislaus, 127.
26 Sr Stanislaus, 88.
27 Sr Stanislaus, 89.
28 Sr Stanislaus, 89.
29 Sr Stanislaus, 87.
30 https://www.focusireland.ie/about-us/our-history/.
31 Focus Ireland (website). Updated 2020. https://www.focusireland.ie/
32 O'Rourke, *NGO Submission to the UN Committee against Torture in Respect of Ireland*, July 2017, 12–13.
33 *Seanad Éireann Debates* (hereafter *SED*), Criminal Justice Bill, 1960—Second Stage, 13 July 1960.
34 Smith, *Ireland's Magdalen Laundries and the Nation's Architecture of Containment*, 65.
35 'Letter from Superioress of St Vincent's Convent, Cork, December 1934', JFMR Digitised archive. See: http://repository.wit.ie/JFMA/.
36 *IDC Report*, Chapters 9 and 11.
37 *IDC Report*, Chapter 13, Para 50; Chapter 11, Para 211.
38 *IDC Report*, Chapter 14, Para 7. The *IDC Report* notes that 'State authorities were not averse to putting pressure on Magdalen Laundries to reduce prices either in order to renew or retain contracts'.
39 *IDC Report*, Chapter 14, Paras 166–88.
40 *IDC Report*, Chapter 15.
41 *IDC Report*, Chapter 15.

42 Smith, *Ireland's Magdalen Laundries and the Nation's Architecture of Containment*, 87–112.
43 Robert Savage and James M. Smith, 'Sexual Abuse and the Irish Church: Crisis and Responses', *The Church in the 21st Century: Occasional Papers*, Boston College eScholarship, 2003.
44 'Clerical Child Abuse - An Irish Timeline: How the Story of Abuse in Catholic Church Institutions Emerged', *Irish Times*, 13 July 2011.
45 *The Ferns Report* (Dublin: Stationary Office, October 2005).
46 R. F. Foster, *Luck and the Irish: A Brief History of Change, 1970*-2000 (London: Allen Lane, 2007), 57.
47 RTÉ, 'Taoiseach Apologises to Victims of Child Abuse', 11 May 1999.
48 Simon Carswell, 'Abuse Inquiry Error is "Embarrassing" Not Damaging, Academic Says', *Irish Times*, 27 November 2019.
49 www.childabusecommission.ie/ and HYPERLINK 'http://www.rirb.ie' \h www.rirb.ie.
50 *CICA* 2003, 42.
51 *CICA* 2003, 44.
52 *CICA* 2003, 45.
53 Mary Raftery, 'The End of a Decade of Inquiry', *Irish Times*, 16 May 2009.
54 Conall Ó Fátharta, 'Ryan Report That Shocked Nation Offers Much but Gaps in the Detail Still Remain', *Irish Examiner*, 19 May 2019.
55 Raftery, 'The End of a Decade of Inquiry'.
56 *Judicial Appointments Advisory Board Annual Report 2003*, 13; Bruce Arnold, *The Irish Gulag* (Dublin: Gill & Macmillan, 2009), 215–16; 'Barrister Ryan New Chair of Child Abuse Commission', *Irish Examiner*, 26 September 2003.
57 Seán Ryan, *Review into the Working of the Commission to Inquire into Child Abuse* (Dublin: Department of Education and Science, 15 January 2004); Seán Ryan, *Address by the Chairperson Commission to Inquire into Child Abuse*, 7 May 2004, 6–7 and *The Legal Team's Statement*, Commission to Inquire into Child Abuse, 7 May 2004, 2–5.
58 Raftery, 'The End of a Decade of Inquiry'.
59 Ryan, *Address by the Chairperson*, 7.
60 Seán Ryan, *A Position Paper on Identifying Institutions and Persons under the Commission to Inquire into Child Abuse Act 2000*, Commission to Inquire into Child Abuse, 7 May 2004.
61 *CICA Final Report*, Vol. 1 Chapter 7 Para 38, 110.
62 Ryan, *Address by the Chairperson*, 11.
63 A benefit of this shift was that the CICA under Ryan no longer allowed stringent legal cross-examination of survivors. See the United Nations Committee on the Rights of the Child, *Concluding Observations on the Combined Third and Fourth Periodic Reports of Ireland*, 1 March 2016; and Reclaiming Self, *Ryan Report Follow-Up: Submission to the United Nations Committee Against Torture* (hereafter UNCAT), June 2017, 6–8.
64 See UN Committee against Torture, *Summary Record of the 1005th Meeting Held at the Palais Wilson, Geneva*, on Tuesday, 24 May 2011, at 3 pm, UN Doc CAT/C/SR 1005, 24 May 2011, and also United Nations Committee Against Torture, *Concluding Observations on the Second Periodic Report of Ireland* (adopted by the Committee at its sixty-first session), UN Doc CAT/C/IRL/CO/2, 31 August 2017.
65 *CICA Final Report*, Vol. 3 Chapter 2. The Confidential Committee heard from 1,090 survivors. The Investigation Committee heard from a further 552 people, see *CICA Final Report*, Vol. 1 Chapter 5, Para 19.

66 'The Savage Reality of Our Darkest Days', *Irish Times*, 21 May 2009.
67 Raftery's 'End of a Decade', found much to praise in Seán Ryan's chairmanship.
68 *BBC News*, 'Reaction to Irish Abuse Report', 20 May 2009.
69 UNCAT, June 2017, 14–15ff.
70 State report to UNCAT, November 2015, Para 223.
71 Maeve O'Rourke, Máiréad Enright and Sinéad Ring, 'Submission on the Provisions of the Retention of Records Bill 2019', 13 November 2019.
72 O'Rourke, Enright and Ring referring to National Archives Act 1986 (as amended), section 2; *Commission to Inquire into Child Abuse Act 2000*, section 7.
73 O'Rourke, Enright and Ring referring to National Archives Act 1986 (as amended), section 2; *Commission to Inquire into Child Abuse Act 2000*, section 7.
74 O'Rourke, Enright and Ring 9, referencing s34 *CICA Act 2000.*
75 Freedom of Information Bill 2013: Report Stage (Resumed) and Final Stage (16 July 2014); *Freedom of Information Act 2014*, Schedule 1, Part 1.
76 Retention of Records Bill 2019; see also JFMR, Retention of Records Bill 2019 and Patsy McGarry, 'Abuse Documents not to be Destroyed Despite Assurances', *Irish Times*, 28 May 2014.
77 Patsy McGarry, '"Shocking, Shocking": Justice Seán Ryan on the Abuses of Children Uncovered in his Report', *Irish Times*, 20 May 2019.
78 John Banville, 'A Century of Looking the Other Way', *New York Times*, 22 May 2009.
79 McGarry, '"Shocking, Shocking"', 20 May 2019.
80 McGarry, '"Shocking, Shocking"', 20 May 2019. The 'Emergence Hearings' took place over four weeks, June–July 2004 and signalled the restart of the Investigation Committee of the CICA under the new chairmanship of Justice Seán Ryan. *CICA Final Report*, Vol. 1. Chapter 1, Paras 41–6: 7–8.
81 McGarry, '"Shocking, Shocking"', 20 May 2019.
82 McGarry, '"Shocking, Shocking"', 20 May 2019.
83 Mary Regan, 'Taoiseach Makes "long overdue" State Apology', *Irish Examiner*, 12 June 2009.
84 See, for example, Minister of State Aodhán Ó Riordáin, 'There Comes a Stage When the Campaigning Ends and the Winning Begins . . .', *SED*, 4 March 2015.
85 Kitty Holland, 'Caranua Chief Withdraws Comments which Offended Abuse Victims', *Irish Times*, 13 April 2017, updated 20 April 2017; Christina Finn, 'Caranua Boss Withdraws Comments in which She Said Abuse Survivors were "damaged"', *TheJournal.ie*, 14 April 2017; AnneMarie Crean, 'Sorry Doesn't Do it Anymore', *Irish Examiner*, 19 May 2019.
86 Executive Summary, *CICA Final Report*, 2009.
87 Department of Health, *Task Force on Child Care Services: Final Report* (Dublin: Stationery Office, 1980); *Report on the Inquiry into the Operation of Madonna* House (Dublin: The Stationery Office, May 1996).
88 James M. Smith, 'Remembering Ireland's Architecture of Containment: "Telling" Stories in *The Butcher Boy* and *States of Fear*', *Éire-Ireland: An Interdisciplinary Journal of Irish Studies*, 36, nos. 3-4 (2001): 122.
89 Fintan O'Toole, 'Time to Atone for the Sins of the Fathers', *Irish Times*, 28 December 2009.
90 RIRA 2002, section 7(1); A Guide to the Redress Scheme under the Residential Institutions Redress Act, 2002 as amended by the Commission to Inquire into Child Abuse (Amendment) Act, 2005 (3rd edn, RIRB 2005), 7.
91 Oireachtas Joint Committee on Education and Skills, Retention of Records Bill 2019: Discussion, 26 November 2019.

92 RIRA 2002, section 11(8). RIRB Guide 2005, 12, 15–16 and 21–2.
93 RIRA 2002, section 11(8).
94 RIRA 2002, section 11(12); section 13(11).
95 RIRA 2002, section 19.
96 RTÉ Television, Redress: Breaking the Silence, 2–3 March 2020.
97 Compensation Advisory Committee, *Towards Redress and Recovery: Report to the Minister for Education and Science,* January 2002.
98 McGarry, '"Shocking, Shocking"', 20 May 2019.
99 McGarry, '"Shocking, Shocking"', 20 May 2019.
100 UNCAT, Section 3.
101 Ó Fátharta, 'Ryan Report That Shocked Nation Offers Much but Gaps in the Detail Still Remain', 19 May 2019. Also see UNCAT, 2017.
102 UNCAT, 9–10.
103 Ireland, *Residential Institutions Redress Act*, 2002. Irish Statute Book. S28 (6); UNCAT, 2017, and Fergus Finlay, 'We've Passed a Law to Protect Abusers and Punish the Abused', *Irish Examiner*, 9 March 2020.
104 *Industrial Memories Project*, https://industrialmemories.ucd.ie, and Emilie Pine, Susan Leavy and Mark T. Keane, 'Re-reading the Ryan Report: Witnessing via and Close and Distant Reading', *Éire-Ireland*, 52, no. 1 & 2 (2017): 198–215.
105 As of 31 December 2016, the RIRB had received 16,650 applications seeking redress and made 12,016 financial awards, the average for which was €62,250, at a total cost to the taxpayer – including administrative and legal fees – of €1.4 billion. See *Annual Report of the Residential Institutions Redress Board, 2016.* Also see, Patsy McGarry, 'Religious Congregations Indemnity Deal was "a Blank Cheque", Says Michael McDowell', *Irish Times*, 5 April 2019.
106 Michael O'Brien, 'Transcript of *Questions and Answers*', *Irish Central*, 28 May 2009; *Irish Times*, 'Ex-Mayor Tells of Abuse', 27 May 2009.
107 *Report to the Government from the Panel to Assess the Statements of Resources Submitted by Religious Congregations Following Publication of the Report of the Commission to Inquire into Child Abuse (AKA the 'Ryan Report')*, November 2009. Department of Education and Skills, *Contributions by Religious Congregations towards the Costs Incurred by the State in Responding to Residential Institutional Child Abuse: Information note for the Committee of Public Accounts*, July 2018.
108 Patsy McGarry, 'Religious Congregations yet to Fully Honour Compensation Deals', *Irish Times*, 11 May 2019, and Ó Fátharta, 'Ryan Report That Shocked Nation Offers Much but Gaps in the Detail Still Remain', 19 May 2019.
109 Mary Minihan, 'Nuns have "moral duty" to Pay Redress Money, Says Committee Chair', *Irish Times*, 18 April 2017.
110 Mark Paul, 'Who Owns Private Hospitals Behind State's €115m-a-month Deal?', *Irish Times*, 19 April 2020.
111 Patsy McGarry, 'Laundry Orders Run Sex Workers' Aid Group', *Irish Times*, 25 June 2011.
112 Ruairí Quinn, Minister for Education, letter to Sr Sheila Murphy, March 2012, https://www.documentcloud.org/documents/814675-16a-letter-to-sisters-of-our-lady-of-charity.html and Sr Sheila Murphy, Regional Leader, Sisters of Our Lady of Charity, letter to Ruairí Quinn, Minister for Education, 25 April 2012, http://www.documentcloud.org/documents/814645-16b-letter-from-sisters-of-our-lady-of-charity.html both provided by Conor Ryan.
113 Letter, Batt O'Keeffe, Minister for Education & Science to Tom Kitt, TD, 4 September 2009. See also Schedule to Residential Institutions Redress Act, 2002.

114 Smith, *Ireland's Magdalen Laundries and the Nation's Architecture of Containment*, 183–5.
115 Maeve O'Rourke, 'The Justice for Magdalenes Campaign', in *International Human Rights: Perspectives from Ireland*, ed. Suzanne Egan (London: Bloomsbury, 2015), 160.
116 Vivienne Clarke, 'There May Be 15,000 Illegal Adoptions, Barnardo's Head Claims', *Irish Times*, 30 May 2018; *CLANN Report*.
117 O'Toole, 'GPA, Magdalen Women and the Underground Connection'; Edward O'Loughlin, 'Funeral Ceremony Sought for "Magdalenes"', *Irish Times*, 8 September 1993; and Padraig O'Morain, 'Daughters Haunted by Values of Times Past', *Irish Times*, 21 September 1993.
118 Mary Raftery, 'Restoring Dignity to Magdalenes', *Irish Times*, 21 August 2003, and 'Ireland's Magdalene Laundries Scandal Must be Laid to Rest', *Guardian*, 8 June 2011.
119 Anne Enright, 'Antigone in Galway: Anne Enright on the Dishonoured Dead', *London Review of Books* 37, no. 24 (December 2015): 11–14.
120 Smith, *Ireland's Magdalen Laundries and the Nation's Architecture of Containment*, 159–63 and 166–7.
121 Marian Harkin, independent TD for Sligo-Leitrim, is an exception.
122 O'Donnell, Pembroke and McGettrick, Oral History of Kathleen R.; O'Donnell, Pembroke and McGettrick, Oral History of Pippa Flanagan.
123 Including Judy Campbell, Paddy Doyle, Tom Kitt T. D., Samantha Long, Dr Sandra McAvoy, Dr Mary McAuliffe, Sally Mulready, Imelda Murphy, Lorraine Owen and Etta Verma.
124 *Report by Commission of Investigation, into the handling by Church and State Authorities of Allegations and Suspicions of Child Abuse against Clerics of the Catholic Archdiocese of Dublin*, November 2009; Carole Holohan, ed., *In Plain Sight: Responding to the Ferns, Ryan, Murphy and Cloyne Reports* (Dublin: Amnesty International Ireland, 2011).
125 O'Toole, 'Time to Atone for the Sins of the Fathers', 28 December 2009.
126 McNally, 'Probation in Ireland', 5–24; John Cooney, *John Charles McQuaid: Ruler of Catholic Ireland* (Dublin: O'Brien Press, 1999), 140.

Chapter 3

1 See James M. Smith, 'Voices of Our Magdalene Women Washed Out of History for Too Long', *Sunday Tribune*, 12 July 2009; 'Abused in the Past and Abandoned in the Present', *Irish Times*, 5 February 2013; 'Rite and Reason: Brave Magdalene Survivor Leaves Inspirational Trail', *Irish Times*, 29 March 2016.
2 Katherine O'Donnell, S. Pembroke and C. McGettrick, 'Oral History of Catherine Whelan'. *Magdalene Institutions: Recording an Oral and Archival History*. Government of Ireland Collaborative Research Project, Irish Research Council, 2013.
3 James M. Smith, 'Will Mother and Baby Homes Commission Advertise to the Hidden Irish Diaspora?', *Irish Times*, 9 November 2016.
4 Justice for Magdalenes Research website, http://jfmresearch.com/home/resources-for-survivors-and-families/.
5 Catharine A. MacKinnon, 'Engaged Scholarship as Method and Vocation', *Yale Journal of Law & Feminism*, 22, nos. 2–3 (2010): 177–84.
6 Patsy McGarry, 'Call for Apology to Survivors of Laundries', *Irish Times*, 6 July 2009.

7 James M. Smith and Mari Steed, 'Proposed Redress Scheme for Survivors of Ireland's Magdalene Laundries [Draft]', 2 July 2009.
8 *Dáil Éireann Debates* [hereafter *DED*], Ruairí Quinn, 'Institutional Child Abuse Bill, 2009: First Stage', 30 June 2009.
9 *DED*, Ruairí Quinn, 'Institutional Child Abuse Bill, 2009: Second Stage', 7 July 2009.
10 Justice for Magdalenes (JFM), *Restorative Justice and Reparations Scheme*, 27 March 2011.
11 http://www.paddydoyle.com/; Michael O'Brien, 'Questions and Answers', RTÉ 1 Television, 25 May 2009.
12 JFM, *Restorative Justice and Reparations Scheme.*
13 JFM, *JFM Restorative Justice & Reparation Scheme for Magdalene Laundry Survivors*, 14 October 2011.
14 *DED*, Michael Woods, 'Written Answers: Child Abuse', 12 February 2002, Question 459 (John Bruton).
15 Smith, *Ireland's Magdalen Laundries*, 54–72, 195–201.
16 Smith, *Ireland's Magdalen Laundries*, 72–81 and 48–54.
17 *DED*, Oscar Traynor, 'Questions-Oral Answers: Army Laundry Contracts', 7 May 1941 (James Hickey).
18 The DoJ met with a delegation from the MST group in November, see Patsy McGarry, 'Magdalene Women Meet Officials', *Irish Times*, 5 November 2009.
19 Smith, *Ireland's Magdalen Laundries*, 66–72.
20 JFM, 'Department of Justice Contradicts Education Minister on Magdalenes', Press Release, 15 December 2009.
21 Jamie Smyth, 'Minister Considers New Magdalene Evidence', *Irish Times*, 16 December 2009; Claire O'Sullivan, 'Group to Get Redress for Magdalen Laundry Victims', *Irish Examiner*, 17 December 2009.
22 JFM, 'Department of Education Acknowledges Its Awareness of Children in Magdalene Laundries', Press Release, 2 February 2010.
23 Mary Coughlan, Minister for Education, letter to James M. Smith, Boston College, 27 April 2010.
24 *DED*, Mary Coughlan, 'Written Answers: Departmental Correspondence', 5 May 2010, Question 381 (Tom Kitt).
25 Mark Hennessy, Colm Keena and Patsy McGarry, 'Religious Orders Must Reveal Extent of Assets to Government', *Irish Times*, 28 May 2009; Fiachra Ó Cionnaith, Claire O'Sullivan, Paul O'Brien and Scott Millar, 'More Religious Orders to Pay Extra over Abuse', *Irish Examiner*, 28 May 2009.
26 JFM, 'Government Exploring an Apology for Magdalene Survivors While Denying Any State Liability', Press Release, 25 June 2010.
27 *CICA Final Report.*
28 Genevieve Carbury, 'Brady Encourages Magdalene Survivors in Talks with Church', *Irish Times*, 26 June 2010.
29 Batt O'Keeffe, Minister for Education, letter to Tom Kitt, 4 September 2009. Patsy McGarry, 'No Redress for Residents of Magdalen Laundries', *Irish Times*, 18 September 2009.
30 Patsy McGarry, 'O'Keeffe Criticised for Referring to Magdalen Women as "employees"', *Irish Times*, 19 September 2009.
31 Batt O'Keeffe, Minister for Education, letter to Tom Kitt, 23 September 2009.
32 *DED*, Batt O'Keeffe, 'Written Answers: Residential Institutions Redress Scheme', 6 October 2009, Question 1136 (Tom Kitt) and 1281 (Willie Penrose).

33 James M. Smith, Boston College, letter to Taoiseach Brian Cowen, 22 September 2009.
34 *DED*, Brian Cowen, 'Written Answers: Residential Institutions Redress Scheme', 27 April 2010, Question 106 and 107 (Michael Kennedy).
35 *DED*, Mary Hanafin, 'Written Answers: Social Insurance', 4 February 2010, Question 257 (Michael Kennedy).
36 *DED*, Brian Lenihan, 'Written Answers: Tax Collection', 4 February 2010, Question 117 (Michael Kennedy).
37 James M. Smith, Boston College to Mr Brian Lenihan, Minister for Finance, 2 April 2010.
38 *DED*, Dara Calleary, 'Written Answers: Employment Rights', 4 February 2010, Question 102 (Michael Kennedy).
39 *DED*, Brian Cowen, 'Written Answers: Residential Institutions Redress Scheme', 27 April 2010, Questions 106 and 107 (Michael Kennedy); and JFM, 'Taoiseach Dismisses Abuse of Children in Magdalene Laundries – JFM Outraged', Press Release, 28 April 2010.
40 *DED*, Dermot Ahern, 'Written Answers: Departmental Records', 27 May 2010, Questions 129 (Michael Kennedy).
41 JFM, 'All Party Dáil/Seanad Committee on Magdalenes Formed', Press Release, 16 December 2009. Also, Marie O'Halloran, 'Taoiseach Urged to Extend Redress Scheme to Magdalene Women', *Irish Times*, 18 December 2009.
42 *DED*, Alan Shatter, 'Order of Business', 17 December 2009, https://www.youtube.com/watch?v=Avj4cJpDY08.
43 *DED*, Michael Kennedy, 'Order of Business', 17 December 2009.
44 *DED*, Joe Costello, 'Order of Business', 17 December 2009. The women were moved to the OLC's facility at Beechlawn Nursing Home at High Park, Drumcondra.
45 *DED*, 'Order of Business', 17 December 2009.
46 Joan Burton, 'Adjournment Debate: Residential Institutions', 21 January 2010, Dáil Éireann, 4:53, https://www.youtube.com/watch?v=w2AAuqrBw18.
47 James M. Smith, 'Magdalene Girl: "I cried for weeks and weeks. I was nobody. I was 16"', Letter to the Editor, *Irish Examiner*, 31 December 2009.
48 *DED*, Mr Brian Lenihan, 'Written Answers: Tax Collection', 4 February 2010, Question 117 (Michael Kennedy).
49 JFM, 'Justice for Magdalenes Challenges Taoiseach after Meeting with Minister for Health', Press Release, 25 March 2010.
50 James M. Smith, letter to Ms Mary Harney, Minister for Health, 8 February 2010; and Smith, *Ireland's Magdalen Laundries*, 48–54.
51 JFM, 'JFM Calls on Election Candidates to Declare Support for Survivors of Magdalene Laundries', Press Release, 11 February 2011.
52 James M. Smith, 'Government Failed us on All Fronts', Letter to the Editor, *Irish Examiner*, 8 February 2011; and James M. Smith, 'Church Abuse should be a Serious Election Issue', Letter to the Editor, *Irish Times*, 23 February 2011.
53 James M. Smith, letter to Mr Alan Shatter, Minister for Justice and Equality, and Ms Kathleen Lynch, Minister of State, 12 March 2011.
54 *DED*, Alan Shatter, 'Written Answers: Report on Magdalen Laundries', 23 March 2011, Questions 77–9 (Caoimhghín Ó Caoláin).
55 Smith, 'Voices of Our Magdalene Women Washed Out of History for Too Long'.
56 *DED*, Dermot Ahern, 'Written Answers: Magdalene Laundries', 19 January 2010, Questions 547–50 (Ruairí Quinn).

57 Mr Batt O'Keeffe, Minister for Education, letter to James M. Smith, Boston College, 27 January 2010.
58 James M. Smith, 'Court Referrals to the Magdalene Laundries', *Irish Times*, 2 February 2010; 'Redress for Magdalene Survivors Overdue', Letter to the Editor, *Irish Independent*, 25 March 2010.
59 McGarry, 'Call for Apology to Survivors of Laundries'.
60 http://www.paddydoyle.com/.
61 Patsy McGarry, 'Laundries Used "forced labour"', *Irish Times*, 6 July 2011.
62 *DED*, Alan Shatter, 'Written Answers: Magdalene Laundries', 19 July 2011, Questions 389 and 390 (Dara Calleary).
63 Patsy McGarry, 'HSE gives EUR87m to Magdalene nuns', *Irish Times*, 21 June 2011.
64 'AG Asked to Consider Magdalene Report', RTÉ News, 9 November 2010.
65 Patsy McGarry, 'Call for Inquiry into Magdalene Laundries', *Irish Times*, 10 November 2010; Claire O'Sullivan, 'Attorney General to Examine Laundries Report', *Irish Examiner*, 10 November 2010; Shawn Pogatchnik, 'Irish Victims Seek Probe into Catholic Laundries', *Boston Globe*, 10 November 2010.
66 JFM, 'JFM Presents "Restorative Justice and Reparations Scheme" to Government', Press Release, 29 March 2011.
67 Claire O'Sullivan, 'Magdalene Case Goes to UN', *Irish Examiner*, 20 May 2011; Patsy McGarry, 'Magdalene Group to Appeal to UN Body', *Irish Times*, 21 May 2011.
68 Carol Ryan, 'Irish Church's Forgotten Victims Take Case to the U.N.', *New York Times*, 25 May 2011.
69 UN Committee against Torture (UNCAT), Concluding Observations on Ireland, UN Doc CAT/C/IRL/CO/1, 17 June 2011, Para 21.
70 UNCAT, 17 June 2011, Para 33.
71 Patsy McGarry, 'State Must Confront Magdalene Tragedy', *Irish Times*, 7 June 2011; 'Magdalene Scandal—A Just and Swift Remedy Is Required', Editorial, *Irish Examiner*, 7 June 2011; 'Magdalene Laundries Apology Urged', Editorial, *Irish Independent*, 6 June 2011; Pamela Duncan, 'Will Ireland Apologize to the Women of the Magdalene Laundries?' *Time Magazine/World*, 4 July 2011; and Raftery, 'Ireland's Magdalene Laundries Scandal Must Be Laid to Rest', Opinion-Editorial.
72 *DED*, Enda Kenny, 'Leaders' Questions', 7 June 2011 (Mary Lou McDonald); also *DED*, Alan Shatter, 'Written Answers: Magdalene Laundries', 15 June 2011, Questions 433–44 (Mary Lou McDonald).
73 'Leadership Needed on Magdalene Laundries', *Care2 Petitions*, Justice for Magdalenes to An Taoiseach of Ireland, Mr Brian Cowen, 2010, https://www.thepetitionsite.com/1/leadership-needed-on-magdalene-laundries/.
74 JFM, 'Pressure Mounts on Cowen as Fianna Fáil TDs Deliver Petition Demanding Justice for Magdalenes', Press Release, 21 June 2010; also, Patsy McGarry, 'Taoiseach Receives Demand for Magdalene Redress', *Irish Times*, 23 June 2010.
75 'Catherine d', 2014, comment *on Care2 Petitions*, 'Leadership needed on Magdalene Laundries', https://www.thepetitionsite.com/1/leadership-needed-on-magdalene-laundries/.
76 James M. Smith, 'No Time to Lose with Apologies for Magdalenes', *Irish Times*, 11 June 2011.
77 Justice for Magdalenes, letter to An Taoiseach, Mr Enda Kenny, 13 June 2011.
78 James Smith email to JFM group, 10 June 2011, 3:50pm EST.
79 JFM, 'NWCI Urges Women Politicians to Support Justice for Magdalenes', Press Release, 9 July 2010.

80 Sr Bernie Mc Nally, Provincial Leader of the Good Shepherd Sisters, letter to James M. Smith, Boston College, 11 June 2010.
81 Sr Sheila Murphy, Regional Leader of the Sisters of Our Lady of Charity, letter to James M. Smith, Boston College, 23 June 2010.
82 Claire O'Sullivan, 'Brady: Church Wants to Find "just solution"', *Irish* Examiner, 1 April 2010.
83 'JFM Meeting with Cardinal Brady at Ara Coeli, Armagh Thursday 24th June 2010', Notes taken by Claire McGettrick, 24 June 2010.
84 Sarah MacDonald, 'Cardinal Sean Brady Highly Regarded until Abuse Cover-Up Scandal', *Belfast Telegraph*, 14 August 2014.
85 Carbury, 'Brady Encourages Magdalene Survivors in Talks with Church'.
86 James M. Smith, Boston College, letter to Sr Marianne O'Connor, Director General, Conference of Religious of Ireland, 9 July 2010.
87 Marianne O'Connor, OSU, Director General, CORI, email to James Smith, Boston College, 1 October 2010.
88 Conor Ryan, 'Sisters of Mercy made €165m from Sales', *Irish Examiner*, 4 July 2011 and 'Site by Laundry Grave Sold for €61.8m', *Irish Examiner*, 5 July 2011.
89 Conor Ryan, 'Counting the Cost of Abuse Redress', *Irish Examiner*, 1 October 2012.
90 *DED*, Alan Shatter, 'Written Answers: Magdalene Laundries', 3 May 2011, Question 472 (Caoimhghín Ó Caoláin).
91 *DED*, James Reilly, 'Written Answers: Magdalene Laundries', 15 June 2011, Question 630 (Caoimhghín Ó Caoláin). Also, Patsy McGarry, 'HSE gives €87m to Magdalene nuns', *Irish Times*, 21 June 2011.
92 McGarry, 'Laundry Orders Run Sex Workers' Aid Group'.
93 JFM, Meeting Minutes with Archbishop of Dublin, Diarmuid Martin, Archbishop's House, taken by Claire McGettrick, 6 July 2011.
94 JFM, 'Justice for Magdalenes Meets with Archbishop of Dublin, Diarmuid Martin', Press Release, 6 July 2011.
95 Deáglan De Bréadún, 'Church Will Stick to Its Teachings on Abortion—Martin', *Irish Times*, 25 July 2012.

Chapter 4

1 See Steed, 'Justice for Magdalenes'.
2 Colin Smith and April Duff, 'Access to Justice for Victims of Historic Institutional Abuse', *Éire-Ireland: An Interdisciplinary Journal of Irish Studies*, 55, nos. 1–2 (2020): 100–19, 109.
3 Justice for Magdalenes (JFM), 'Submission to the Irish Human Rights Commission', 10 June 2010; and JFM, 'Justice for Magdalenes Submits Human Rights Application', Press Release, 24 June 2010.
4 *Witness: Sex in a Cold Climate*, Prod. by Steve Humphries, aired 16 March 1998, Testimony Films for Channel 4; *Liveline*, aired 28 and 29 September 2009 on RTÉ Radio 1.
5 League of Nations 1926 Slavery Convention; the 1957 United Nations Supplementary Convention on the Abolition of Slavery, the Slave Trade, and Institutions and Practices Similar to Slavery; the International Labour Organization (ILO) 1930 Forced Labour Convention; and the ILO 1957 Convention on Abolition of Forced Labour.

6 Convention for the Protection of Human Rights and Fundamental Freedoms (adopted 4 November 1950, entered into force 3 September 1953) 213 United Nations Treaty Series 222, Article 4 (AKA European Convention on Human Rights).
7 *Bunreacht na hÉireann*, Article 40.3.
8 Maeve O'Rourke, 'Slavery, Forced Labour and the Magdalene Laundries', *Human Rights in Ireland* (blog), 13 July 2010.
9 Irish Human Rights Commission, *Assessment of the Human Rights Issues Arising in Relation to the 'Magdalen Laundries'*, 10 November 2010, 27–8.
10 Sinéad Lucey, IHRC Senior Enquiry and Legal Officer, 'Presentation of Assessment's Conclusions', 10 November 2020.
11 Maurice Manning, IHRC President, 'Closing Remarks', 10 November 2010.
12 Olive Braiden, IHRC Commissioner, 'Opening Remarks', 10 November 2010.
13 McGarry, 'Call for Inquiry into Magdalene Laundries'.
14 *DED*, 'Adjournment Debate: Report on Magdalen Laundries', 9 November 2010, and https://www.youtube.com/watch?v=BsGULZDLpGo.
15 *DED*, 'Adjournment Debate', 9 November 2010.
16 Maeve O'Rourke and James M. Smith, 'Justice for Magdalenes: Official Response to Irish Human Rights Commission Findings', Blog post, *Human Rights in Ireland* (blog), 14 November 2010.
17 Maeve O'Rourke, 'Submission to the United Nations Committee against Torture', May 2011; Maeve O'Rourke, 'Submission to the United Nations Working Group on the Universal Periodic Review', October 2011. Also, Pamela Duncan, 'Magdalene Survivors in UN Plea', *Irish Times*, 23 April 2011; Maeve O'Rourke, 'Lack of Redress for the Magdalene Laundries Abuse – A Continuing Violation of UNCAT', *Human Rights in Ireland* (blog), 3 May 2011.
18 Maeve O'Rourke, 'Submission to the United Nations Committee against Torture' (UNCAT), Appendix IV, 22–42.
19 O'Rourke, Submission to UNCAT, Appendix II, 18–9 and Appendix III, 20–1.
20 See, for example, *A.A. v Azerbaijan*, Communication No 247/2004, 25 November 2005.
21 *DED*, An Taoiseach, Enda Kenny, 'Questions: Church-State Dialogue', 11 May 2011 (Gerry Adams).
22 Maeve O'Rourke et al., *Justice for Magdalenes (JFM) Statement.* Geneva, Switzerland, UN Committee against Torture (UNCAT), NGO Briefing Session, 20 May 2011.
23 Seán Aylward, 'Opening Statement for the Consideration of Ireland's First Periodic Report under Article 19 of the Convention against Torture', 23 May, 2011.
24 UN Committee against Torture, *Summary Record of the 1002nd Meeting Held at the Palais Wilson, Geneva*, UN Doc CAT/C/SR.1002. 23 May 2011.
25 Jamie Smyth, 'State Defends Response to Ryan Report', *Irish Times*, 24 May 2011; Jennifer Hough, 'UN Committee Urges State to Set Up Magdalene Probe', *Irish Examiner*, 24 May 2011.
26 Mr Aylward's remarks on 24 May 2011, https://www.youtube.com/watch?v =tSrDbeO5wYs; also, UN Committee against Torture, *Summary Record of the 1005th Meeting Held at the Palais Wilson, Geneva.*
27 Aylward, 24 May 2011; United Nations Convention Against Torture and Other Cruel, Inhuman or Degrading Treatment or Punishment (adopted 10 December 1984, entered into force 26 June 1987) 1465 UNTS 85, Articles 12 and 13; Abad v Spain, Communication No. 59/1996, UN Doc CAT/C/20/D/59/1996, 14 May 1998, Para 8.6; Parot v Spain, Communication No. 6/1990, 2 May 1995, Para 10.4.

28 Ed O'Loughlin, '50 Years Later, a Victim of Ireland's "Laundries" Fights for Answers', *New York Times*, 26 October 2018; Elizabeth Coppin, BBC Radio, Outlook, 'Confronting the Nun Who Despised Me', 14 November 2018; Kitty Holland, 'Magdalene Survivor: "It feels like Ireland is abusing us again"', *Irish Times*, 17 February 2020.
29 Aylward, 24 May 2011.
30 JFMR YouTube Channel: 'Myrna Kleopas Magdalene Laundries UNCAT Questioning 24-05-11', 24 May 2011; 'Nora Sveaass Magdalene Laundries UNCAT Questioning 24-05-11', 24 May 2011; 'Xuexian Wang Magdalene Laundries UNCAT Questioning 24-05-11', 24 May 2011.
31 JFMR YouTube Channel: Felice Gaer, 'Magdalene Laundries UNCAT Questioning 24-05-11', 24 May 2011, 6:29.
32 UN Committee against Torture (UNCAT), Concluding Observations on Ireland, UN Doc CAT/C/IRL/CO/1, 17 June 2011, Para 33.
33 Justice for Magdalenes, 'Dear Cabinet: Magdalene Survivors Need Justice Now', *Irish Times*, 2 May 2011; *DED*, Alan Shatter, 'Written Answers: Magdalene Laundries', 3 May 2011, Question 450 (Michael McGrath), Question 472 and 632 (Caoimhghín Ó Caoláin), Question 480 (Clare Daly); An Taoiseach Enda Kenny, 'Questions: Church-State Dialogue', 11 May 2011 (Gerry Adams); 'Other Questions: Magdalene Laundries', 18 May 2011 (Michael Colreavy).
34 Patsy McGarry, 'Magdalene Operators Vow to Cooperate with Any Inquiry', *Irish Times*, 11 June 2011; Dan Buckley and Claire O'Sullivan, 'Religious Agree to Help Magdalenes', *Irish Examiner*, 11 June 2011.
35 Department of Justice and Equality, *Statement on the Magdalene Laundries*, 14 June 2011.
36 Department of Justice, 'Oifig an Aire Dli agus Cirt agus Athchdirithe Dli Memorandum for the Government Magdalen Laundries', 13 June 2011 [hereafter DoJ Memorandum]. Also, Conall Ó Fátharta, 'Magdalene Laundries: Dodging Liability Is Still the Name of the Game', *Irish Examiner*, 27 March 2017.
37 Conall Ó Fátharta, 'Government "conscious of redress" for Magdalene Survivors', *Irish Examiner*, 18 November 2014. The 'DRAFT: 3rd Draft: March 2011' memorandum is embedded in this article online.
38 Ó Fátharta, 'Government "conscious of redress" for Magdalene Survivors'.
39 *DED*, Alan Shatter, 'Order of Business', 17 December 2009.
40 DoJ Memorandum, 13 June 2011, 1, 3.
41 DoJ Memorandum, 13 June 2011, 2.
42 DoJ Memorandum, 13 June 2011, 4.
43 DoJ Memorandum, 13 June 2011, 3.
44 DoJ Memorandum, 13 June 2011, 8. Also, Conall Ó Fátharta, 'Magdalene Laundries: Dodging Liability . . .'.
45 DoJ Memorandum, 13 June 2011, 12. We recognize that these 'Observations' were drafted by senior departmental officials prior to presentation by ministers.
46 DoJ Memorandum, 13 June 2011, 15.
47 DoJ Memorandum, 13 June 2011, 9.
48 DoJ Memorandum, 13 June 2011, 11.
49 DoJ Memorandum, 13 June 2011, 12.
50 DoJ Memorandum, 13 June 2011, 12.
51 DoJ Memorandum, 13 June 2011, 7–8.
52 JFM group email exchange, Monday, 13 June 2011.

53 Department of Justice and Equality, *Statement on the Magdalene Laundries*, 14 June 2011. Also, JFM, 'JFM Welcomes Magdalene Inquiry Announcement and Pledges to Participate', Press Release, 14 June 2011. The IDC's final report was published on 5 February 2013, see *IDC Report*.
54 Maeve O'Rourke, letter to Alan Shatter, Minister for Justice, 17 June 2011.
55 Merrion Street, 'Appointment of Chairperson of Inter-Departmental Committee into Magdalene Laundries – Shatter', 1 July 2011. Also, Eoin Burke Kennedy, 'McAleese to Chair Magdalene Group', *Irish Times*, 1 July 2011.
56 'IP Comment: Appointment of Dr McAleese a Mistake', Editorial, *Irish Post*, 13 July 2011.
57 JFM, 'JFM Welcomes Appointment of Chair for Inter-Departmental Committee on Magdalene Laundries', Press Release, 1 July 2011.
58 Alan Shatter, Minister for Justice, letter to James M. Smith, Boston College, 20 June 2011.
59 James M. Smith, *A Narrative of State Interaction with the Magdalene Laundries*, 2011.
60 Department of Justice, 'Notes of Meeting with Representatives of Justice for Magdalenes (JFM) and Irish Women Survivors Support Network UK', 4 July 2011, Department of Justice, Dublin, signed and dated 'LB, 8 July 2011', 6 pages, np [hereafter DoJ Notes]. FOI Data Request, 2015.
61 DoJ Notes, 8 July 2011.
62 James M. Smith, Boston College, letter to Senator Martin McAleese, Seanad Éireann, 12 July 2011.
63 Senator Martin McAleese, letter to James M. Smith, Boston College, 24 August 2011.
64 JFM, meeting minutes with Inter-Departmental Committee, taken by Claire McGettrick, 9 September 2011, Montague Court, Dublin 2 (hereafter JFM Minutes).
65 Smith, *A Narrative of State Interaction with the Magdalene Laundries*, 2011.
66 Including Mr Jimmy Martin (Department of Justice), Ms Mary McGarry (Department of Education), Ms Mary Moylan (Department of the Environment), Mr Denis O'Sullivan (Department Children), Ms Bairbre Nic Aonghusa (Department of Health), and Mr Francis Rochford (Department of Jobs Enterprise & Innovation).
67 See also, Sorcha Pollak, 'Magdalene Redress Scheme to be Widened', *Irish Times*, 3 June 2018.
68 JFM minutes, 9 September 2011.
69 Katherine summed this up best: 'Extremely loathe though I am to say it, I think we will need high quality survivor testimony to blow them way, way off this course,' see Katherine O'Donnell, email to JFM Group, 11 September 2011.
70 James M. Smith, letter to Alan Shatter, Minister for Justice, 8 June 2011.
71 http://www.hiqa.ie/social-care/find-a-centre/nursing-homes/beechlawn-house-nursing-home.
72 Claire McGettrick, JFM PRO, to Kathleen Lynch, Minister of State for Older People, Department of Justice and Equality, 18 August 2011.
73 Justice for Magdalenes Research website, http://jfmresearch.com/home/resources-for-survivors-and-families/.
74 *DED*, Alan Shatter, 'Written Answers: Data Protection', 2 November 2011, Question 369 (Dominic Hannigan).
75 See Adoption Rights Alliance resources, http://adoption.ie/records/.
76 Carol Ryan, 'Seeking Redress for a Mother's Life Spent in a Workhouse', *New York Times*, 7 February 2013.

77 Inter-Departmental Committee to establish the facts of State involvement with the Magdalen Laundries, *Interim Progress Report*, 20 October 2011, 5 (hereafter *IDC Interim Report*).
78 Statutory Instrument, S.I. No. 486 of 2011, *Data Protection Act, 1988 (Section 2B) Regulations 2011* (Dublin: Stationery Office, 2011). 2.
79 S.I. No. 486, 3.
80 Eugene F. Collins Solicitors, letter to the Department of the Environment, 'Exhumation Licence for Grave Ground at High Park Convent', 12 May 1993. FOI Data Request, 2015.
81 *IDC Interim Report*, 7. See James M. Smith, 'Commission of Investigation Act Inhibits Truth-Telling about Past and Present', *Irish Times*, 20 October 2018.
82 *IDC Interim Report*.
83 *DED*, Alan Shatter, 'Written Answers: Data Protection', 2 November 2011, Question 369 (Dominic Hannigan).
84 JFM, 'Justice for Magdalenes Cautiously Welcomes Magdalene Inter-Departmental Committee Report', JFM Press Release, 26 October 2011.
85 *DED*, Alan Shatter, 'Priority Questions: Magdalene Laundries', 13 March 2012, Question 62 (Maureen O'Sullivan), and https://www.youtube.com/watch?v=uinusEKSE4I.
86 Monckton Chambers, 'Raymond Hill Nominated for Bar Pro Bono Award', 11 October 2012; Monckton Chambers, 'Victims of the Magdalene Laundries Finally Receive a Full Apology', 1 March 2013.
87 United Nations, *Principles on the Effective Investigation and Documentation of Torture and Other Cruel, Inhuman or Degrading Treatment or Punishment*, Recommended by General Assembly resolution 55/89 of 4 December 2000.
88 Mr Kenny nominated Dr McAleese to An Seanad on 11 May 2011.
89 *IDC Report*, Chapter 2, 4–14.
90 *DED*, Alan Shatter, 'Written Answers: Magdalene Laundries', 19 July 2011, Questions 289 and 390 (Dara Calleary); and Alan Shatter, 'Written Answers: Magdalene Laundries', 4 October 2011, Question 455 (Mary Lou McDonald).
91 *IDC Interim Report*, 7.
92 Dr Jacinta Prunty accessed relevant archives at the OLC and SGS mother-houses in France that are not referred to in the *IDC Report*. See Jacinta Prunty, *The Monasteries, Magdalen Refuges and Reformatories and Reformatory Schools of Our Lady of Charity in Ireland* (Dublin: Columba Press, 2017).
93 Committee Against Torture, *General Comment No 3, Implementation of Article 14 by States Parties*, UN Doc CAT/C/GC/3, 13 December 2012, Para 30.
94 We provided contact details for Patricia Burke Brogan, Mary Raftery, Maria Luddy, Diarmaid Ferriter, Eoin O'Sullivan, Evelyn Glynn, a former doctor at one laundry and the former manager of another. We also forwarded scholarly articles and book chapters; Patricia Burke Brogan, *Eclipsed* (Galway: Salmon Publishing, 1994) and *Stained Glass at Samhain* (Galway: Salmon Publishing, 2003); Evelyn Glynn, curator, *Breaking the Rule of Silence*, 2011, Limerick College of Art.
95 James Smith, email to Nuala Ní Mhuircheartaigh, 'Transfers', 27 October 2011, 7:56 pm; 'A New Form of State Interaction', 26 January 2012, 1:17 pm; 'Charitable Donations & Bequests', 1 & 2, 2 April 2012, 5:24pm; 'Stanislaus Kennedy Book', 4 April 2012, 10.23 am; 'Newspapers-Claire McGettrick', 2 April 2012, 5:25 pm; and 'Criminal Convictions-Claire McGettrick', 2 April 2012, 5:26 pm. JFM also submitted

more material on five CDs in July 2012: Disc 1 - Census of Production; Disc 2 - Court Committals; Disc 3 - Various articles_State Interaction; Disc 4 - Sundays Well; Disc 5 - Development_Land Sales.

96 James M Smith, Boston College, letter to Senator Martin McAleese, Independent Chairperson IDC, 16 February 2012. Also, National Archives, Department of Health File A 124/9, 'Foster Mothers'.

97 Department of Health File 124/34 'Children and Mothers in Special Homes, Annual Returns'. Also, J. P. Rodgers, *For the Love of My Mother: A Memoir* (Williamstown, Co. Galway: MacRuairi Art, 2005).

98 James M Smith, Boston College, letter to Senator Martin McAleese, Independent Chairperson IDC, 14 March 2012. Also, National Archives, Department of Health, File L112/212, b, 'Mayo Returns, Children and Unmarried Mothers'; File A21/158/v.2 (b) 'Mayo Returns'; File AL113/21 'Children and Unmarried Mothers, Returns'; and File A11/342/v.2 'Galway, Children and Unmarried Mothers in Institutions, Returns 1952-57'.

99 James M. Smith, 'Knowing and Unknowing Tuam: State Practice, the Archive, and Transitional Justice', *Éire-Ireland: An Interdisciplinary Journal of Irish Studies*, 55, no. 1–2 (Spring/Summer 2020): 142–80.

100 *DED*, Richard Bruton, 'Written Answers: Legislative Provisions', 23 June 2011, Question 92 (Caoimhghín Ó Caoláin).

101 James Smith, email to Nuala Ní Mhuircheartaigh, 26 January 2012; and Letter, James M. Smith, Boston College to Senator Martin McAleese, Independent Chairperson IDC, 16 February 2012.

102 Irish Statute Book, *Factories Act, 1955* (Dublin: Stationery Office, 1955). Sec. 84; *SED*, 'Factories Bill, 1954 – Committee', 11 May 1955.

103 James Smith, email to Nuala Ní Mhuircheartaigh, "Email 1_Factories Act," 17 May 2012, 11.43 am.

104 Maeve O'Rourke, email to JFM, 'Pre-1955 Factories Act Legal Framework', 2 July 2012, 00:13 am; Maeve O'Rourke, Memo to JFM, 'Pre-1955 Factories Act Legal Framework', 2 July 2012.

105 James Smith, email to Nuala Ní Mhuircheartaigh, 'Email_1: Factories Inspectorate Memo to Government', 2 April 2012, 5:04 pm.

106 James Smith, email to Nuala Ní Mhuircheartaigh, 'Email_2: Prosecutions of Laundries, Factories Inspectorate', 2 April 2012, 5:19 pm.

107 http://jfmresearch.com/home/oralhistoryproject/.

108 http://jfmresearch.com/home/oralhistoryproject/transcripts/ohpresources/.

109 http://jfmresearch.com/home/oralhistoryproject/transcripts/.

110 Claire McGettrick, email to JFM Group, 'McAleese Meeting Notes', 16 February 2012. We met Senator McAleese for a third time on 18 April 2012.

111 Claire McGettrick meeting notes, 16 February 2012.

112 Evelyn Glynn, curator, *Breaking the Rule of Silence*, 2011, Limerick College of Art.

113 James M Smith, Boston College, letter to Senator Martin McAleese, Independent Chairperson IDC, 27 March 2012; and James M. Smith, Boston College, letter to Mr Alan Shatter, Minister for Justice and Ms Kathleen Lynch, Minister of State, 27 March 2012.

114 Email, Nuala Ní Mhuircheartaigh to James Smith, 'Letter for Senator McAleese', 29 March 2012, 12:13 pm.

115 Claire McGettrick, JFM PRO, letter to Senator Martin McAleese, Independent Chairperson IDC, 28 May 2012.

116 JFM, 'Justice for Magdalenes and Survivors meet with Senator McAleese', Press Release, 6 June 2012; Fiachra Ó Cionnaith, 'Magdalenes Demand Apology', *Irish Examiner*, 7 June 2012.

117 JFM, 'Irish Human Rights Commission, Women's Human Rights Alliance and Justice for Magdalenes (JFM) Address UN Human Rights Council on Magdalene Laundries Abuse', Press Release, 15 March 2012.

118 Maeve O'Rourke, *Follow-Up Report to the United Nations Committee against Torture*, May 2012.

119 UN Committee against Torture (UNCAT), *Information Received from Ireland on the Implementation of the Committee's Concluding Observations*, UN Doc CAT/C/IRL/CO/1/Add.1 (31 July 2012). Para 22–3.

120 UNCAT, 31 July 2012, Para 22.

121 Patsy McGarry, 'Magdalene Group Urges Action', *Irish Times*, 24 May 2012.

122 James M. Smith and Raymond Hill, 'State Involvement with the Magdalene Laundries: A Summary of JFM's Submissions to the Inter-Departmental Committee', May 2012. Also, Conall Ó Fátharta, 'Magdalene Group Hits Out at Government', *Irish Examiner*, 25 May 2012.

123 Felice Gaer, Director of the New York-based Jacob Blaustein Institute for the Advancement of Human Rights and Vice-Chair of the UN Committee against Torture (speaking in a personal capacity), Key Note Address, 'Preventing Ill-Treatment and Securing Accountability: The Impact in Ireland of the UN Convention Against Torture (UNCAT)', 28 May 2012, Dublin.

124 'Justice for Magdalenes on RTÉ Nine News', aired 28 May 2012 on RTÉ 1.

125 Joe Little, 'State-Run Homes Sent Women to the Magdalene Laundries', 28 May 2012, RTÉ News.

126 JFM, 'One Year after UN Recommendation Magdalene Women Are no Closer to an Apology or Redress', JFM Press Release, 28 May 2012.

127 For video of Ms Gaer's remarks, see https://vimeo.com/43021127, at 21:46.

128 Conall Ó Fátharta, '500 Pages of New Testimony on Magdalene Laundries', *Irish Examiner*, 29 May 2012; Kitty Holland, 'Magdalene Lobby Group Criticises Coalition Inaction', *Irish Times*, 29 May 2012.

129 *Fifth Report of the Special Rapporteur on Child Protection: A Report Submitted to the Oireachtas, 2011 Report* (Copyright 2012, Geoffrey Shannon), 76, 78.

130 Principal Submission. A redacted version was circulated to Oireachtas members on 23 September 2012, and a version made available online on 16 February 2013.

131 JFM submitted three separate tranches of testimony – 13 testimonies on 28 May 2012; an additional eight testimonies as part of the 'Principal Submission'; and a further three testimonies submitted in late August/early September 2012, including eleven survivors, four daughters, three family members and four others witnesses, for a total of twenty-two testimonies. We submitted an additional seven testimonies gathered by Evelyn Glynn.

132 'Principal Submission', 7.

133 'Principal Submission', 8–9.

134 Pamela Duncan, 'Inquiry Chaired by McAleese Cost Just over €11,000', *Irish Times*, 6 February 2013.

135 Department of Justice, 'Shatter Statement on Magdalen Laundries', 11 September 2012; also *DED*, Kathleen Lynch, 'Magdalen Laundries: Motion [Private Members]', 25 September 2012.

136 Patsy McGarry, 'State "failing" Magdalene Women as Report Delayed', *Irish Times*, 12 September 2012.
137 JFM, 'JFM Says McAleese Report Delay should not Prevent State Action on Magdalenes', Press Release, 11 September 2012.
138 JFM, 'JFM Demands Immediate Government Action for Magdalene Survivors', Press Release, 18 September 2012.
139 Justice for Magdalenes, letter to Ms Kathleen Lynch, Minister of State, 17 September 2012.
140 JFM, 'JFM Says McAleese Report Delay should not Prevent State Action on Magdalenes'. Also, Patsy McGarry, 'Magdalene Group Seeks Action on Redress', *Irish Times*, 21 September 2012.
141 *RTÉ Prime Time*, 'Prime Time Investigates: The Magdalenes', Prod. Tanya Sillem, aired 25 September 2012, Dublin: RTÉ.
142 Fintan O'Toole, 'Dark Stain of Irish Gulag System Still not Addressed', *Irish Times*, 25 September 2012.
143 James M. Smith, 'Magdalene Survivors Still Held Hostage to Politics', *Irish Times*, 26 September 2012.
144 *DED*, Mary Lou McDonald, 'Magdalene Laundries: Motion [Private Members]', 25 September 2012.
145 JFM, 'JFM Calls for Dignified Debate on Magdalene Laundries', Press Release, 25 September 2012.
146 O'Toole, 'Dark Stain of Irish Gulag System Still not Addressed'.
147 *DED*, Kathleen Lynch, 'Magdalene Laundries: Motion [Private Members]', 25 September 2012.
148 *DED*, 25 September 2012. Also, 'Minister Kathleen Lynch Says Calls for Magdalene Apology "premature"', 25 September 2012, RTÉ News; Clare O'Sullivan, 'Magdalene Laundries Motion "premature"', *Irish Examiner*, 26 September 2012; and Michael O'Regan, 'Magdalene Laundries Report due Later in the Year', *Irish Times*, 26 September 2012.
149 *DED*, 25 September 2012.
150 *DED*, Mary Lou McDonald, 'Magdalene Laundries: Motion (Resumed) [Private Members]', 26 September 2012.
151 'Magdalene Laundries Apology Motion Defeated', 26 September 2012, *RTÉ News*.
152 This precedent was replayed during the Private Members debate in February 2013 when Dara Calleary declared, 'I believe Maisie. I believe Attracta. I believe all the women,' *DED*, Dara Calleary, 'Magdalene Laundries: Motion [Private Members]', 12 February 2012.
153 Claire O'Sullivan, 'Interviews Lacked Transparency, Says Victims Group', *Irish Examiner*, 7 February 2013.
154 Nuala Ní Mhuircheartaigh, email to Claire McGettrick, 28 November 2012, 3.31 pm.
155 Nuala Ní Mhuircheartaigh, email to Mari Steed, 'Meeting with Magdalene Survivors', 2 December 2012, 11.42 am.
156 Nuala Ní Mhuircheartaigh, email to Mari Steed, 'Re: Meeting with Magdalene Survivors', 3 December 2012, 11.25 am.
157 Secretary for State Hillary Rodham Clinton, 'Frontlines and Frontiers: Making Human Rights A Reality', 8 December 2012, Dublin City University, Dublin, Ireland.
158 Claire McGettrick, email to JFM Group, 'Survivor Meeting Yesterday', 7 December 2012, 9.06 am.

159 McGettrick, email, 7 December 2012.
160 Survivor Elizabeth Coppin has reflected on her experience of this process as follows: 'When I think about it now, I am very upset that I said "No" when Senator McAleese asked me if I ever saw abuse in the Magdalene Laundries. I should have said, "I didn't see it, I lived it." Neither Senator McAleese nor Nuala explained what they meant the word "abuse" to mean. I think I have always associated the word "abuse" with the physical beatings I grew up with on a daily basis in the Industrial School. I didn't believe that the act of dragging me to the padded cell, or the detention and forced labour I experienced, would be classed as abuse.' See *Elizabeth Coppin v Ireland*, Witness Statement of Elizabeth Coppin dated 12 July 2018, Para 63.
161 McGettrick, 'Survivor Meeting Yesterday', 7 December 2012.
162 Department of Justice, 'Shatter Statement on Magdalen Laundries', 11 September 2012; *DED*, Taoiseach Enda Kenny, 'Order of Business', 19 December 2012 (Mary Lou McDonald).
163 Ireland, Department of Justice and Equality, 'Shatter Statement Regarding Report on Magdalen Laundries', 9 January 2013; and 'Report on the Magdalene Laundries is to be Brought to Government by Justice Minister', 9 January 2013, RTÉ News.
164 *DED*, Taoiseach Enda Kenny, 'Order of Business', 23 January 2013 (Mary Lou McDonald); 'Topical Issue Matters', 24 January 2013 (Maureen O'Sullivan); and Tánaiste Eamon Gilmore, 'Order of Business', 24 January 2013 (Dara Calleary).
165 *DED*, An Taoiseach Enda Kenny, 'Order of Business', 29 January 2013 (Mary Lou McDonald).
166 Claire McGettrick, JFM PRO, letter to survivors, 30 January 2013.
167 Stephen O'Brien, 'Judgment day for Inmates of Magdalenes', *Sunday Times* (London), 27 January 2013; Mark Hennessey, 'Justice for the Daughters of the Laundries', *Irish Times*, 2 February 2002; and Rachel Cooper, 'The Forgotten Women of Ireland's Magdalene Laundries', *Telegraph* (London), 4 February 2013.
168 Sinead O'Carroll, '"Margaret died of her slave-related injuries": A Magdalene Daughter Shares Her Story', *journal.ie*, 3 February 2013.
169 Carol Ryan, 'Dublin Journal: Seeking Redress for a Mother's Life in a Workhouse', *New York Times*, 6 February 2013.
170 James Smith email to JFM Group, 'Priority: McAleese Phone Call', 30 January 2013, 2.36 pm.
171 Stephen Collins, 'McAleese Resigns his Seat in Seanad', *Irish Times*, 1 February 2013.
172 JFM, 'Justice for Magdalenes (JFM) Awaits the Release of the Inter-Departmental Committee Investigating State Involvement with the Magdalene Laundries', Media Advisory, 3 February 2013.
173 James Smith, email to Raymond Hill, 'Magdalene Laundries', 5 February 2013, 4.49 am est.
174 Smith, 'Abused in the Past and Abandoned in the Present'.

Chapter 5

1 Principal Submission.
2 Mari Steed, email to JFM, 'After a Phone Call with Dr McAleese', 2 February 2013.
3 *IDC Report*, Chapter 4, Para 16, 54.
4 *IDC Report*, Chapter 19, Para 63, 959.

5 *IDC Report*, Introduction, Para 17, vi.
6 *IDC Report*, Chapter 19, Para 33, 932.
7 *IDC Report*, Chapter 19, Para 34, 932.
8 *IDC Report* Chapter 20, Para 2, 994.
9 Notes taken on behalf of JFM by Katherine O'Donnell, 5 February 2013.
10 Katherine O'Donnell, 'Academics Becoming Activists: Reflections on Some Ethical Issues of the Justice for Magdalenes Campaign', in *Irishness on the Margins*, ed. Pilar Villar-Argáiz (Cham: Palgrave Macmillan, 2018), 77–100.
11 JFM, 'Senator Martin McAleese's Report Finds That the Irish State was Directly Involved in the Magdalene Laundry System', Press Release, 5 February 2013. *Dáil Eireann Debates* (hereafter *DED*), 'Topical Issue Matters', 5 February 2013.
12 *DED*, Enda Kenny, 'Leaders' Questions', 5 February 2013.
13 *IDC Report*, Executive Summary, XIII.
14 *IDC Report*, Chapter 8, Para 9 and 10. The available field of information for analysis of duration of stay consisted of 11,198 cases. This is greater than the number of women the report considers.
15 Footage included in RTÉ *Prime Time* programme, 5 February 2013.
16 JFM, 'Urgent: Justice for Magdalenes Clarification on Taoiseach Statement', Press Release, 5 February 2013.
17 Claire McGettrick interview with Bryan Dobson, RTÉ *Six One* News, 5 February 2013.
18 Maeve O'Rourke, 'Laundries Apology Is Now Needed', *Irish Examiner*, 6 February 2013.
19 RTÉ *Prime Time*, 5 February 2013.
20 RTÉ *Prime Time*, 5 February 2013.
21 TV3 News at 5.30, 5 February 2013.
22 Jack Wall, 'Labour Oireachtas Members Call for Justice for Magdalene Women', *Labour News and Media*, 6 February 2013.
23 John Drennan, 'Labour Narrowly Averted Walkout over Kenny's Magdalene "apology"', *Sunday Independent*, 10 February 2013.
24 Nuala Ní Mhuircheartaigh, email to Claire McGettrick, 8 February 2013, 3.37 pm.
25 Claire McGettrick, James Smith, Mari Steed, Katherine O'Donnell and Maeve O'Rourke, letter to Nuala Ní Mhuircheartaigh, 8 February 2013. The letter was copied to An Taoiseach Enda Kenny; An Tánaiste, Eamon Gilmore; Minister for Justice, Alan Shatter; Minister of State for Older People, Kathleen Lynch; Mary Lou McDonald; Maureen O'Sullivan; Dara Calleary.
26 Justine McCarthy, 'Laundry Survivors Snub the Taoiseach', *Sunday Times*, 10 February 2013.
27 *IDC Report*, Chapter 19, Para 14, 928.
28 *IDC Report*, Chapter 19, Para 15, 928–9.
29 Gavin Sheridan, 'Taoiseach's Diary 2013', *TheStory.ie*, 22 January 2016.
30 Mary Minihan, 'Magdalene Survivors Expect Apology', *Irish Times*, 11 February 2013.
31 *IDC Report*, Chapter 19, Paras 79–138, pp. 963–86.
32 *IDC Report*, Chapter 19, Paras 60–78, pp. 958–63.
33 *DED*, Dara Calleary, 'Private Members Motion', 12 February 2013.
34 *DED*, 'Private Members Motion', 13 February 2013.
35 Sheridan, 'Taoiseach's Diary'.
36 Sheridan, 'Taoiseach's Diary'.
37 Maeve O'Rourke, 'Take this Chance, Taoiseach – Apologise to Each and Every One', *Irish Independent*, 16 February 2013.

38 Written by Johnny Mulhern.
39 *DED*, 'Magdalen Laundries Report: Statements', 19 February 2013. See also, https://www.youtube.com/watch?v=hOQyl7ZpoH8, 19:04. Mr Kenny's speech did not acknowledge the relatives of Magdalene women (including sons and daughters lost to adoption).
40 *DED*, 19 February 2013.
41 RTÉ *Prime Time*, 13 February 2013.

Chapter 6

1 Banville, 'A Century of Looking the Other Way', A 21.
2 For example, in the case of the *IDC Report*, its bulk is largely down to extraneous research notes and historical archives being indiscriminately presented. For example, Chapter One should have been an appendix, it merely explains the use of terms used in the report; Chapter Three is a collection of rudimentary notes towards writing a very general history of Magdalene institutions in Ireland; Chapter Six: Archive of the Committee's Work; Chapter Fourteen (C) Defence forces use of the laundry services provided by the Magdalen Laundries which repeats a lot of the archive trawl from 14 (B) merely to restate (without analysis or criticism) evidence of the Defence Forces' use of Magdalen Laundries; Chapter 15 Financial (C): Taxation, Commercial Rates and Social Insurance for a history of the law governing charitable tax relief since 1634.
3 *IDC Report*, Chapter 7, Para 34, pp. 150–1.
4 *IDC Report*, Chapter 7, Para 20–3, pp. 148.
5 See S.I. No. 486 of 2011, http://www.irishstatutebook.ie/eli/2011/si/486/made/en/pdf.
6 *IDC Report*, Executive Summary, XIII; see also Chapter 7 Par. 27, 30, pg. 149 & 150. JFM brought numerous examples to the IDC's attention of women listed on the 1901 and 1911 censuses who died in Magdalene Laundries post-1922, some as late as 1961, 1967 and as late as 1985: Maggie M. died in the care of the nuns after the closure of the Limerick institution, having spent seventy-four years there.
7 *IDC Report*, Chapter 8, Para 19, p.163.
8 *IDC Report*, Executive Summary, XIII.
9 *IDC Report*, Chapter 8, Para 19, p. 163.
10 McNally, 'Probation in Ireland', 12ff.
11 *IDC Report*, Executive Summary, XIII.
12 The *IDC Report*, Chapter 8, Para 6, p. 159, explains that 14,607 entry records were available to it, not including records of entries prior to 1922 or to the Magdalene Laundries in Dún Laoghaire or Galway. The Executive Summary, XIII explains that the 14,607 entry records relate to 10,012 women. Chapter 8 provides statistics that relate to individual entry records, not individual women. In other words, it does not collate entry records that concern the same woman and present them as a whole.
13 *IDC Report*, Chapter 8, Para 7, p. 159.
14 *The Magdalen Commission Report* (Dublin: Department of Justice and Equality, May 2013), Para 4.10, 5.
15 *IDC Report*, Chapter 16, Para 37, pp. 790–1.
16 *IDC Report*, Chapter 8, Para 29 and table, 168, notes that duration of stay was discernible only for 6,151 'women' which should read 'entries' or 'admissions' because it is acknowledged to be 6,151 from a database of 11,198 entries. The dataset of 11,198

entries is explained in Chapter 8, Para 7, pp. 159–60, to be a subset of the overall database of 14,607 known admissions (not including entries prior to 1922 or entries to the Magdalene Laundries in Galway or Dún Laoghaire).

17 *IDC Report*, above note 8, Chapter 8, Para 31, p. 169.

18 http://jfmresearch.com/home/magdalene-names-project/.

19 The IDC's failure to consider the testimony of the former Magdalene women is a classic example of what Miranda Fricker describes as 'epistemic injustice', whereby those who suffer from socially stigmatized identities are not considered to be expert or merely reliable witnesses, even when they offer accounts of their own experiences. This 'testimonial injustice' means that swathes of people are discounted in the process of forming public knowledge, even (or perhaps particularly) when that public knowledge concerns their own lives. Miranda Fricker, *Epistemic Injustice: Power and the Ethics of Knowing* (Oxford: Oxford University Press, 2007).

20 *IDC Report*, Introduction, VII.

21 *IDC Report*, Introduction, VIII.

22 *IDC Report*, Chapter 19, Para 15, pp. 928–9.

23 Enright, 'Antigone in Galway'.

24 *IDC Report*, Chapter 19, Para 60–138, pp. 958–86.

25 *IDC Report*, Introduction, Para 5–6, p. I.

26 For example, see *IDC Report*, Introduction, Para 10–11, IV; also Para 18, VII, and Para 23–4, X.

27 *IDC Report*, Chapter 19, Section B, p. 958, emphasis added.

28 *IDC Report*, Chapter 19, Para 134, p. 985.

29 *IDC Report*, Chapter 19, Para 135, p. 985.

30 *IDC Report*, Chapter 19, Para 16, p. 929.

31 *IDC Report*, Chapter 19, Para 35, p. 933.

32 *IHRC Assessment*; Sr Stanislaus Kennedy, *But Where Can I Go?*.

33 Sr Stanislaus, 29.

34 *IDC Report*, Chapter 19, Para 77, p. 963.

35 The authors' early readings of the *IDC Report* were informed by Simon McGarr's blog post: *How to Read the McAleese Report into the Magdalen Laundries*.

36 *IDC Report*, Chapter 9, Para 281, p. 308.

37 *IDC Report*, Chapter 9, Para 282, p. 308.

38 *IDC Report*, Chapter 9, Para 294, p. 313.

39 *IDC Report*, Chapter 5, summary, p. 70.

40 *IDC Report*, Chapter 5, Para 2, p. 71.

41 Indeed, the State's own Department of Justice as late as June 2010 insisted that the only statutory provision for the State sending a woman to a Laundry was the *1960 Criminal Justice Act*, and it referred specifically to one institution and only for remand cases.

42 *IDC Report*, Chapter 18: Non-State Routes of Entry to the Magdalen Laundries (Part B), Para 97, p. 920.

43 *IDC Report*, Chapter 12, summary, p. 523.

44 *IDC Report*, Chapter 12, Para 152, p. 575.

45 *IDC Report*, Chapter 12, Para 141, p. 570.

46 *IDC Report*, Chapter 12, Para 182, p. 585.

47 *IDC Report*, Chapter 20, summary, p. 993.

48 *IDC Report*, Chapter 15, Para 38, p. 754.

49 *IDC Report*, Chapter 15, Para 62–5, p. 762.

50 *IDC Report*, Chapter 15, Para 66–123, pp. 762–78.
51 *IDC Report*, Chapter 15, Para 66, p. 763.
52 *IDC Report*, Chapter 15, Para 96, p. 771–2.
53 *IDC Report*, Chapter 15, Para 102–9, pp. 773–4.
54 *IDC Report*, Chapter 15, Para 107, p. 774.
55 *IDC Report*, Chapter 20, Para 2, p. 994.
56 *IDC Report*, Chapter 20, Para 4, p. 994.
57 *IDC Report*, Chapter 20, Para 5, p. 994.
58 *IDC Report*, Chapter 20, Para 49, p. 1006.
59 *IDC Report*, Chapter 20, Para 51, p. 1007.
60 The authors are indebted to notes provided by Raymond Hill, incorporated in JFMR's submissions to UN Commission on the Status of Women in August 2014: Maeve O'Rourke, *Justice for Magdalenes Research: Submission to UN Commission on the Status of Women* (JFM Research, 1 August 2014).
61 Felice D Gaer, Rapporteur for Follow-up on Concluding Observations, Committee against Torture, letter to Mr Gerard Corr, Permanent Representative of Ireland to the United Nations Office at Geneva, 22 May 2013.
62 Mr Gerard Corr, Ambassador Extraordinary and Plenipotentiary, Permanent Representative of Ireland to the United Nations Office in Geneva, letter to Ms Felice D. Gaer, Rapporteur, Office of the United Nations High Commissioner for Human Rights, Committee Against Torture Secretariat, 8 August 2013.
63 United Nations, *Ireland, Second Periodic Report to the Committee Against Torture*, UN Doc CAT/C/IRL/2, 20 January 2016, Para 241; United Nations, *Ireland, Information on Follow-Up to the Concluding Observations of the Committee against Torture on the Second Periodic Report of Ireland*, UN Doc CAT/C/IRL/CO/2/Add.1, 28 August 2018, Par. 15; United Nations, Human Rights Committee, *Replies of Ireland to the List of Issues*, UN Doc CCPR/C/IRL/Q/4/Add.1, received 27 February 2014, published 5 May 2014; United Nations, *Ireland, Information on Follow-Up to the Concluding Observations of the Human Rights Committee on the Fourth Periodic Report of Ireland*, UN Doc CCPR/C/IRL/CO/4/Add.1, 15 August 2017, Par. 5 (third round); United Nations, *Ireland, Follow-Up Material to the Concluding Observations of the UN Human Rights Committee on the Fourth Periodic Review of Ireland under the International Covenant on Civil and Political Rights*, 17 July 2015, 3 Ireland, *Combined Sixth and Seventh Periodic Reports to the United Nations Committee on the Elimination of All Forms of Discrimination Against Women*, 30 September 2016, 8.
64 UN, HRC, *Replies of Ireland to the List of Issues*, 5 May 2014; *Follow-Up Material to the Concluding Observations of the UN Human Rights Committee on the Fourth Periodic Review of Ireland*, 17 July 2015, 3; *Submission by Ireland of Further Information to the UN Human Rights Committee following Ireland's Fourth Periodic Review under the International Covenant on Civil and Political Rights*, 13 June 2016; *Information on Follow-Up to the Concluding Observations of the Human Rights Committee on the Fourth Periodic Report of Ireland*, 15 August 2017, Par. 5 (third round); *Information on Follow-Up to the Concluding Observations of the Committee against Torture on the Second Periodic Report of Ireland*, 28 August 2018, Para 15.
65 *Replies to the Human Rights Committee's List of Issues*, 5 May 2014, Para 54.
66 *Second Periodic Report to CAT*, 20 January 2016, Para 248.
67 *Second Periodic Report to CAT*, 20 January 2016, Para 237.
68 United Nations Committee against Torture, *Elizabeth Coppin v Ireland*, Complaint No. 879/2020. Response of Ireland on the Question of Admissibility, Para 6.

69 *DED*, Written Answers, 'Department of Justice and Equality: Magdalen Laundries Issues', Question No 46766/13, 5 November 2013.
70 *DED*, Department of Justice and Equality: Magdalen Laundries Issues', 5 November 2013.
71 *DED*, Written answers, 'Department of Justice and Equality: Magdalen Laundries Report', 30 June 2015.
72 *DED*, written Answers, 'Department of Justice and Equality: Restorative Justice', Questions 9731/17, 9732/17, 9733/17, 9734/17, 9735/17, 9736/17, 9737/17 and 9738/17, 28 February 2017; also *DED*, written answer of Frances Fitzgerald, TD, Minister for Justice, to Clare Daly, TD, Question 4964/17, 2 February 2017. See also *DED*, written answers to Catherine Connolly, 8 February 2017.
73 *DED*, written answer of Richard Bruton TD, Minister for Education and Skills, to Catherine Murphy TD (Question 42230/17), 10 October 2017.
74 *Magdalen Commission Report*, 8, Para 3.03, 5.09, 5.13.
75 Irish Human Rights Commission, *Follow-Up Report on State Involvement with Magdalen Laundries* [hereafter *IHRC Follow-Up Report*], June 2013, Executive summary, 4.
76 *IHRC Follow-Up Report*, Para 76. Emphasis added.
77 *IHRC Follow-Up Report*, Para 171.
78 *IHRC Follow-Up Report*, Para 185.
79 *IHRC Follow-Up Report*, Para 229.
80 *IHRC Follow-Up Report*, Para 237.
81 *IHRC Follow-Up Report*, Para 254.

Chapter 7

1 *DED*. 'Magdalen Laundries Report: Statements', 19 February 2013.
2 Alan Shatter, letter to Mr Justice Quirke, 20 February 2013.
3 *Collins Dictionary*, s.v. 'ex gratia', n.
4 *Magdalen Commission Report*, 40.
5 *Magdalen Commission Report*, 36–7.
6 *Magdalen Commission Report*, 36.
7 JFM. *JFM Restorative Justice & Reparation Scheme for Magdalene Laundry Survivors*. 14 October 2011, 6.
8 Residential Institutions Redress Act 2002, sections 11(12) and 13(11); *DED*, Residential Institutions Redress (Amendment) Bill 2011: Second Stage, 14 July 2011.
9 *Magdalen Commission Report*, 5.
10 Claire McGettrick et al., 'Survivor Guide to Magdalen Commission', *Justice for Magdalenes*, 24 March 2013.
11 Claire McGettrick, 'Guide for Relatives of Deceased Women', *Justice for Magdalenes*, 24 March 2013, updated 2016; JFM, 'Justice for Magdalenes publishes Survivor Guide to Magdalen Commission', Press Release, 25 March 2013.
12 *Magdalen Commission Report*, 27, 8, Para 5.13; Para 3.03; and Para 5.09.
13 *Elizabeth Coppin v Ireland*, Witness Statement.
14 Katherine O' Donnell, Sinead Pembroke and Claire McGettrick, *Magdalene Institutions: Recording an Oral and Archival History*, Government of Ireland

Collaborative Research Project, Irish Research Council, 2013, 'Oral History of Pippa Flanagan'. Emphasis in original.

15 Oral History of Kathleen. This 'Kathleen' is not the same woman as 'Kathleen R.' referred to later in the chapter.

16 *Magdalen Commission Report*, 25.

17 Alan Shatter, 'Address by Alan Shatter TD, Minister for Justice, Equality and Defence on the publication of the Report of Mr Justice Quirke', Department of Justice, 26 June 2013.

18 *Magdalen Commission Report*, 6.

19 *Magdalen Commission Report*, 33–4.

20 *Magdalen Commission Report*, 37.

21 *Magdalen Commission Report*, 38.

22 Justice for Magdalenes, *Submission to Mr Justice John Quirke, Magdalen Commission*, 13 March 2013.

23 Email from Katherine O'Donnell to JFM, 'Re: Letter to survivors', 13 March 2013.

24 Justice for Magdalenes, 'Justice for Magdalenes to End Its Political Campaign', Press Release, 17 May 2013.

25 JFM Press Release, 17 May 2013; Maeve O'Rourke (on behalf of Justice for Magdalenes), *Submission to the UN Committee against Torture regarding Follow-up to Ireland's most recent State Party Report and List of Issues for Ireland's next State Party Report*, 7 March 2013.

26 Newspaper and Magazine Articles; Books; Academic Journal Articles and Book Chapters available at www.jfmresearch.com/bookarchive; O' Donnell et al., *Magdalene Institutions: Recording an Oral and Archival History*, 2013.

27 Opinion Editorials; Press Releases/Statements; Radio. Interviews/Documentaries/ Podcasts; Television Documentaries; Dáil and Seanad Éireann Debates/Questions; Briefings Memoranda/Minutes/Notes available at www.jfmresearch.com/ bookarchive.

28 Letters; Emails; Non-Governmental Organizations (NGO) and JFM/R Reports available at www.jfmresearch.com/bookarchive.

29 Non-Governmental Organizations (NGO) and JFM/R Reports; Emails available at www.jfmresearch.com/bookarchive.

30 Irish Government and Statutory Bodies: Documents and Reports; Non-Governmental Organizations (NGO) and JFM/R Reports. NGOs and bodies include the Irish Human Rights and Equality Commission, Amnesty International available at www.jfmresearch.com/bookarchive.

31 Coppin v Ireland, United Nations Committee against Torture, Complaint No. 879/2020. Mrs Coppin is also represented by Michael Lynn SC, Colin Smith BL, Jennifer MacLeod (Brick Court Chambers, London), Lewis Mooney BL, Wendy Lyon, Solicitor, and Hogan Lovells International LLP.

32 Brenda McVeigh, Department of Finance, memo to Jimmy Martin, 16 August 2013. This record was generously shared by Conall Ó Fátharta.

33 *Report of the Inter Departmental Group on the Implementation of the Recommendations of Judge Quirke contained in his report 'On the establishment of an ex gratia Scheme and related matters for the benefit of those women who were admitted to and worked in the Magdalen Laundries'.* September 2013. [Hereafter *IDG Report*]. These records were generously shared by Conall Ó Fátharta.

34 *IDG Report*, 8.

35 *IDG Report*, 17–18.

36 *IDG Report*, 18.
37 *Opportunity Lost: An Investigation by the Ombudsman into the administration of the Magdalene Restorative Justice Scheme* (Dublin: Office of the Ombudsman, 2017), 9.
38 The women in the UK received extra money for a solicitor to set up a personal injury trust. See the *Magdalen Commission Report*.
39 'Address by Alan Shatter', 26 June 2013.
40 Ryan Moling, email to Jimmy Martin, 8 July 2013.
41 *IDG Report*, 20.
42 Maeve O'Rourke, Email to Ombudsman, 'Magdalene Ex Gratia Scheme: Ongoing Problems', 6 June 2019; Justice for Magdalenes, letter to Frances Fitzgerald, 1 September 2014. See also *DED*, Charlie Flanagan, Questions 107 and 109, 30 November 2017.
43 *IDG Report*, 3, 4; Minutes of the First Meeting of the Inter-Department Committee on Implementation of Quirke Report – Magdalen Laundries (membership), Thursday 4 July 2013, 10am in Montague Court. These records were generously shared by Conall Ó Fátharta.
44 *Magdalen Commission Report*, 29; JFM, *Submission to Justice John Quirke, Magdalen Commission*, 13 March 2013, 3.
45 *DED*, Catherine Murphy, Deputy, addressed to the Minister for Justice and Equality, Question No. 170, 6 March 2013.
46 'Address by Alan Shatter', 26 June 2013.
47 Mary Christian, letter to Minister for Justice and Equality, 25 June 2013; Sr Bernadette McNally, letter to Mr Jimmy Martin, Assistant Secretary, Department of Justice and Equality, 27 June 2013; Sr Bernadette McNally, letter to Mr Jimmy Martin, Assistant Secretary, Department of Justice and Equality, 2 August 2013; Sr Sheila Murphy, letter to the Minister for Justice and Equality, 28 June 2013; Sr Sheila Murphy, letter to the Minister for Justice and Equality, 13 August 2013; Sr Margaret Casey, email to James Martin,1 July 2013; Sr Margaret Casey, letter to Christopher Quattrociocchi, Private Secretary to the Minister for Justice and Equality, 20 August 2013. This correspondence was generously shared by Conall Ó Fátharta.
48 Sir Nigel Rodley, Statement at Human Rights Committee examination of the fourth periodic report of Ireland, 15 July 2014.
49 United Nations Convention against Torture and Other Cruel, Inhuman or Degrading Treatment or Punishment, *Consideration of Reports Submitted by States Parties under Article 19 of the Convention Pursuant to the Optional Reporting Procedure, Second Period Report of States Parties due in 2015, Ireland,* 23 November 2015, 223.
50 Ireland, *Commissions of Investigation Act*, 2004, Irish Statute Book, Section 19.
51 James Gallen. 'Historical Abuse and the Statute of Limitations.' *Statute Law Review*, 39, no. 2 (2018): 103, 104–9; Colin Smith and April Duff, 'Access to Justice for Victims of Historic Institutional Abuse', *Éire-Ireland: An Interdisciplinary Journal of Irish Studies*, Special Issue: 'Toward Transitional Justice in Ireland? Addressing Legacies of Harm', eds. Katherine O'Donnell, Maeve O'Rourke and James M Smith, 55, nos. 1–2 (2020): 100–19, 109; *O'Dwyer v. The Daughters of Charity of St Vincent de Paul & Ors* IECA 226 (2015) (Court of Appeal), Para 45; *EAO v. Daughters of Charity of St Vincent de Paul & Ors.* IEHC 68 (2015) (High Court); *Elizabeth Anne O'Dwyer v The Daughters of Charity of St Vincent de Paul, the Sisters of Our Lady of Charity of Refuge, and the Health Service Executive* IESCDET 12 (2016) (unreported) (22 January 2016 Supreme Court).
52 Smith and Duff, 'Access to Justice for Victims of Historic Institutional Abuse', 109.

53 Free Legal Advice Centres, *Submission to the Joint Oireachtas Committee on Justice and Equality: Access to Justice & Costs*, November 2019.
54 Smith and Duff, 'Access to Justice for Victims of Historic Institutional Abuse', 100–19.
55 See *Freedom of Information Act*, 2014 sections 2, 11.
56 *IDC Report (AKA the McAleese Report)*, 5 February 2013, 137, 140; Letter from Eamonn Molloy, Assistant Secretary General, Department of the Taoiseach, to Maeve O'Rourke, 13 November 2018 (Ref FOI/2018/0351). See JFMR Briefing Note Re McAleese Archive for further details of our efforts to access these records.
57 Letter from Cillian Doyle, Department of the Taoiseach, to Maeve O'Rourke, 25 September 2018 (Ref FOI/2018/0351). This decision was upheld on appeal by the internal reviewer.
58 Molloy, letter, 13 November 2018.
59 *DED*, Frances Fitzgerald, TD, Minister for Justice and Equality, reply to Maureen O'Sullivan, TD, 23 February 2017; Minister Flanagan issued a similar statement in November 2018: *DED*, Charlie Flanagan TD, Minister for Justice and Equality, to Catherine Connolly TD, Questions 98 and 101, 22 November 2018.
60 *Ms P. v. the Department of the Taoiseach*, Case No OIC-53487-S3Q7X3 (24 January 2020).
61 *Elizabeth Coppin v Ireland*. Submission of the government of Ireland on the Merits of the Communication to the Committee Against Torture Made by Elizabeth Coppin, Para 156.
62 *CLANN Report*, Section 5; CLANN, 'Clann Publishes Findings of Three-Year Project on Adoption and Mother and Baby Homes', 15 October 2018; Conall Ó Fátharta, 'Commission Says they Are Prohibited from Telling Surviving Family Members about Burial Locations', *Irish Examiner*, 19 April 2019.
63 Ireland, *Retention of Records Bill*, 2019, Oireachtas; JFMR, 'Retention of Records Bill 2019' (webpage), *Justice For Magdalenes Research*, updated 2020.
64 Creative Cultures and Associates, *National Archives, Ireland: A Comparative Management Survey for Fórsa, Archivists' Branch*', Fórsa, 2019, 4.
65 Creative Cultures and Associates, *Comparative Management Survey for Fórsa*, 22.
66 Creative Cultures and Associates, *Comparative Management Survey for Fórsa*, 35.
67 See *National Archives Act*, 1986, sections 1, 2, 13 (as amended). The *National Archives Act 1986* says nothing about the records of non-State bodies which provide State-funded services.
68 Creative Cultures and Associates, *Comparative Management Survey for Fórsa*, 33.
69 United Nations, *Ireland, Information on follow-up to the Concluding Observations of the Committee against Torture*, 28 August 2018, Para 28.
70 Ireland, *Adoption (Information and Tracing) Bill*, 2016, Section 7.
71 See the letters above from the orders concerning their cooperation with the scheme. Ireland, *Information on follow-up to the Concluding Observations of the Committee against Torture*, 28 August 2018; see also for example *DED*, written reply by Frances Fitzgerald, TD, Minister for Justice and Equality, to Maureen O'Sullivan, TD, 23 February 2017; UN Committee against Torture, *Summary Record of the 1551st Meeting*, UN Doc CAT/C/SR.1551, 28 July 2017.
72 Conall Ó Fátharta, 'Four Years on, Questions Continue to be Asked of Report into Magdalene Laundries', *Irish Examiner*, 1 November 2017.
73 See, for example, Conall Ó Fátharta, 'Tusla Considers Damage Release of Personal Information can Cause', *Irish Examiner*, 16 July 2019.
74 'Address by Alan Shatter', 26 June 2013.

75 McDonagh, Gerry, Prisons and Probation Policy Division, to the Secretary General and Jimmy Martin, 29 May 2013.
76 Department of Justice and Equality, Note regarding 'Restorative Justice Scheme', Restorative Justice Implementation Team, 26 June 2013.
77 JFMR, 'JFM Research Welcomes UNCAT List of Issues, Citing Grave Concerns about Magdalene Scheme', 28 November 2013.
78 Claire McGettrick, Mari Steed, James M. Smith, Maeve O'Rourke, and Katherine O'Donnell. 'Restorative Justice for Magdalenes', *Irish Examiner*, 19 February 2014.
79 By 6 June 2014, the combined pressure of a solicitor writing to the Department on Maisie's behalf, Jim's efforts and Maureen O'Sullivan's advocacy resulted in a letter from the Department making an offer.
80 Justice for Magdalenes, letter to Frances Fitzgerald, 1 September 2014.
81 Niall O'Sullivan. 'Only 67 British-Based Magdalene Survivors Seek Redress Despite "majority" Claim', *Irish Post*, 21 July 2014.
82 Justice for Magdalenes, letter to Frances Fitzgerald, 1 September 2014.
83 Kathy Sheridan, 'Minister with a Mission to Deliver', *Irish Times*, 1 November 2014.
84 JFMR, Notes, Meeting with Minister Frances Fitzgerald. 20 October 2014. Department of Justice, Stephen's Green.
85 Maeve O'Rourke, Claire McGettrick, Mari Steed, Katherine O'Donnell and James M Smith, letter to Minister Frances Fitzgerald, TD, 19 November 2014. On 19 December 2014 we received a reply from the minister's private secretary, responding only to a small number of our queries and stating that 'the interview process for cases where there is insufficient documentary evidence to make a determination on a case is well advanced'. See also: *DED*, Residential Institutions, 18 November 2014.
86 JFMR, Notes, Meeting with Minister Frances Fitzgerald. 20 October 2014. Department of Justice, Stephen's Green.
87 *DED*, Maureen O'Sullivan, Healthcare Bill 2nd stage, 28 January 2015. See also, for example, *DED*, Catherine Murphy, 29 January 2015.
88 *DED*, Frances Fitzgerald, 'Redress for Women Resident in Certain Institutions Bill 2014: Second Stage', 28 January 2015.
89 *SED*, 'Redress for Women Resident in Certain Institutions Bill 2014: Report and Final Stages', 11 March 2015; See for a related response: *DED*, Written Answers, 'Department of Justice and Equality: Restorative Justice', 28 February 2017.
90 *Opportunity Lost*, 8.
91 *Opportunity Lost*, 41.
92 *Opportunity Lost*, 41. Emphasis in original.
93 *Opportunity Lost*, 44.
94 *Opportunity Lost*, 45.
95 *Opportunity Lost*, 44. Emphasis in original.
96 *Opportunity Lost*, 44. Two years before the Ombudsman's report was published, JFMR had provided the DoJ with research on electoral registers in support of one survivor's application. See Comparison between names of religious sisters supplied by — and the names of religious sisters appearing in the electoral registers for Limerick city. *Compiled by Claire McGettrick, JFM Research.* Report on file with authors to protect survivor's identity.
97 *Opportunity Lost*, 44.
98 *DED*, Written Answers, 'Charles Flanagan to Mary Lou McDonald', 24 April 2018.
99 According to the DoJ's website in June 2020.

100 O'Rourke, Email to Ombudsman, 'Magdalene Ex Gratia Scheme: Ongoing Problems', 6 June 2019.
101 Letter from Brenda R Ryan, Restorative Justice Implementation Unit, Department of Justice and Equality, to [Caitríona] enclosing Preliminary Assessment of Mary O'Toole SC, both dated 16 September 2019.
102 Department of Justice, letter to survivor, 16 April 2014; Department of Justice, letter to survivor, 14 May 2014.
103 Residential Institutions Redress Board, *A Guide to the Redress Scheme under the Residential Institutions Redress Act, 2002*, 3rd edn, December 2005.
104 Ombudsman, email to survivor, 20 June 2014; Ombudsman, letter to survivor, 20 June 2014.
105 Jim Smith, email to Maureen O'Sullivan, 13 May 2014. See *DED*, Leaders' Questions, 29 May 2014.
106 Maeve began to work with the Public Interest Law Alliance of the Free Legal Advice Centres to arrange free legal assistance for women who came to our attention, and solicitors Simon McGarr and Declan Duggan, along with the London office of international law firm, Hogan Lovells, and solicitors in A&L Goodbody in Dublin, volunteered as well.
107 Conall Ó Fátharta, 'Special Investigation: Centre and Laundry "one and the same"', *Irish Examiner*, 4 June 2015. This article includes excerpts from the JFMR statement.
108 Ó Fátharta, 'Special Investigation', 4 June 2015; see also, Conall Ó Fátharta, 'Mother and Baby Homes: "Bizarre" Reasoning for Refusal to Uphold Appeals', *Irish Examiner*, 6 August 2015.
109 Ann O'Loughlin, 'Woman Challenges Magdalene Redress Refusal', *Irish Examiner*, 27 January 2016.
110 *MKL and DC v Minister for Justice and Equality* [2017] IEHC 398.
111 *MKL and DC v Minister for Justice and Equality* [2017] IEHC 398 Para 34.
112 JFMR, 'High Court Challenge to Magdalene Redress Scheme Reveals DoJ Being Investigated by Ombudsman', Press Release, 26 January 2017.
113 Conall Ó Fátharta, 'Verdict in Magdalene Case May be Far-Reaching', *Irish Examiner*, 1 June 2017.
114 *MKL and DC v Minister for Justice and Equality* [2017] IEHC 398, Affidavit of James Martin, 1 February 2017, Exhibit JM 1.
115 Personal communication, Conrad Bryan.
116 *Report of the Commission of Inquiry into the Reformatory and Industrial School System (AKA Kennedy Report)* (Dublin: Government Publications, 1970), 39.
117 *MKL and DC v Minister for Justice and Equality* [2017] IEHC 398, Affidavit of James Martin, 1 February 2017, Exhibit JM 1.
118 *DED*, Residential Institutions Statutory Fund (Amendment) Bill 2016: Second Stage [Private Members], 2 March 2017; *DED*, Donnchadh Ó Laoghaire, Question nos, 97 and 98; *DED*, questions addressed to the Minister for Justice and Equality (Deputy Frances Fitzgerald) by Deputy Catherine Connolly, 8 February 2017; *DED*, Frances Fitzgerald, Minister for Justice and Equality, to Catherine Connolly TD, Question 21307/17, 4 May 2017.
119 *MKL and DC v Minister for Justice and Equality* [2017] IEHC 398 Paras 12–15.
120 *MKL and DC v Minister for Justice and Equality*, Para 35.
121 *Opportunity Lost*, 10.

122 *DED*, DoJ and Equality, Magdalen Laundries Report, Clare Daly to Minister Flanagan, Question Numbers 51323/17, 51324/17, 51325/17, 30 November 2017; *DED*, response to Jim O'Callaghan, Priority Questions, 5 December 2017.
123 *DED*, Joint Oireachtas Justice Committee on Justice, Defence, and Equality, Administration on Magdalen Restorative Justice Scheme: Report of Ombudsman, 31 January 2018.
124 Maeve O'Rourke, ICCL, JFMR, NWCI, Amnesty International Ireland, and Sage Support and Advocacy, letter to Minister Charlie Flanagan, 11 January 2018; Jim O'Callaghan, letter to Charlie Flanagan, 12 February 2018; JFMR, letter to An Taoiseach, 16 February 2018; Maeve O'Rourke, 'Magdalene Laundry Survivors Have Waited Too Long for Redress', *Irish Examiner*, 21 February 2018; JFMR, Memo to Minister for Justice Charlie Flanagan, 'Re: Women Excluded from Magdalene Scheme', 27 March 2018; *DED*, 'Priority Questions: Magdalen Laundry Report', 17 April 2018; *DED*, 'Questions on Promised Legislation', 18 April 2018; See further *DED*, Written Answers, 'Charles Flanagan to Mary Lou McDonald', 24 April 2018.
125 See, for example, *DED*, questions by Catherine Connolly and Mary Lou McDonald, Dáil, 6 November 2018; *DED*, Catherine Connolly to Leo Varadkar, Question 6, 23 October 2018; *DED*, Mary Lou McDonald to Leo Varadkar, 6 November 2018.
126 Department of Justice and Equality, *Addendum to the Terms of Magdalen Restorative Justice Ex Gratia Scheme in Respect of Women Who Worked in the Laundries in the 12 'Magdalen' Institutions and Who were Resident in One of the 14 Adjoining Institutions*, November 2018.
127 *DED*, Mary Lou McDonald to Charlie Flanagan, 27 November 2018; *DED*, 'Department of Justice and Equality: Magdalen Laundries', 28 November 2018; *DED*, 'Department of Justice and Equality: Magdalen Laundries', 29 November 2018; Conall Ó Fátharta, 'Eight Redress Payments made to Magdalene Survivors', *Irish Examiner*', 17 June 2019; *DED*, 'Department of Justice and Equality: Magdalen Laundries', 13 March 2019; O'Rourke, Maeve, email to the Ombudsman, 6 June 2019.
128 *Opportunity Lost*, 49.
129 *Opportunity Lost*, 9.
130 *Opportunity Lost*, 49.
131 *SED*, 'Redress for Women Resident in Certain Institutions Bill 2014: Committee Stage', 4 March 2015.
132 *DED*, Frances Fitzgerald, written answer to Jim O'Callaghan, Questions No 9731-8/17, 28 February 2017.
133 Oireachtas Public Accounts Committee, Annual Report of the Comptroller and Auditor General and Appropriation Accounts Vote 24 – Justice and Equality, 4 April 2019, emphasis added.
134 *Magdalen Commission Report*, 50; Ireland, Law Reform Commission, *Vulnerable Adults and the Law* (Law Reform Commission, Dublin: Ireland, 2006).
135 *IDG Report*, 24.
136 DoJ and Equality, 'Minister Fitzgerald Announces government Approval for Legislation to Provide for Women Who Worked in Magdalen Laundries', Press Release, 24 June 2014; *DED*, Frances Fitzgerald TD, Minister for Justice and Equality, Written Response to Maureen O'Sullivan, TD, Question No 27176/14, 24 June 2014.
137 DoJ and Equality, *General Scheme of Bill: Redress for Women who were in Certain Institutions Bill*, 8 August 2014.
138 Ireland, 'Redress for Women Resident in Certain Institutions Bill', 2014.

139 JFM Research, National Women's Council of Ireland, Irish Council for Civil Liberties, Amnesty International (Ireland), 'Briefing Note: Redress For Women Resident In Certain Institutions Bill 2014', 19 January 2015; JFM Research, National Women's Council of Ireland, Irish Council for Civil Liberties, Amnesty International (Ireland), Press Release, 19 January 2015.
140 *DED*, Frances Fitzgerald, 'Redress for Women Resident in Certain Institutions Bill 2014: Second Stage', 28 January 2015.
141 *DED*, answer from Frances Fitzgerald TD, Minister for Justice and Equality, to Róisín Shortall TD, Question No 3815/15, 27 January 2015; *DED*, answer from Frances Fitzgerald TD, Minister for Justice and Equality, to Finian McGrath TD, Question No 4750/15, 3 February 2015; *DED*, answer from Frances Fitzgerald TD, Minister for Justice and Equality, to Terence Flanagan TD, Question No 4883/15, 3 February 2015.
142 Kitty Holland, 'Mental Health Commission has "serious concerns" over Delays in Opening Service', *The Irish Times*, 27 January 2020.
143 *DED*, Oireachtas Public Accounts Committee, 26 April 2018.
144 Email from Wendy Lyon to Maeve O'Rourke, 15 January 2021.
145 Dr Michael Browne, 'Independent Advocacy in Ireland: Current Context and Future Challenge: A Scoping Document' (Safeguarding Ireland, September 2018); Ireland, Law Reform Commission, *Issues Paper: A Regulatory Framework for Adult Safeguarding* (Law Reform Commission, 2019).
146 Ireland, Law Reform Commission, *Issues Paper: A Regulatory Framework for Adult Safeguarding* (Law Reform Commission, 2019), 153 citing: Sarah Lonbay and Toby Brandon, 'Renegotiating Power in Adult Safeguarding: The Role of Advocacy', *The Journal of Adult Protection*, 19, no. 2 (2017): 84.
147 *Magdalen Commission Report*, 49.
148 JFM Submission to Justice John Quirke, 21.
149 O'Donnell, Pembroke and McGettrick, Oral History of Sara W.
150 O'Donnell, Pembroke and McGettrick, Oral History of Bridget Flynn.
151 Personal letter to James M. Smith.
152 O'Donnell, Pembroke and McGettrick, Oral History of Maisie K (b).
153 Maeve O'Rourke, email to Anne Ferris, 2 February 2015, including list of proposed amendments.
154 *DED*, 'Redress for Women Resident in Certain Institutions Bill 2014', Committee Amendments, 3 February 2015; *DED*, 'Redress for Women Resident in Certain Institutions Bill 2014', Report Amendments, 9 February 2015; *SED*, 'Redress for Women Resident in Certain Institutions Bill 2014', Committee Amendments, 4 March 2015; *SED*, 'Redress for Women Resident in Certain Institutions Bill 2014', Report Amendments, 11 March 2015.
155 *DED*, 'Redress for Women Resident in Certain Institutions Bill 2014: Report Stage'. See also *DED*, answer from Frances Fitzgerald, Minister for Justice and Equality, to Finian McGrath TD, Question No 6150/15, 10 February 2015; *SED*, 'Redress for Women Resident in Certain Institutions Bill 2014: Second Stage', 24 February 2015; *DED*, 'Redress for Women Resident in Certain Institutions Bill 2014: Report Stage (Resumed)', 17 February 2015; See also Minister Flanagan's position in January 2018: Charlie Flanagan, letter to Maeve O'Rourke, ICCL, JFMR, NWCI, Amnesty International Ireland, and Sage Support and Advocacy, 28 January 2018.
156 *DED*, answer from Frances Fitzgerald, Minister for Justice and Equality, to Anne Ferris, TD, Question No 9863/15, 5 March 2015; *DED*, answer from Minister Frances Fitzgerald to Joan Collins TD, 25 March 2015.

157 To enter care settings, make inquiries, attend meetings and make representations relating to their client, supported by a statutory obligation on care providers to cooperate with the advocate – albeit this service was designated only for persons with disabilities under sixty-five years of age. The National Advocacy Service for People with Disabilities (NAS) operates under the remit of the Citizens Information Board on a non-statutory basis. Safeguarding Ireland reported in 2018 that 'NGOs working with vulnerable adults are at times frustrated in assisting people they believe to be vulnerable because of the lack of a statutory framework within which the role of independent advocates is recognised and acknowledged'. See Browne, 'Independent Advocacy in Ireland', 17.
158 *Magdalen Commission Report*, 33–4.
159 *Magdalen Commission Report*, 36.
160 Maeve O'Rourke and James M. Smith, 'Magdalene Survivors Are Still Waiting for Restorative Justice', *Irish Times*, 6 February 2014.
161 Terms of an ex gratia scheme for women who were admitted to and worked in Magdalen Laundries, St Mary's Training Centre Stanhope Street and House of Mercy Training School Summerhill, Wexford, December 2013, Para 36. In November 2013, a written answer by Alan Shatter to Maureen O'Sullivan had indicated, too, that the government did not intend to provide healthcare to women abroad: *DED*, written answers, Question 48860/13, 19 November 2013.
162 Alan Shatter, 'Payments for Magdalene Women', *Irish Times: Letters*, 13 February 2014.
163 *Redress for Women Resident in Certain Institutions Bill 2014, as initiated.*
164 Justice for Magdalenes Research, NWCI, ICCL, Amnesty International (Ireland), 'Advocacy and rights groups join in criticising government's Magdalene Bill as unacceptable, unfair and full of broken promises to survivors', 19 January 2015.
165 O'Donnell, Pembroke and McGettrick, Oral History of Kathleen R.
166 Email from Claire McGettrick to JFMR, 23 December 2014.
167 *DED*, 'Redress for Women Resident in Certain Institutions Bill 2014'.
168 Sarah Clancy and Mark Conroy, contact.ie campaign, Magdalene Women have no time to waste please take action to help them, 25 January 2015.
169 *DED and SED*, 'Redress for Women Resident in Certain Institutions Bill 2014'; Dáil Éireann, *Standing Orders Relative to Public Business*, 2016. Edition, S.O. 179(3).
170 *SED*, 'Redress for Women Resident in Certain Institutions Bill 2014: Committee Stage', 4 March 2015.
171 *SED*, 'Redress for Women Resident in Certain Institutions Bill 2014: Second Stage', 24 February 2015.
172 *DED*, 'Redress for Women Resident in Certain Institutions Bill 2014: Report Stage (Resumed)', 17 February 2015.
173 *DED*, 'Redress for Women Resident in Certain Institutions Bill 2014: Committee Stage', 4 February 2015.
174 *DED*, 'Redress for Women Resident in Certain Institutions Bill 2014', Committee Amendments, 2 February 2015.
175 *DED*, 'Redress for Women Resident in Certain Institutions Bill 2014: Second Stage', 28 January 2015. Appendix G of Judge Quirke's report contained no mention of 'angel healing'. The Minister's comments appeared erroneously to connect the concept of complementary therapies to the previous autumn's public controversy over alleged misspending of State funding (unrelated to the HAA Card) by the Hepatitis C support organization, 'Positive Action'. See Paul Hosford, 'Gardaí Investigate Support

Group's Spend on Gifts, Angel Healing and Dog Kennels', *thejournal.ie*, 23 October 2014.

176 *DED*, Redress for Women Resident in Certain Institutions Bill 2014: Second Stage (Resumed)', 29 January 2015.

177 *DED*, 'Redress for Women Resident in Certain Institutions Bill 2014: Report Stage (Resumed)', 17 February 2015.

178 *DED*, 'Redress for Women Resident in Certain Institutions Bill 2014: Committee Stage', 4 February 2015.

179 *DED*, Frances, Fitzgerald, 'Redress for Women Resident in Certain Institutions Bill 2014: Second Stage', 28 January 2015: 'Some NGOs have incorrectly stated that the Bill will not provide for these services.'

180 *SED*, 'Redress for Women Resident in Certain Institutions Bill 2014: Committee Stage', 4 March 2015.

181 Gillian McGuire, letter to Restorative Justice Implementation Unit, Department of Justice and Equality, 28 May 2015. (Recipient's name withheld to protect her privacy).

182 Jimmy Martin, memo, 31 May 2013.

183 Jimmy Martin, email to Conan McKenna, Department of Justice, 'Observations of Department of Health', 4 July 2013.

184 Carol Baxter, Civil Law Reform, Note, 'Meeting with D/Health on Magdalen Redress Scheme', 8 July 2013.

185 Fintan Hourihan, email to Katherine O'Donnell, 13 July 2014.

186 JFMR, 'JFM Research Says Magdalene Healthcare Provisions Are a Betrayal of Survivors' "trust"', 14 July 2015.

187 Dr Padraig O'Reachtagain, Dr Maurice Quirke, Dr Desmond Kennedy. Letter to the Editor. *Journal of the Irish Dental Association* 61, no. 4 (August/September 2015): 164.

188 Sarah Clancy and Mark Conroy, contact.ie campaign, Magdalene Laundry Survivors: Just Say Yes Ministers, 16 July 2015.

189 Claire McGettrick, email correspondence with Margaret Gannon, August–October 2015. On file with authors to protect the survivor's privacy.

190 Personal communication, Kathleen R.

191 Claire McGettrick, email correspondence with Margaret Gannon, August–October 2015. On file with authors to protect the survivor's privacy.

192 McGettrick, email correspondence, August–October 2015.

193 Pro bono legal services were provided by Wendy Lyon, Colin Smith BL and Siobhan Phelan SC; the pro bono psychiatric report was provided by Jo Campion.

194 John Hennessy, National Director, Primary Care, HSE, letter to Wendy Lyon, 16 February 2016.

195 As we wrote to senators on 24 June 2019, we have raised the problem of healthcare provision to Magdalene survivors numerous times since the *RWRCI Act 2015* was enacted, including in writing to Ministers for Justice and DoJ officials on 27 July 2016, 11 January 2018 and 26 April 2019; in writing to the Ombudsman on 16 February 2017 and 6 June 2019; in writing to the Taoiseach on 16 February 2018; and to the government through our written submissions to several UN human rights bodies, including CESCR in 2015, CEDAW in 2017, and CAT in 2017. On 25 February 2016 JFMR wrote to the National Director of Primary Care at the HSE to ask for written clarification of all ways in which Magdalene survivors' entitlements under the *RWRCI* card differ from those already available under the standard medical card. We received an acknowledgement letter on 15 March 2016 but have received no substantive response to date.

196 James M. Smith, 'Will Mother and Baby Home Commission Advertise to the Hidden Irish Diaspora'? *Irish Times*, 9 November 2016.
197 JFMR, email to Senators, 24 June 2019; JFMR Amendments to the Redress for Women Resident in Certain Institutions (Amendment) Bill 2019; JFMR, email to TDs, 9 July 2019.
198 *SED*, 'Redress for Women Resident in Certain Institutions (Amendment) Bill 2019: Committee Stage', 27 June 2019.
199 *SED*, 'Redress for Women Resident in Certain Institutions (Amendment) Bill 2019: Report and Final Stages', 3 July 2019.
200 *DED*, Charlie Flanagan TD, to Stephen Donnelly, Minister for Health, 20 October 2020.

Chapter 8

1 Raftery, 'Restoring Dignity to Magdalens', 14.
2 Claire McGettrick, 'In Memory of the Magdalens', *AdoptionIreland Yahoo! Group*, 1 September 2003.
3 Claire McGettrick, 'Magdalene Names Project', http://jfmresearch.com/home/magdalene-names-project/.
4 Fiona Ward, Evelyn Glynn, Pauline Goggin, Jennifer O'Mahoney, Nancy Rochford Flynn and Maxine Keoghan generously photographed Magdalene graves on behalf of JFM(R).
5 This figure includes twenty-two women exhumed from High Park for whom there are no identifying details available.
6 Enright, 'Antigone in Galway', 11–14.
7 Flowers for Magdalenes is the brainchild of Áine Downes and events are coordinated in conjunction with JFMR. http://jfmresearch.com/home/flowers-for-magdalenes/ updated 2021.
8 O'Toole, 'GPA, Magdalen Women and the Underground Connection'.
9 McGettrick et al., 'Death, Institutionalisation & Duration of Stay', 19 February 2015.
10 JFMR submitted several applications to OLC for access to their archives. The Sisters ignored all but one (registered) letter, in which they refused our request. Sr Ethna McDermott, letter to Claire McGettrick, 28 January 2020. The Sisters suggested that Dr Prunty's book and the *IDC Report* may be of assistance to our research.
11 Department of Justice and Equality (hereafter DoJ), *IDC Report*, 5 February 2013.
12 In 1993, DCC was known as Dublin Corporation.
13 Since the 1970s, the 'Environment' portfolio has been housed in a number of differently named Departments. We use 'Department of the Environment' (DoEnv) throughout.
14 Dr Jacinta Prunty, letter to Dave Corcoran, Assistant Principal, DoEnv, 27 August 2010.
15 *IDC Report*, Chapter 16, Para 108, p. 811.
16 *IDC Report*, Chapter 16, Para 75–6, p. 802.
17 *IDC Report*, Chapter 16, Para 110, pp. 810–11.
18 *IDC Report*, Chapter 16, Para 113, p. 812.
19 The first licence was for 133 bodies and the second was for 'all human remains' at the graveyard.

20 Circular Letter ENV 3/89, Jack Killane to each sanitary authority, 'Re: Exhumation Licences', 8 February 1989; Circular Letter ENV 11/90, Jack Killane to each sanitary authority, 'Re: Applications for Exhumation Licences', 5 October 1990.
21 *IDC Report*, Chapter 16, Para 100, p. 809.
22 *IDC Report*, Chapter 16, Para 19–26, pp. 785–8.
23 *IDC Report*, Chapter 16, Para 100, p. 811.
24 *IDC Report*, Chapter 16, Para 118, p. 813.
25 FOI request to DCC, 24 August 2015; FOI request to the DoEnv, 24 August 2015; FOI request to the DoJ, 27 August 2015; FOI request to the DoEnv, 17 October 2015 (records could not be found); FOI request to the GRO, 21 October 2015, (records could not be found); FOI request to Dublin City Coroner, 21 October 2015 (request refused); FOI request to the State Pathologist's Office, 9 November 2015 (request refused, alleging no records held); FOI request to the DoT, 25 February 2016. Unless stated otherwise, all records cited in this chapter are sourced from these FOIs. Claire also visited the Dublin Diocesan Archives and viewed planning applications at the DCC public counter.
26 Most deaths up to 1969 were located via searches of the civil registration records available online at www.irishgenealogy.ie. Deaths after 1969 were located manually in the Research Room of the GRO. We are extremely grateful to Kathy Finn and Judy Campbell for their assistance in this work.
27 Smith, *Ireland's Magdalen Laundries*, 39–40; Prunty, *The Monasteries, Magdalen Asylums and Reformatory Schools of Our Lady of Charity in Ireland*, 468.
28 Michael Lavery, 'A Nun's Story', *Evening Herald*, 15 September 1993, 6.
29 Katherine O'Donnell, Sinéad Pembroke and Claire McGettrick, 'Oral History of Ann Kelly', *Magdalene Institutions: Recording an Oral and Archival History*, Government of Ireland Collaborative Research Project, Irish Research Council, 2013.
30 Prunty, *The Monasteries, Magdalen Asylums and Reformatory Schools of Our Lady of Charity in Ireland*, 169.
31 Photograph in: Nell McCafferty, 'They Lived in Silence to Wash Away Our Shame', *Irish Press*, 9 September 1993, 16. We are very grateful to Bryan Meade who shared his photographs taken in 1993.
32 Sr Angela Fahy, 'Cemetery Removals', letter to the editor, *Irish Independent*, 6 September 1993, 19.
33 www.rip.ie.
34 www.rip.ie.
35 Sr Ann Marie Ryan, letter, 'Re: Grave ground at St Mary's, High Park, Drumcondra, Dublin', 9 July 1992.
36 *IDC Report*, Chapter 16, Para 80, p. 803.
37 Eugene F. Collins Solicitors, letter to Anne Clarke, DoEnv, 'Re: Exhumation licence for grave ground at High Park Convent', 28 January 1993.
38 Collins, letter, 28 January 1993; Joseph McDonnell, General Register Office, letter to Graham Hanlon, Eugene F. Collins Solicitors, 14 January 1993.
39 DoEnv, internal memorandum, Local Services Section to Assistant Secretary Cullen, 'Re Exhumation Licence Application, High Park Convent', 19 April 1993.
40 DoEnv, file note, Anne Clarke to Colm Keenan, 30 March 1993.
41 DoEnv, Local Services Section, Draft letter to Eugene F. Collins Solicitors, 'Re: Exhumation Licence for Grave Ground at High Park Convent', April 1993.
42 Handwritten note on DoEnv internal memorandum, Local Services Section to Assistant Secretary Cullen, 29 April 1993.

43 David Dalton, letter to Claire McGettrick, 'Re: FOI request FOI-2015-309', 9 November 2015.
44 Handwritten note, DoEnv internal memorandum, 29 April 1993.
45 OLC's solicitors said they had been in 'constant communication' with the GRO about locating death certificates. Eugene F. Collins Solicitors, letter to the DoEnv, 'Exhumation Licence for Grave Ground at High Park Convent', 12 May 1993.
46 *Ministerial Order for the Exhumation of the Remains of the Deceased Persons Listed in the Schedule*, Ref LSS 66/29/93, 25 May 1993.
47 Mary Lee, Environmental Health Officer, letter to Graham Hanlon, Eugene F. Collins Solicitors, 'Proposed exhumations at St Mary's Private Graveyard, High Park, Drumcondra, Dublin 9', 9 June 1993.
48 Eugene F. Collins Solicitors, letter to Patrick Massey Funeral Directors, 'Re: Exhumation of 133 Bodies at Grave Ground, High Park Convent, Drumcondra', Mary Raftery Archive, 16 June 1993.
49 Patrick Massey, letter to Eugene F. Collins Solicitors, 'Re: Exhumation of 133 Bodies at Grave Ground, High Park Convent, Drumcondra', Mary Raftery Archive, 13 July 1993.
50 Eugene F. Collins Solicitors, letter to Patrick Massey Funeral Directors, 'Re: Exhumation of 133 Bodies at Grave Ground, High Park Convent, Drumcondra', Mary Raftery Archive, 11 August 1993.
51 The Canon Law Society of Great Britain and Ireland, *The Code of Canon Law* (London: Collins Liturgical Publications, 1983), 207.
52 Mary Raftery, letter to Sr Ann Marie Ryan, Sisters of Our Lady of Charity of Refuge, 14 April 2003; Sr Ann Marie Ryan to Mary Raftery, 'Statement for Mary Rafferty [*sic*]', n.d., circa August 2003.
53 Mary Lee, Environmental Health Section, Dublin City to Oliver Devitt, Principal Environmental Health Officer, 'Re: Exhumations at St Mary's private graveyard, High Park, Drumcondra, Dublin 9', 14 September 1993. Attempts to contact Ms Lee have been unsuccessful.
54 'Exhumation of the Remains of a Deceased Person' (webpage), Citizens Information Board, Updated 21 November 2018, https://www.citizensinformation.ie/en/death/sudden_or_unexplained_death/exhumation_of_the_remains_of_a_deceased_person.html.
55 Lee, letter, 14 September 1993.
56 Thus far, we have been unable to obtain a copy of this map.
57 Lee, letter, 14 September 1993.
58 Ms Lee contended that twenty women could not be identified; however, having examined *List One* in careful detail, we argue the number should be twenty-two.
59 Mary Lee, letter, 14 September 1993; Eugene F. Collins Solicitors, letter to the DoEnv, 'Exhumation Licence for Grave Ground at High Park Convent', 30 August 1993.
60 In 1993, Charlotte was identified only as Magdalene of St Bernadine. Her given name was revealed in Dr Prunty's report. See Prunty, letter, 27 August 2010.
61 Dublin Poor Law Union Admission and Discharge Registers (BG 78/G 59), accessed via www.findmypast.ie.
62 Lee, letter, 14 September 1993.
63 Collins, letter, 30 August 1993.
64 Collins, letter, 30 August 1993.
65 Lee, letter, 14 September 1993.
66 Collins, letter, 30 August 1993.

67 Eugene F. Collins Solicitors, draft letter to Colm Keenan and Jim Lillis, DoEnv, 'Re: Exhumation Licence for Grave Ground at High Park Convent', 27 August 1993.
68 *Ministerial Order Granting a Licence for the Exhumation of All Remains at St Mary's Private Graveyard, High Park*, LSS 66/29/93, 31 August 1993.
69 Mary Lee, letter 14 September 1993.
70 Lavery, 'A Nun's Story'.
71 Jo Corcoran, 'Nuns' Housing Project Opposed', *Irish Independent*, 23 February 1990, 30; Jo Corcoran, '266 Houses Proposed for South Dublin', *Irish Times*, 28 September 1990, 21.
72 Ann Marie Ryan, letter, 9 July 1992; DoEnv file note, Anne Clarke, 30 March 1993.
73 Cliff Taylor, 'Ryan to Step Down as Head of GPA', *Irish Times*, 30 August 1993, 1; O'Toole, 'GPA, Magdalen Women and the Underground Connection'.
74 *Irish Independent*, 'Abandoned Women Exhumed in Convent Land Sale', 23 August 1993, 6; Paulette O'Connor, 'Remains of 133 "abandoned" Women Exhumed at Convent', *Irish Press*, 24 August 1993.
75 Patrick Massey, Funeral Directors, to Sr Ann Marie Ryan, Sisters of Our Lady of Charity, Mary Raftery Archive, 9 September 1993.
76 Lee, letter, 14 September 1993. Ms Lee's report states that 116 coffins were used; however, it is 115 as she appears to have inadvertently skipped coffin 85 on *List One*.
77 Patrick Massey, letter, 9 September 1993; Eugene F. Collins, letter to Patrick Massey Funeral Directors, 'Re: Exhumations at High Park', Mary Raftery Archive, 1 November 1993.
78 Fahy, 'Cemetery Removals', 19.
79 Frank Doherty, '"Unwanted" Bodies Dug Up as Convent Land Sold for Housing', *Sunday Business Post*, 29 August 1993; Cliodhna O'Donoghue, '£3m Hotel for nun's [*sic*] Magdalen Site in D9', *Irish Independent*, 6 May 1994.
80 Elsewhere, Sr Fahy claimed the graveyard was worth £9,000. See: Bairbre Power, 'Order Rejects Burial Claims', *Irish Independent*, 13 September 1993, 4.
81 See Regan Developments, *Planning Application to Dublin Corporation*, Reference 0686/94, 18 April 1994; Regan Developments, *Planning Application to Dublin Corporation*, Reference 2326/99, 13 July 1994.
82 See DCC planning application number 2326/99.
83 Fahy, 'Cemetery Removals', 19.
84 McGettrick, 'Death, Institutionalisation and Duration of Stay'. Grave locations are ascertained from searches of Glasnevin's genealogy service. See: https://www.glasnevintrust.ie/genealogy.
85 Collins, letter, 12 May 1993.
86 Liz Allen, 'Family's Fight to Give their Grandmother a "proper" Burial', *Evening Herald*, 13 September 1993, 3.
87 Mary Raftery, 'Taking Mary Home', *Irish Times*, 15 August 2004, 14.
88 Frank Brehany, email to Claire McGettrick, 'Message from Frank Brehany', 5 June 2020, 12:52pm.
89 O'Connor, 'Remains of 133 "abandoned" Women Exhumed at Convent', 6.
90 *Kenny Live*, aired September 1993, RTÉ (exact date could not be determined). Video kindly provided by Gabrielle O'Gorman, a Magdalene survivor who appeared on the show.
91 Paul O'Kane, 'Magdalens Reinterred in Common Grave', *Irish Times*, 13 September 1993, 4.

92 Margo Kelly, personal communication, 6 May 2020; Eugene Moloney, 'Jeep in Place of a Hearse', *Evening Herald*, 11 September 1993, 3.
93 Susan McKay, 'Relatives Condemn nuns' Exhumation of Bodies', *Sunday Tribune*, 29 August 1993; Maeve Sheehan, 'Families "not notified" of Reinterment', *Sunday Tribune*, 12 September 1993.
94 McKay, 'Relatives Condemn nuns' Exhumation of Bodies'; Sheehan, 'Families not Notified of Reinterment'.
95 Bairbre Power, 'Women's Reburial Defended by nun', *Evening Herald*, 13 September 1993, 3.
96 Fahy, 'Cemetery Removals', 19.
97 Margo Kelly, personal communication.
98 Aoife MacEoin, 'Church Funds "unlikely for Magdalen memorial"', *Irish Press*, 9 September 1993, 4.
99 O'Kane, 'Magdalens Reinterred in Common Grave', 4.
100 Margo Kelly, personal communication.
101 Eamonn Holmes, 'Tears Flow at Meeting on "Magdalens"', *Irish Press*, 13 September 1993, 4.
102 Kathleen Mulready, 'Poor, Female and Dependent', letter to the editor, *Irish Times*, 8 September 1993, 11.
103 The Ruhama Women's Project, Form A1 and Memorandum of Association, 13 September 1993.
104 Sample Exhumation Licence Application, Mary Raftery Archive.
105 DoEnv, internal notes regarding Mary Raftery, query, n.d., circa March 2003.
106 Margaret Killeen, email, 'Re: Fwd: More Queries', 28 March 2003, 10:22am; Eugene F. Collins, letter 12 May 1993.
107 Raftery, 'Restoring Dignity to Magdalens'; *DED*, Written Answers: Unregistered deaths, Finian McGrath to Martin Cullen, Question: 1259, 30 September 2003; Eugene F. Collins, letter 30 August 1993.
108 Garda Commissioner Fachtna Murphy, letter to Sean Aylward, Secretary General, Department of Fachtna Murphy, 19 May 2010. Both Garda Headquarters and Whitehall Garda Station commenced separate enquiries around this time; however, Whitehall Garda Station subsequently took over the investigation. See Department of the Environment internal note of phone call from An Garda Síochána, 16 September 2003; Department of the Environment internal note of conversations with An Garda Síochána, 19 September 2003.
109 G. Blake, Chief Superintendent, Legal Section, Garda Headquarters, letter to Betty Moriarty, Assistant Principal, 'Re: Exhumation licence: Sisters of Our Lady of Charity of Refuge', 2 September 2003; DoEnv, Internal file note re visit of An Garda Síochána, 24 September 2003; Fachtna Murphy, letter, 19 May 2010. The Coroner said he was 'satisfied' that licence conditions were complied with, that all human remains were female, that they were buried correctly and that the 'condition of the remains was in keeping with what one would expect to find'.
110 DoJ Memorandum, 13 June 2011.
111 Sean Aylward, letter to Garda Commissioner Fachtna Murphy, 16 November 2009.
112 Murphy, letter, 19 May 2010.
113 May 2010 Garda report states that

> On 21 September 2003, Gardaí met with the Superior of the Sisters of Our Lady of Charity who confirmed that the Order had been in residence at High Park since 1853 and from the late 1800s the Order had provided hotel/residential services to the

> marginalised female members of the community who for one reason or another were unwanted, homeless or slurred. Some were placed in the care of the Order by their families, while others were there voluntarily.

This wording is almost identical to OLC's solicitor's language in their 1993 letter to the DoE:

> The Sisters of Our Lady of Charity have been in residence in High Park for 140 years. From the late eighteen hundreds until recently, the Sisters of Our Lady of Charity have, as part of their community and charitable vocation, provided a hostel/residential service to marginalised members of the community who for one reason or another were unwanted, shunned or made homeless.

See Collins, letter, 12 May 1993; Murphy, letter, 19 May 2010.

114 Murphy, letter, 19 May 2010; Mr James Martin, Assistant Secretary, DoJ, letter to Prof. James Smith, Associate Professor, Boston College, 25 June 2010.

115 DoJ, 'Memorandum for the Government: Magdalen Laundries'.

116 Prunty, *The Monasteries, Magdalen Asylums and Reformatory Schools of Our Lady of Charity in Ireland.*

117 Crowe, 'Valuable Addition to History of Magdalene Laundries Uses "private records"'.

118 Dave Corcoran, letter to Sr Teresa Burke, 19 August 2010. See also: DoEnv Memorandum, Miriam Tiernan, Local Services Section to Dave Corcoran, Assistant Principal, Local Services Section, 'Re: Exhumation at St Mary's, High Park, Drumcondra, 1993', 24 June 2010.

119 Corcoran, letter, 19 August 2010; Prunty, letter, 27 August 2010.

120 Prunty, letter, 27 August 2010.

121 Irish Human Rights Commission, *Assessment of the Human Rights Issues Arising in relation to the 'Magdalen Laundries'*, November 2010; Jimmy Martin, letter to Fachtna Murphy, 'Re: Magdalen Laundry issues – IHRC report Issued Today', 10 November 2010.

122 IHRC *Assessment*, 25–7.

123 Martin, letter, 10 November 2010.

124 Martin Callinan, Garda Commissioner, letter to Jimmy Martin, 'Re Investigation in respect of bodies exhumed in 1993 from the site of a former Magdalene Laundry at High Park, Drumcondra', 2 February 2011.

125 Assistant Garda Commissioner Derek Byrne, letter to Jimmy Martin, Assistant Secretary General, DoJ, 'Magdalen Institutions. – St Mary's High Park, Drumcondra, Dublin – Exhumation of bodies in 1993', 16 October 2012.

126 Murphy, letter, 19 May 2010. The 2012 report repeats the same portions of text almost verbatim from OLC's 1993 letter to the DoEnv.

127 *IDC Report*, Chapter 16, Para 107–8, pp. 810–11.

128 *IDC Report*, Chapter 16, Para 112, p. 812 citing Letter to the Department of Environment, Heritage and Local Government dated 27 August 2010, File Ref Id.

129 Corcoran, letter, 19 August 2010; Prunty, letter, 27 August 2010.

130 Prunty, letter, 27 August 2010, emphasis added.

131 In another instance (that of Jane M.) Dr Prunty erroneously claims there was a duplication on the exhumation licence.

132 Prunty, letter, 27 August 2010.

133 Prunty, letter, 27 August 2010.

134 See Victoria Perry, 'Report on the Archives of the Sisters of Our Lady of Charity of Refuge', *Journal of the Catholic Archives Society*, no 27 (2007): 54–61.

135 Lee, letter, 14 September 1993.
136 Lee, letter, 14 September 1993.
137 Mary Raftery's archive contains a copy of Edith H.'s cremation form, stating that Edith died in 1972. Sr Sheila Murphy of OLC signed the form. Edith H. is not listed on the exhumation licence schedule, nor is she included in Dr Prunty's database. In 2003, Mary Raftery asked OLC why Edith's name was on their handwritten list but not on the exhumation licence? The question was ignored. Mary Raftery, letter, 14 April 2003; Mary Raftery, Application for cremation of Edith H., Mary Raftery Archive, 1 September 1993.
138 Sisters of Our Lady of Charity. Handwritten list, 'Names of other women buried in St Mary's', Mary Raftery Archive, August to September 1993.
139 A further four women on this list were always buried in Glasnevin, and never buried at St Mary's.
140 Prunty, letter, 27 August 2010, emphasis added.
141 Prunty, letter, 27 August 2010.
142 Glasnevin Trust Genealogy web service. https://www.glasnevintrust.ie/genealogy/.
143 Prunty, letter 27 August 2010.
144 Two of these are women are among the seven on Dr Prunty's database for which Glasnevin is cited as the source.
145 Prunty, letter 27 August 2010, emphasis added.
146 Collins, letter, 12 May 1993.
147 *Evening Herald*, 'Dublin Inquest', 13 January 1933, 2.
148 Gerry Farrell, 'A Bohemian Life - Through the Eyes of Mick Morgan' (blog post). *The Bohemian Football Club.* https://bohemianfc.com/?page_id=12611.
149 'Mary Morgan' (webpage), *Find a Grave*, Updated 2021, https://www.findagrave.com/memorial/189739029/mary-morgan.
150 Additional searches for all females with the surname Morgan anywhere in Ireland who died in 1933 turned up no relevant entries. JFMR volunteer Kathy Finn also checked the 1933 *Register of Deaths* and confirmed that there was no late registration for another Mary Morgan.
151 McGettrick, 'Death, Institutionalisation and Duration of Stay'.
152 Prunty, letter, 27 August 2010.
153 Kathleen Fahey, letter to Frank Brehany, 'Re: Request for records of deceased person, Mary Brehany (RIP)', 3 December 2019.
154 Dublin City Council, *Chief Archaeologist's Report to Area Planner*, Re 4198/19, 'The Bonnington Hotel site on Swords Road, Whitehall, Dublin 9', 28 November 2019, http://www.dublincity.ie/AnitePublicDocs/00858932.pdf.
155 Michelle Fagan, An Bord Pleanála, *Board Order*. ABP-306721-20. 21 September 2020.
156 Lee, letter, 14 September 1993, emphasis added.
157 Smith, *Ireland's Magdalen Laundries*, 40. To become a consecrate, a woman had to undergo a number of probationary steps, including becoming a Child of Mary.
158 Sixty-four of these women are named on the exhumation licence.
159 *DED*, Mary Lou McDonald TD to Minister for Health, Question Number 537, Question Reference13487/20 30 June 2020.
160 John Orme, letter to Claire McGettrick, 'Re: Our Reference: DRCD-FOI-2020-0032', 12 August 2020.
161 Marie Ryan, letter to Claire McGettrick, 'Re: FOI Request on the HSE Policy Concerning Exhumations', 4 August 2020.

Conclusion

1 Nora Sveaass and Nils Johan Lavik, 'Psychological Aspects of Human Rights Violations: The Importance of Justice and Reconciliation', *Nordic Journal of International Law*, 69 (2000): 35, 43.
2 Sveaass and Lavik, 'Psychological Aspects of Human Rights Violations', 35, 43.
3 Sveaass and Lavik, 'Psychological Aspects of Human Rights Violations', 48.
4 *Elizabeth Coppin v Ireland*, Admissibility Decision.
5 *CLANN Report*.
6 Alice M. Panepinto, 'The Right to the Truth in International Law: The Significance of Strasbourg's Contributions', *Legal Studies*, 37, no. 4 (2017): 739.
7 Committee against Torture, *General Comment No 3, Implementation of Article 14 by States Parties*, 13 December 2012. United Nations General Assembly, Resolution 60/147, 'Basic Principles and Guidelines on the Right to a Remedy and Reparation for Victims of Gross Violations of International Human Rights Law and Serious Violations of International Humanitarian Law', UN Doc A/RES/60/147, 16 December 2005.
8 *IHRC Follow-Up Report*, 111.
9 *IHRC Follow-Up Report*, 125–7.
10 O'Donnell, McGettrick et al., *Dublin Honours Magdalenes Listening Exercise Report Vol 1*, 30; *Elizabeth Coppin v Ireland*, Legal Submissions.
11 Katherine O'Donnell, Maeve O'Rourke and James M. Smith, 'Editors Introduction: Toward Transitional Justice in Ireland? Addressing Legacies of Harm', *Éire-Ireland: An Interdisciplinary Journal of Irish Studies*, 55, nos. 1 & 2 (Spring/Summer 2020): 9–16, citing an extensive scholarly literature addressing transitional justice including, for example, Ruti G. Teitel, *Transitional Justice* (Oxford: Oxford University Press, 2000); Pablo De Greiff, 'A Normative Conception of Transitional Justice', *Politorbis*, 50, no. 3 (2010): 17–29; Juan E. Méndez and Catherine Cone, 'Transitional Justice', in *Routledge Handbook of International Human Rights Law*, eds Scott Sheeran and Nigel Rodley (London: Routledge, 2013), 761.
12 JFM, *JFM Restorative Justice & Reparation Scheme for Magdalene Laundry Survivors*, 14 October 2011; Maeve O'Rourke, James M. Smith, Raymond Hill, Claire McGettrick, Katherine O'Donnell et al., *Follow-Up Report to the UN Committee Against Torture*, May 2012.
13 *Towards Transitional Justice: Recognition, Truth-Telling and Institutional Abuse in Ireland* (Boston College, Boston, 1–2 November 2018); 'Towards Transitional Justice' special issue, *Eire-Ireland* 55, especially Mary Harney, Mari Steed, Caitríona Palmer, Terri Harrison, Rosemary Adaser, Conrad Bryan, Susan Lohan and Connie Roberts, 'Testimony', 17–34; Claire McGettrick, '"Illegitimate Knowledge": Transitional Justice and Adopted People', 181–200; and Caitríona Palmer, '"It steadies me to tell these things": Memoir and the Redemptive Power of Truth-Telling', 299–314.
14 Ruth Rubio-Marín (ed.), *The Gender of Reparations: Unsettling Sexual Hierarchies While Redressing Human Rights Violations* (Cambridge: Cambridge University Press, 2009); *Nairobi Declaration on Women's and Girls' Right to a Remedy and Reparation* (Nairobi: International Meeting on Women's and Girls' Right to a Remedy and Reparation, proceedings, 19–21 March 2007); United Nations Human Rights Council, *Report of the Special Rapporteur on Violence against Women, Its Causes and Consequences*, Rashida Manjoo, on reparations to women who have been subjected to violence in contexts of both peace and post-conflict, UN Doc A/HRC/14/22, 23 April 2010; Inter-American

Court of Human Rights, *Case of González et al ('Cotton Field') v Mexico*, Judgment of 16 November 2009 (Preliminary Objection, Merits, Reparations, and Costs).

15 JFMR, 'Statement Re Donnybrook Magdalene Laundry', 1 March 2016; Mannix Flynn, 'Protect Me, I Am the Donnybrook Laundry' (blog post), *Mannix Flynn*, 2 March 2016; Dublin City Council, *Archaeological Assessment at The Crescent, Donnybrook, Dublin 4*, 2016, 11. See also 'Abandoned Magdalene Laundry in Donnybrook, Dublin, Ireland', *YouTube*.

16 *Archaeological Assessment at The Crescent, Donnybrook*, 11; 'Abandoned Magdalene Laundry in Donnybrook, Dublin, Ireland'; Laura McAtackney, 'Materials and Memory: Archaeology and Heritage as Tools of Transitional Justice at a Former Magdalene Laundry', *Éire-Ireland: An Interdisciplinary Journal of Irish Studies* 55, nos. 1 & 2 (Spring/Summer 2020): 223–46.

17 Faith Bailey and Brenda Fuller, 'Archaeological Assessment at the Crescent, Donnybrook, Dublin 4 on behalf of Pembroke Partnership' (Irish Archaeological Consultancy, July 2016).

18 Justice for Magdalenes Research, *Submission to Dublin City Council Regarding the Proposed Property Development at the Former Magdalene Laundry at Donnybrook, Dublin 4*, 4 October 2016.

19 There had been efforts by councillors in 2013 to suggest a substantial memorial at Seán McDermott Street: Paul O'Donoghue, 'Gone for Good: Last Magdalene Laundry to be Converted into Houses and Sold', *Journal.ie*, 25 May 2013.

20 Ellen Coyne, 'Kenny "broke promise" on Dublin Arts Centre', *Times (Ireland Edition)*, 6 February 2017.

21 Maeve O'Rourke, email to Donnchadh Ó Laoghaire, Stephen Todd and Olive Sloan, 8 February 2017.

22 Emergency Motion presented in the name of Cllr. Gary Gannon and Cllr Críona Ní Dhálaigh submitted with the agreement of all group leaders on Dublin City Council, 6 March 2017 (on file with Maeve); Ruairi Casey, 'Battle over Ireland's Last Magdalene Laundry', *Deutsche Welle*, 19 March 2017.

23 For example, Katherine O'Donnell, email to Gary Gannon and Brendan Kenny, 8 March 2017; meeting 22 March 2017 between Katherine O'Donnell, Maeve O'Rourke, Claire McGettrick, Gary Gannon, Declan Dunne (Respond!) and Rose Kenny (DCC Deputy Area Manager).

24 *DED*, Frances Fitzgerald, Minister for Justice, written answer to Jim O'Callaghan TD, 28 February 2017; *DED*, Alan Shatter, Minister for Justice, Topical Issue Debate, 27 June 2013.

25 Katherine O'Donnell and Maeve O'Rourke, *Proposal to Dublin City Council and Lord Mayor*, 12 April 2017.

26 Conall Ó Fátharta, 'Magdalene Laundries Report "not accurate or respectful" to Women Who Suffered', *Irish Examiner*, 5 May 2016.

27 Katherine O'Donnell, Maeve O'Rourke and Claire McGettrick, letter to An Tánaiste Frances Fitzgerald, Minister for Justice and Equality RE: Dublin Honours Magdalenes, 10 April 2017 (by post and email).

28 Katherine O'Donnell, Maeve O'Rourke and Claire McGettrick, letter to Taoiseach Enda Kenny RE: Dublin Honours Magdalenes, 9 May 2017 (by post and email, cc'd to An Tánaiste Frances Fitzgerald).

29 See 'Dublin Honours Magdalenes Facebook Page', March 2017. Facebook (short film). July 2017. 'Honouring Magdalenes', Twitter account, created March 2017. Among the artists and activists were Jason Byrne and Lauren Larkin, and the students were

Ashley Perry, Julia Canney, Erin Dunleavy, Michelle Dunne, Rory Geoghegan, Mary Haasl, Oisin MacCannaa, Roisin O'Sullivan and Neil Rafter.

30 David Bayley and Faith Bailey, *Archaeological Assessment at Sean MacDermott St & Railway St, Dublin 1 for Dublin City Council*, July 2017.

31 Claire McGettrick, email to JFMR, 24 October 2017.

32 See *CLANN Report.*

33 JFMR, *Submission to Cork City Council Re Development at Sundays Well. Application Reference: 1737279*, 20 March 2017. In December 2017 the City Council issued 'conditional permission'; see Cork City Council, 'Notification of Decision to Grant Permission Subject to Conditions under Section 34 of the Act of 2000', Ref No 17/37279, 14 December 2017.

34 Gary Gannon, email to Maeve O'Rourke, 9 December 2017.

35 Irish Council for Civil Liberties, Amnesty International Ireland, the National Women's Council of Ireland, Sage Support and Advocacy Service and Justice for Magdalenes Research, letter to Charlie Flanagan, 20 December 2017. Ed O'Loughlin, 'A Blot on Ireland's Past, Facing Demolition', *New York Times*, 15 January 2018.

36 Brendan Kenny, email to Katherine O'Donnell and Maeve O'Rourke, 23 January 2018.

37 Maeve O'Rourke email to Brendan Kenny, 2 February 2018.

38 Maeve O'Rourke, email to Caoimhghín Ó Caoláin, 31 January 2018.

39 Caoimhghín Ó Caoláin, email to Maeve O'Rourke, 7 February 2018. Maeve O'Rourke, email to Mícheál MacDonncha, 15 February 2018.

40 Maeve O'Rourke, email to Norah Casey, 10 February 2018.

41 JFMR, 'Government Called on to Help Honour Hundreds of Magdalene Survivors', Press Release, 6 March 2018. See also Claire McGettrick, Katherine O'Donnell and Maeve O'Rourke, email to Brendan Kenny and DCC Group and Party Leaders, 6 March 2018.

42 JFMR, 'Minister for Justice's Offer to Actively Support Event to Honour Magdalene Survivors Is Warmly Welcomed', Press Release, 9 March 2018.

43 Zoë Kelly was event manager, Louise Stanley, Maria Walsh and Lily Casey were assistant organizers and Darryl Downey was artist liaison. Michelle O'Shea from Norah's staff also gave of her time as executive assistant. The artists included Christy Moore, the Hothouse Flowers, Madeleine Seiler, Damien Scallon, The Three Tenors Ireland, John Conway, Fionnuala Monks, Philomena Begley, Mary Byrne, Dana Rosemary Scallon, Pauline McLynn, Róisín Ó, Paul Harrington, Dónal Lunny, Paddy Glackin, Julian Erskine, Kila, Colm Ó Snodaigh, Kathy Cullinan, Brian Cunningham, Mary Coughlan, Mary Black, Phil Coulter, Moya Doherty and Riverdance.

44 A full list of volunteers and contributors is available in O'Donnell, McGettrick et al., *Dublin Honours Magdalenes Listening Exercise Report Vol 1.*

45 It was not possible to assign a pseudonym to some participants as they either chose not to use names, or they did not identify themselves.

46 O'Donnell, McGettrick et al., *Dublin Honours Magdalenes Listening Exercise Report Vol 1*, 78–82. See also pages 83–5 for speech by Minister for Justice, Charlie Flanagan.

47 'Coming Home: When Dublin Honoured the Magdalenes'. New Decade Productions. Aired 25 June 2019 on RTÉ One.

48 O'Donnell, McGettrick et al., *Dublin Honours Magdalenes Listening Exercise Report Vol 1.*

49 The audio recordings were initially transcribed by Dr Clare Moriarty, Aodhán Peelo and Sophie Gough.

50 O'Donnell, McGettrick et al., *Dublin Honours Magdalenes Listening Exercise Report Vol 1* (All ensuing quotes from survivors come from this volume unless otherwise noted); Katherine O'Donnell, Claire McGettrick et al., *Dublin Honours Magdalenes Listening Exercise Report Vol 2: Transcripts* (Dublin: Justice for Magdalenes Research, 2020).
51 Caelainn Hogan, 'Mary's Story: The Magdalene Laundry Survivor Who Still Lives there', *Irish Times*, 30 August 2020.
52 O'Donnell, McGettrick et al., *Dublin Honours Magdalenes Listening Exercise Report Vol 2*, 1338.
53 O'Donnell, McGettrick et al., *Dublin Honours Magdalenes Listening Exercise Report Vol 1*.
54 RTÉ Nine News, 28 June 2018, 17:50.
55 Sean Murray, '€1.6 Million on Stewards and €76k on Catering: How Much the Pope's Visit Cost the Taxpayer', *Journal.ie*, 22 November 2018.
56 Taoiseach Leo Varadkar, 'Speech of An Taoiseach, Leo Varadkar, on the Occasion of the Visit of Pope Francis', Merrion Street Irish Government News Service, 25 August 2018. *RTÉ News*, 'Varadkar Asks Pope to Ensure Justice for Abuse Survivors', 25 August 2018.
57 Cónal Thomas, 'Calls for Pope to Acknowledge Seán MacDermott Street Laundry', *Dublin Inquirer*, 15 August 2018.
58 Sarah Burns, 'Pope Francis "shocked" upon Hearing about Mother-and-Baby Homes', *Irish Times*, 26 August 2018. This was despite Philomena Lee meeting the Pope in February 2014 (Ronan McGreevy, 'Philomena Lee brings Campaign to the Vatican', *Irish Times*, 6 February 2014) and the Holy See engaging with several UN human rights treaty bodies in relation to the Magdalene Laundries.
59 *Irish Times*, 'Pope Francis Asks for Forgiveness for Abuses and Exploitation', 26 August 2018.
60 Colm O'Gorman, Twitter comment, 'Stand for Truth', 18 August 2018.
61 Christina McSorley, 'Attempts to Block Sale of Magdalene Laundry Building', *BBC News NI*, 3 September 2018.
62 John Mulligan, 'Abbeville's Japanese Owner Back in Profit during 2017', *Irish Independent*, 4 May 2018.
63 Dublin City Council, *Report on the Proposed Development of the Former Convent/ Magdalene Laundry Site at Seán MacDermott Street Lower, Dublin 1. (0.82 hectares, 2.04 acres)*, September 2018.
64 Gary Gannon, interview. 'DCC Members Vote to Halt Sale of Magdalene Laundry Site'.
65 Francis Timmons, email to Maeve O'Rourke, 20 August 2020, '10 December 2018 motion re Sean McDermott Street'.
66 Katherine O'Donnell, email to Grafton Architects, 1 October 2018.
67 Open Heart City: www.openheartcitydublin.ie.
68 *CICA Final Report*, Recommendation 4.
69 *CLANN Report*.
70 Department of Children and Youth Affairs, *Recommendations from the First Report of the Collaborative Forum of Former Residents of Mother and Baby Homes*, December 2018, Para 1.2.
71 Barbara Walshe and Catherine O'Connell, *Consultations with Survivors of Institutional Abuse on Themes and Issues to be Addressed by a Survivor Led Consultation Group*, Department of Education, July 2019, 13.

72 In April 2015 the Joint Committee on Education and Social Protection held a pre-legislative scrutiny hearing on the general scheme of the Retention of Records Bill 2015 with officials from the Department of Education and Skills only. See *DED*, Houses of the Oireachtas, Joint Committee on Education and Social Protection, 'General Scheme of Retention of Records Bill 2015', Discussion, 15 April 2015. For the written submissions to the Oireachtas Joint Committee on Education and Skills in November 2019 by Tom Cronin, Dr Mary Lodato, Carmel McDonnell-Byrne, Anne Grehan, Rosemary Adaser, Eileen Molloy, Elizabeth Coppin, Mary Harney, Conrad Bryan, AnneMarie Crean, Maeve O'Rourke, Máiréad Enright, Sinéad Ring, Fred Logue, James Gallen, Catríona Crowe and Sarah-Anne Buckley, see JFMR, 'Retention of Records Bill 2019' (webpage), *Justice for Magdalenes Research*. For the transcript of the committee hearing on 26 November 2019, see *DED*, Houses of the Oireachtas, Joint Committee on Education and Skills, 'Retention of Records Bill 2019', Discussion 26 November 2019.

73 JFMR, 'National Archive: General Election 2020: Survivors, academics and practitioners call on every election candidate and political party to commit to a National Archive of Historical Institutional and Care-Related Records' (webpage).

74 Sean O'Rourke, *Today with Sean O'Rourke*, 'Retention of Records' and 'Mr Justice Sean Ryan', Aired 16 December 2019, RTÉ Radio.

75 O'Rourke, Enright and Ring, Submission on the provisions of the Retention of Records Bill 2019, 13 November 2019; Conor O'Mahony, Fred Logue, Maeve O'Rourke et al., Opinion on the application of the Irish Constitution and EU General Data Protection Regulation to the Adoption (Information and Tracing) Bill 2016 and the Government's 'Options for Consideration' dated 5 November 2019; *CLANN Report*, Section 4; Maeve O'Rourke, Submission to the UN Special Rapporteur on truth, justice, reparations and guarantees of non-recurrence, 24 January 2020.

76 See, in addition to the *Dublin Honours Magdalenes Listening Exercise Report*, the *CICA Final Report*, Recommendations 1–4; *Magdalen Commission Report* (AKA Quirke Report), 6th Recommendation; Department of Children and Youth Affairs; Walshe and O'Connell, *Consultations with Survivors of Institutional Abuse*; *CLANN Report*. See also Harney et al., 'Testimony', 17–34.

Bibliography

For an individualised list and copies of documents referred to in each chapter's endnotes, please visit www.jfmresearch.com/bookarchive

ARCHIVES

Conall Ó Fátharta Papers.
Department of Health Data Management Centre.
Dublin Diocesan Archives.
Dublin Register of Electors, 1954-1964. Pearse Street Library, Dublin.
Limerick Register of Electors, 1961-1983. Limerick City Library.
Mary Raftery Papers. Private Archive. Held privately by Sheila Ahern.
Mike Milotte Papers (Banished Babies). Held privately by Adoption Rights Alliance.
National Archives of Ireland.

DIGITAL REPOSITORIES

British and Irish Legal Information Institute: https://www.bailii.org
Clann: Ireland's Unmarried Mothers and their Children: Gathering the Data: www.clannproject.org
Court Service of Ireland: www.courts.ie
Department of Justice: http://www.justice.ie
Dublin Honours Magdalenes: http://jfmresearch.com/home/restorative-justice/dublin-honours-magdalenes
Find My Past: http://findmypast.ie
Glasnevin Trust Genealogy Service: https://www.glasnevintrust.ie/genealogy
Glynn, Evelyn, curator. *Breaking the Rule of Silence*, 2011. Limerick College of Art: http://www.magdalenelaundrylimerick.com
Industrial Memories Project: https://industrialmemories.ucd.ie
Inter-American Court of Human Rights: https://www.corteidh.or.cr
Irish Statute Book: http://www.irishstatutebook.ie
Justice for Magdalenes, archived at: https://web.archive.org/web/20130606020611/http://www.magdalenelaundries.com
Justice for Magdalenes Research: www.jfmresearch.com
Justice for Magdalenes Archive, Waterford Institute of Technology: http://repository.wit.ie/JFMA
Magdalene Institutions: Recording an Oral and Archival History: www.magdaleneoralhistory.com
Office of the Information Commissioner: www.oic.ie/decisions

Open Heart City: http://openheartcitydublin.ie
Residential Institutions Redress Board: http://www.rirb.ie
Right to Know: https://www.righttoknow.ie
TheStory.ie: https://www.thestory.ie
The Waterford Memories Project: https://www.waterfordmemories.com
United Nations Office of the High Commissioner for Human Rights: www.ohchr.org
United Nations Official Document System: www.documents.un.org

MEMORANDA/MINUTES/NOTES/BRIEFINGS

(Archived at: http://jfmresearch.com/bookarchive)

Aylward, Mr. Seán. 'Opening Statement for the consideration of Ireland's First Periodic Report under Article 19 of the Convention Against Torture'. 23 May 2011.

Baxter, Carol, Civil Law Reform. Note, 'Meeting with D/Health on Magdalen Redress Scheme'. 8 July 2013.

Department of the Environment. Circular Letter ENV 3/89. Jack Killane to each sanitary authority, 'Re: Exhumation licences'. 8 February 1989.

Department of the Environment. Circular Letter ENV 11/90. Jack Killane to each sanitary authority, 'Re: Applications for exhumation licences'. 5 October 1990.

Department of the Environment. File note. Anne Clarke to Colm Keenan. 30 March 1993.

Department of the Environment. Local Services Section. Draft letter to Eugene F. Collins Solicitors. 'Re: Exhumation Licence for grave ground at High Park Convent'. April 1993.

Department of the Environment. Internal memorandum. Local Services Section to Assistant Secretary Cullen. 'Re: Exhumation licence application, High Park Convent'. 19 April 1993.

Department of the Environment. Handwritten note. On internal memorandum, Local Services Section to Assistant Secretary Cullen, 'Re: Exhumation licence application, High Park Convent'. 29 April 1993.

Department of the Environment. Ministerial Order for the exhumation of the remains of the deceased persons listed in the schedule. Ref LSS 66/29/93. 25 May 1993.

Department of the Environment. Ministerial Order granting a licence for the exhumation of all remains at St Mary's Private Graveyard, High Park. LSS 66/29/93. 31 August 1993.

Department of the Environment. Internal notes regarding Mary Raftery, query. No date, circa March 2003.

Department of the Environment. Internal file note re visit of An Garda Síochána. 24 September 2003.

Department of the Environment. Memorandum, Miriam Tiernan, Local Services Section, to Dave Corcoran, Assistant Principal, Local Services Section. 'Re: Exhumation at St Mary's, High Park, Drumcondra, 1993'. 24 June 2010.

Department of the Environment. Sample Exhumation Licence Application. Mary Raftery Archive. No date, circa 2003.

Department of Justice. 'Oifig an Aire Dli agus Cirt agus Athchdirithe Dli Memorandum for the Government Magdalen Laundries'. 13 June 2011.

Department of Justice. 'Notes of meeting with representatives of Justice for Magdalenes (JFM) and Irish Women Survivors Support Network UK'. 4 July 2011. Department of Justice, Dublin.

Department of Justice. Minutes of the First Meeting of the Inter-Departmental Group on the Implementation of Quirke Report – Magdalen Laundries (membership). 4 July 2013, Montague Court.

Department of the Taoiseach. *Memo from the Department of Taoiseach*. 25 April 1957.

Hill, Raymond, Barrister. 'Magdalene Laundries – Summary of Points to Check in Final Report'. 3 February 2012.

Justice for Magdalenes. Meeting Minutes with Officials from Department of Justice. Taken by Claire McGettrick. 14 December 2009.

Justice for Magdalenes. Notes from Meeting with Department of Education Officials. Taken by Claire McGettrick. 2 February 2010.

Justice for Magdalenes. Meeting Notes with DoH. Taken by Claire McGettrick. 25 March 2010.

Justice for Magdalenes. Meeting Notes with Cardinal Brady at Ara Coeli, Armagh. Taken by Claire McGettrick. 24 June 2010.

Justice for Magdalenes. Meeting Notes with Dept Justice, 25 June 2010. Taken by Claire McGettrick, 25 June 2010.

Justice for Magdalenes. 'JFM Meeting with Ministers Alan Shatter and Kathleen Lynch'. Department of Justice, Stephen's Green, Dublin, Notes taken by Claire McGettrick, JFM, 4 July 2011.

Justice for Magdalenes. Meeting Notes with Dara Calleary, FF Spokesperson on Justice. Taken by Claire McGettrick. 5 July 2011. Leinster House.

Justice for Magdalenes. Meeting Minutes with Archbishop of Dublin, Diarmuid Martin, 6th July 2011, Archbishop's House. Minutes taken by Claire McGettrick. 6 July 2011.

Justice for Magdalenes. Meeting Minutes with Interdepartmental Committee. Taken by Claire McGettrick. 9 September 2011. Montague Court, Dublin 2.

Justice for Magdalenes. Meeting Notes, Senator McAleese. 16 February 2012.

Justice for Magdalenes. JFM Meeting Minutes with Nuala Ní Mhuircheartaigh. Taken by Claire McGettrick. 18 April 2012.

Justice for Magdalenes. Notes regarding meetings with Dr McAleese and survivors. Taken by Claire McGettrick. February 2013.

Justice for Magdalenes. Notes from Meeting with Frances Fitzgerald Minister for Justice and Equality. Taken by Claire McGettrick. 20 October 2014.

Justice for Magdalenes. Briefing Note on the Redress for Women in Certain Institutions Bill. 6 March 2015.

Justice for Magdalenes. A Briefing Note on 'Implementation of the Magdalene "Restorative Justice" Scheme: Where are we now?'. 12 March 2017.

Justice for Magdalenes. Meeting with Jim O'Callaghan, TD. 23 March 2017.

Justice for Magdalenes. Meeting with Charlie Flanagan, Minister for Justice and Equality. 27 March 2018.

Justice for Magdalenes. Briefing Note on the Archive of the Inter-Departmental Committee to Establish the Facts of State Involvement with the Magdalen Laundries. April 2018.

Justice for Magdalenes. Meeting with Charlie Flanagan, Minister for Justice and Equality. 26 April 2019.

Justice for Magdalenes Research, National Women's Council of Ireland, Irish Council for Civil Liberties, Amnesty International (Ireland). 'Briefing Note: Redress for Women Resident in Certain Institutions Bill 2014'. 19 January 2015.

Justice for Magdalenes Research and National Women's Council of Ireland. 'Briefing Note: Redress for Women Resident in Certain Institutions Bill 2014'. March 2017.

Martin, Jimmy. Memo. 31 May 2013.

McVeigh, Brenda, Department of Finance. Memo to Jimmy Martin. 16 August 2013.
O'Donnell, Katherine, Maeve O'Rourke, Claire McGettrick. Briefing to Seanad Eireann. 26 February 2015.
O'Rourke, Maeve. Briefing to Minister for Justice. April 2018.
O'Rourke, Maeve. Briefing to Minister for Justice. 26 April 2019.
Prunty, Jacinta. Statement for Gardaí, 1 April 2010. In Department of Justice, 'Oifig an Aire Dli agus Cirt agus Athchdirithe Dli Memorandum for the Government Magdalen Laundries'. 13 June 2011.
Raftery, Mary. 'Questions for Sister Ann Marie Ryan, Sisters of Our Lady of Charity of Refuge, High Park, Drumcondra'. Mary Raftery Archive. 14 April 2003.
Sisters of Our Lady of Charity. Handwritten list, 'Names of other women buried in St Mary's'. Mary Raftery Archive. August to September 1993.
Sisters of Our Lady of Charity. Application for cremation of Edith H. Mary Raftery Archive. 1 September 1993.
Smith, James. Briefing to U.S. Immigration Subcommittee. April 2016.

CORRESPONDENCE

Correspondence archived at: http://jfmresearch.com/bookarchive

OFFICIAL PUBLICATIONS

Irish Government and Statutory Bodies: Documents and Reports (Chronological)

Report of the Commission of the Relief of the Sick and Destitute Poor, Including the Insane Poor. Dublin: Stationery Office, 1928.
Report of the Committee on the Criminal Law Amendment Acts. Unpublished, 1931.
Report of the Commission of Inquiry into the Reformatory and Industrial School System. Dublin: Stationery Office, 1936.
Report of the Commission on Emigration and Other Population Problems 1948–54. Dublin: Stationery Office, 1955.
Some of Our Children: A Report on the Residential Care of Deprived Children in Ireland. London: Tuairim, 1966.
Report of the Commission of Inquiry into the Reformatory and Industrial School System. Dublin: Government Publications, 1970.
Department of Health, Task Force on Child Care Services: Final Report. Dublin: Stationery Office, 1980.
Report on the Inquiry into the Operation of Madonna House. Dublin: The Stationery Office, May 1996.
Compensation Advisory Committee. *Towards Redress and Recovery: Report to the Minister for Education and Science*. January 2002.
Commission to Inquire into Child Abuse. *Commission to Inquire into Child Abuse Third Interim Report*. Dublin: Stationary Office, 2003.

Judicial Appointments Advisory Board Annual Report. 2003.
Ryan, Seán. *Review into the Working of the Commission to Inquire into Child Abuse*. Dublin: Department of Education and Science, 15 January 2004.
Commission to Inquire into Child Abuse. *The Legal Team's Statement*. 7 May 2004.
Ryan, Seán. *Address by the Chairperson*. Commission to Inquire into Child Abuse. 7 May 2004.
Ryan, Seán. *A Position Paper on Identifying Institutions and Persons under the Commission to Inquire into Child Abuse Act 2000*. Commission to Inquire into Child Abuse. 7 May 2004.
The Ferns Report. Dublin: Stationary Office, October 2005.
Residential Institutions Redress Board. *A Guide to the Redress Scheme under the Residential Institutions Redress Act, 2002*. 3rd edn. December 2005.
Law Reform Commission. *Report: Vulnerable Adults and the Law*. Law Reform Commission. Dublin: Law Reform Commission, 2006.
Commission to Inquire into Child Abuse. *Final Report of the Commission to Inquire into Child Abuse*. Dublin: Stationary Office, 20 May 2009.
Report by Commission of Investigation into the handling by Church and State Authorities of Allegations and Suspicions of Child Abuse against Clerics of the Catholic Archdiocese of Dublin. November 2009.
Report to the Government from The Panel to Assess the Statements of Resources Submitted by Religious Congregations Following Publication of the Report of the Commission to Inquire into Child Abuse (Ryan Report). November 2009.
Irish Human Rights Commission. *Assessment of the Human Rights Issues Arising in Relation to the 'Magdalen Laundries'*. November 2010.
Inter-Departmental Committee to establish the facts of State involvement with the Magdalen Laundries. *Interim Progress Report*. 20 October 2011.
Shannon, Geoffrey. *Fifth Report of the Special Rapporteur on Child Protection: A Report Submitted to the Oireachtas*. 2011. Copyright 2012.
Inter-Departmental Committee to establish the facts of State involvement with the Magdalen Laundries. *Report of the Inter-Departmental Committee to Establish the Facts of State Involvement with the Magdalen Laundries*. 5 February 2013.
The Magdalen Commission Report. Dublin: Department of Justice and Equality. May 2013.
Irish Human Rights Commission. *Follow-up Report on State Involvement with Magdalen Laundries*. June 2013.
Report of the Inter Departmental Group on the Implementation of the Recommendations of Judge Quirke Contained in His Report 'On the establishment of an ex gratia Scheme and related matters for the benefit of those women who were admitted to and worked in the Magdalen Laundries'. September 2013.
Irish Human Rights Commission. *Submission to the UN Human Rights Committee on the Examination of Ireland's Fourth Periodic Report under the International Covenant on Civil and Political Rights*. June 2014.
Department of Justice and Equality. *General Scheme of Bill: Redress for Women Who were in Certain Institutions Bill*. 8 August 2014.
Irish Human Rights and Equality Commission. *Submission to UN Human Rights Committee on Ireland's One-Year Follow-up to Its Fourth Periodic Review under ICCPR*. September 2015.
Irish Human Rights and Equality Commission. *Submission to UN Committee on the Elimination of all forms of Discrimination against Women, List of Issues Prior to Reporting on Ireland's Combined 6th and 7th Report under CEDAW*. October 2015.
Dáil Éireann. *Standing Orders Relative to Public Business*. 2016.

Dublin City Council. *Archaeological Assessment at The Crescent*, Donnybrook, Dublin 4. 2016.
Residential Institutions Redress Board. *Annual Report of the Residential Institutions Redress Board*. 2016.
Irish Human Rights and Equality Commission. *Submission to the United Nations Committee on the Elimination of Discrimination Against Women on Ireland's Combined Sixth and Seventh Periodic Reports*. January 2017.
Bayley, David and Faith Bailey. *Archaeological Assessment at Sean MacDermott St & Railway St, Dublin 1 for Dublin City Council*. July 2017.
Irish Human Rights and Equality Commission. *Submission to the United Nations Committee against Torture on Ireland's Second Periodic Report*. July 2017.
Opportunity Lost: An Investigation by the Ombudsman into the administration of the Magdalene Restorative Justice Scheme. Dublin: Office of the Ombudsman, 2017.
Department of Education and Skills. *Contributions by Religious Congregations Towards the Costs Incurred by the State in Responding to Residential Institutional Child Abuse: Information note for the Committee of Public Accounts*. July 2018.
Dublin City Council. *Report on the Proposed Development of the Former Convent/ Magdalene Laundry Site at Seán MacDermott Street Lower, Dublin 1. (0.82 hectares, 2.04 acres)*. September 2018.
Department of Justice and Equality. *Addendum to the Terms of Magdalen Restorative Justice Ex Gratia Scheme in Respect of Women Who Worked in the Laundries in the 12 'Magdalen' Institutions and Who were Resident in One of the 14 Adjoining Institutions*. November 2018.
Department of Justice and Equality. *Terms of an Ex Gratia Scheme for Women Who were Admitted to and Worked in Magdalen Laundries, St. Mary's Training Centre Stanhope Street and House of Mercy Training School Summerhill Wexford*. Updated November 2018.
Department of Children and Youth Affairs. *Recommendations from the First Report of the Collaborative Forum of Former Residents of Mother and Baby Homes*. December 2018.
Law Reform Commission. *Issues Paper: A Regulatory Framework for Adult Safeguarding*. Law Reform Commission, 2019.
Walshe, Barbara and Catherine O'Connell. *Consultations with Survivors of Institutional Abuse on Themes and Issues to be Addressed by a Survivor Led Consultation Group*. Department of Education, July 2019.
Dublin City Council. *Chief Archaeologist's Report to Area Planner*, Re 4198/19. 'The Bonnington Hotel site on Swords Road, Whitehall, Dublin 9'. 28 November 2019.
Irish Human Rights and Equality Commission. *Submission to the United Nations Committee Against Torture for the List of Issues Prior to Reporting in Respect of Ireland for the 69th Session*. January 2020.
Fagan, Michelle. An Bord Pleanála, *Board Order*. ABP-306721–20. 21 September 2020.

JFM/R REPORTS (Chronological)

Archived at www.jfmresearch.com/bookarchive

Justice for Magdalenes. *Submission to the Irish Human Rights Commission, State Complicity and Constitutional Rights*. 10 June 2010.
Justice for Magdalenes. *Restorative Justice and Reparations Scheme*. 27 March 2011.

Justice for Magdalenes. *Restorative Justice & Reparation Scheme for Magdalene Laundry Survivors*. 14 October 2011.

Justice for Magdalenes. *Submission to Mr Justice John Quirke, Magdalen Commission*. 13 March 2013.

Justice for Magdalenes Research & Boston College Institute for the Liberal Arts. 'Toward Transitional Justice: Recognition, Truth-telling, and Institutional Abuse in Ireland'. International Conference, Boston College, 1–2 November 2018.

Justice for Magdalenes Research & Boston College Institute for the Liberal Arts. 'Amendments to the *Redress for Women Resident in Certain Institutions (Amendment) Bill*'. 2019.

Landy, Ciara and Anna O'Duffy. (On behalf of Justice for Magdalenes Research). *Follow-up Report to the UN Committee against Torture*. August 2018.

McGettrick, Claire. *Submission to Dublin City Council Regarding the Proposed Property Development at the Former Magdalene Laundry at Donnybrook, Dublin 4*. 4 October 2016.

McGettrick, Claire. *Submission to Dublin City Council Re Development at Donnybrook. Application Reference: 3621/16*. 2016.

McGettrick, Claire. *Submission to Cork City Council Re Development at Sundays Well. Application Reference:* 1737279. 20 March 2017.

McGettrick, Claire. *Submission to An Bord Pleanála. Lands at Bonnington Hotel, Swords Road, Whitehall, Dublin. Case Reference: PL29N.306721*. 13 March 2020.

McGettrick, Claire. *Supplementary Submission to An Bord Pleanála. Lands at Bonnington Hotel, Swords Road, Whitehall, Dublin. Case References: PL29N.306721; PL29N.307366*. 18 August 2020.

McGettrick, Claire and Justice for Magdalenes Research. 'Death, Institutionalisation and Duration of Stay: A Critique of Chapter 16 of the Report of the Inter-Departmental Committee to Establish the Facts of State Involvement with the Magdalen Laundries and Related Issues'. 19 February 2015.

O'Donnell, Katherine and Maeve O'Rourke. Proposal to Dublin City Council and Lord Mayor, 12 April 2017.

O'Donnell, Katherine, and Claire McGettrick with James M. Smith, Maeve O'Rourke and Clare Moriarty. *Dublin Honours Magdalenes Listening Exercise Report Vol 1: Report on Key Findings*. Dublin: Justice for Magdalenes Research, 2020.

O'Donnell, Katherine, and Claire McGettrick with James M. Smith, Maeve O'Rourke and Clare Moriarty. *Dublin Honours Magdalenes Listening Exercise Report Vol 2: Transcripts*. Dublin: Justice for Magdalenes Research, 2020.

O'Mahony, Conor, Fred Logue, and Maeve O'Rourke with James Gallen, Eoin Daly, Máiréad Enright, Sinéad Ring, Rossa McMahon and Laura Cahillane. *Opinion on the application of the Irish Constitution and EU General Data Protection Regulation to the Adoption (Information and Tracing) Bill 2016 and the Government's 'Options for Consideration'*. 5 November 2019.

O'Rourke, Maeve. (On behalf of Justice for Magdalenes). *Ireland's Magdalen Laundries and the State's Duty to Protect*. 2010.

O'Rourke, Maeve. *Submission to the United Nations Committee Against Torture*. May 2011.

O'Rourke, Maeve. *Justice for Magdalenes Statement*. Geneva: UN Committee Against Torture, NGO Briefing Session. 20 May 2011.

O'Rourke, Maeve. *Submission to the United Nations Universal Periodic Review*, Twelfth Session of the Working Group of the UPR Human Rights Council. 6 October 2011.

O'Rourke, Maeve. *Follow-up Report to the United Nations Committee against Torture*. May 2012.

O'Rourke, Maeve. *Submission to the UN Committee against Torture regarding Follow-up to Ireland's most recent State Party Report and List of Issues for Ireland's next State Party Report*. 7 March 2013.

O'Rourke, Maeve. (On behalf of Justice for Magdalenes Research). *Follow-Up Submission to the UN Human Rights Committee in respect of Ireland. 111th Session*. July 2014.

O'Rourke, Maeve. *Submission to UN Commission on the Status of Women*. 1 August 2014.

O'Rourke, Maeve. *NGO Submission to the UN Committee on the Elimination of Discrimination Against Women in respect of Ireland for List of Issues Prior to Reporting*. 2015.

O'Rourke, Maeve. *Parallel Report to the United Nations Committee on Economic, Social and Cultural Rights for Its examination of Ireland, 55th Session*. June 2015.

O'Rourke, Maeve. *NGO Submission to the UN Committee on the Elimination of Discrimination Against Women in respect of Ireland*. February 2017.

O'Rourke, Maeve. *NGO Submission to the UN Committee Against Torture in respect of IRELAND (for the session)*. July 2017.

O'Rourke, Maeve. (On behalf of the Irish Council for Civil Liberties). *NGO Submission to the United Nations Committee against Torture*. 23 November 2018.

O'Rourke, Maeve. *Ireland's Experience of Memorialisation in the Context of Serious Violations of Human Rights and Humanitarian Law: A Submission to the United Nations Special Rapporteur on the Promotion of Truth, Justice, Reparations and Guarantees of Non-recurrence*. 24 January 2020.

O'Rourke, Maeve and Claire McGettrick. (On behalf of Justice for Magdalenes Research). *Submission to the Council of Europe Commissioner for Human Rights*. 18 November 2016.

O'Rourke, Maeve, Claire McGettrick, Rod Baker, and Raymond Hill with James M. Smith, Colin Smith, Susan Lohan, Katherine O'Donnell and Tara Casey. *CLANN: Ireland's Unmarried Mothers and their Children: Gathering the Data: Principal Submission to the Commission of Investigation into Mother and Baby Homes*. Dublin: Justice for Magdalenes Research, Adoption Rights Alliance, and Hogan Lovells, 15 October 2018.

O'Rourke, Maeve, Máiréad Enright and Sinéad Ring. 'Submission to the Joint Oireachtas Committee on Education and Skills regarding the provisions of the Retention of Records Bill 2019'. 13 November 2019.

Smith, James M. (On behalf of Justice for Magdalenes). *A Narrative of State Interaction with the Magdalene Laundries*. 2011.

Smith, James M., Maeve O'Rourke, Raymond Hill, Claire McGettrick, with additional input from Katherine O'Donnell and Mari Steed. *State Involvement in the Magdalene Laundries. JFM's Principal Submissions to the Inter-departmental Committee to Establish the Facts of State Involvement with the Magdalene Laundries*. 18 August 2012.

Smith, James M. and Mari Steed. *Proposed Redress Scheme for Survivors of Ireland's Magdalene Laundries* [Draft]. 2 July 2009.

Smith, James M. and Raymond Hill (on behalf of Justice for Magdalenes). 'State Involvement with the Magdalene Laundries: A Summary of JFM's submissions to the Inter-departmental Committee to establish the facts of state involvement with the Magdalene Laundries'. May 2012.

Steed, Mari and Claire McGettrick. 'Magdalene Laundries/Mother and Baby Homes and the Adoption/Fostering Connection', email submission to Irish Human Rights Commission. July 2010.

NON-GOVERNMENTAL ORGANIZATION PUBLICATIONS

Reference material is fully listed at www.jfmresearch.com/bookarchive

Adoption Rights Alliance: www.adoption.ie
Amnesty International, Ireland: www.amnesty.ie
Care2 Petitions: www.care2.com
Clann: Ireland's Unmarried Mothers and their Children: Gathering the Data: www.clannproject.org
Citizens Information Board: www.citizensinformation.ie
Contact.ie: www.contact.ie
Focus Ireland: www.focusireland.ie
Fórsa: www.forsa.ie
Free Legal Advice Centres: www.flac.ie
International Federation for Human Rights (FIDH): www.fidh.org
Irish Centre for Human Rights: www.nuigalway.ie/irish-centre-human-rights
Irish Council for Civil Liberties: www.iccl.ie
McGarr Solicitors: www.mcgarrsolicitors.ie
Monckton Chambers: www.monckton.com
National Women's Council of Ireland: www.nwci.ie
Reclaiming Self: https://twitter.com/rsadvocacyirl
Safeguarding Ireland: www.safeguardingireland.org
Sr. Stanislaus Kennedy--Visionary and Social Innovator: www.srstan.ie
Uplift: People Powered Change: www.uplift.ie
Women's Human Rights Alliance.

DÁIL AND SEANAD ÉIREANN DEBATES / QUESTIONS

Dáil Éireann Debates. Volumes 1–994. 1919–2020.
Seanad Éireann Debates. Volumes 1–269. 1922–2020.

JOURNALISM AND COMMENTARY

Reference material is fully listed at www.jfmresearch.com/bookarchive

Aljazeera.
America Magazine.
BBC News.
BBC News NI.

Belfast Telegraph.
Boston Globe (USA).
BreakingNews.ie.
CatholicCulture.org (USA).
CllrMannixFlynn.blog.
Daily Mail (UK).
Daily Mirror (London).
Deutsche Welle (DE).
Dublin Inquirer.
Evening Herald (Dublin).
Extra.ie.
Harvard Law Today (USA).
Human Rights @Harvard Law (USA).
Human Rights in Ireland.
Huffington Post (USA).
Globe and Mail (CA).
Guardian (UK).
Independent (UK).
Irish Central (USA).
Irish Examiner.
Irish Independent.
Irish Legal News.
Irish Mirror.
Irish News (Belfast).
Irish Post (UK).
Irish Press.
Irish Times.
Irish Voice (New York).
Journal.ie.
Journal of the Irish Dental Association.
London Review of Books.
Magill Magazine.
Mayo News.
Meath Chronicle.
Medium.
National Catholic Reporter (USA).
New Statesman (UK).
New York Times.
Philadelphia Magazine (USA).
Press Association of Ireland.
RTÉ News.
Sun (UK).
Sunday Business Post.
Sunday Telegraph (UK).
Sunday Times (London).
Sunday Tribune.
Telegraph (London).
Time Magazine/World.

Times (Ireland Edition).
Times (London).
Twitter.
Washington Post (USA).
UN-Truth.com.
Vox.com.

JFM/R OPINION EDITORIALS & LETTERS TO THE EDITOR (Chronological)

Justice for Magdalenes. 'Dear Cabinet: Magdalene survivors need justice now'. *Irish Times*, 2 May 2011.

McGettrick, Claire. 'Government Apology a Watershed Moment, but Fairness and Respect Must Follow'. *Meath Chronicle*, 2 March 2013.

McGettrick, Claire. 'Magdalene Survivors are Still Seeking Justice'. *Irish Examiner*, 14 July 2014.

McGettrick, Claire. 'Adoption: The Secrets, Lies and Myths'. *Irish Examiner*, 9 August 2014.

McGettrick, Claire. 'Mother and Baby Homes: It's Time for the State to Realise de Valera's Ideals'. *Irish Examiner*, 25 August 2014.

McGettrick, Claire. 'Magdalene Laundries: Truth Hidden Behind a Wall of Silence'. *Irish Examiner*, 12 January 2015.

McGettrick, Claire. 'Justice for Magdalenes Continue to Advocate for Survivors'. *Public Interest Law Alliance Bulletin*, 3 June 2015.

McGettrick, Claire. 'Remembering the Magdalene Women on International Women's Day'. *Human Rights in Ireland (blog)*, 8 March 2016.

McGettrick, Claire. '1916 Centenary'. *NWCI Blog*, 29 March 2016.

McGettrick, Claire. 'Magdalene Laundries Survivors Denied What was Promised by the State'. *Irish Examiner*. 20 March 2018.

McGettrick, Claire, Mari Steed, James M. Smith, Maeve O'Rourke and Katherine O'Donnell. 'Restorative Justice for Magdalenes'. *Irish Examiner*, 19 February 2014.

O'Donnell, Katherine. 'State Must Force Orders to Apologise'. *Irish Independent*, 6 February 2014.

O'Donnell, Katherine. 'Let's Listen Attentively to Survivors of Magdalene Laundries'. *Irish Times*, 5 June 2018.

O'Rourke, Maeve. 'Slavery, Forced Labour and the Magdalene Laundries'. *Human Rights in Ireland (blog)*, 13 July 2010.

O'Rourke, Maeve. 'Lack of Redress for the Magdalene Laundries Abuse – A Continuing Violation of UNCAT'. *Human Rights in Ireland (blog)*, 3 May 2011.

O'Rourke, Maeve. 'Laundries Apology Is Now Needed'. *Irish Examiner*, 6 February 2013.

O'Rourke, Maeve. 'Take this Chance, Taoiseach – apologise to Each and Every One'. *Irish Independent*, 16 February 2013.

O'Rourke, Maeve. 'Magdalene Survivors Are Still Waiting for Restorative Justice'. *Irish Times*, 6 February 2014.

O'Rourke, Maeve. 'Broken Promises and Delays for Magdalenes: A Response to Minister Alan Shatter'. *Human Rights in Ireland*. 26 February 2014.

O'Rourke, Maeve. 'It's Time We Learnt the Truth about Magdalene Laundries'. *Irish Independent*, 5 July 2014.

O'Rourke, Maeve. 'Taoiseach must Honour Promise to Magdalene Survivors'. *Irish Independent*, 24 January 2015.

O'Rourke, Maeve. 'Magdalene Laundry Survivors Have Waited Too Long for Redress'. *Irish Examiner*, 21 February 2018.

O'Rourke, Maeve. '10 Ways Institutional Abuse Details Are Still being Kept Secret' (online article and multimedia post). *RTÉ Brainstorm*. Updated 2 March 2020.

O'Rourke, Maeve and James M. Smith. 'Justice for Magdalenes: Official Response to Irish Human Rights Commission Findings'. *Human Rights in Ireland*. 14 November 2010.

Smith, James M. '"Irish Society Colluded in Betrayal of Magdalen Women": Opinion-Editorial'. *Irish Times*, 1 September 2003.

Smith, James M. 'Voices of Our Magdalene Women Washed Out of History for Too Long'. Opinion- Editorial. *Sunday Tribune*, 12 July 2009.

Smith, James M. 'Redress for Magdalene Laundry Inmates'. Letter to the Editor. *Irish Times*, 9 November 2009.

Smith, James M. 'Magdalene Girl: "I cried for weeks and weeks. I was nobody. I was 16"'. Letter to the *Editor. Irish Examiner*, 31 December 2009.

Smith, James M. 'Court Referrals to the Magdalene Laundries'. *Irish Times*, 2 February 2010.

Smith, James M. 'Magdalene Victims Awaiting Apology'. *Irish Times*, 26 February 2010.

Smith, James M. 'Redress for Magdalene Survivors Overdue'. *Irish Independent*, 25 March 2010.

Smith, James M. 'Redress for Magdalene Victims'. *Irish Times*, 25 March 2010.

Smith, James M. 'Magdalene Victims Redress'. *Irish Times*, 19 April 2010.

Smith, James M. 'State in Denial Over Magdalenes'. *Irish Times*, 5 July 2010.

Smith, James M. 'Abuse Files must be Preserved'. Letter to the *Editor. Irish Examiner*, 12 July 2010.

Smith, James M. 'Response to Magdalene Survivors'. Letter to the Editor. *The Irish Times*, 14 December 2010.

Smith, James M. 'Government Failed us on All Fronts'. *Irish Examiner*, 8 February 2011.

Smith, James M. 'Church Abuse should be a Serious Election Issue'. *Irish Times*, 23 February 2011.

Smith, James M. 'Ireland's Magdalene Laundries: Time to Put An End to the Continued Abuse'. *Political World: Group Blog for Political World*, 25 April 2011.

Smith, James M. 'We Need Justice for Magdalene Survivors Now'. Opinion-Editorial. *Hibernia Times: Ireland's Internet Newspaper*, 9 June 2011.

Smith, James M. 'No Time to Lose with Apologies for Magdalenes'. Opinion-Editorial. *Irish Times*, 11 June 2011.

Smith, James M. 'We Need Clarity on Magdalene Laundries'. Letter to the Editor, *The Irish Independent*, 25 June 2011.

Smith, James M. 'Legacy of a Campaigning Journalist: Mary Raftery'. Letter to the Editor, *The Irish Times*, 13 January 2012.

Smith, James M. 'Magdalene Survivors Still Held Hostage to Politics'. *Irish Times*, 26 September 2012.

Smith, James M. 'Abused in the Past and Abandoned in the Present'. Opinion-Editorial. *Irish Times*, 5 February 2013.

Smith, James M. 'Fair Compensation must Follow Magdalene Apology'. Opinion-Editorial. *Irish Times*, 19 February 2013.

Smith, James M. 'Inquiry Needed to Compel Congregations to Reveal Truth about Treatment of Magdalenes'. Opinion-Editorial, *Irish Times*, 24 July 2013.
Smith, James M. 'Rite and Reason: Brave Magdalene Survivor Leaves Inspirational Trail'. Opinion- Editorial. *Irish Times*, 29 March 2016.
Smith, James M. 'Will Mother and Baby Homes Commission Advertise to the Hidden Irish Diaspora?'. Opinion-Editorial. *Irish Times*, 9 November 2016.
Smith, James M. 'Two Cathartic Days for 200 Dignified Magdalene Survivors'. Opinion Editorial. *Irish Examiner*, 5 June 2018.
Smith, James M. 'Dublin Honours Magdalenes Too Late for Catherine but She would have Liked It'. Opinion Editorial. *Irish Times*, 6 June 2018.
Smith, James M. 'Commission of Investigation Act Inhibits Truth-Telling about Past and Present'. *Irish Times*, 20 October 2018.

PRESS RELEASES / STATEMENTS

JFM/R Press Releases Available at: http://jfmresearch.com/bookarchive

Government Statements Available at: Merrion Street: Irish Government News Service.

BOOKS

Arnold, Bruce. *The Irish Gulag*. Dublin: Gill & Macmillan, 2009.
Bourke, Joanna. *Husbandry to Housewifery: Women, Economic Change, and Housework in Ireland, 1890–1914*. Oxford: Clarendon, 1993.
Boylan, Peter C. *In the Shadow of the Eighth*. Dublin: Penguin Ireland, 2019.
Burke Brogan, Patricia. *Eclipsed*. Galway: Salmon Drama, 1994.
Burke Brogan, Patricia. *Stained Glass at Samhain*. Galway: Salmon Drama, 2003.
Canon Law Society of Great Britain and Ireland, The. *The Code of Canon Law*. London: Collins Liturgical Publications, 1983.
Cooney, John. *John Charles McQuaid: Ruler of Catholic Ireland*. Dublin: O'Brien Press, 1999.
Delay, Cara. *Irish Women and the Creation of Modern Catholicism, 1850–1950*. Manchester: Manchester University Press, 2019.
Doyle, Paddy. *The God Squad*. London: Corgi-Penguin Books, 1989.
Earner-Byrne, Lindsey. *Mother and Child: Maternity and Child Welfare in Dublin, 1922–60*. Manchester: Manchester University Press, 2007.
Finnegan, Frances. *Do Penance or Perish*. Piltown, Co. Kilkenny: Congrave Press, 2001.
Fitzgerald, Maureen. *Habits of Compassion: Irish Catholic Nuns and the Origins of New York's Welfare System, 1830–1920*. (Women in American History). Urbana and Chicago: University of Illinois Press, 2006.
Foster, R. F. *Luck and the Irish: A Brief History of Change, 1970–2000*. London: Allen Lane, 2007.
Fricker, Miranda. *Epistemic Injustice: Power and the Ethics of Knowing*. New York: Oxford University Press, 2009.

Goulding, June. *The Light in the Window*. Dublin: Poolbeg, 1998.
Holland, Kitty. Savita: *The Tragedy that Shook a Nation*. Dublin: Transworld Ireland, 2013.
Holohan, Carole, ed. *In Plain Sight: Responding to the Ferns, Ryan, Murphy and Cloyne Reports*. Dublin: Amnesty International Ireland, 2011.
Inglis, Tom. *Moral Monopoly: Rise and Fall of the Catholic Church in Modern Ireland*. 2nd edn. Dublin: University College Press, 2019.
Joyce, James. *Ulysses*. 1922. Harmondsworth: Penguin, 1986.
Kennedy, Sr. Stanislaus. *But Where Can I Go?: Homeless Women In Dublin*. Dublin: Arlen House, 1985.
Lee, Joseph J. *Ireland, 1912-1985, Politics and Society*. Cambridge: Cambridge University Press, 1989.
Luddy, Maria. *Women and Philanthropy in Nineteenth Century Ireland*. Cambridge: Cambridge University Press, 1995.
Luddy, Maria. *Prostitution and Irish Society: 1800–1940*. Cambridge: Cambridge University Press, 2007.
Luddy, Maria and James M. Smith, eds. *Children, Childhood and Irish Society: 1500 to the Present*. Dublin: Four Courts Press, 2014.
McGee, Hannah, Rebecca Garavan, Mairead de Barra, Joanne Byrne and Ronan Conroy. *The SAVI Report – Sexual Abuse and Violence in Ireland: A National Study of Irish Experiences, Beliefs and Attitudes Concerning Sexual Violence*. Dublin: Liffey Press, 2002.
Milotte, Mike. *Banished Babies*. Dublin: New Island Books, 2012.
Novick, Ben. *Conceiving Revolution: Irish Nationalist Propaganda during the First World War*. Dublin: Four Courts Press, 2001.
O'Donnell, Ian and Eoin O'Sullivan. *Coercive Confinement in Post-Independence Ireland: Patients, Prisoners and Penitents*. Manchester: Manchester University Press, 2012.
O'Donnell, Katherine, Maeve O'Rourke and James M. Smith, eds. 'Toward Transitional Justice in Ireland? Addressing Legacies of Harm'. Special Issue. *Eire-Ireland: An Interdisciplinary Journal of Irish Studies* 55, nos. 1 & 2 (Spring/Summer 2020): 1–341.
Ó Gráda, Cormac. *Ireland: A New Economic History, 1780–1939*. Oxford: Clarendon Press, 1995.
Ó hÓgartaigh, Margaret. *Kathleen Lynn*, Irishwoman, Patriot, Doctor. Dublin: Irish Academic Press, 2006.
O'Leary, Don. *Vocationalism and Social Catholicism in Twentieth-Century Ireland: The Search for a Christian Social Order*. Dublin: Irish Academic Press, 2000.
Palmer, Caitríona. *An Affair with My Mother: A Story of Adoption, Secrecy and Love*. London: Penguin, 2016.
Peckham Magray, Mary. *The Transforming Power of the Nuns: Women, Religion, and Cultural Change in Ireland, 1750–1900*. Oxford: Oxford University Press, 1998.
Prunty, Jacinta. *The Monasteries, Magdalen Asylums and Reformatory Schools of Our Lady of Charity in Ireland 1853–1973*. Dublin: The Columba Press, 2017.
Raftery, Mary and Eoin O'Sullivan. *Suffer the Little Children*. Dublin: New Island Books, 1999.
Redmond, Jennifer. *Moving Histories, Irish Women's Emigration to Britain from Independence to Republic*. Liverpool: Liverpool University Press, 2019.
Rodgers, John P. *For the Love of My Mother*. Williamstown, Co. Galway: MacRuairi Art, 2005.
Rubio-Marín, Ruth, ed. *The Gender of Reparations: Unsettling Sexual Hierarchies While Redressing Human Rights Violations*. Cambridge: Cambridge University Press, 2009.

Smith, James M. *Ireland's Magdalen Laundries and the Nation's Architecture of Containment*. South Bend: Notre Dame Press, 2007/Manchester: Manchester University Press, 2008.
Teitel, Ruti G. *Transitional Justice*. Oxford: Oxford University Press, 2000.
Valiulis, Maryann Gialanella and Mary O'Dowd, eds. *Women & Irish History: Essays in Honour of Margaret MacCurtain*. Dublin: Wolfhound Press, 1997.
Walsh, Barbara. *Roman Catholic Nuns in England and Wales, 1800–1937*. Dublin and Portland: Irish Academic Press, 2002.
Wills, Clair. *That Neutral Island: A Cultural History of Ireland During the Second World War*. London: Faber & Faber, 2007.
Yeates, Padraig. *A City in Wartime: Dublin 1914–1918*. Dublin: Gill & Macmillan, 2011.

ACADEMIC JOURNAL ARTICLES & BOOK CHAPTERS

Daly, Mary E. 'Turn on the Tap: The State, Irish Women and Running Water'. In *Women & Irish History: Essays in Honour of Margaret MacCurtain*, edited by Maryann Gialanella Valiulis and Mary O'Dowd, 206–19. Dublin: Wolfhound Press, 1997.
Daly, Mary E. 'Marriage, Fertility and Women's Lives in Twentieth-Century Ireland (c. 1900–c. 1970)'. *Women's History Review* 15, no. 4 (2006): 571–85.
De Greiff, Pablo. 'A Normative Conception of Transitional Justice'. *Politorbis* 50, no. 3 (2010): 17–29.
Earner Byrne, Lindsey. 'Mother and Child Scheme Controversy' History Hub Podcast.
Enright, Máiréad. '"No. I Won't Go Back": National Time, Trauma and Legacies of Symphysiotomy in Ireland'. In *Law and Time*, edited by Sian Beynon-Jones and Emily Grabham. London: Routledge, 2018.
Enright, Máiréad and Sinéad Ring, 'State Legal Responses to Historical Institutional Abuse: Shame, Sovereignty, and Epistemic Justice'. *Éire-Ireland: An Interdisciplinary Journal of Irish Studies* 55, nos. 1 & 2 (Spring/Summer 2020): 68–100.
Gallen, James. 'Historical Abuse and the Statute of Limitations.' *Statute Law Review* 39, no. 2 (2018): 103–17.
Garrett, Paul Michael. 'Excavating the Past: Mother and Baby Homes in the Republic of Ireland'. *British Journal of Social Work* 47 (2017): 358–74.
Grimes, Brendan. 'Funding a Roman Catholic Church in Nineteenth-Century Ireland'. *Architectural History* 52 (2009): 147–68.
Harney, Mary, Mari Steed, Caitríona Palmer, Terri Harrison, Rosemary Adaser, Conrad Bryan, Susan Lohan and Connie Roberts. 'Testimony'. *Éire-Ireland: An Interdisciplinary Journal of Irish Studies* 55, nos. 1 & 2 (Spring/Summer 2020): 17–34.
Henderson, Stuart. 'Religion and Development in Post-Famine Ireland'. *Economic History Review* 72, no. 4 (2019): 1251–85.
Howell, Philip. 'Venereal Disease and the Politics of Prostitution in the Irish Free State'. *Irish Historical Studies* 33, no. 131 (2003): 320–41.
Larkin, Emmet. 'Economic Growth, Capital Investment, and the Roman Catholic Church in Nineteenth Century Ireland'. *The American Historical Review* 72, no. 3 (1967): 852–84.
Lonbay, Sarah and Toby Brandon. 'Renegotiating Power in Adult Safeguarding: The Role of Advocacy'. *The Journal of Adult Protection* 19, no. 2 (2017): 78–91.
Luddy, Maria. 'The Wrens of the Curragh: An Outcast Community'. *Women's History Review* 1, no. 3 (1992): 341–55.

Luddy, Maria. 'Magdalene Asylums in Ireland, 1880–1930, Welfare, Reform, Incarceration?' In *Armenfürsorge und Wohltätigkeit. Ländliche Gesellschaften in Europa, – Poor Relief and Charity. Rural Societies in Europe, 1850–1930*, edited by Inga Brandes and Katrin Marx-Jaskulski, 283–305. Frankfurt am Main: Peter Lang, 2008.

Luddy, Maria. 'Unmarried Mothers in Ireland, 1880–1973'. *Women's History Review* 20, no. 1 (2011): 109–26.

Luddy, Maria. 'Possessed of Fine Properties': Power, Authority and the Funding of Convents in Ireland, 1780–1900'. In *The Economics of Providence*, edited by M. Van Dijck and J. De Maeyer, 227–46. Leuven: Leuven University Press, 2012.

MacCurtain, Margaret. 'Late in the Field: Catholic Sisters in Twentieth-Century Ireland and the New Religious History'. *Journal of Women's History* 6&7, nos. 4 & 1 (1995): 49–63.

McAtackney, Laura. 'Materials and Memory: Archaeology and Heritage as Tools of Transitional Justice at a Former Magdalene Laundry'. *Éire-Ireland: An Interdisciplinary Journal of Irish Studies* 55, nos. 1 & 2 (Spring/Summer 2020): 223–46.

McAvoy, Sandra L. 'The Regulation of Sexuality in the Irish Free State, 1929–1935'. In *Medicine, Disease and the State in Ireland, 1650–1940*, edited by Greta Jones and Elizabeth Malcolm, 253–66. Cork: Cork University Press, 1999.

McCarthy, Joan. 'Reproductive Justice in Ireland, A Feminist Analysis of the Neary and Halappanavar Cases'. In *Ethical and Legal Debates in Irish Healthcare: Confronting Complexities*, edited by Mary Donnolly, Rob Kithcin and Claire Murray, 9–23. Manchester: Manchester University Press, 2016.

McGettrick Claire. '"Illegitimate Knowledge": Transitional Justice and Adopted People'. *Éire-Ireland: An Interdisciplinary Journal of Irish Studies* 55, nos. 1 & 2 (Spring/Summer 2020): 181–200.

McNally, Gerry. 'Probation in Ireland: A Brief History of the Early Years'. *Irish Probation Journal* 4, no. 1 (2007): 5–24.

Méndez, Juan E. and Catherine Cone. 'Transitional Justice'. In *Routledge Handbook of International Human Rights Law*, edited by Scott Sheeran and Nigel Rodley, 761–80. London: Routledge, 2013.

Niamh NicGhabhann, 'How the Catholic Church Built Its Property Portfolio'. RTÉ Brainstorm podcast 27 August 2018.

O'Donnell, Katherine. 'Academics Becoming Activists: Reflections on Some Ethical Issues of the Justice for Magdalenes Campaign'. In *Irishness on the Margins*, edited by Pilar Villar-Argáiz, 77–100. Cham: Palgrave Macmillan, 2018.

O'Donnell, Katherine, Maeve O'Rourke and James M. Smith, eds. 'Editors' Introduction: Toward Transitional Justice in Ireland? Addressing Legacies of Harm'. *Éire-Ireland: An Interdisciplinary Journal of Irish Studies* 55, nos. 1 & 2 (Spring/Summer 2020): 9–16.

O'Rourke, Maeve. 'Ireland's Magdalene Laundries and the State's Duty to Protect'. *Hibernian Law Journal* 10 (2011): 200–37.

O'Rourke, Maeve. 'The Justice for Magdalenes Campaign'. In *International Human Rights: Perspectives from Ireland*, edited by Suzanne Egan, 145–68. London: Bloomsbury, 2015.

O'Rourke, Maeve. 'O'Keefe v. Hickey'. In *Northern/Irish Feminist Judgments*, edited by Mairéad Enright, Julie McCandless and Aoife O'Donoghue, 334–44. Oxford: Hart, 2017.

O'Rourke, Maeve. 'Prolonged Impunity as a Continuing Situation of Torture or Ill-Treatment? Applying a Dignity Lens to So-Called "Historical" Cases'. *Netherlands International Law Review* 66 (2019): 101–41.

O'Rourke, Maeve and James M. Smith. 'Ireland's Magdalene Laundries: Confronting a History not yet in the Past'. In *A Century of Progress? Irish Women Reflect*, edited by Alan Hayes and Máire Meagher, 107–34. Dublin: Arlen House, 2016.

Palmer, Caitríona. '"It steadies me to tell these things": Memoir and the Redemptive Power of Truth-Telling'. *Éire-Ireland: An Interdisciplinary Journal of Irish Studies* 55, nos. 1 & 2 (Spring/Summer 2020): 299–314.

Panepinto, Alice M. 'The Right to the Truth in International Law: The Significance of Strasbourg's Contributions'. *Legal Studies* 37, no. 4 (2017): 739–64.

Perry, Victoria. 'Report on the Archives of the Sisters of Our Lady of Charity of Refuge'. *Journal of the Catholic Archives Society*, no. 27 (2007).

Pine, Emilie, Susan Leavy and Mark T. Keane. 'Re-reading the Ryan Report: Witnessing via and Close and Distant Reading'. *Éire-Ireland: An Interdisciplinary Journal of Irish Studies* 55, nos. 1 & 2 (2017): 198–215.

Raftery, Deirdre. 'The "mission" of Nuns in Female Education in Ireland, c.1850–1950'. *Paedagogica Historica* 48, no. 2 (2012): 299–313.

Redmond, Jennifer. '"Sinful Singleness"? Exploring the Discourses on Irish Single Women's Emigration to England, 1922–1948'. *Women's History Review* 17, no. 3 (2008): 455–76.

Savage, Robert and James M. Smith. 'Sexual Abuse and the Irish Church: Crisis and Responses'. In *The Church in the 21st Century: Occasional Papers*. Boston College eScholarship (online publication), 2003.

Smith, Colin and April Duff. 'Access to Justice for Victims of Historic Institutional Abuse'. *Éire-Ireland: An Interdisciplinary Journal of Irish Studies* 55, nos. 1–2 (2020): 100–19.

Smith, James M. 'Remembering Ireland's Architecture of Containment: "telling" Stories in *The Butcher Boy* and *States of Fear*'. *Éire-Ireland: An Interdisciplinary Journal of Irish Studies* 55, nos. 3 & 4 (2001): 111–30.

Smith, James M. 'The Politics of Sexual Knowledge: The Origins of Ireland's Containment Culture and the Carrigan Report (1931)'. *Journal of the History of Sexuality* 13, no. 2 (2004): 208–33.

Smith, James M. '*The Magdalene Sisters*: Evidence, Testimony…Action?'. *Signs* 32, no. 2 (2007): 431–58.

Smith, James M. 'The Justice for Magdalenes Campaign'. In *In Plain Sight: Responding to the Ferns, Ryan, Murphy and Cloyne Reports*, edited by Carole Holohan, 373–77. Dublin: Amnesty International Ireland, 2011.

Smith, James M. 'Knowing and Unknowing Tuam: State practice, the Archive, and Transitional Justice'. *Éire-Ireland: An Interdisciplinary Journal of Irish Studies* 55, nos. 1–2 (Spring/Summer 2020): 142–81.

Sveaass, Nora and Nils Johan Lavik. 'Psychological Aspects of Human Rights Violations: The Importance of Justice and Reconciliation'. *Nordic Journal of International Law* 69, no. 1 (2000): 35–52.

Whelan, Bernadette. 'Women on the Move: A Review of the Historiography of Irish Emigration to the USA, 1750–1900'. *Women's History Review* 24, no. 6 (2015): 900–16.

Wills, Clair. 'Joyce, Prostitution, and the Colonial City'. *South Atlantic Quarterly, Special Issue*: *Ireland and Irish Cultural Studies*, edited by John Paul Waters 95 (1996): 79–95.

AUDIO VISUAL

(Including JFM/R radio and television interviews, podcasts; documentaries; films)

Archived at: http://jfmresearch.com/bookarchive

Index